Dear Genius
The Letters of Ursula Nordstrom

Ursula Nordstrom, 1969

PHOTOGRAPH BY PAUL WILKES

Dear Genius

The Letters of Ursula Nordstrom

COLLECTED AND EDITED BY LEONARD S. MARCUS

HARPERCOLLINS*PUBLISHERS*

All letters by Ursula Nordstrom not written expressly in her role as
an employee of Harper reprinted by permission of Mary Griffith.

Letters from Ursula Nordstrom to Georges Duplaix,
dated July 17, 1941, and October 10, 1942, from Harper Papers,
Rare Book and Manuscript Library, Columbia University.

Letters to Crockett Johnson, November 2, 1944; E. B. White, April 2, 1952; Ruth Krauss,
January 20, 1954; Mary Chalmers, October 24, 1957; Maurice Sendak, October 17, 1960;
Louise Fitzhugh, September 2, 1966; and John Steptoe, June 19, 1967, first appeared in
Hungry Mind Review, Summer 1997.

Photographs of Ursula Nordstrom by Paul Wilkes.

Photograph of Clement Hurd and Margaret Wise Brown
reprinted by permission of Thacher Hurd.

Photograph of Maurice Sendak copyright © 1968 by Nancy Crampton and used by permission.

Photograph of Crockett Johnson by Jerome Weidman and used by permission.

Photograph of E. B. White and Katharine S. White
reprinted by permission of Joel White
and the Division of Rare and Manuscript Collections, Cornell University Library.

Line drawing of Ursula Nordstrom by Marc Simont
reprinted by permission of Marc Simont.

From "Not Waving but Drowning" by Stevie Smith.
From *Collected Poems of Stevie Smith*. Copyright © 1998 by Stevie Smith.
Used by permission of Oxford University Press, Inc.

Every effort has been made to locate the copyright holders of all copyrighted materials and secure
the necessary permission to reproduce them. In the event of any questions arising as to their use,
the publisher will be glad to make necessary changes in future printings and editions.

Jacket painting by Maurice Sendak based on a photograph by Sidney Fields.

Dear Genius: The Letters of Ursula Nordstrom

Library of Congress Cataloging-in-Publication Data
Nordstrom, Ursula
    Dear genius : the letters of Ursula Nordstrom / collected and edited by Leonard S. Marcus
        p.   cm.
    Includes bibliographical references (p.   )
    ISBN 0-06-023625-6. — ISBN 0-06-446235-8 (pbk.)
    1. Nordstrom, Ursula—Correspondence.   2. Publishers and publishing—United States—
Correspondence.   3. Children's literature—Publishing—United States—History—20th century.
4. Book editors—United States—Correspondence.   I. Marcus, Leonard S., 1950–   . II. Title.
Z473.N68A4   1998   97-18895
070.5'092—dc21   CIP
[b]

Typography by Al Cetta
❖

FOR MY MOTHER

AND

IN MEMORY OF MY FATHER

CONTENTS

ACKNOWLEDGMENTS

I wish to express my thanks and appreciation to the following individuals who generously sat for interviews, made available letters not in the Harper files, responded to requests for information, or supplied critical research materials when needed: Harriett Barton, Barbara Borack, John Briggs, the late Dorothy Briley, Donna Brooks, Mary M. Burns, Natalie Savage Carlson, Mary Chalmers, Margaret N. Coughlan, Nancy Crampton, Barbara Alexandra Dicks, Peggy Doherty, Michel Duplaix, Sara Ann Freed, Jean Craighead George, Rosalie Slocum Goldberg, Margaret Bloy Graham, the late Mary Griffith, Dorothy Hagen, Deborah Hallen, Esther Hautzig, the late Ethel Heins, Kevin Henkes, Susan Hirschman, Phyllis Hoffman, Thacher Hurd, Nina Ignatowicz, Olivia Kahn, Karla Kuskin, Jane Langton, Robert Lipsyte, Anita Lobel, Joanna Rudge Long, Ellen Loughran, Fran Manushkin, Marilyn E. Marlow, William Maxwell, Julie McAlpine, Margaret K. McElderry, James McMullan, Stuart Miller, William C. Morris, Doris Orgel, the late Margret Rey, Elizabeth M. Riley, Joan Robins, Mary Rodgers, Glen Rounds, Miriam Schlein, Maurice Sendak, the late Shel Silverstein, Anita Silvey, Marc Simont, Christopher Stephens, Javaka Steptoe, Mary Stolz, Zena Sutherland, Lucille Thomas, Ann Tobias, Jeanne Vestal, Lisa Von Drasek, Margaret Warner, Robert Warren, Meredith Mundy Wasinger, Ann Armistead White, the late Joel White, Elizabeth Winthrop, Paul O. Zelinsky, and Charlotte Zolotow.

Copies of letters and help with research were provided by Albert Brayson, The Lake Grove School; Lucy B. Burgess, Rare and Manuscript Collections, Cornell University Library; Bernard Crystal, Rare Book and Manuscript Library, Columbia University; the Exeter, New Hampshire, Public Library; Karen Nelson Hoyle, the Kerlan Collection, University of Minnesota Libraries; Dolores B. Jones, the de Grummond Children's Literature Research Collection, McCain Library, University of Southern Mississippi; Dorothy G. Knaus, Special Collections, University of Oregon Library; Carolyn Kupisz, American Library Association; Angeline Moscatt, Central Children's Room, the New York Public Library; the Alumni Services Office, Northfield Mount Hermon School; and Lorett Treese, College Archivist, Mariam Coffin Canaday Library, Bryn Mawr College. My thanks go to these individuals and their institutions for their gracious assistance.

I wish to thank Marilyn Kriney, former publisher of HarperCollins Children's Books, for her early interest in this project, and Susan Katz for her enthusiastic and steadfast support of it. Donna Slawsky de Leon, Library and Records Manager, and Stephen Fleming, Corporate Librarian, HarperCollins, provided invaluable help with research and, on many days, a much-appreciated quiet workplace. My editor, Antonia Markiet, has been a good guide and friend throughout the years that it has taken to complete the manuscript, and I am grateful for all she has done. Renée Cafiero copyedited the manuscript with great care and skill, and this book is the better for her efforts.

I thank my wife, Amy, and my son, Jacob, for their love and friendship.

* * *

While at work on an earlier project, I was fortunate to have met, and heard many stories about Ursula Nordstrom from, the late Clement Hurd, the late Edith Thacher Hurd, the late Ruth Krauss, the late Lucille Ogle, the late Harriet F. Pilpel, the late William R. Scott, Leonard Weisgard, and the late Garth Williams, all of whom knew her well. Invariably, when the editor's name came up, the first thing said was "She wrote such wonderful letters!" I took note of the fact, and of the expressions of utter delight that came over the faces of these friends and colleagues of hers at the mere mention of her letters. Thoughts of editing a book of Ursula Nordstrom's correspondence had their origin in those memorable encounters.

The two years during which I read the many tens of thousands of letters written by Ursula Nordstrom as Harper's editor would have been well spent if only for the immense enjoyment I gleaned from the experience. The letters also, however, have much to tell about the arts of writing, illustrating, and editing; the social history of the twentieth century; and the pivotal role that books, and a love of books, can play in children's lives. To read the letters is to receive a many-faceted education from a teacher of rare insight, high good humor, and lively humanity. I am glad that readers will now have the chance to share in the experience.

1910   Born to Marie Ursula Nordstrom and Henry E. Dixie, February 1, in New York City.

c.1917–   Attends Winnwood School, Lake Grove, New York.
1926

1926–   Attends Northfield Seminary, East Northfield, Massa-
1928   chusetts.

1928–?   Takes business course at Scudder School, New York.

1931   Hired as clerk in College Textbook department, Harper & Brothers, New York.

1936   Appointed assistant to Ida Louise Raymond, director of Harper Books for Boys and Girls.

1939   In anticipation of Raymond's retirement the following year, shares management responsibilities for the Department of Books for Boys and Girls.

1940   Becomes director of the department.

1954   Becomes the first woman elected to the Board of Directors, Harper & Brothers.

Serves one-year term as president of The Children's Book Council.

Laura Ingalls Wilder, author of the Little House books, is honored by the American Library Association as the first recipient of a medal named for her and intended as a lifetime achievement award in children's literature.

1955   Meindert DeJong wins the Newbery Medal for *The Wheel on the School*, illustrated by Maurice Sendak.

1957   Marc Simont wins the Caldecott Medal for *A Tree Is Nice*, by Janice May Udry.
The I Can Read Book series is launched with the publication, in August, of *Little Bear*, by Else Holmelund Minarik, illustrated by Maurice Sendak.

1960   Becomes the first woman elected a vice president of Harper & Brothers.
The Secret Language, by Ursula Nordstrom, illustrated by Mary Chalmers, published by Harper Books for Boys and Girls.

1962   Harper & Brothers merges with Row, Peterson & Company, of Evanston, Illinois, a publisher of music and school texts, to form Harper & Row.
Meindert DeJong wins the international Hans Christian Andersen Medal honoring the body of his work as a writer for children.

1964   Maurice Sendak is awarded the Caldecott Medal for *Where the Wild Things Are*; Emily Cheney Neville wins the Newbery Medal for her novel *It's Like This, Cat*.

1968   Nordstrom is corecipient with Evan Thomas, publisher and editor-in-chief of Harper Trade Books, of the first annual Gold Medal Award, given by Harper & Row to reward outstanding editorial achievement. Nordstrom's department is renamed Harper Junior Books.

1969   Meindert DeJong wins the first National Book Award for Children's Literature, for *Journey from Peppermint Street*, illustrated by Emily Arnold McCully.

1970   Nordstrom named senior vice president of Harper & Row and publisher, Junior Books.

Maurice Sendak wins the Hans Christian Andersen Medal for Illustration.

E. B. White is honored with the Laura Ingalls Wilder Award.

William H. Armstrong wins the Newbery Medal for *Sounder*, illustrated by James Barkley.

1971 E. B. White receives the National Medal for Literature.

Harper Junior Books launches its paperback imprint, Harper Trophy.

1972 Nordstrom receives the Constance Lindsay Skinner Award, given by the Women's National Book Association in recognition of her contribution to the world of books and to society through books.

1972 Harper & Row moves out of its longtime offices at 49 East 33rd Street to new, larger quarters at 10 East 53rd Street.

1973 Nordstrom takes early retirement; becomes senior editor of Ursula Nordstrom Books, her own imprint within the department.

Jean Craighead George wins the Newbery Medal for *Julie of the Wolves*, illustrated by John Schoenherr.

1980 On March 1 relinquishes the title of senior editor and becomes a consultant to the department.

1980 Nordstrom becomes the first woman, and the first person in the children's book field, to win the Curtis Benjamin Award, given by the Association of American Publishers in recognition of innovation and creativity in publishing.

1988 After a long illness, Nordstrom dies of ovarian cancer on October 11, in New Milford, Connecticut.

INTRODUCTION

Ursula Nordstrom, director of Harper's Department of Books for Boys and Girls[1] from 1940 to 1973, was children's literature's Maxwell Perkins, the single most creative force for innovation in children's book publishing in the United States during the twentieth century. A high-strung, voluble, tartly witty woman, Nordstrom brought devotion and verve to the quest for originality and honesty in books for young people, a readership she believed had long been ill served by the sentimental illusions and false pieties of their elders.

Certainly vast quantities of tamely imagined reading matter for children had been published prior to Nordstrom's entrance into the field as an editorial assistant in 1936—the same year, as it happens, in which the mildly satirical *The Story of Ferdinand*[2] became a national phenomenon and feisty *Caddie Woodlawn*[3] won the Newbery Medal. If by the late 1930s, however, the genteel tradition had lost some of its stifling hold on American children's literature, it remained for an editor of Nordstrom's maverick temperament, high-voltage intellect, and grand

1. On May 1, 1962, Harper & Brothers merged with Row, Peterson & Company, a publisher of music books and textbooks, to form Harper & Row. The name of Nordstrom's department changed from Harper Books for Boys and Girls to Harper Junior Books at the start of 1968.
2. *The Story of Ferdinand*, by Munro Leaf, illustrated by Robert Lawson, Viking, 1936.
3. *Caddie Woodlawn*, by Carol Ryrie Brink, Macmillan, 1935.

ambition to reexamine, and often to reject, the shopworn taboos and conventions of the genre, and to propel American children's literature headlong into the modern age.

A partial list of the authors and illustrators whose work Nordstrom championed reveals the extent to which her unorthodox vision of "good books for bad children"[4] eventually swept the field. It was she who published many or all of the children's books of Margaret Wise Brown, E. B. White, Garth Williams, Ruth Krauss, Crockett Johnson, Charlotte Zolotow, Maurice Sendak, Mary Stolz, Tomi Ungerer, Louise Fitzhugh, Else Holmelund Minarik, Mary Rodgers, Karla Kuskin, Russell Hoban, John Steptoe, and Shel Silverstein. Put another way, it was Nordstrom who edited a major portion of the children's classics of our time, including *The Runaway Bunny*, *The Carrot Seed*, *Stuart Little*, *Goodnight Moon*, *Charlotte's Web*, *Harold and the Purple Crayon*, *Where the Wild Things Are*, *Harriet the Spy*, *Little Bear*, *Bedtime for Frances*, and *The Giving Tree*.

Like most editors, Nordstrom—known to friends and colleagues as UN—generally preferred to operate in literature's margins, to make her mark as it were with invisible ink. Unlike some of her colleagues, however, she also possessed, at least partly by reason of inheritance, a powerful gift for self-dramatization. To range over the vast expanse of her professional correspondence is not only to glimpse a great editor at work but also to witness the creation of an artfully drawn, unfailingly vivid character named Ursula Nordstrom, a literary persona by turns leonine and Chaplinesque, cocksure and beguilingly off-balance.

Not surprisingly, Nordstrom herself saw the parallel between her own pathfinding career and that of Scribner's legendary editor who had risen to preeminence a generation earlier.

---

4. Nordstrom often used this phrase to contrast the edgy, challenging books she published for children with more conventional sorts of children's books that sentimentalized childhood.

"If [novelist Meindert DeJong] wants to play Thomas Wolfe to my Maxwell Perkins, well, I'll live with it,"[5] she wrote George Woods, children's book editor at *The New York Times Book Review*, following DeJong's bitter break with her after more than three decades of close professional association. But to judge from the letters, the Perkins comparison seems hardly to have obsessed her. Was she not, after all, Ursula Maelstrom . . . Ursula Norcross . . . Ursula Carroll Moore . . . Ursa Major . . . *The* Ursula Nordstrom[6]? The Harper editor who liked to say that she personally had been "Established in 1817"[7] for many years shared a Greenwich Village apartment with a Yorkshire terrier named, perhaps not irrelevantly, Perkins.

Nordstrom's father, Henry E. Dixie, was one of the most famous American actors of his generation, a gaslight-era matinee idol best known for his performance in the title role of *Adonis*, a "burlesque in two acts" co-authored by the actor and William Gill. Dixie was about fifty when he met a beautiful nineteen-year-old actress named Marie Ursula Nordstrom, his costar in something called *Mary Jane's Pa*; the couple married in time for the birth of their daughter in New York City on February 1, 1910.

Dixie's sparkling manner delighted the young girl and left

5. See letter to George Woods, July 18, 1969, page 276.
6. Margaret Wise Brown called UN "Ursula Maelstrom." UN sometimes called herself "Ursula Norcross," a reference to the frequent misspelling of her name and to a well-known greeting-card company that produced sentimental cards that would not have been very much to her liking. "Ursula Carroll Moore" was UN's teasing reference to Anne Carroll Moore, the New York Public Library's superintendent of work with children, with whom UN often disagreed about books. "Ursa Major" was Russell Hoban's variation on UN's name. Karla Kuskin recalls that during the 1960s, when "Ms." was just coming into use as a term of address and still sounded awkward, she addressed a letter to her editor not as "Miss" or "Ms." but *The* Ursula Nordstrom."
7. A reference to the company's logo bearing that legend.

its bittersweet imprint after the parents divorced, when Ursula was seven. Packed off to boarding school, she spent holidays with her mother and rarely again saw her fun-loving father. The dashing Dixies' bespectacled only child would forever regard herself as an ugly duckling born of swans.

For the next eight years she attended the Winnwood School, a Long Island repository for the children of theater people. Settling in at Winnwood, she felt "terribly ashamed" at first about the failure of her parents' marriage. But as Nordstrom recalled years later for the novelist Janette Sebring Lowrey: "I used to wonder if all the other children knew my parents were divorced . . . . . and then gradually I found out most of the parents of the children at that school were divorced, and that's why we were all there, really."[8] At sixteen, following a botched chemistry exam and some long-forgotten piece of school-age mischief, she quietly transferred to the Northfield Seminary in East Northfield, Massachusetts. Asked on the Northfield application to state whether she had formed any "purpose in life," Ursula responded: "to be a writer."

The dean of her new school regarded her as a leader and commended her to her mother as "the life of the table." The dean worried, however, over the illness-prone girl's fitful sleeping and eating habits, and over her mystifying reports of voices heard ringing in her head with alternating words of reproach and approval.[9]

Nordstrom's mother had remarried by then. Ursula's stepfather, Elliott Robinson Brown, was a steady sort of man and a businessman of modest means. Notwithstanding the admonishments of a favorite English teacher, Miss Alta J. Becker, who recognized her student's intellectual promise, the Browns chose

---

8.   Letter to Janette Sebring Lowrey, October 15, 1956. HarperCollins archives. The whereabouts of letters that are quoted from in the Introduction, but not included in the collection itself, have been individually noted, as here.

9.   Information provided by Northfield Mount Hermon School.

not to send their daughter to college but urged her instead to acquire secretarial skills. She did as she was told. With elaborate irony, Nordstrom would later say that it was not just *any* college that she had never attended, but Bryn Mawr.

In the fall of 1931 Harper & Brothers hired Nordstrom as a clerk in the College Textbook department. Her interviewer, Frank S. MacGregor[10], recalled her as a painfully shy young woman; for the next five years she bided her time in a job she found largely unrewarding. During that period Nordstrom became friends with Ida Louise Raymond, assistant to the editor of Harper's small Department of Books for Boys and Girls. In 1936, when Raymond became head of the department, she chose Nordstrom to assist her.

Nordstrom loved her new work and seems quickly to have hit her stride in professional confidence. Writing to Laura Ingalls Wilder, the department's star author, she mustered an admirable degree of poise in circumstances that had to have been utterly embarrassing to a newcomer: ". . . I know [Louise Raymond] would want me to write you and try to apologize for that inexcusably stupid mistake in the dummy for *On the Banks of Plum Creek.* . . . It certainly won't appear again! Miss Raymond, and all of us, were upset about it because, very frankly, every single bit of copy written for your lovely book has been worked over with enthusiasm and affection."[11] Although Nordstrom's correspondence over the next forty-odd years would be peppered with declarations of her editorial fallibility and professional self-doubt—many of these cast, however, in the most wildly exaggerated and thus ambiguous terms—she seems rarely to have questioned her fundamental fitness for her work. Asked pointedly by Anne Carroll Moore, the New York Public Library's powerful superintendent of work with

10. Head of the College Textbook department and later president of Harper & Brothers.
11. See letter to Laura Ingalls Wilder, September 9, 1937, page 3.

children, what qualified her, a nonlibrarian, nonteacher, non-parent, and noncollege graduate to publish children's books, Nordstrom just as pointedly replied, "Well, I am a former child, and I haven't forgotten a thing."[12]

Ursula Nordstrom belonged to the second generation of editors to head the children's book departments of America's major publishing houses. In 1926 Harper & Brothers joined the growing roster of firms that had established such departments, largely in response to the national movement for specialized service to children at the public libraries. Professionally staffed children's reading rooms, a new phenomenon at the end of the last century, had become a standard feature of libraries throughout the United States by the 1910s, and publishers (even those like Harper with a long and noteworthy history in the juvenile field) were eager to understand, and profit by ministering to, the children's librarians' special needs. Harper's department, typical in size for the time, consisted of an editor, her assistant, and a secretary, each with a desk and a telephone.

The pioneering women who took these jobs earned lower wages than their male counterparts in trade, college, and religious publishing and had to be willing to tolerate the patronizing slights of the men of the house. Those women who paid the price enjoyed an enviable freedom to publish what they wished and had the further satisfaction of advancing professionally in a field that, prior to the seventies, remained otherwise largely closed to women.

Harper's founding juvenile editor, Virginia Kirkus, had come to the house with a background in teaching and magazine work. She led the department for its first seven years before

12. Charlotte Zolotow, "Ursula Nordstrom," *The Calendar* [of The Children's Book Council], November 1981; Roni Natov and Geraldine DeLuca, "Discovering Contemporary Classics: An Interview with Ursula Nordstrom," *The Lion and the Unicorn*, Vol. 3 (Spring 1979), 122.

turning it over to Raymond, a recent Bryn Mawr graduate from Virginia. On taking charge from Raymond, Nordstrom inherited a list of authors and artists that included Laura Ingalls Wilder and picture-book artist Clare Turlay Newberry, whom Kirkus had been the first to publish; and, from Raymond's era, novelist Meindert DeJong and a rising star among writers for the nursery age named Margaret Wise Brown.

Ambitious, mercurial, and prolific, Brown felt unbound by the stately publishing tradition of lifelong association between an author and a single house—and freely published her work with whomever she liked. In this, Nordstrom's first experience of so unpredictable an author, she proved herself easily the equal to Brown's own sporting temperament and force of will. Her occasional battles with Brown—"Miss Genius," "my favorite author," as Nordstrom called her, not always with affection—proved a harbinger of things to come in the increasingly profitable business of juvenile publishing.

After Simon & Schuster launched its wildly successful Little Golden Books imprint in 1942, dramatically underpricing and outdistributing their books to the alarm of everyone in the industry, Nordstrom's letters bristled with irritable references to the new competitor with its truckloads of money and determination to lure authors from her own and other lists. In 1950 the advent of Random House's popular history and biography series, Landmark Books, would furnish Nordstrom with a second nemesis. In an apparently rare case of pressure from above, Harper's management prodded the Department of Books for Boys and Girls to devise a rival history series. Nonfiction had never interested Nordstrom greatly, and perhaps for that reason the Breakthrough Series, the first volumes of which finally made their appearance in 1962 under the general editorship of Walter Lord, failed to take hold.

More often than not, however, it was Nordstrom who led the competition, at times courting controversy as the publisher of books that tested the limits and expanded the boundaries of the field in which, as she remarked only half in jest, she "prais[ed] the Lord in [her] own fashion."[13] *A Hole Is to Dig*—with its quirky text based on preschoolers' comments and its (for then) oddly unpretty illustrations—typifies the kind of risky book for young children that Nordstrom found of compelling interest. When *A Hole Is to Dig* drew criticism for a line of text that reads: "A face is to make faces with"—some adults having taken this as a green light to their youngsters for rude behavior—Nordstrom responded by saying, "Well, they're going to make faces whether you want them to or not."[14] Her approach to young adult fiction was just as firmly grounded in psychological realism and an openhearted respect for the young person's point of view. Reflecting on the sodden tradition of the teen novel prior to the 1960s, with its shadowless depictions of home, school, and community life and its stifled acknowledgments of sexuality, Nordstrom wrote:

> Is there a real world where young people *always* respect their always respectable parents? Where Dick Faversham *always* asks Patty Fairchild to the Senior Prom? Where Dan Baxter, the bully, and Mumps, his toady, *always* get their comeuppance? The "rigid world of good and bad" is infinitely easier to write about than the real world. Because the writer of books about the real world has to dig deep and tell the truth.[15]

However impatient she sometimes became with the guardians of tradition, Nordstrom was too canny a businesswoman

13. See letter to Meindert DeJong, March 4, 1953, page 63.
14. "Ursula Nordstrom—and How Harper's Children's Books Come to Be," *The House of Harper* (company newsletter), August 1963, 3.
15. Ursula Nordstrom, "Honesty in Teenage Novels," *Top of the News*, Vol. 21 (November 1964), 35.

simply to dismiss what the critics said. She defined this part of her job as that of "get[ting the books] past the adults who buy" them,[16] and she did so faithfully, in the belief that "most children . . . will react creatively to the best work of a truly creative person."[17]

Year after year she worked the library and school conventions like a seasoned campaigner, nodding and smiling while keeping a sharp eye on the book budgets of those to whom she apportioned her time. She secured endorsements when necessary from psychologists, educators, and others for a book deemed risky—or risqué. She sent out special letters to booksellers and librarians, fine-tuned advertising copy, and held meetings with key review editors, all with something like martial precision. Preparations for the publication of John Donovan's *I'll Get There. It Better Be Worth the Trip.*, a novel that included the first reference, in a book for young adults, to a homosexual experience, succeeded beyond Nordstrom's wildest hopes in securing for the book a levelheaded and generally favorable reception. The same had been true for *It's Like This, Cat* by Emily Neville, a purposefully grim contemporary urban novel for teens about faltering family relationships, which went on to win the 1964 Newbery Medal; and it would again be true for books containing equally dicey material by Louise Fitzhugh, M. E. Kerr, and others.

When controversy could not be averted, as in the case of the objections raised to Maurice Sendak's depiction of a naked boy in the illustrations for *In the Night Kitchen*, Nordstrom stood her ground with immense dignity and an unshakeable resolve. She responded with outrage to a report that a Louisiana librarian had, in the name of public decency, made alterations in her library's copy of Sendak's book. In an open letter to the children's book

16. See letter to John Donovan, August 5, 1968, page 259.
17. See letter to Mary V. Gaver, November 21, 1963, page 168.

community, Nordstrom condemned the librarian's "act of censorship by mutilation rather than by obvious suppression" and declared that such behavior "must not be allowed to have an intimidating effect on creators and publishers of books for children."[18] Throughout her career, Nordstrom responded personally to letters of complaint received by her department, taking the thoughtful ones as occasions for reaffirming, and sometimes rethinking, her convictions as a publisher, and allowing herself some raffish fun with the letters written by quacks.

A publishing innovation that drew universal praise was Nordstrom's introduction, in the late summer of 1957, of the I Can Read Books, an essentially new genre in American children's literature, designed and written for children newly able to read on their own.[19] Nordstrom had been contemplating the need for such books, and the form they might take, for years, when an unknown writer named Else Holmelund Minarik came to see her with a manuscript that Nordstrom recognized at once was just right for the sort of book she wanted. Minarik's *Little Bear*, with Maurice Sendak's illustrations, would, she realized, set a brilliant standard for all the I Can Read Books to follow, and the editor could not have been more pleased. In the months prior to publication, Nordstrom's sense of triumph came crashing down, however, when Random House launched its own somewhat similar series with a Dr. Seuss book called *The Cat in the Hat.* Suddenly faced with unwelcome competition, Nordstrom went to work, composing more letters to more librarians, booksellers, and on and on. It was back once more into the "eye of the hurricane"[20] for her; but that after all was where Nordstrom felt at home.

* * *

18. See Harper press release, containing letter from UN, June 9, 1972, pages 333–35.
19. See letter to Virginia Haviland, May 7, 1957, footnote 2, page 96.
20. See letters to Russell Hoban, January 16, 1974, page 352, and to Barbara Alexandra Dicks, December 26, 1974, page 361.

Ursula Nordstrom's entrance into the field of juvenile publishing in the late 1930s coincided with the popularity of nationally syndicated comic strips like *Dick Tracy* and *Little Orphan Annie*, and with the advent of a rival mass-medium format that proved to be spectacularly successful, the comic book. Children's librarians condemned the comics in the most vigorous terms as formulaic, subliterary, and excessively violent. On becoming Harper's editor, Nordstrom, however, decided to "find out what the children like[d] so much in them. So I got Dick Tracy, Orphan Annie, anything that was going, and I got hooked myself."[21] She found that "strong characters, funny names and a lot of action" were common elements, and that some strips were in fact "very well drawn." She also enjoyed, and on some level desperately needed, the Wonderland rush of venturing headlong into territory marked off-limits by the authorities. In conversation and by letter, Nordstrom issued license after license for her authors to do the same.

On taking charge of the department, Nordstrom made it her policy that no artist or writer wishing to present his or her work would be turned away, with or without an appointment. If she sensed that the visitor had talent—her antennae for this remained permanently extended—time and the telephone, and the daunting stacks of manuscripts and mail, ceased to exist for as long as the get-acquainted session lasted. Nothing but the young aspirant's thoughts and confidences mattered to her, or so she made one visitor after another feel. The sheer extravagance with which Nordstrom professed her eagerness to listen gave to these free-form meetings thrilling overtones of an impromptu experiment in self-revelation, a stripping down to one's own raw center as a means toward discovering the core material from which a deeply felt book might emerge. "You've come home!" she told more than one thunderstruck visitor in

21. Natov and DeLuca, 126.

whom she had detected promise, accepting the author in advance of the work. A gifted young person could hardly have asked for more.

Such blanket acceptance afforded the editor wide latitude when criticizing, and sometimes rejecting, an author's subsequent efforts. The marginal note that everyone who worked with her remembers—"N.G.E.F.Y.," or Not Good Enough For You—implied, deftly enough, that if a word or passage or even an entire manuscript did not pass muster, it was not because the author was a failure but because the piece of work in question had, in that particular instance, somehow failed to rise to his or her own high and praiseworthy standard.

A superlative line editor, Nordstrom detested cant and what she called "stuffiness" in writing. This applied not only to books but to office memoranda and to the letters that she and her staff daily wrote and that circulated throughout the department in what were called carbon folders for all to see. When a pedantic memo made the rounds stating that "pic" (publishing shorthand for "picture") was not to be confused with the plural "pix," Nordstrom scribbled in the margin: "(Another good thing to know is that a humming bird weighs less than a penny. UN)"[22]

She rooted out cloying, babyish language along with pomposity, and was keenly aware of the magnitude of the achievement, in literary terms, of a simple-seeming text like Margaret Wise Brown's *The Runaway Bunny*, a book for preschoolers that captures the essence of a young child's need for unconditional love. "There is a great deal of difference," Nordstrom mildly observed, "between this story and what most of us would do if we set out to write a book about a rabbit."[23]

Whether in person or by letter, she coaxed authors toward perfection by a dazzling variety of means, including flattery,

22. Memo supplied by Charlotte Zolotow.
23. "Ursula Nordstrom—and How Harper's Children's Books Come to Be," 3.

exhortation, extravagant praise, outrageous wit, guilt, self-parody, and self-deprecation.

"Don't you want to have *fun* with this?"[24] Nordstrom asked Mary Rodgers when they met to talk over the manuscript of *Freaky Friday*. The author had become bogged down, and her writing showed it. "Sure I want to have fun," Rodgers replied, trying on the thought. Nordstrom's question proved to be just the nudge that Rodgers needed to get on with her work.

She also said little when Jean Craighead George, the natural-science writer and novelist, came to see her following the retirement of George's longtime editor at Thomas Y. Crowell, Elizabeth Riley. This author, a Newbery Honor winner, knew precisely what she was about, and Nordstrom understood this.

George recalled:

> I climbed the wooden steps to the Children's Department in the old Harper building on Thirty-third Street and entered a large room partitioned off into offices by glass walls and bookcases. It smelled of paper, rubber cement and printer's ink; its colors were red, yellow and blue against smoky brown. I felt at home.
>
> Pat[25] led me along a winding course to Ursula Nordstrom's office deep inside the busy labyrinth. She was bent over her desk in concentration, her gray hair grooved where her fingers had pressed. Hearing us, she turned around and her penetrating eyes met mine head-on. She nodded to say she knew who I was and why I was there.
>
> "I want to write a book," I said, "about an Eskimo girl who is lost on the Arctic tundra. She

24. Interview with author, December 4, 1996.
25. Pat Allen, the department's business manager; she became associate publisher with Charlotte Zolotow in 1976.

survives by communicating with a pack of wolves in their own language."

"Will it be accurate?"

"Yes."

"I'll write you up your contract and advance now. Who is your agent?"

Never before had I been offered a contract and advance before a word had been written. . . . I went home and began writing *Julie of the Wolves.*"[26]

In contrast to these minimalist contacts, Nordstrom's letter to Else Holmelund Minarik of May 26, 1970, pages 299–300, exemplifies the gently probing manner in which, on other occasions, the editor put out long, patient lines of questions in the hope of prompting some observation or glimmer of interest in an author unsure of how to proceed.

As coach and fan, confessor and healer, surrogate mother and devoted friend, Nordstrom lived through authors' divorces, financial crises, depressions. When an author was short of cash, she did what she could to help out, paying some authors an annual general allowance (as opposed to the more usual kind of advance payment that is tied to a specific book under contract), or offering an advance based on little more than her belief that the promising artist or writer in question would deliver a worthy book sooner or later. Nordstrom could afford to enter into such unconventional arrangements on occasion only because she kept such a tight rein on department finances overall. Harper rewarded her contribution to the house by electing her in 1955 to its board of directors (she was the only woman to have reached this level within the firm up to that time); by naming her its first woman vice president in 1960; and

26. Jean Craighead George, *Journey Inward* (New York: Dutton, 1982), 213–14. George's novel *Julie of the Wolves*, illustrated by John Schoenherr, won the 1973 Newbery Medal.

by a succession of subsequent promotions and honors. Nonetheless, she seems never to have risen entirely above the second-class status traditionally accorded women in publishing. At one board meeting when a colleague asked her, the only woman present, to make the coffee, Nordstrom had curtly replied she did not know how.

Nordstrom had an earthy, robust laugh, a piercing gaze, and a knowing look of amused skepticism. She had a messy desk and a messy office, with a "confused table" for manuscripts about which she could not yet think intelligently. She typed her own letters, having found dictation a drag on her prized spontaneity; she typed very rapidly though not very accurately, and was forever lampooning herself as an editor in need of editing. Time and again she apologized to correspondents for the "messy" or "bad" letter she was about to send off to them. She loved playing the part of the hard-boiled publisher barking orders to subordinates as she pounded away at her keyboard and as the telephone—her word for this—constantly "exploded."

"Answer that!" she growled if an office telephone continued to ring for too long. "That could be the next Mark Twain."[27] It was a good joke, but it was also for that reason that Nordstrom generally answered her own telephone.

She had a witty remark for most occasions. When an artist new to her spoke pompously of having illustrated the Bible, Nordstrom replied, "Good text."[28] Served a plate of rabbit stew at dinner during a business trip to London, she reportedly sighed, "I'm sorry but I can't eat this. I publish rabbits!"[29]

She kept a pair of miniature boxing gloves in her desk drawer, to be taken out when tempers boiled over, and told friends that if she wrote a memoir, she would call the book *I'm*

27. Charlotte Zolotow, interview with author, January 4, 1994.
28. Ibid.
29. Mary Stolz, interview with author, May 10, 1996.

Glad I Never Knew Shakespeare. The editor who established the Nordstrom Award for the Most Amiable Author of the Year had come to expect that creative people would be difficult to work with at times; she had come to thrive on the difficulty. Her complete sympathy for the underdog extended not only to children as a group but to creative artists in need of support and understanding, and to all victims of prejudice and discrimination.

Authors showed their devotion not just by publishing their books on the Harper list, but by playing talent scout. Margaret Wise Brown, who—their occasional skirmishes aside—was deeply fond of Nordstrom, introduced the editor to illustrators Clement Hurd, Charles G. Shaw, and Leonard Weisgard. Brown may also have sent Ruth Krauss to Harper. Margret and H. A. Rey introduced Nordstrom to Jesse Jackson, whose 1945 novel *Call Me Charley* would make history as one of the first books for young people to address the issue of racial prejudice in contemporary American life from an African-American point of view. Louise Fitzhugh sent M. E. Kerr. Tomi Ungerer sent Shel Silverstein. Maurice Sendak encouraged Nordstrom to approach Edward Gorey and Stephen Sondheim, the latter of whom turned out not to want to write for children but was glad to put Nordstrom in touch with Mary Rodgers, who did.[30]

Maurice Sendak had come to the editor's notice thanks not to a Harper author but to the book buyer at F.A.O. Schwarz, Frances Chrystie. New York's preeminent toy store had one of the city's best children's book departments; for that reason Nordstrom had made a point of getting to know Chrystie. In 1951 Sendak was a shy, high-school-educated artist-in-the-making with a day job in Schwarz's window-display department. In what has become an oft-told tale, Chrystie arranged

---

30. As Rodgers recalls, Nordstrom often found authors by simply "sending letters off like messages in bottles." Interview with author, December 4, 1996.

for Nordstrom to see the young man's sketchbook drawings.[31] The editor promptly hired the Brooklyn lad to illustrate Marcel Aymé's *The Wonderful Farm*.

Several years later, when Nordstrom sailed to Europe on a trip combining vacation time with business, she arranged to travel with Frances Chrystie. Always a nervous, irritable traveler, she was glad for the companionship of someone as unflappable as her bookseller friend. In Greece they stopped at Epidaurus to visit the ancient amphitheater famed for its perfect acoustics. As Nordstrom recalled the scene for Janette Sebring Lowrey: "Frances climbed to the very top seat of the theatre and she asked me to speak in a normal tone of voice where the actors stood, to let her find out for herself how good the acoustics were. So when she was finally seated at the very top, I said to this fine book buyer: 'Buy Harper books.' And she called down coldly: 'At the proper discount I will.'"[32]

When asked to explain how she chose the books that Harper published, Nordstrom often said: "If I can resist a book, I resist it." As a reader, however, she seems to have had an appetite for almost everything. "Would Virginia Woolf be sickened to know that she is loved by one who also reads *Confidential*?" she slyly wrote novelist Mary Stolz, having just sorted through her personal library for a move.[33] Letters dated December 7th often bore the notation "Pearl Harbor Day and Willa Cather's birthday." She read Thurber with relish and Melville with a blue pencil, and regarded *The Oxford Book of English Verse*[34] as a kind of bible, to be consulted for solace and quoted from memory. A passage summing up Martha Graham's advice to

31. See footnote 2, page 41 to letter to Ruth Krauss, October 15, 1951.
32. Letter to Janette Sebring Lowrey, November 30, 1959. HarperCollins archives.
33. See letter to Mary Stolz, January 2, 1957, page 90.
34. *The Oxford Book of English Verse, 1250 1918*, chosen and edited by Arthur Quiller-Couch, Clarenden Press, 1939.

self-doubting artists came to have the importance for her of a professional credo, to be shared with authors and reread to herself, from a crumpled slip of paper she carried in her purse, at her "most tired and disillusioned [moments]:"[35]

> There is a vitality, a life force, an energy, a quickening that is translated through you into action and because there is only one of you in all of time this expression is unique. And if you block it, it will never exist through any other medium and it will be lost. It is not your business to determine how good it is, nor how valuable, nor how it compares with other expressions. It is your business to keep it yours, clearly and directly, to keep the channel open."[36]

The central idea expressed in these lines explains a great deal about Nordstrom's view of herself professionally, including her approach to letter writing, which had less to do with the art of the essay than with the act of giving an unguarded response to her authors' work and personal news. Not all her business letters were written in this freeflowing, straight-from-the-heart style, but the wonder is how very many of them were. Letter writing was a form of theatrical improvisation for Nordstrom. Her letters were her stage.

Nordstrom belonged to the last generation of devoted letter writers. She took immense pleasure in the act, often writing to authors when there was no obvious necessity of doing so, except for the all-important necessity of keeping a "channel open" to them. Although she naturally did much of her editorial work with local authors in person or by phone, she also sent long, funny, perceptive letters to those with whom she had just

35.   Letter to Else Holmelund Minarik, November 19, 1973. HarperCollins archives.
36.   Quoted in Agnes de Mille, *Dance to the Piper*, Little, Brown, 1952, p. 256.

spoken by telephone or just that day met for lunch. Time and again, she simply could not resist the temptation to write.

When she was working with authors who lived at a great distance from New York, letter writing was a basic necessity. Two sets of correspondence in this category deserve special mention, not only for their sheer volume but also for the representative places they occupy within the body of Nordstrom's correspondence.

Nordstrom first corresponded with Meindert DeJong as Ida Louise Raymond's assistant in 1938. DeJong, who was then employed as the janitor of a Grand Rapids, Michigan, church, had an unwavering determination to raise himself out of obscurity and to perfect his art; that being the case, Nordstrom was fully prepared to play correspondence-school Pygmalion with him. The DeJong file eventually ran to ten massive folders containing hundreds of impassioned, rambling letters of bareknuckle candor and mutual regard:

"Please don't desert children's books (as you threaten to) for a long, long time . . . "[37];

". . . I am dying—dieing—dyeing (?) to see the *Unhappy Bull* ms. If it is as good as you say you won't have to worry about your bank account again. . . ."[38]; and, during a particularly discouraging time following his return from wartime service, when DeJong was writing nothing publishable and the editor desperately hoped that he would not give up:

"Ah, come on, Mick. I can't be <u>this</u> wrong."[39]

Years later, after DeJong had won all the major prizes, he broke definitively with her in a painful turning for the editor who had remained so loyal to him for so long. It was then that Nordstrom thought to invoke the comparison between Maxwell

37. Letter to Meindert DeJong, January 28, 1941. HarperCollins archives.
38. Letter to Meindert DeJong, February 17, 1942. HarperCollins archives. The manuscript referred to was published as *Billy and the Unhappy Bull*, by Meindert DeJong, 1946.
39. See letter to Meindert DeJong, July 22, 1947, page 16.

Perkins and herself; it was all she could do to put a good face on what was perhaps the saddest experience of her career.

Nordstrom had her next-longest correspondence with Janette Sebring Lowrey, a writer from San Antonio, Texas, who, like DeJong, first published with Harper as one of Louise Raymond's authors. During the early 1940s Lowrey made something of a name for herself as the author of the popular Little Golden Book *The Poky Little Puppy*[40]. But Nordstrom recognized in her the sensibility of a young-adult novelist of the first order, and was convinced that Lowrey lacked only the willingness—"ruthlessness" was Nordstom's word—to put work before family considerations for long enough to fulfill her enormous promise. If DeJong stood apart as the archetypal "willing subject," Lowrey presented a rather different, and perhaps still more urgent, case—that of the talented author in danger of wasting her talent. All forms of waste horrified Nordstrom, self-styled "daughter of the Depression"; in the hierarchy of her concerns, a squandered creative gift counted as the worst kind of waste imaginable.

She pressed Lowrey onward, with only very limited success, for the better part of her own career. In the course of exchanging scores of letters, Nordstrom came to regard Lowrey as a kindred spirit and an appreciative audience for picaresque tales of her business travels, her appalled observations as a novice television viewer, and her latest lament for the star-crossed presidential candidacies of Adlai E. Stevenson. Gradually, Lowrey's fiction writing became more or less a fiction in itself, a slender, if necessary, pretext for letter writing.

A running theme of Nordstrom's editorial correspondence is that of family life as an impediment to creativity. She expressed herself on this subject in the most broadly comical

40. *The Poky Little Puppy*, by Janet Sebring Lowrey, illustrated by Gustaf Tenggren, Simon & Schuster, 1942.

terms, being fully aware, of course, of the churlish and absurdly contradictory implications of her viewpoint. Nordstrom nonetheless clearly would have preferred that her authors, artists, and for that matter her staff had left marriage, and the bearing and raising of children, to others.

Nordstrom herself shared a quiet private life with her longtime companion, Mary Griffith. Authors visited them over the years at their various homes in and around New York. During the 1960s UN held court in an apartment in chic U.N.—United Nations—Plaza, where their neighbors included Truman Capote and Robert Kennedy. By the time New York had become "Fun City" to some, however, Nordstrom no longer found it so, and she and Griffith moved to a small house with a pool in rural Connecticut, on a backwoods road not easily located even with the aid of a map.

Ursula Nordstrom wrote only one book of her own, a middle-grade novel for girls called *The Secret Language*, based on her memories of boarding school. "Sooner or later," she began her book, "everyone has to go away from home for the first time. Sometimes it happens when a person is young. Sometimes it happens when a person is old. But sooner or later it does happen to everyone. It happened to Victoria North when she was eight."[41]

Nordstrom agonized over the manuscript and its publication. The book was well received, and a sequel, undertaken reluctantly at the insistence of friends, came within a chapter of completion. Unable to decide on an ending for *The Secret Choice*, however, and torn with self-doubt, she burned the manuscript in a sullen act of self-deprecation that for once lacked the saving grace of her trademark sense of fun.

Nordstrom had by then taken early retirement as director

41. Ursula Nordstrom, *The Secret Language*, illustrated by Mary Chalmers, 1960, p. 1.

of the department. In August 1973 she relinquished the directorship to become "senior editor" of Ursula Nordstrom Books (she seems never to have spoken of the imprint that bore her name with anything but embarrassment); then, in March of 1979, she became a "consultant" to the department, an honorific that signaled the effective end of her career, though books continued to be published under her imprint.

Her reasons for leaving the directorship early are not entirely clear. She told her authors that she had chosen to do so in order to have more time to edit manuscripts, and to free herself of the mounting burden of administrative paperwork that had in fact laid claim to an ever-larger portion of time. This plainly was not the whole story, however. As John Tebbel, the historian of American book publishing, has recorded, by the late 1960s, with the departure of Harper's patrician chairman of the executive committee, Cass Canfield Sr., both the tone and power structure of the company dramatically changed: "There was one aspect of these changes that did not escape observers of the publishing scene. The house was now in the hands of business-oriented people, while those who combined business with editorial creativity were out of control."[42] Nordstrom belonged to the latter group and understood what that meant.

During Nordstrom's thirty-three-year tenure as director, the department steadily grew from an original staff of three to more than forty by the time the house moved uptown, in the spring of 1972, to greatly expanded new quarters at 10 East 53rd Street. Moreover, as Nordstrom noted with pride in a letter to her old Northfield teacher Alta Becker written shortly before her retirement, the Junior Books department under her directorship had achieved "the highest profit percentage of any in this House."[43]

As the department expanded, its operations necessarily

42. John Tebbel, *Between Covers: The Rise and Transformation of Book Publishing in America* (New York: Oxford University Press, 1987), p. 371.
43. Letter to Alta J. Becker, January 30, 1973. Northfield Mount Hermon School.

changed. By 1960 Nordstrom was overseeing the publication of many books that she herself had not edited. In later years there were entire layers of staff to whom she rarely spoke; the "Tot Department," as she called it, had assumed something of the hothouse atmosphere of a boarding school, a fertile but feverish subculture of cliques and favorites. "There were [usually] tears around [the office] somewhere—not hers!"[44] one longtime staff member recalled. Only the strong survived, and those who did, having proven themselves a match for Nordstrom's leviathan bursts of temper, received an education in publishing. A remarkable number of the people she trained went on to head departments or take other senior positions within the field.[45]

The chief legacy of the Great Depression for Ursula Nordstrom was that it had made a supremely self-sufficient working woman of her while denying her the chance to attend college. Nordstrom may have mentored a generation of editors, but she never overcame her feelings of inferiority at having failed to complete her own education. The Depression also left its mark on her letter writing. As a Harper clerk during that period of scarcity, she learned to treat paper as a precious commodity; reinforced by wartime rationing, this became a lifelong habit. When typing a letter, she set narrow margins and rarely pulled the sheet from her machine before she had transformed the page into a solid, single-spaced wall of words.

Nordstrom's thrift yielded unintended dividends in the case of the many letters in which she concluded her business only partway down the page. It was often only then, when faced with an expanse of leftover paper, that the editor felt free (because,

44. Leonard S. Marcus, "An Interview with William C. Morris," *The Horn Book*, Vol. 71 (January/February 1995), 39.
45. In addition to those mentioned in her letter to Maurice Sendak, August 25, 1966, page 226, there were Janet Chenery (Simon & Schuster and Doubleday), Ferd Monjo (Coward, McCann), and Charlotte Zolotow (Harper), among others.

in a sense, obligated) to write on nonbusiness matters, to offer up a personal aside, a digression about politics, some tidbit of gossip, or childhood reminiscence, nearly always followed by words of apology: "Please forgive the autobiographical tone of this. . . ." It is often in these last paragraphs that the reader gets the most telling glimpses of Nordstrom herself, fragments of the memoir she was unlikely ever to have written.

Ursula Nordstrom was a devoted reader as well as writer of letters. It was she who, after a thirty-year-long correspondence with E. B. White, first urged the author to publish a book of his letters. (Thereafter, when authors failed to respond to her own communications, she reminded them that they too might have a letters book one day, if only *they* would write to her more regularly.) She read for pleasure (as well as no doubt with a consuming professional curiosity) the published correspondence of Katherine Mansfield, Edna St. Vincent Millay, Maxwell Perkins, and others. Following the announcement in 1962 that Meindert DeJong had won the international Hans Christian Andersen Medal, she assisted her staff in the preparation of excerpts from her own correspondence with DeJong for possible use in conjunction with the event. During the last years of her life she even contemplated the publication of a book such as the present one but found it easy enough to postpone work on a project that would have cast her again in the limelight role of author.

A NOTE ON THE LETTERS

The letters that follow represent the full range of Ursula Nordstrom's professional correspondence. I have chosen letters that illuminate Nordstrom's many-faceted approach to her work as editor; that offer insights into the creation of a wide range of books and the development of a great variety of authors' and artists' careers; and that stand on their own as examples of the letter-writer's art.

All but a few of the letters that follow are given in their entirety. In the handful of instances in which deletions have been made in the interest of privacy, breaks in the original text are clearly indicated by the insertion of boldface ellipses enclosed in boldface brackets: **[. . .]**.

Dots of ellipsis were also, as it happens, a favorite element of Nordstrom's own informal style of punctuation—her way of signaling an interruption in her thoughts or change of subject or sudden descent into a tactful—or exasperated—silence. All ellipses that occur in the text, apart from those in boldface, are Nordstrom's own. She often exceeded, and occasionally fell short of, the three-dot standard, a detail that has seemed worth preserving for whatever it may suggest as a seismic gauge of her mood at the time of writing.

Nordstrom also sometimes used longer than usual spaces between sentences to mark changes of focus not significant enough to merit a paragraph break. These gaps have also been preserved here.

Minor spelling mistakes attributable to haste in typing have been corrected. The dating of letters has been standardized as, for example, September 9, 1937, despite the fact that Nordstrom sometimes wrote September 9th, 1937, or 9/9/37.

Because italics were not available on her typewriter, Nordstrom most often highlighted the titles of books and periodicals in full capital letters as the easiest way of setting them off. Occasionally, she underlined titles, placed them within quotes, or simply did not bother to set them off at all. For clarity's sake, all titles of works have been rendered here in standard format: italics for books, periodicals, films, and other major works, and quotes for poems and other short works.

In places, however, where Nordstrom underlined a phrase or used full capitals for emphasis or other visual effects, those treatments have been preserved.

In the annotations that accompany the letters, the recipient's initials have often been substituted for the full name; UN always stands for Ursula Nordstrom.

For reasons of space, signatures have been omitted except in the case of departures from the standard "Ursula" or "Ursula Nordstrom." Less has been lost in doing so than might at first appear, as it is almost always possible to surmise from the letters themselves the tenor of their author's relationship with her correspondent. The rare instances when she felt it necessary to include her title have been preserved.

For reasons of privacy, the names of readers and other correspondents outside the publishing world have been deleted.

Unless otherwise indicated, all titles cited in the notes were published by Harper & Brothers (up to 1962) and by Harper & Row (thereafter).

Nordstrom composed all but a few of the letters in Harper's offices. Exceptions are indicated by the insertion of a place name—the letter's point of origin—above the date.

All but a few of the letters have been transcribed from carbon copies on file in HarperCollins' archives, New York. Other sources are identified by a notation at the head of the letter placed after the recipient's name. The following is a key to the abbreviations:

CoU	Harper Papers, Rare Book and Manuscript Library, Columbia University, New York, New York
CZo	Charlotte Zolotow
MiS	Miriam Schlein
MNC	Margaret N. Coughlan
MRo	Mary Rodgers
USM	de Grummond Children's Literature Research Collection, McCain Library & Archive, University of Southern Mississippi, Hattiesburg, Mississippi
ZSu	Zena Sutherland

The Letters

TO LAURA INGALLS WILDER[1] September 9, 1937

My dear Mrs. Wilder:

Miss Raymond[2] received your letter last Friday afternoon and she planned to answer it at once. Unfortunately, however, she is not well and is out of the office for about a week.

I know she would want me to write you and try to apologize for that inexcusably stupid mistake[3] in the dummy for *On the Banks of Plum Creek*[4]. She was extremely sorry that the error wasn't caught but I'm glad to be able to write you that it appeared only in the synopsis for the dummy. It certainly won't appear again! Miss Raymond, and all of us, were upset about it because, very frankly, every single bit of copy written for your lovely book has been worked over with enthusiasm and affection.

Plans for the poster are being worked out now, but doubtless Miss Raymond will write you herself as soon as she is back at her desk.

Sincerely yours,
Department of Books for Boys and Girls
Assistant to Miss Raymond

1. Laura Ingalls Wilder published *Little House in the Big Woods*, the first in her series of autobiographical novels of American pioneer life, in 1932, when she was sixty-five years old.
2. Ida Louise Raymond, director of Harper Books for Boys and Girls, 1936–1940.
3. As UN later recalled (see letter to Doris K. Stotz, January 11, 1967, page 234), *On the Banks of Plum Creek* was the first book for which she wrote flap copy, and she was nervous throughout the ordeal.
4. *On the Banks of Plum Creek*, by Laura Ingalls Wilder, illustrated by Helen Sewell and Mildred Boyle, 1937. This, the fourth of the Little House books, won a Newbery Honor in 1938.

TO GEORGES DUPLAIX[1] (CoU)   July 17, 1941

Dear Sir:

I am at a loss to understand your leaping to the conclusion that because your book[2] (of which I have only heard vague rumors) is on the first page of our catalogue, we are short of really good books. I am not so naive as to think that your comment denotes modesty. No, it is disagreeable, unfriendly, vicious, and—how do they say?—lousy.

Kindly do not feel concerned for the House of Harper because your book, or rather your alleged book, appears on the first page of our Tot Catalogue. An excess of good nature on my part should not indicate that there is cause to worry about this house. (As a matter of fact, Mr. Gergely's barge was what swung the first page for the book.)

Fortunately I am too proud to be vindictive, as the poet hath said. I therefore remain, honored sir,

Yours cordially,

Ursula (Anne Carroll) Nordstrom[3]

1. Author, illustrator, and publisher. As production manager at Artists & Writers Guild, a subsidiary of Western Printing Company, Duplaix oversaw the publication of books for his own company and packaged books for other houses, including Harper.
2. *The Merry Shipwreck*, by Georges Duplaix, illustrated by Tibor Gergely, 1942.
3. UN here made playful reference to Anne Carroll Moore, the influential superintendent of children's work at the New York Public Library, whose strongly voiced opinions on children's literature were often at odds with her own.

TO MARGARET WISE BROWN[1]   October 28, 1941

Dear Margaret:

It was good to see you this morning and I think the text of *The Runaway Bunny*[2] is now perfect. Will you please sign the enclosed contract, and then send it on to Mr. Hurd? As soon as it comes back to us from him our signed copy will go to you, and your half of the advance of $400.00. His advance will be paid on delivery of completed, acceptable illustrations.

I enclose the text of *Night and Day*[3] I'm glad you think it is "too loose," as you said this morning. You're right that it shouldn't be a real story but it does need pulling together and polishing.* I'm eager to see what you do to it.

Yours sincerely,

*"More matter with less art"—as the bard said.[4]

TO GEORGES DUPLAIX (CoU)   October 10, 1942

Dear Georges[5]:

Your gracious invitation and the beautiful drawing have brightened up a whole gloomy Saturday morning. I look forward with pleasure to luncheon on Wednesday.

1. One of the great innovators in the field of literature for the very young, Brown published her first book, *When the Wind Blew*, illustrated by Rosalie Slocum, in 1937, while Raymond headed Harper's juvenile department. When Nordstrom read *The Runaway Bunny* in manuscript, she told Brown that the ending needed work. From Maine the author cabled Harper a witty closing line that delighted Nordstrom: "'I have a carrot,' said the mother bunny."
2. *The Runaway Bunny*, by Margaret Wise Brown, illustrated by Clement Hurd, 1942.
3. *Night and Day*, by Margaret Wise Brown, illustrated by Leonard Weisgard, 1942.
4. Handwritten at bottom of page.
5. UN crossed out "Georges" and wrote "Mr. Genius."

I hope you are pleased by Mr. MacGregor's[1] desire to bring a goose, and a photographer, and get the book[2] some publicity. I wish it would make you once and for all infatuated with the enterprise and general sprightliness of this distinguished organization. (I <u>desperately</u> hope that you will not feel instead that we are acting out of turn in trying to arrange to have a goose at your luncheon…)

Mr. MacGregor's telephone call to *Variety* about the goose, and in fact the whole situation, has made me a little light-headed and rather hysterical. Unaccustomed as I am to having a vice-president busy himself with details connected with this department, I think I surely must have died and gone to Heaven. Now I long to persuade Arthur (Dimples) Rushmore[3] to come as Little Boy Blue. Mr. Burger[4], the old thing, could come as Georgie Porgie; Mr. MacGregor could be Pretty Bobby Shaftoe; Mr. Hoyns[5] could be Jack Sprat; I could be the cow with the crumpled horn. The possibilities are endless…. But, as I say, I am a bit hysterical.

Have you decided what to do about Miss Barksdale[6] and Mrs. Becker[7]?

I must tell you again that we are proud and happy to have *The Tall Book of Mother Goose* on our list. I'm so glad you are going to see more of Harpers on Wednesday. Everyone here thinks the book is brilliant and now they will tell you so them-

1. Frank S. MacGregor, vice president, Harper & Brothers.
2. *The Tall Book of Mother Goose*, illustrated by Feodor Rojankovsky, 1942. Artists & Writers Guild packaged the book for Harper.
3. Arthur W. Rushmore, head of book production and design, Harper & Brothers, and proprietor of the Golden Hind Press.
4. Adam W. Burger, sales manager, Harper & Brothers.
5. Henry Hoyns, chairman of the board, Harper & Brothers.
6. Lena Barksdale, manager of the children's book department at the Doubleday, Doran Book Shop, New York, and review editor of the influential *Publishers' Weekly* "Forecast of Children's Books."
7. May Lamberton Becker, children's book editor, the *New York Herald-Tribune*.

selves. They also think you are brilliant. As for me, I love you with all my heart.

Yours,
Department of *The Tall Book of Mother Goose*

TO CROCKETT JOHNSON[1]   November 2, 1944

Dear Mr. Johnson:

We loved the pictures for *The Carrot Seed*[2]. Thanks a lot for a beautiful job. It's going to be a beautiful book. We're having the type set now and proofs will be sent to you as soon as possible.

You're awfully busy, I know, and so we hesitate to raise even a small point about the pictures. But here it is. The little boy is perfect in most of the pictures but we are hoping that you will feel, as we do, that he shouldn't look surprised or doubtful in <u>any</u> of them. One of the most charming and touching things in the original little dummy was the feeling that from start to finish the child was absolutely confident. But it seemed to us that in a few of the finished drawings that sense of sublime assurance was lacking. He looked dubious. What do you think? We're hoping that you will agree and that you will have time to put back that very splendid certainty. Will you?

Best wishes to you and our author.

Sincerely,

1. Pen name of David Johnson Leisk, author and illustrator; husband of the writer Ruth Krauss. Johnson's first recognition came in 1942 as the creator of the syndicated comic strip *Barnaby*.
2. *The Carrot Seed*, by Ruth Krauss, illustrated by Crockett Johnson, 1945. This book marked Johnson's debut as a children's book artist.

TO KATHARINE S. WHITE[1]   March 30, 1945

Dear Mrs. White:

Here is our contract for Mr. White's *Stuart Little*[2]. We followed, except for the royalty and advance clauses, the Trade Department's contract for *One Man's Meat*[3] and do hope that you will find it correct in every respect.

Don Freeman[4] has just sent in several rough sketches. They are enclosed. He is a good artist, but he sees Stuart as a rather zoot-suited character and I'm afraid that you will be disappointed in his sketches. Will you let me know how you feel about them?

I also enclose some drawings by Garth Williams[5]. He wants me to be sure to tell you that we didn't give him much time to prepare them. He feels that if he is given the job he will be able to work out something much closer to what he thinks you want. I told him that you had spoken of Ernest Shepard's[6] way of enlarging the proportions of Toad and Mole, and he said that at first he had wanted to give that effect. But when he got down to work he found that difficult, because Stuart's size is mentioned so often. Mr. Williams felt that since, for instance, a dime can come up to Stuart's waist he (Mr. Williams) should be pretty consistent in the

---

1. Fiction editor at *The New Yorker*; wife of E. B. White. KSW often corresponded with Harper about business matters on her husband's behalf.
2. *Stuart Little*, by E. B. White, illustrated by Garth Williams, 1945.
3. *One Man's Meat*, by E. B. White, 1944. A collection of White's columns for *Harper's Magazine*.
4. Freeman was at this time known primarily for his illustrations chronicling the New York theater scene.
5. The son of two British-born artists, Williams won the Prix de Rome for sculpture in 1936. Settling in New York following the start of World War II, he published a number of drawings in *The New Yorker* that pleased E. B. White, prompting the author to suggest Williams as a potential illustrator for *Stuart Little*.
6. The English illustrator of Kenneth Grahame's *Wind in the Willows* and of A. A. Milne's Pooh books.

proportions in most of the pictures. (This sounds very dull and literal, I'm afraid, but Mr. Williams didn't mean it that way and, in fact, said it all much better than I am saying it.) I think that if you'd been here and talked with him you'd feel rather hopeful about him for the book. I may be quite wrong, of course; perhaps you will think his sample drawings not at all right. Now I wish we'd told him to take more time on them but we are hurrying so to get the artist problem settled we didn't dare. Anyhow, here are his drawings and we're eager to have your comments on them. He wanted very much to be able to do more but couldn't. We are sending on reproductions of some of his drawings for an adult book (not yet published) and two other drawings you might like to see.

You will see that in the sample drawings for *Stuart Little* Mr. Williams did one picture in different techniques. We like the more detailed technique, don't you? He was careful about lots of small but important details. For instance, in the picture of the doctor examining Stuart, Stuart is standing up. Mr. Williams had him lying down in the first sketch but changed it because he was afraid he might look like a little dead mouse if he were lying down. (That is probably a silly detail to pass on to you, but it was somehow encouraging to us.)

We have two other artists working on sketches and I'll send them on as soon as they are turned in. But one is Aldren Watson[1], and we're afraid, with you, that he won't be right for the book. The other artist has never done a book but he is a fine artist and "well known in the art world." He is such a long shot, though, that I better wait to see his samples before saying any more. I checked again on Robert Lawson[2] and unfortunately he

1. Author, illustrator, art editor, and muralist.
2. Author and artist, perhaps best known as the illustrator of *The Story of Ferdinand*, by Munro Leaf, Viking, 1936; winner of the 1941 Caldecott Medal for *They Were Strong and Good*, Viking, 1940, and of the 1945 Newbery Medal for *Rabbit Hill*, Viking, 1944. Lawson had ongoing relationships with Little, Brown and Viking and may have felt bound not to work for any other house.

is not allowed to do any work at all. Have you thought of anyone else?

We hope you will find the contract entirely satisfactory. But if there is any question about any point in it, please let me know.

Yours sincerely,

TO E. B. WHITE   September 12, 1945

Dear Mr. White:

I enclose a letter from a Mr. Stuart Little of 16 East 48th Street. At first I thought it was a joke. I thought some low character had had a special letterhead printed. But he really exists. I telephoned the number given, asked guardedly for Stuart Little, and was connected with him. We had quite a pleasant talk. I promised him a copy of the book and he said all he asked was one signed copy for him. You won't mind doing that, will you?

Mr. Aswell[1] tells me you have offered your barn for the storage of unsold copies of *Stuart Little*. Thanks a lot, but we won't need any space for your book. The advance sale has increased the past few days and we think we'll have to increase the order from 50,000 to 60,000. We're not absolutely sure, but it looks probable.

Yours sincerely,

---

1. Edward C. Aswell, editor in Harper's Trade department.

Dear Reys:

The librarian I wish you would meet in Chicago is Miss Agatha Shea, of the Chicago Public Library, main branch. I've written her that you may get in touch with her and that I hope you will meet each other even if briefly.

Miss Shea is a perfectly grand woman, with a sensible, vigorous, intelligent approach to children's books. I think I mentioned over the 'phone that several of the New York librarians are not overly fond of her, because she has locked horns with them on several occasions. She is the librarian who told me years ago not to worry about what this librarian and that librarian thought, that her advice to me was to go ahead and do the books I liked and believed in, and let the various library cliques take them or leave them. Perhaps I shouldn't write this (please burn the letter) but I've always appreciated her hearty and friendly comments on Harper children's books. She and I haven't always agreed on various books but even when we've argued, I've never felt she was stuffy about them.

Margret, Miss Shea is not young and beautiful like you. But she is well worth knowing. I told her, in my letter, that you and Rey might telephone but added that if you didn't it would just be because you hesitated to interrupt one of her busy days. So if your time in Chicago is too rushed, don't worry about getting in touch with her.

1. Author/illustrator team. The Reys had been living in Paris at the time of the Nazi invasion. Fleeing to America, they took an apartment in New York's Greenwich Village not far from UN's. Harper became the Reys' second publisher after Houghton Mifflin, which had been lucky enough in 1941 to secure American rights to *Curious George*. The Reys' Harper books included *Pretzel* (1944) and *Spotty* (1945), both written by Margret and illustrated by her husband; in addition, H. A. Rey illustrated Charlotte Zolotow's first book, *The Park Book*, published by Harper in 1944.

I hope you have lots of fun. Please remember every single thing so you can describe the trip to me in detail. I hope you are impressed with the Mississippi River.

Affectionately,

P.S. Margret, let Rey do most of the talking.

TO MARGARET WISE BROWN   January 25, 1946

Dear Margaret:

I tried to 'phone you this afternoon but apparently you disregarded my advice to you to stay home. I feel this was very unwise and I must ask you to take better care of your health—at least until you have a satisfactory text for the *Little Fur Family*[1].

This is to ask whether or not you can let me have another copy of *Goodnight Moon*[2]. I'd like to try out another artist and haven't a copy for him. Will you let me know about this right away?

Yours,

TO MARGARET WISE BROWN   August 28, 1946

Dear Margaret:

Thanks for your letter which was waiting for me when I returned to this horrible hideous city. I love to think of you

1. *Little Fur Family*, by Margaret Wise Brown, illustrated by Garth Williams, 1946. See also letter to Garth Williams March 30, 1950, footnote 1, page 33.
2. *Goodnight Moon*, by Margaret Wise Brown, illustrated by Clement Hurd, 1947.

sailing and wish we could have a publicity picture of our Little Golden Little Fur author at the tiller[1].

Miss Renshaw[2] is devoting some time and a great deal of interest to *The First Story*[3]. We hope to locate some smooth-coated stock in the not too distant future (I'm purposely vague here) and I'll keep you informed.

Little Fur Family will be ready, the Manufacturing Department assures me, on or about September 3rd. I'll rush a copy to you in Maine but will hold the rest of your copies until I know for sure where you want them sent. The printed sheets are not bad but they are not as good as we'd hoped. However, everyone loves the book and the advance [sale] will be at least 50,000 copies. Young Books ordered 1,000 and F.A.O. Schwarz ordered 2,500. Publication is September 25th.

We must get together with Mr. Hurd[4] when you both get back and settle problems about *Goodnight Moon*. How long will you be in Maine? (I'm <u>not</u> glad to hear that you have not written any more stories.)

It is awful to be back in New York. I hate it. No, I didn't find a house but I'm not looking very seriously any more. I'm sure that even if I found just what I wanted the adjoining property would belong to a librarian or one of our more unreasonable authors (not you).

Did you get your new dog? Describe him, please.

1. UN here makes pointed reference to the fact that Brown, who was vacationing at her summer home at Vinalhaven, Maine, was then at work on a number of Little Golden Books for the rival house of Simon & Schuster.
2. Raine Renshaw, of Harper's manufacturing department.
3. *The First Story*, by Margaret Wise Brown, illustrated by Marc Simont, 1947.
4. Clement Hurd, illustrator and painter. As editor of William R. Scott, Inc., in the late 1930s, Brown first suggested to Hurd that he try his hand at illustrating children's books. Brown herself wrote the text for his first book, *Bumble Bugs and Elephants* (Scott, 1938). The following year he won the plum assignment of illustrating Gertrude Stein's fantasy for children, *The World Is Round* (Scott, 1939).

TO MARGARET WISE BROWN   September 12, 1946

Dear Margaret:

It was good to see you yesterday. I enjoyed you and your dogs and luncheon very much.

I'll write Clem and try to find out when he can come down for one more session with you and me and the Manufacturing Department. I'll also write him to make both creatures bunnies, instead of humans.

Will you start thinking right away about the second fur book[1]? Let's have a good story for it soon. In the meantime I'll start working at this end.

Yours,

TO MEINDERT DEJONG[2] (*telegram*)

(early October) 1946

YOU CRAZY MICK OF COURSE SEND MANUSCRIPT HAVE PUT CANDLE IN WINDOW FOR OUR WAN-DERING BOY STOP HERE IS WHERE YOU BELONG LOVE

URSULA

---

1. A sequel to *Little Fur Family*, the original edition of which was bound in real rabbit's fur, never materialized. Brown's text for the follow-up book was, however, published posthumously by Harper in a conventional picture-book edition as *Three Little Animals*, illustrated by Garth Williams, in 1956.
2. Dutch-born American author, primarily of middle-grade fiction. For many years DeJong worked as a janitor at a Grand Rapids, Michigan, church, writing in his spare time. Wartime service in China interrupted DeJong's literary efforts and left him with troubling doubts as to his future as a writer; it was only with considerable coaxing by UN that he began writing again.

November 14, 1946

Dear ——————:

I am taking the liberty of writing you to ask your help. We have received a letter from a girl in the Sixth Grade in Washington School, ——————. She mentions you as her library teacher in the letter.

The child is extremely angry at Jesse Jackson[1], the author of *Call Me Charley*. She says that if he is colored (he is) "it is a shame the way he writes about his own people, calling them niggers." I am terribly distressed to realize that the child is so upset by the book. I think what she is referring to is a bit on Page 8. George Reed, a very stupid and ignorant boy tells Charley that they don't like "niggers" around there—and immediately another character tells George to take "that trashy talk" away. George is a problem to Charley throughout most of the book and, of course, the author used that sort of a character to help make his point.

I've written —————— trying to explain why Mr. Jackson did that. I enclose a copy of my letter to her. I can't believe the child finished the book. But I hope with all my heart that she will read it carefully and feel differently about it. I'm writing you because, as you will see, I suggested that she talk the matter over with you. If she does will you try to help her understand that, as I wrote her, Jesse Jackson and we feel exactly the way she feels about Negroes?

I'll be very grateful to you if you will try to straighten her out on this and I do hope you will find a few minutes to write me a letter. Will you? I am really horrified to hear that even one

---

1. Margret Rey introduced UN to Jesse Jackson, a postal worker and reporter whom she had met at the Bread Loaf Writers' Conference in Vermont. *Call Me Charley*, which Harper published in 1945, with illustrations by Doris Spiegel, was among the first novels for young readers to address the issue of racism in contemporary American society.

child was disturbed by anything in that book, and that is why I am presuming to ask for your help.

Yours sincerely,

TO MEINDERT DEJONG   July 22, 1947

Dear Mick:

It will be good to see you in October and talk over your doubts and qualms with you and maybe shout and swear at you. My belief that you are on the verge of doing your best book is NOT due to wishful thinking, Mick. Kindly do not accuse me of "holding out the sponge of vinegar," dear sir.

I know you can do something which is even better than anything you've ever done, if you don't get discouraged and say the hell with it. It is absolutely unnecessary for you to be discouraged. I admit it is a bad time for you in your writing life, but it won't last forever. You know and I know that you can write and feel and think better books than any of the poor bloodless competition and you must remember that and get back to work and know that sooner or later it will once more come out right and warm and good DeJong. And if it is any help, remember that I'm here in New York convinced of that and, how shall I say this, and, well, just sitting this one out with you and confidently waiting for the orchestra to play even better than it used to. Wow, what a sickening flight.... Shall we dance? Ah, come on, Mick. I can't be this wrong.

I'll let you know as soon as I can whether it will be middle or late October. I'm looking forward to seeing you. You'll get out of this damned bog, Mick. I know it.

Love,

TO GARTH WILLIAMS   September 18, 1947

Dear Garth:

Mrs. Wilder's agent, George Bye, is very happy to hear about the new edition of the Little House books. He has been in touch with Mrs. Rose Wilder Lane, (the author's daughter), and she will be glad to see you. Will you get in touch with her directly? Her address is Route 4, Box 42, King Street, Danbury, Connecticut. The telephone number is Danbury 1684 W3. I'm sure it will be very worthwhile to have a talk with her. Tell her about the possibility of your going to see her mother, will you? I know she will be pleased about everything, and hope you and she have a good visit together.

I like to think of you and Dorothea[1] in the country now; the weather is so wonderful. Take a deep breath of fresh air for me, will you? I am chained to this cement island and hate it.

                                        Best to you both,

TO ESTHER AVERILL[2]   October 6, 1947

Dear Miss Averill:

Thanks for the final text and dummy for *Jenny's First Party*[3]. I simply love the story and the pictures are the best yet. The moonlit dance picture is wonderful, and so is the one on Page 21 (Jenny sitting on the box while Florio and Pickles go off with

---

1. Dorothea Williams, the artist's wife.
2. Author, illustrator, publisher. While living in Paris during the 1930s, EA established the Domino Press, a small press whose first publication was the landmark *Daniel Boone*, by Esther Averill and Lila Stanley, illustrated by Feodor Rojankovsky, 1931; Harper reissued this book in 1946. In later years EA lived in Brooklyn, New York, and became known as an author-illustrator of stories for younger children about cats.
3. *Jenny's First Party*, by Esther Averill, 1948.

Alice Featherlegs.) And the one on Page 22 is just right. I wish there could be a picture, just a small picture, for "All that could be seen was one black front paw appearing from behind the basket and then disappearing..." but I suppose there isn't room, and it isn't really necessary, but it could be a wonderful picture.

One thought—maybe I'm wrong to suggest this but on Page 31 could there be something very short about Jenny bidding Alice Featherlegs goodnight? You do say the three cats said goodnight to everyone but it might be fine for Jenny to say goodnight especially to Alice Featherlegs. I certainly don't mean anything especially loving, I hasten to add, just a few words which could express Jenny's sweet dignity. What do you think? There wasn't any hard feeling in Jenny's heart, I believe? Jenny always seems to be able, sooner or later, to rise above usual human smallness and it might be a good idea to insert something on Page 31. You've done a wonderful job of revision, Miss Averill, and I wouldn't make any more suggestions but I think this one more touch could be wonderful.

Perhaps you will call me Tuesday to let me have your reaction?

Again, I'm very happy over the story and I'm so glad you were willing to make it a party of cats instead of humans. Thanks for another fine job!

Yours sincerely,

TO CLARE TURLAY NEWBERRY[1]

November 28, 1947

Dear Clare:

The dummy[2] arrived safely and Mary[3] and I went over it together. It is going to be a superb and delicious book and I love it. Mary's letter will reach you before mine so I'll probably telegraph you today not to be disturbed by any comments on the story. We are so crazy about the pictures, Clare, that it seems silly to say anything about the text. What I have to say about the little story is that I hope you will let more of you into it as you work on the pictures. It seems a little perfunctory at present and I think you can have a lot more fun with it than you think you can.

Mary and I and several other persons here agree that the title is too long. If you can feature Smudge more just his name would make a good title, as Mary wrote you. You certainly don't need a big, involved, dramatic plot. Some of Beatrix Potter's[4] wonderful little stories are absolutely simple. But your text as it stands now is somehow boneless—can't think of the right word, there, I'm sorry.

Don't let our comments about the text make you edge-y, Clare dear. I think it can be as short as it is but I also think you can make it sound less perfunctory. This may be silly but would you be willing not to say the new kittens looked like mice? They do, and everyone knows it, but to some people

---

1. Picture-book author and illustrator. Newberry, whose specialty as an illustrator was the utterly lifelike depiction of small, furry animals, was Harper's leading picture-book artist at the time that UN became department head. Newberry's *Barkis* (1938), *April's Kittens* (1940), and *Marshmallow* (1942) were all Caldecott Honor winners.
2. *Smudge*, by Clare Turley Newberry, 1948.
3. Mary Squire Abbot, Newberry's agent at McIntosh & Otis, Inc.
4. The renowned English author-illustrator's little books were widely regarded as models of picture-book making for the very young.

the connotations are unpleasant[1] and we wish you'd omit that comparison. Another small point, which I hesitate to make, is that we wish you'd not call the mother Pussums. It sounds baby-talkish and therefore not like that brilliant and amusing Mrs. Newberry.

We're returning the dummy by registered first-class mail. We don't want to trust it to airmail. Let me hear from you, will you?

I've just seen the first proof of the orange, green-eyed cat, in the cloth book[2] and it is so close to the original that I'm ecstatic. I'll get an extra one for you and send it on as soon as I can. I know you'll be pleased.

Affectionately,

TO MARGARET WISE BROWN

Ten o'clock, a.m.
December 2, 1947

Dear Margaret:

The prescription from Bendel's has arrived and I am deeply touched and appreciative. The box created quite a riot in the Tot Department and now everyone wants to go home with me tonight and take baths in my apartment. I feel that this prescription will mean a great deal to me in the days ahead and that now anything can happen. I'll certainly have to meet a whole new group of people. No one I know at present is nearly elegant enough to go with this addition to my life,

---

1. E. B. White's *Stuart Little*, which Harper published two years earlier, had met with criticism on this score from the New York Public Library's Anne Carroll Moore, who, on reading White's fantasy in manuscript, went so far as to urge that the book be suppressed.
2. *What's That?*, by Clare Turlay Newberry, 1948.

except you, of course, and <u>perhaps</u> one or two librarians.
Thank you very much, dear friend and author.

I beg to remain,
yours sincerely,
Ursula Nordstrom
who is about to
smell <u>divinely</u>.

TO CLARE TURLAY NEWBERRY   December 17, 1947

Dear Clare:

Thanks for your last letter. Mary and I are glad that you agree about *Smudge*. We agree with you that your New York trip should be timed so that you can see the proofs. Everything else can be handled by mail. I'll find out the best way for you to send stuff. The horrors of New York cannot be exaggerated. It is hideous and noisy and confusing and the traffic is impossible, and everyone hates everyone else.

I don't understand the stores in Santa Fe, and have given our Sales Manager a memorandum asking him to check up on this[1]. The ads for your books were nice, we thought. Mary [Squire Abbot] sent you copies, didn't she?

Do you still love it in Taos? How is your health? I've just discovered that chronic bronchitis is probably psycho-somatic in origin so I'm rapidly getting over it. I don't want anyone to think ANYTHING happened to me when I was five months old.... Everything I read also applies to hay-fever and asthma. What about this???

Yes, it will be all right for you to indicate the second color on blues. We'll make the blues as soon as possible after we

---

1. CTN had complained that Santa Fe bookstores did not seem to stock her books.

receive the black and white pictures, and rush them to you.

You are so kind to want me not to die, and I appreciate your honest statement of how inconvenient it might be for you. Take care of your health, too, won't you? There are so many author-artists I'd rather have in New Mexico, rather than you. But the ones I have in mind stay right here in New York. Last year I established the Nordstrom Award for the Most Amiable Author of the Year, and I must send you yours soon. Mr. [Arthur] Rushmore designed and hand-set a very impressive certificate for this Award. It is fun awarding it and it is MUCH more fun notifying the authors who did NOT win it. Thus: "So sorry you didn't win it this year, Mrs. Rey, but better luck next time. Why don't you <u>try</u> for it next year, dear? All authors are eligible." Etc. Etc. Margret Rey didn't scream over the telephone to me for at least a week afterward. The Reys ask after you often. What is the news from Stephen[1]? How is he? And where? Send me some personal news, Mrs. Newberry. Are you having a fine life?

I hope you have a good Christmas.

Love,

TO MARGARET WISE BROWN (*telegram*)

August 24, 1948

SORRY CANNOT ACCEPT GRACIOUS INVITATION. WISH I COULD. HAVE IMPORTANT DATE WITH IMPORTANT LIBRARIAN ABOUT IMPORTANT BOOK. WILL WRITE WHEN I AM LESS IMPORTANT[2].

LOVE

1. The artist's son.
2. UN here refers to MWB's *The Important Book*, then a work in progress, which Harper published, with illustrations by Leonard Weisgard, in 1949.

TO MARY STOLZ[1]   September 7, 1949

Dear Mrs. Stolz:

We'd like very much indeed to see your teen-age girls' novel[2]. We do do teen-age books, but if it appears to us, after looking at it, that it's "above" our level, we can then pass it on to the regular Editorial Department.

Thanks again for writing us about it, we'll look forward to seeing it.

Sincerely yours,

TO ELIZABETH NOWELL[3]   November 10, 1949

Dear Nowell:

This is like old times, and thank God to be writing to you again about Mick.

He's written me about *House Sixty*[4] and I'll certainly send the manuscript to you as soon as I can find it. I should start this letter by saying that I have had a complete upheaval in my department what with one young lady getting married, one leaving for a better job, one having a mental breakdown ten days ago. So my desk is piled high with requests for review

1. Novelist, primarily of young-adult fiction. Stolz was to become one of UN's closest friends.
2. *To Tell Your Love*, by Mary Stolz, 1950.
3. Literary agent best known for having represented Thomas Wolfe and, in later years, as Wolfe's biographer and as the editor of his letters. EN was Meindert DeJong's agent during the years of his prewar apprenticeship. She retired in 1941; then in 1949 she reentered the book world as a freelance editorial consultant and, briefly again, as an agent, in which dual capacities she advised UN and DeJong with regard to the latter's manuscripts.
4. DeJong's *The House of Sixty Fathers* went through several more drafts before it was finally published by Harper, with illustrations by Maurice Sendak, in 1956.

copies, howls from irate authors, suggestions for possible books from possible authors and—well, you know the mess! I can't find ANYTHING these days but I promise to dig out *House Sixty* from the vault and send it on as soon as possible. I also want to send you a copy of some of the correspondence I've had with Mick since his return from the wars and copies of some of the letters he received from that nice agent he had for a time. But that will take a while. I want you to see the correspondence because I think you will see from it that it was hard, in fact it was god damn difficult, to coax Mick along after his stretch in the Army. He wasn't writing "good DeJong" and my problem was to try to keep him sending stuff along even though I was having to reject it with tears and anguish. All I could do was write him that I knew he was about to write something splendid and not to get discouraged and not to etc. etc. etc. As you know, this finally paid off in *Good Luck Duck*[1], which the Jr. [Junior Literary] Guild has taken, and which I think is one of the very best things he's ever written. (In all the correspondence which I was looking over a month or so ago I found in one of my letters declining one of his bum manuscripts a sentence from us saying "the little duck on the Ferris wheel is delightful and perhaps you should think of doing something about him."[2] I'm mentioning this not to make you think I think I'm any good as an editor—I am, though—but to help show you that he has had the most loving and tender attention all along since you left us.)   I think that probably somewhere sometime there'll be a book in *House Sixty* but it is going to take a lot of work to find it—and when I did decline it I received such a blast from him that I had no heart (I mean I'd run out of mental energy for a bit) to try anything. When we get *Good Luck Duck* to press and *The Cat Forlorn*[1] all set and I have

1. *Good Luck Duck*, by Meindert DeJong, illustrated by Marc Simont, 1950.
2. By hand on original: "This isn't exact but we did single out duck and Ferris wheel."

a bit more time I DEFINITELY WANT TO GO BACK AT *House Sixty* and see what we can do here to help tell Mick why it doesn't seem "good DeJong" to us.   He wrote me that you were furious that we'd passed it up and wanted to send it elsewhere. I think it would be a damn pity if some other publisher got the chance to work on this when we've gone along so long and so well, I think, with Mick. No one realizes that when you're laboring on the pictures, lay-out, number of colors, illustrator, for *Good Luck Duck*, and at the same time reading and thinking about *Cat Forlorn* and engaging in correspondence about *Cat*, (and also doing that with about twenty other authors at least) there simply isn't the time or energy to give to *House Sixty* until the immediate and obviously publishable manuscripts are handled intelligently.

I wish I were there or you were here so we could talk. This letter is turning into a disgusting one. I'm simply trying to say that when I can I'd like with all my heart to go back over *House Sixty* and give Mick some possibly helpful comments on it. It could be a really great book, but it certainly isn't now. And when I had to decline it regretfully he was in no state of mind for anything from me. I'll just have to dig up the correspondence and type a copy of it for you myself. I think then you'll certainly see the care and thought Mick has always had from us (as every author should, of course) and that *House Sixty* was certainly not rejected because it is a "war book." I never heard anything so ridiculous in my life as <u>that</u>.....

He is really hitting on all sixteen cylinders now with *Good Luck Duck* and *Cat Forlorn*. I'm sending you a set of galleys of *Duck* with the earnest plea that you PLEASE return them when you've read it. I'm sorry to have to ask you to bother but we're short of galleys and I want these back to send to *Kirkus* and

1. UN was dissatisfied with *The Cat Forlorn* as a title. The book was published as *The Tower by the Sea*, by Meindert DeJong, illustrated by Barbara Comfort, 1950.

others for pre-publication notices. I think you will love it. I am crazy about it.

I so hoped to get to Grand Rapids this week but with all these explosions in the department I couldn't.

Well, forgive this long rambling letter—too full of a whimpering self-justifying tone. (It makes me sick, too, dear.) But please don't go rushing to another publisher with *House Sixty* as it stands until Mick's devoted old Ursula has a chance to go back at it.

Hurry up and write me a letter.

And, again, I'm glad to be in touch with you again. We've really missed you, Nowell.

As ever,

P.S. Someone named Gwen Campbell 'phoned. Couldn't have sounded more delightful but alas the jobs are all filled AT THIS MOMENT. However, anything can happen to this department so I've asked Miss Campbell to come in to see me after Book Week is over, in case something turns up in the future. Thanks for asking her to call. She sounds wonderful.

TO ELIZABETH NOWELL   December 9, 1949

Dear Nowell:

(1). Please don't address me as "Dear Baby." I was young and eager when you knew me but now I'm a large, middle-aged woman even though my last anguished letter to you didn't sound very mature. (2). It was wonderful to have your good crazy sensible letter.

I'm sending you *House 60* today. Will you do me a big favor and let me know what you think of it before you send it to any other publisher? As I wrote you, when I regretfully declined his first revision of it I would have suggested possible ways of further improvement. But he was in no mood to consider any more changes then, as the records of that unhappy correspondence show. He rushed it off via Ives[1] to Reynal and Hitchcock, as you probably know. Then when he came back to home and mother when Reynal declined *House 60* he let me have the ms. back—and went to work on something else. I've just written him that now that he's working so well, and we're all happier together, I'd like to have your advice on it and he given the chance here to make one more try to see if it can't be turned into the magnificent book it can be and by God isn't at this stage.

You wrote me about some of Mick's manuscripts: "What the hell, kid, if you don't like em, just decline em." Would that the decisions on the material he's sent me since his return from the wars could have been as simple! I'll say no more.

Mrs. Campbell came in and I couldn't have liked her more. As I wrote you, all the jobs are now filled and the new staff seems to be working out well. But I'll certainly remember her the next time the wedding bells ring out in the Juvenile Department and will also let her know if and when there is any opening in any other dept. in Harpers. She impressed me mightily.

Please don't have secrets with Mick about *House Sixty* and don't have secrets with me about it. He seems in a good frame of mind these days, and God knows <u>I'm</u> as cheerful as all hell. (Joke.)

Love,

Baby

---

1. Marion Ives, a friend of Elizabeth Nowell's, who served for a time as DeJong's agent. Frustrated by UN's unwillingness to accept *The House of Sixty Fathers* for publication, DeJong tried his luck elsewhere, a serious step in an era when authors typically built career-long relationships with a single house.

March 9, 1950

Dear Mick:

The copy-editor brought the revised ms. of *Cat* back this morning and I've been gulping it down with such excitement that I'm almost incoherent. I'm only up to Page 37 but Oh Lord, Mick, what a magnificent thing it is now! The introduction of Crazy Alice is <u>beautifully</u> done. She is so touching and lonely and strange and tragic. I'd postpone this note until I finish the ms. but I have to leave in about ten minutes to go to a big luncheon, and want to get some word off to you immediately—sort of to relieve my own excitement and tension! Forget—as I have completely—my few reservations when I read the first version. This is too magnificent and powerful a story for anyone to worry over whether it will scare some timid adults. I'm ashamed that I ever had the slightest fear on that score. You should be very very proud of it and I'm so proud it will be on the Harper list I can hardly type.....

Now, I wrote you about the new artist[1] I've found. I think she will do a wonderful job. While we were waiting for the copy of the revision (AND DON'T FORGET TO SEND ME THE CARBON COPY OF THE ORIGINAL) about all she could do was to do research on magpies, wooden shoes, reed cages, graveyards, etc. etc. Have you any sort of material which would help her, and me? I want her to get the feeling of that olden time, and of that old village. But as she does her research what period of costumes, and architecture do you have in mind? We don't want any trite Hans Brinker job done. So any old books or any old pictures you can tell us about will be extremely valuable. Also, tell me about when you thought of the story as taking place.

Mick, I am honestly so excited I'm chittering like the cat.

1. Barbara Comfort.

When the copy-editor brought the ms. in he told Gloria Miller, my assistant, that it was one of the most beautiful stories he'd ever read.

Must stop and dash to that darn luncheon. I'll finish the ms. as soon as I come back. But I just had to get this letter off to you so you'll have it Friday a.m.   And please do send us any hints you can for the artist. She too is tremendously excited by the story. Gosh, I have to draw up a contract for it—I forgot that up to now. And you can have some advance on it too if I haven't sent you any already I'll check up on all this later today. In the meantime love and congratulations and Oh I cannot possibly wait until this book is published.

One last thought. Think the Cat need not be mentioned in the title. Makes it sound like a younger book than it is.

Love,

TO MEINDERT DEJONG   March 9, 1950
4.30 p.m.

Dear Mick:

I finished it and still think it is magnificent. Your letter also arrived about an hour ago and I'm glad you're keeping the carbon of the revision. Because I think two things in the first version were better. (I'm writing in terrible rush to get this into the airmail thing by five.)

I like the disposal of the burgomaster's whereabouts much better in the first version than in the revision. Refer to Page 63 OF THE FIRST VERSION. Then, in the revision I think the ending is weakened by having the burgomaster appear on the sea in a boat with Crazy Alice. There should be nothing on that sunlit sea but the cradle and the cat leaping. Let Alice drown.

Keep the scene with the black mass of the people on the beach watching the cat and the cradle on the sunlit sea, with the burgomaster's wife and the wise old woman. Keep the father coming back on horseback. It is honestly more powerful and dramatic that way, Mick. It is all right for poor crazy Alice to drown. And the first version's treatment of that almost unbearable scene on the beach is VASTLY better than in the revision.

Oh, dear <u>dear</u> Mick. I'm so happy about this book.....

To change these couple of places in the revision back to the way they were in your first version won't be too hard, Mick, so don't get at all discouraged. I'm sure that you'll see what we mean about these two places. Don't get that sunlit sea all crowded with burgomaster and boat and Crazy Alice and oars, and so forth. Just let that cradle come nearer and nearer with the cat leaping on it, and everyone on the dunes—and then the burgomaster wades out for the baby. Oh gosh, it is so good.

About the title—the book isn't about "The Cat Forlorn," no matter what the subtitle might do to liven that up. The book is about some of the most important things in the world, of course, and I think that—as I wrote in my morning's letter—the word "cat" should be left out of the title. The perfect one will come to us in time.

Glad you're so happy to be banned by Zondervan.[1] As for "religious" book my God I didn't mean the sort of thing you seemed to fear at all.[2] I'll dig up some examples of some lovely

1. Harper's Chicago salesman had written to UN to report that the Zondervan Book Store refused to stock DeJong's *Good Luck Duck* because any title "containing the words 'good luck'" implied that "the authority of God" was not "full and complete." In a previous letter to the author, UN had passed on this information to DeJong for his amusement.

2. In that previous letter, UN had gone on to suggest that DeJong, who was a man of deep religious faith, might want to consider writing about religious matters for young readers. Here UN hastened to add that she did not mean to imply that DeJong should ever contemplate writing the type of dogmatic, straitlaced book that a bookseller like Zondervan was sure to favor.

books and send them on. In the meantime, go over these spots in *Cat*, and write me what you think. Much love and much much gratitude for a wonderful book.

P.S. OH ALMOST FORGOT. What happened to the beginning with the two lines of that lovely old song about the cradle rocking rocking??? Have reread the first version in a great gulp and realized that those lovely lines should be kept in.

NOW DON'T LET THIS FINAL TIDYING UP OF LOOSE ENDS DISTURB YOU! It shouldn't be too time-consuming or thought consuming after all your good work, and it will make the book even finer than it is at this writing.

TO GARTH WILLIAMS   March 29, 1950

Dear Garth:

Well, Gentry[1], Bradley[2], Mergendahl[3] and Nordstrom have now had their session.

After fifty minutes Bradley and Gentry gave in and agreed that we would have to do the eight Wilder books by offset in view of the fact that Nordstrom was so pig-headed as to insist on the carbon pencil technique.

It was the funniest session, and Bud and I wished you could have been here. Bradley would say "But this and thus may happen if we do it offset, and it would be much simpler and easier to do

---

1. Helen Gentry, cofounder and part owner of Holiday House. In addition to overseeing all design and production at her own firm, Gentry occasionally served as a consultant for other publishers.
2. Daniel F. Bradley, head of production, Harper & Brothers. Bradley joined Harper in 1942 as Arthur W. Rushmore's assistant and succeeded Rushmore on the latter's retirement in 1950. UN's department did not yet have its own production staff.
3. Bud Mergendahl, of Harper's manufacturing department.

them letterpress." And I'd say "Yes, I know, but there is no simple and easy way to do these books." And then Gentry would throw in her two cents worth about the fact that the type might not be as black in offset as it would be in letterpress. And I'd say "Yes, but I can't believe children care so much about having absolutely black type, and I know they would like the carbon pencil technique." And then Bradley would think up another argument about how much trouble it would be to do the books offset. And I'd agree wholeheartedly and say there just wasn't any really simple way to do the books, that Mrs. Wilder had gone to a lot of trouble to write them, that you were going to a great deal of work to illustrate them, that all of us would just have to put ourselves to a bit of extra trouble to publish them, and so forth and so forth and so forth. At long last Bradley said "Well, O.K. We'll just have to do them by offset." Which I could have told them in the first place. Bud and I had a hard time keeping our faces straight. He feels as strongly as I do about your beautiful carbon pencil technique, so he and I are happy now, and hope you are too.

Gentry will be writing you, but this is a special line from me to say we're going ahead with the carbon pencil and God bless you.

Garth, do you need to have us go back to the $500.00 per month? I know that Harwood[1] will be sympathetic if all your recent troubles make that necessary. So let me know.

The books I'm sending Dorothea are a strange selection but I don't know her tastes in reading. But I'm pretty sure she will enjoy *Herself Surprised* and *The Horse's Mouth*[2]. *The Horse's Mouth* is about an artist, and you both should enjoy it, I hope. I sent a copy of one of my new books, *Good Luck Duck*, because it is a sweet book and I love it.

Write me a line soon.

Love,

1. Raymond C. Harwood, executive vice president, Harper & Brothers.
2. *Herself Surprised*, by Joyce Cary, 1941; *The Horse's Mouth*, by Joyce Cary, 1944.

Dear Garth:

We want to re-issue *Little Fur Family* in the size of the orig-inal paintings,[1] and with a regular cloth binding. I telephoned Bruce Bliven[2] this morning and he explained how your originals were stored in the ceiling—or some such place. He says that it would be a life-time task to go through all the stuff stored in the ceiling but that if you can give me any sort of hint as to approx-imately where those *Fur Family* pictures are, he will locate them and give them to me.

I am praying that you have some sort of chart in your head at least, and that you will be able to airmail me some instruc-tions to pass on to Bruce. I should have decided to do this new printing several months ago but have to confess that I would think of it only when I woke up in the middle of the night from time to time, and never got started on it. So now will you write me just as soon as possible and give me any information you can?

I think a new edition in a larger size and without any wormy or moth-eaten fur will sell very well and make you and Margaret some money. We'd get the very best offset printer possible and make a beautiful book of it. Do you think the same type face as in the fur-bound edition—only larger—would be suitable? Any ideas from our dear artist will be gratefully received.

We'll probably also have to have a jacket picture—unless we

1. The diminutive 1946 rabbit-fur-bound edition had proven difficult to store (moths got into Harper's warehouse, destroying a large quantity of the first printing), and even more difficult to sell to libraries, which favored standard-size books in standard bindings. (It was reissued in 1951 in a standard format, then in 1968 in a new, fur-jacketed mini-edition, and finally in 1985 in a small format bound in fake fur.)

2. Bruce Bliven, Jr., journalist, and friend of Margaret Wise Brown and Garth Williams. Bliven's profile of Brown, "Child's Best-Seller," was published in the December 2, 1946, issue of *Life*. Bliven was staying in Williams' Manhattan apart-ment while the artist and his family were living in Rome.

use the picture we used on the box. It is a darling picture, certainly.

I hope you receive this Saturday, April 1st, and that you will write me as soon as possible so I get some hint as to the whereabouts of the originals as early as possible next week. I go to Ashville, North Carolina, for a Childhood Education convention on April 8th, and will be there for a week—so do try to get some word to me before I leave the office Friday April 7th.

Love to all. And tell Margaret[1] to write me too, as well as you. Send me a joint letter—text and pictures by my favorite author and my favorite artist. I might be able to publish it.....

"ROUGH NOTES ON TALK WITH MARY STOLZ"
August 14, 1950

Gave her back ms. of *Organdy Cupcakes*[2] and told her it could and should be much much better than it is now. Warned her that she can make her stuff sound awfully slick if she isn't careful. Said Gretchen is, in spite of the author, the girl you're interested in, and that she should make it her story, with Nelle and Rosemary more incidental than they are now. Mrs. Gibson, Nelle's mother, much too stock a character, needs toning down. Rosemary completely unsympathetic, unreal, and irritating whenever you come upon her. Suggested that what is known to the reader about Nelle and Rosemary could largely be what is known about them to Gretchen (not as now to the author) and that perhaps that would automatically take care of the problem. She agreed to all this. Warned her too about some mannerisms

1. Margaret Wise Brown visited GW in Rome that April.
2. *The Organdy Cupcakes*, by Mary Stolz, 1951.

of style she is developing—omitting the pronoun in sentence after sentence—very Mignon Eberhart-ish[1] and done to death in *Organdy Cupcakes*. Mrs. Stolz took the ms. home, will reread and then rework so that Gretchen is more important and so that Rosemary is made more believable and interesting, will fix Mrs. Gibson, and other parts marked, etc.

TO MARY STOLZ   November 1, 1950

Dear Molly:

Please stay after school and write 500 times "I promise always to make a carbon copy of all my manuscripts in the future."

Yours sincerely,

TO E. B. WHITE   March 19, 1951

Dear Mr. White:

Thanks for your letter telling me that you've recently finished another children's book[2]. That's the best news I've had in a long long time.

We assume that you will want Garth Williams to illustrate it and I'm warning him to keep his schedule as flexible as possible. We know you can't possibly say when you think "the body heat" will go out of your story, and we'll welcome it whenever it comes. I'll just keep hoping that Garth won't be in the middle of

1. Mignon Eberhart, prolific author of romance mysteries, several of which were turned into movies.
2. *Charlotte's Web*, by E. B. White, illustrated by Garth Williams, 1952.

anything with an urgent deadline for Simon & Schuster[1]. Any Harper book he ever does is given to him with the understanding that he can stop work on it the minute the E. B. White manuscript arrives. I wish I could speak as firmly for S & S!

I've been a little afraid to answer your letter. I don't want to write anything that might seem pushy. I hope I haven't.

Yours sincerely,

TO RUTH KRAUSS[2]   May 2, 1951

Dear Ruthless:

Damn it, why don't you EVER stay home in the afternoon so a frantic rushed ch. bk. ed. can telephone you instead of having to write a letter!

Marc[3] telephoned me to say that he is not doing the second adult book for Schuman right away (you remember that YOU introduced him to That Other Publisher) and Marc said that another publisher wants him to illustrate a children's book right away. So here he is, with time suddenly to do a book, and he'll probably do the other publisher's book if I don't have something for him IMMEDIATELY.

Now Ruth, I cannot bear to put him on any other publisher's

---

1. The lucrative financial arrangements that Simon & Schuster's Golden Books imprint was offering top-drawer illustrators and authors like Garth Williams and Margaret Wise Brown had long since become the bane of UN's existence.
2. Picture-book writer and poet; wife of Crockett Johnson. Krauss, like Margaret Wise Brown before her, had been a member of the Bank Street College of Education's experimental Writers Laboratory, an association that brought her into direct contact with groups of nursery-school children and with a variety of experts in early childhood development. As UN's salutation suggests, editor and author delighted in teasing each other; but see also UN's letter to Janette Sebring Lowrey, June 4, 1965, pages 191–92, on the absolute necessity for authors to be ruthless about their work.
3. Marc Simont, French-born American illustrator. Simont had received a Caldecott Honor for his illustrations for Krauss' *The Happy Day*, 1949.

book unless I am absolutely sure that there is no Krauss book for him to illustrate. Have you by chance done a lot more on that wonderful definitions book[1]? If not is there any chance that you could get it into some sort of final shape by, say, next week? I told Marc not to take the other job, that I'd give him something rush from Harper & Brothers. But I'd love it to be a Krauss book.

Forgive awful, rushed letter. The operator says you won't be home until 5.30 and I'll be on my commuter's train to Irvington. I moved last Friday, and am dead. My fox terrier acts as though she'd handled the entire move alone, though. She drags around, thin and worn, with dark shadows under her eyes. I love to commute and all

Phone me RUSH

TO RUTH KRAUSS August 22, 1951

Dear Ruth:

Now about this participation book[2] you brought back in this morning: I hope you will read this letter in the loving and respectful spirit in which it is written, dear Ruth, and don't think I am just a dope to suggest anything as stupid as the following will probably seem to you. I am making suggestions in sheer desperation because (1) so much of this book is convulsively funny that I love it (2) you love it and (3) I have grave doubts about

---

1. *A Hole Is to Dig*, by Ruth Krauss, illustrated by Maurice Sendak, 1952.
2. This manuscript, in revised form, was published as *Is This You?*, by Ruth Krauss, illustrated by Crockett Johnson, Scott, 1955. RK continued to experiment with unconventional ways of enlisting young readers' active participation. In *How to Make an Earthquake*, illustrated by Crockett Johnson, 1954, for instance, she wrote a mischievous parody of how-to books aimed at encouraging children to entertain and think for themselves; in *A Moon or a Button: A Collection of First Picture Ideas*, illustrated by Remy Charlip, 1959, RK offered a series of playful starting points for children's own drawings.

a book with blank pages to-be-drawn-on-by-children being wise for you or for the distinguished House for which I labor.

But if you would be willing to give a little, and shift your angle on this book, I'd be very happy, and I think you might have just as funny a book, and honestly a more valuable one because it would get looked at, which the drawing-on-book wouldn't get, probably.

When I said you could make it a participation-in-partici-pating book I meant—and oh Lord, I hope you don't scream with exasperation over this—how about a book <u>within</u> a book. It could be the way it is now within a book (a couple of extra pages at the beginning and maybe one at the end) and your wonderful stuff could all be used. You could get some wonder-ful ideas for the beginning—you know, about once there was a boy named so-and-so who got a funny (crazy? ridiculous? un-usual?) book for his birthday. The name of it was—and then there could be a second title page with the title of this crazy book, your name, artist's name, etc., and he looked at it and it said "Is this your name" and then show that page, and then So-and-So wrote his name. And the next page said "Is this where you live" and show all that crazy page, and so then So-and-So drew a picture of where he lived. And so forth. And on the right hand pages instead of blank spaces for the actual child to draw in you could show what So-and-So drew—and so on right through. "His" drawings could be in quite a different style, of course, in just black and white.   Oh, I've just reread this paragraph and it doesn't describe what I mean. The thing is that you're so set on the actual child participating in this book and I think that is a good but half-baked idea. Why should a child participate by drawing in a book? There are other ways of par-ticipating. And if you did have it changed around in a book about a funny book a boy got for his birthday you could keep all the funny stuff, show his participation, and still not have the present thing of blank pages to be drawn on.

He could be rather a serious looking little boy, which would make it funnier, as he went through the cock-eyed book. And you could think of a wonderful ending, Ruth. I was just showing Bud [Mergendahl] the lay-out you left (still safe, still pristine) and he loved the idea but agreed with me about having it be a drawing-in-book. He thought it would be just as good making it participation-by-proxy. I mention what he said because you love Bud (so man-crazy in general) and maybe his opinion would influence you more than mine. Seriously, I'd ask John Appleton[1] too but do you really want to mix business with pleasure?

I'm afraid that writing this was harder (even) than trying to talk it over with you would have been. But do please at least think about it. I'm sure the suggestion will seem horrid, heavy-handed, obvious, uninteresting to you at first. But really think about it over night. It honestly could be very funny if you make it a book within a book. I love the idea of the second title-page and everything. And it would be fine to have a children's book about a children's book. The title of the book could be different from the title of the book within the book, of course.

Please please think about this, Ruth. And don't think that I'm "scared" of the drawing-in-book just because it is so different. I just think it doesn't come off and would do nothing for your reputation or your financial situation, and also wouldn't add lustre to you or the publisher. Yet I hate to lose all the really deeply funny stuff in it. And that's why I've floundered around in my head trying to think of an acceptable solution. You know we're not scared of <u>different</u> books, I hope.

Let me hear from you soon.

Your friend and admirer,

---

1. Editor, Trade department, Harper & Brothers.

Dear Ruth:

Thanks for calling back last Thursday afternoon. I can't tell you how sorry I am that I caved in Thursday morning. I should let Harper & Brothers get a pleasant placid phlegmatic children's book editor, shouldn't I. At any rate they shouldn't have one who seems to be equipped only to play in a third-rate company production of *Medea*, and suddenly starts to rehearse in an office. The real salt in the wound is, as I said over the telephone, that I contributed so much to the distasteful stereotype of the woman in business.

Well, I appreciated your telephone call, and am glad that you and Miss Sillcox[1] felt that, it being understood that no precedent is being set for the future, the Definitions contract[2] can go through without that one phrase in it. Mrs. Howley[3] is re-doing the contract now and I hope it will be ready to be enclosed in this note. All the other changes are being incorporated in it. I hope you can better the final delivery date of March 1, 1952, for the final text and I think you can, can't you?

Did you read that copy I gave you of Bettina's[4] letter? I am sure she wasn't so lovely about *The Bundle Book*[5] just because she knew you liked her *Castle in the Sand*[6].

---

1. Luise M. Sillcox, executive secretary of the Authors' League, who provided legal advice on contractual matters to RK, Margaret Wise Brown, and other League members.
2. That is, RK's contract for *A Hole Is to Dig*.
3. Dorothea F. Howley, secretary to UN; later the person who looked after rights and permissions matters.
4. Bettina Ehrlich, author-illustrator who published several picture books with Harper as Bettina.
5. *The Bundle Book*, by Ruth Krauss, illustrated by Helen Stone, 1951.
6. *Castle in the Sand*, by Bettina, 1951.

Well, Ruth, once more I'm terribly sorry about last Thursday and I hope it won't come between you and Harpers. As an editor who tries to do her best most of the time, I have the Harper children's book list now at the point where I do not want to lose any of the authors. And Abou Ben Kraussie's[1] name is way up at the top of the list of authors I would not care to part with. It is too bad, because I have often remarked cynically in the past that almost as exciting to an editor as finding a good author is the moment at which the editor decides she (or he) is willing to lose a certain author. But I am not at that point with you and I believe I never could be at such a point. As I tried to say last Thursday, I honestly have such a real reverence for creative talent that I am willing to do anything for anyone who possesses it. And it mixes me up when house-policy says I can't go 100% of the way. What the dickens, all I want to do is the best I can to see some four or five year old people get a wonderful definitions book, written by you and illustrated by Maurice[2], and published by Harper & Brothers, established 1817.

Affectionately, your friend and editor,

I'm so <u>damn</u> sorry.[3]

---

1. The reference is to Leigh Hunt's poem "Abou Ben Adhem," which tells the story of a good man whose name "led all the rest" of the list of those "whom the love of God had blest."
2. Maurice Sendak, artist; later also author, essayist, designer for the opera and theater. Sendak was a self-described "twenty-two-and-a-half"-year-old, working in the window display department of F.A.O. Schwarz when, in the spring of 1950, the store's children's book buyer, Frances Chrystie, arranged a meeting between him and UN. A day after seeing his sketches, the editor offered Sendak the assignment of illustrating *The Wonderful Farm*, by Marcel Aymé, which Harper published with his drawings the following year.
3. Handwritten at bottom.

TO RUTH KRAUSS   January 29, 1952

Dear Ruth:

Your list of suggested titles arrived this morning. I like *A Hole Is to Dig*, *A First Book of First Definitions*. You like it the best. The ladies in this department like it the best. And the Advertising Manager likes it the best. So let's use it. I'll get hold of Maurice today by 'phone and tell him.

Have you and he discussed the jacket at all, Ruth? What sort of a drawing?

I was tempted by *Stars and Mashed Potatoes* but it really is adult in a smart-alecky way. I think *A Hole Is to Dig* is fine.

I hope he'll (M.S.) have all the drawings ready by the end of the week, and of course I can give him a letter saying he can have an extra week for the jacket. But perhaps that won't be necessary. However, if it is I'll write it.

Last week-end I saw a television program (yes, I have a tv set and the other children's book editors think I'm horrible to have one but I just toss my lovely head and act defiant) and on it was the most attractive 4 year old boy I've ever seen. Very close, manly hair cut, and a darling face with dimples. The repulsive master of ceremonies said to him: "Tell me, Craig, when did you get those dimples?" and the m.c. grinned a baby-talk sort of grin, and the audience of adults giggled lovingly. And the kid looked at him and said: "When I got my face." His tone of voice was reasonable and courteous and trying not to indicate what a silly question that one was…. Doesn't look so wonderful written down, but it was wonderful. A Krauss Kid, I thought happily to myself.

Your sincere friend and admirer,

Dear Andy:

I am glad you are too exhausted to call me Miss Nordstrom any longer. We will save a great deal of typing time.

The copy of *American Spiders* came and we sent it right down to Garth. We also sent him the New York Public Library slip on the McCook books. As you have probably heard from him, he loves *Charlotte's Web* as much as I do and is at work on the illustrations. You'll see some soon.

The Advertising Department is preparing copy for *Charlotte's Web* and we will send it to you for your comments. There is no rush for jacket copy, of course, but there is for catalogue copy.

No, I have never encountered any story plot like *Charlotte's Web*. I do not believe that any other writer has ever told about a spider writing words in its web. Perhaps I should ask some of the children's book ladies who go back even further in time than I do, but I am sure nothing even remotely like this has been written. I believe Charlotte is the first spider since Miss Muffet's.

Yours sincerely,

TO KATHARINE S. WHITE   April 10, 1952

Dear Mrs. White:

I enjoyed dining with you and your husband last night. I think I made notes of all suggestions for the catalogue copy, and revised copy will be sent to you soon.

Garth and I had a talk over the 'phone this morning. He

says he is starting slowly and is making many sketches now. He was on his way to the Natural History Museum when I telephoned. I gathered that Fern will appear in many drawings, and I think you will both like her. I think that he meant he didn't want to show Fern in <u>all</u> the drawings simply because if he does Charlotte and the other creatures will have to be so small. At any rate, you will both see sketches and I know you will find Garth still open to all suggestions. I guess he won't have anything to show until the end of next week.

I hope neither of you minded my bringing up the chapter title "Charlotte's Death."[1] I hesitated to mention it but thought it could do no harm. (When I got home last night I looked in my copy of *Little Women*. The chapter in which Jo learns that Beth is going to die is called "Beth's Secret," and the chapter in which Beth does die is called "The Valley of the Shadow.")

Best wishes to you both.

Yours sincerely,

TO E. B. WHITE   April 28, 1952

E. B. W.[2]

Here are some rough sketches and a few finished drawings of Charlotte.

I am extremely worried about Charlotte's face in all drawings on sheet marked "A" but if you like any of them I will know I am wrong.

---

1. The author retitled the book's penultimate chapter "Last Day."
2. UN wrote in the upper left-hand corner of this memo to White, "If you like Charlotte ignore all this."

Garth wants to meet the challenge of doing a close-up of a spider, he says. But when he comes right up to it he doesn't meet it by giving her a <u>face</u>. I told him this morning that I would send the drawings over to you, for your comments. I also told him that I thought he had managed to make Charlotte a more <u>spider-y</u> attractive figure. But I said you might like Charlotte and if so she would be all right with us, of course.

On drawing marked (1) Charlotte has 8 eyes, which apparently she should have. Two on the top of her head, two low on the sides of her head, two where eyes usually are, and two where Garth has indicated a nose. I think that if the nose dots were made larger (as her eyes would be) and the line he has put in for a mouth were omitted, she would be still attractive but more of a spider. I put a small piece of paper over that line of her mouth and she looked better (less like a person).

On the side of the page, the drawing marked (2) would, if the mouth line were blanked out, be a rather accurate picture of a wolf spider, Garth tells me. Will you put a small piece of paper over the mouth on picture marked (2) and see what you think?

On the <u>reverse</u> of the sheet marked A is a very rough pencil sketch marked (3). Garth did this in my office this morning and though it is almost too rough to see I think it is somehow more attractive than the faces on the side of the sheet marked A. What do you think? After all, Charlotte <u>is</u> a spider.

The drawing of Wilbur is darling, I think. How do you like Fern? Please be absolutely frank about Fern because Garth can make her any sort of a little girl you want. The other rough drawings are labelled. I like Lurvy and also Mr. Arable.

Please forgive this note. I am rushing to get it off to you by messenger with the drawings. Will you telephone me this afternoon if you possibly can? If time were not so short I'd send the drawings with no comments of my own. You may possibly love Charlotte with a face. But in case you don't, let me know right away. Garth agreed with me and said that if <u>you</u> wanted less of an actual face he'd do some more samples. He and I would like to get Charlotte and Fern definitely settled before you go to Maine, and I'm sure you would too.

I hope you will be able to telephone me this afternoon.

TO RUTH KRAUSS   May 1, 1952

Dear Ruth:

So sorry I missed your last telephone call. I am assured that we will have printed sheets for the wonderful book *A Hole Is to Dig* on Monday, May 5. Is that one of your days in town? If so do telephone me so I can tell you definitely whether or not the sheets are here. They will HAVE to come some time Monday because our Sales Conference is 10 a.m. Tuesday. I simply cannot possibly wait to see the sheets and I can imagine that you are about 150 times as eager as I am, if possible. Mr. Maurice Sendak should be back by then, and perhaps he will come in too.

Now, Miss Krauss, I would like to know if you are going to do another book for Harper & Brothers for 1953 and if so which one you think it will be. Crazy House book[1]? Or what? Or do you feel you have drifted too far away from me? (I could never drift too far from you and your loony books, dear.) You always say that you don't want to do any more picture books, and I can understand that because twice a year when I'm getting ready for a Sales Conference I say I never want us to publish any more picture books. And if from the point of my much less involved

1. *A Very Special House*, by Ruth Krauss, illustrated by Maurice Sendak, 1953.

involvement I feel that way occasionally, I can certainly understand how Author Krauss can feel that way. But after all we should not take our personal problems into consideration but think instead of the CHILDREN. Think of all the babies born in 1949 who, by the fall of 1953, will be just the right age to love your 1953 book. Good Heavens, think of the babies being born at this very minute on May 1, 1952! They too will be wandering around in 1956 looking for a new Krauss book. (Several have been born since I stopped typing that very last sentence, wondering how the dickens to wind up this crazy but heartfelt paragraph.)

Anyhow, let me hear from you if you're in town Monday. I pray the brown will be the right color. I pray the paper is really the most beautiful ever seen before in a book.

As soon as the pressure of the fall books and the Sales Conference lets up we must get together with Ad Reinhardt[1] and figure out what to do about *A Good Man and His Good Wife*, a fine book which opened up a whole new field of literature so many many years ago .....

Sincerely, very sincerely,

---

1. Ad Reinhardt, the nonobjective painter associated with the New York School, illustrated RK's picture book *A Good Man and His Good Wife*, 1944. Although copies of the book, RK's first, later became highly collectible, it sold poorly when published. Marc Simont reillustrated the book for a new edition published in 1962.

TO NATALIE SAVAGE CARLSON[1]   June 13, 1952

Dear Natalie:

Thanks a lot for the carbon of *Alphonse*[2]. I will be sure to see that the changes in the carbon copy are made in the original copy.

I am glad you have ideas for two new books and I wish I were the sort of omniscient editor who could tell you firmly which is the one for you to work on next. I understand that there are such editors in existence but I do not know how they function. It really depends on which one you are yourself eager to write. Either or both of them might be completely charming. Since you do ask for advice from me perhaps I should say that the one about the little French sailor sounds perhaps more like Natalie Carlson but I hate to say even that much. The horse story in which you say you could include autobiographical incidents might be wonderful. I really would like to leave it up to you. We are still new at working together so you will have to tell me more about how you like to work. Would you like to do a little bit on one or both ideas and let me see them again before you put too much time on either?

Please know that I am not trying to avoid my editorial responsibility, but I think it is always unfortunate that an editor decides what an author should do next. I certainly don't want to sound stuffy but I do think you should do the one you really want to do. I never want to forget that if Lewis Carroll had asked me whether or not he should bother writing about a little girl named Alice who fell asleep and dreamed that she had a lot

1. Natalie Savage Carlson, novelist and reteller of traditional tales. The author's first book, *The Talking Cat and Other Stories of French Canada*, illustrated by Roger Duvoisin, 1952, won the prestigious *New York Herald-Tribune* Spring Book Festival award for the best book for children of eight to twelve.
2. The manuscript for what was going to be Carlson's second Harper book proved unsatisfactory to UN. See letter to Natalie Savage Carlson, December 9, 1952, pages 59–60, and footnote 1, page 60.

of adventures down a rabbit hole, it would not have sounded awfully tempting to any editor.

I am putting through the voucher for the last two expense accounts and the check will go to you next week. I am so terribly sorry that your trip to New York took place at the same time as this department's move from the sixth floor to the fourth floor. I did want to see more of you. I was certainly proud of my author on that radio broadcast and I am happy to be able to enclose a billet doux for you from Miss McBride[1] in her own sacred handwriting. I also enclose a good review from the *Worcester Telegram* and one from *The Miami Herald*.

Sincerely,

TO E. B. WHITE   June 20, 1952

Dear Andy:

Garth brought the pictures in this morning, and I hope the photostats will be ready to send you late this afternoon. Garth was not satisfied with one drawing and is going to re-draw it this week-end. But all the others are in. I think you will like them. Garth assured me that if you want changes he can make them after he arrives in Colorado. That will be about July 5th.

The fair drawing is good, I think, don't you? One thing does bother me about that drawing—the word "ices" on one of the booths. It seems English to me, but Garth thinks it isn't, necessarily. (I suppose that if the English publisher uses Garth's pictures he will prefer it to "cones.") What do you think? I haven't been to a country fair in one hundred years but "ices" bothered me.[2]

---

1. Mary Margaret McBride, one of the period's leading radio personalities.
2. The word was changed to "ice."

I hope the lettering in the web is all right with you but if it isn't it can be changed. I asked Garth about the word TERRIFIC in the web. He thinks it is legible. Do you? I also spoke to him about the front right foot in the picture of Wilbur weeping, and he asked me to send you the enclosed small reproduction of that drawing. He thinks that when the drawing is reduced it does look as though Wilbur has his head on one foot, but if you still want it taken out let me know and we'll do it.

How do you like the drawing of Wilbur crying to the little spiders "Come back, children!" I had thought there would be more little spiders. But perhaps it is all right as it is now. The picture of Templeton which you saw last Friday is more ratty now. Do you like it now? And do you think Garth has done quite well by Charlotte? There is no detailed close-up of her but I think there are enough drawings of her, don't you? Do you like the one of her wrapping up the fly?

I asked Garth why he hadn't shown Wilbur at the fair, and he said that he'd tried several and then decided that he should make the fair sequence quite different from the farm. He pointed out that he did do a couple of pictures of the writing in the web, and Wilbur looking happy, back on the farm, and he said that when he started to draw another of Wilbur at the fair it seemed to bring the whole thing back to the feeling of the farm. Oh, I'm not writing this as fluently as he said it to me. But what he said seemed to make sense. However, if you definitely would like another picture just let me know.

I do hope you will like the pictures, but please know that changes can and will be made. I'll have a corrected proof of the jacket to send you soon. Everyone here loves the jacket and I think you will like it, too.

Best wishes to you both.

Yours sincerely,

Some of the pictures are double spreads. I'll try to indicate them clearly when I send the photostats late today.[1]

TO E. B. WHITE   July 10, 1952

Dear Andy:

Here is a rough proof of the jacket. I've been hoping to get a corrected proof to send you but guess I'll send this uncorrected one now. The green will be brighter, and will therefore brighten the entire jacket. Do you like it? Everyone here loves it and we hope you both will too.

I would have thanked you before this for your promptness in commenting on the photostats of Garth's pictures, but 5000 librarians met in convention here on June 28th. The convention ran through July 5th, and I was out of the office all that time, smiling at each of the 5000 librarians and, of course, telling them about *Charlotte's Web*. There is a great deal of advance interest and enthusiasm for the book, of course. One earnest lady said to me: "Miss Nordstrom, do you realize that Charlotte is the third spider to appear in children's literature? There was Miss Muffet's; there was Robert Bruce's[2]; and now there is Charlotte." I said I realized it.

We removed the foot here, and changed the lettering on the carnival picture, and we are about to find a good place for that picture of Templeton. You are right about not putting him opposite the title page, of course, and we should have realized it ourselves.

The pictures to be changed were sent to Garth in Colorado the day we heard from you. I'm sure he will make the necessary

1. Handwrtten note in left-hand margin.
2. See UN to EBW, July 17, 1952, following.

corrections and return them promptly. We'll send you photostats of them as soon as we receive them.

If I go away for a vacation Mary Russell, my assistant, will send the corrected drawings to you. Best wishes to you both.

Sincerely,

TO E. B. WHITE   July 17, 1952

Dear Andy:

I enclose proofs of the pictures Garth re-drew. Are they all right? The Manufacturing Department had cuts made (instead of photostats) but please know that changes can still be made if the three new pictures are not exactly right! On #1 Garth changed the position of the door. On #2 he re-did it so that Fern has hair more consistent with the other drawings. On #3 he re-drew it so Mrs. Arable looked less like a young girl, and more like herself in other drawings. (On #3, if you agree, I feel Mrs. Arable looks a bit whisker-y and we <u>can</u> have a couple of the little lines taken out. I may be imagining it, though.)

Yes, I meant Robert the Bruce[1]. All I remember from my 2nd grade reader is: Robert the Bruce was losing some war, and he was discouraged, and he was about to give up, and he flung himself down in a meadow to think things over. At that point in his life he saw a spider spinning a web. Something suddenly tore her web (a branch? the wind? some animal?) and though it was ruined she started to spin another. Just as she was about to finish the second web something else came along and tore it. So

1. Robert the Bruce, early-twelfth-century Scottish king, who fought to free Scotland from English rule. MacGregor's version of the legend, as given here, is the more nearly accurate one, but UN also had the gist of the tale. Robert the Bruce was in hiding, not in prison, when he saw the spider said to have inspired him to fight on.

she started to do it a third time, and the third time she was successful. So Robert the Bruce thought to himself that if that spider wasn't discouraged he shouldn't be either, and he picked himself up off the grass and went off and won the war, or something like that. (The prose style in my reader was better, of course.) Now I'm not at all sure that is the right story, so I asked the President of Harper & Brothers, the great Scot— Frank S. MacGregor. He says my reader was all wrong and that Robert the Bruce was in exile, in a cell, and he saw the spider in his cell try over and over again to spin a web, and that the spider inspired him to escape, and he eventually won the war.   (However, it goes, it isn't much of a story and <u>no</u> competition, of course, for <u>your</u> spider.)

Please forgive this messy letter. It is late on Friday and I want to mail these proofs to you for your approval or disapproval.

I'm so glad you liked the jacket. The endpaper came in yesterday from Garth and I am sure you will love it. I'll send you a proof as soon as possible. As always please remember that it can be re-done if not just what you thought it would be.....

Yours sincerely,

TO ——————   October 14, 1952

Dear ——————:

Your letter to Mrs. [Laura Ingalls] Wilder, the author of *Little House on the Prairie*[1], came several weeks ago. We took the liberty of opening it as we do many of the letters that are addressed to Mrs. Wilder. Often we can send the writers the

1. *Little House on the Prairie*, by Laura Ingalls Wilder, illustrated by Helen Sewell, 1935. This was the second Little House book.

photographs and biographical material they want. Mrs. Wilder is now in her late eighties and we try to handle much of the correspondence here.

We were indeed disturbed by your letter. We knew that Mrs. Wilder had not meant to imply that Indians were not people and we did not want to distress her if we could possibly avoid it. I must admit to you that no one here realized that those words read as they did. Reading them now it seems unbelievable to me that you are the only person who has picked them up and written to us about them in the twenty years since the book was published. We were particularly disturbed because all of us here feel just as strongly as you apparently feel about such subjects, and we are proud that many of the books on the Harper list prove that. Perhaps it is a hopeful sign that though such a statement could have passed unquestioned twenty years ago it would never have appeared in anything published in recent years.

Instead of forwarding your letter to Mrs. Wilder I wrote her about the passage and said that in reprinting we hoped that she would allow us to change it. I have just received her answer. She says: "You are perfectly right about the fault in *Little House on the Prairie* and have my permission to make the correction you suggest. It was a stupid blunder of mine. Of course Indians are people and I did not intend to imply they were not." We are changing the next printing to read "There were no settlers."[1]

We appreciate your letter, but we are terribly sorry that ————— could not have the book for her eighth birthday. The new printing will be available for her ninth one though, and we are making a note now to be sure that you receive a complimentary copy. As a children's book editor, I was touched by your

1. The passage in question appears in the opening chapter. As revised it reads as follows: "There the wild animals wandered and fed as though they were in a pasture that stretched much farther than a man could see, and there were no settlers. Only Indians lived there."

not wanting ———————— to know only the *Saggy, Baggy Elephant*[1]
and I was therefore all the more upset by your very reasonable
complaint about Mrs. Wilder's book.

I am sorry this is not a better letter and I am particularly
sorry that I have not written you long before this. I wanted to
wait though, until I had written Mrs. Wilder and received her
answer.

Yours sincerely,

TO E. B. WHITE   October 23, 1952

Dear Andy:

Thanks for your letter. I enclose a review which will appear
in the next issue of *The Horn Book*.

And thanks for the grave comment of Caroline Angell[2]. I
am absolutely sure that most children will love the book, even
more than *Stuart Little*. The children I know love it, including
one tough nine-year-old boy who states it is his favorite book.
Please don't worry at all about the children.

Rumors have reached me that Miss Anne Carroll Moore
has certain reservations about *Charlotte's Web*[3]. As her reservations about *Stuart Little* preceded a wonderful success for that

1. *The Saggy Baggy Elephant*, by Kathryn and Byron Jackson, illustrated by Gustaf
   Tenggren, Simon & Schuster, 1947. This picture book was number 36 in the Little
   Golden Books series.
2. The author's step-granddaughter, age four and a half, had listened attentively as her
   father read *Charlotte's Web* aloud, then commented that a simpler solution to Wilbur's
   dilemma might have been to feed him less, thereby rendering him unfit for slaughter.
3. Moore did indeed have reservations. In a letter to UN dated June 2, 1952, she stated
   that while she found the book "entrancing" on the whole, she thought that EBW
   had not developed the character of Fern adequately and that he had produced a
   hybrid work that confusedly mingled realism and fantasy. Moore restated her objections in print in *The Horn Book*, December 1952, page 394.

book I am taking all this as good news for *Charlotte's Web*. (I would not mention this but someone may quote Miss Moore to you.) Well, Eudora Welty[1] said the book was perfect for anyone over eight or under eighty, and that leaves Miss Moore out as she is a girl of eighty-two.

I will stop writing you so many letters soon.

Yours,

TO PHYLLIS WEISGARD[2]   November 19, 1952

Dear Phyllis:

I'm so angry at myself for not recognizing you immediately yesterday at the Roosevelt thing[3]! Good heavens, you are one of my favorite people. Please blame it on the fact that I was wearing the wrong glasses. I have two pairs—one to look at manuscripts with, and one to look at those who write the manuscripts with (my life is extremely limited, as you can see) and I had the manuscript glasses on. Anyhow, it was good to have even a brief glimpse of you and I hope you will let me come down soon to see you and meet Abigail[4] and see Leonard, if he isn't uptown at Simon and Schusters that day....

Forgive me for talking stupidly today. I was at my worst but blame it on Anne Carroll Moore.

Yours,

---

1. The distinguished writer reviewed *Charlotte's Web* in *The New York Times Book Review*, October 9, 1952, page 49. She loved the book.
2. Wife of artist Leonard Weisgard; he illustrated many books for Harper, including several written by Margaret Wise Brown.
3. An event at the Roosevelt Hotel, in mid-Manhattan, celebrating Children's Book Week.
4. The Weisgards' daughter.

TO MIRIAM SCHLEIN[1] (MiS)   November 24, 1952

Dear Miss Schlein:

Your idea for a Margaret Wise Brown Library for Children is a lovely one. There isn't anything we, or you, or any of her non-librarian admirers could do about it, I'm afraid. But perhaps sooner or later a branch library could be named after her. I <u>don't</u> mean to sound defeatist, please know! A couple of libraries have been named after Laura Ingalls Wilder, but the idea came from the librarians. Anyhow, this is just a note to say that I think it would be wonderful but I'm not too hopeful about such recognition in the near future.

(I like to think of what Margaret's own idea for such a library would be. I'm sure she'd want the children to talk or sing whenever they wanted to, paint the furniture, draw with crayons on the walls, jump on the tables, kick any interfering adult on the ankle.....when they weren't looking at books. It would be a fine library.)

This is a bad letter. I'm sorry. I just wanted to say thanks for your good one.

Yours sincerely,

P. S. And congratulations again on the good reviews.[2]

1. Author whose work, like Margaret Wise Brown's, reflects the influence of the experientially based "here and now" approach to writing for young children first developed at the Bank Street College of Education. News of Brown's death on November 13, while she vacationed in France, had reached New York only days earlier. Brown had died of an embolism following surgery for the removal of an ovarian cyst. She was forty-two.
2. The author's *Shapes*, illustrated by Sam Berman, Scott, 1952, received strong notices in, among other publications, *The New York Times Book Review*, which, in its November 16, 1952, number called *Shapes* a "brilliant little book."

TO MEINDERT DEJONG   December 8, 1952

                                        (late afternoon)

Dear Mick:

    Sendak just telephoned and wants me to send you an
S.O.S.[1] Do people in Holland wear their wooden shoes in the
house? I think the answer is no, they don't. But if they don't
what do they wear? Little soft slippers? Or what? He's drawn
several interiors (over the week-end) and had people wearing
wooden shoes indoors but a friend of his came by and told him
that was all wrong.

    Now of course he can go to the library and look all this up
but it will take time away from his drawing table so he thought
perhaps you could answer this question quickly for him and
save us all time.

    He hasn't found a picture of a dyke as yet, but he will. Of
course if you know a book which has a wonderful picture of a
dyke in it we'd be grateful to have the title of it. Sendak was so
funny the other day (I mean droll, not "funny"). He said
thoughtfully that now he was doing your book laid in Holland,
had done *Maggie Rose*[2], laid in Maine, had started with *The
Wonderful Farm*, laid in France, "and me, I'm from Brooklyn,"
he said sadly....   So any help on wooden shoes or dykes
will be much appreciated by him and by me.

                                        Love, in a rush

1. Maurice Sendak was working on the illustrations for MDeJ's novel *Shadrach*, pub-
    lished by Harper in 1953.
2. *Maggie Rose: Her Birthday Christmas*, by Ruth Sawyer, illustrated by Maurice Sendak,
    1952.

Dear Natalie:

With a heavy heart I must write you that we still think *Alphonse* (revised version) is not a worthy successor to *The Talking Cat*.

This makes me sad. I read it, and so did Miss Powers[1] and Miss Russell[2]. So we are all sad. We understand that you will want to send it to another publisher and of course we all wish you luck with it.

Declining this book is a tough decision, because of course it probably will be taken elsewhere and so you will probably feel any future books by you should go to the publisher that accepts *Alphonse*. So we are in the unfortunate position of being sorely tempted to take *Alphonse* so that we will keep you on the list. But we shouldn't accept it and try to publish it on that basis because it, in our judgment—and we may be wrong, doesn't come up to the high standard of *The Talking Cat*. So we have decided that in spite of everything we must regretfully decline this manuscript. I can't tell you how sorry I am, Natalie.

If by any remote chance it is not taken by one of the top publishers we certainly hope that you will send us something else by you in the future. Let me know what happens, will you? I have been happy to think of you as a Harper author up to now. Coming unexpectedly upon the delightful manuscript of *The Talking Cat*, and publishing it so successfully, was one of the high spots in my experience as an editor. Well, let me know who takes *Alphonse*, if you are willing, will you? By the way, I hear via the grapevine, that Harcourt turned down *The Talking Cat* and I think they would be <u>extremely</u> glad to have a chance at

---

1. Ann Powers, reader in the Department of Books for Boys and Girls.
2. Mary Russell, UN's editorial assistant. Russell eventually made a specialty of editing nonfiction, a category that did not interest UN greatly.

Alphonse. You know Miss McElderry[1], don't you? She does lovely books.

We return the manuscript herewith. Please don't disappear into the blue now. Let me hear from you and tell me how things go with you and with the manuscript.

Yours sincerely,

TO MAURICE SENDAK   March 3, 1953

Dear Mr. Sendak:

I'm writing you this note, instead of telephoning you, because I don't want to disturb you or sound too urgent or desperate. I am not really desperate, but I just have to ask you something and get an answer soon. However, I don't want to slow up your final touches on *Crazy House*[2], or whatever the title is to be. And now, after that cautious beginning, I will continue: I know that you are working hard on the Ruth Krauss book and that you also have worked hard on DeJong's *Shadrach* and that as soon as you can you want to do the pictures for that book by your friend[3]. And so I am sure this is not a good time to bring up the possibility of your doing illustrations for yet another book but I HAVE TO BRING IT UP NOW in fairness to the author.

This is Meindert DeJong's new story, about a dog.[4] The

---

1. Margaret K. McElderry, children's book editor, Harcourt, Brace. Harcourt did publish NSC's *Alphonse: That Bearded One*, illustrated by Nicolas Mordvinoff, in 1954. UN and NSC remained on friendly terms; the author published many subsequent books with Harper.
2. UN still thought of Ruth Krauss' *A Very Special House* by its working title.
3. *The Tin Fiddle*, by Edward Tripp, illustrated by Maurice Sendak, Oxford University Press, 1954.
4. *Hurry Home, Candy*, by Meindert DeJong, illustrated by Maurice Sendak, 1953.

manuscript came in late yesterday and Miss Powers read it at once and tells me she thinks it is the best book she's ever read in manuscript, so far, better than any of DeJong's previous books including *Tower by the Sea* and *Shadrach*. I will read it myself next but I'm pretty sure from what Miss Powers tells me that I will be just as enthusiastic as she is. The question now is: do you think you could illustrate it before you go to Europe[1]? I am not pressing you, Maurice dear. But I can't even think of giving it to another artist unless I ask you first to do it. I know that DeJong wants you to do it and of course you know I want you to. However, I do not want to turn into a big pushy woman who is pushing the brilliant young artist all the time. What you did for *Shadrach* was one of the high points of my life as an editor, as surely you know, and obviously you would be perfect for this new story. (I've skimmed enough of it to see that it is DeJong at his best.) The manuscript is over 200 pages long so we couldn't possibly have too many pictures in it or the book would turn out to be too long and too expensive. So before you say yes or no will you think about it and remember that we probably couldn't have more than 15 or 20 pictures in it at the most? Once again, I hate to bother you right now and if you just don't see how you can possibly do it in view of your friend's manuscript and the lovely trip abroad please tell me so. I have to know one way or the other soon because if you can't do it I will have to start finding someone else immediately. By the way, little research would be involved as it is about a dog and some children and the country and a farm, and is laid right here in this country. No dikes, no fancy aprons or capes, or towers. Oh gosh, I hope you can do it!

Yours,

1. MS made his first trip abroad later that year.

Dear Mick:

Darn it, I had to snatch the manuscript from Miss Powers after she finished it, and rush it by messenger up to Helen Ferris[1] who is going home for three days to read manuscripts. So I am the underprivileged editor here and I'm so anxious to get a carbon copy from you, so I can read it, that I'm probably going to develop a migraine headache any moment. I can imagine that this slight delay in hearing from your good gray editor is sort of frustrating to you too, dear. Don't think I don't understand!

If it is any help, Miss Powers has never been so enthusiastic about any manuscript by any author, including you. Her report on *Hurry Home Candy* is a poem of praise. I trust her judgment, as you know, and so I can assure you that I will love it too. I may have a few mild points to make but I'm sure I will be as enthusiastic about it as Miss Powers is. I glanced through a little bit of it before I had to send it to Miss Ferris and it looks like good good better best wonderful right and inevitable DeJong. I cannot wait to read it word for word and I am going crazy without a duplicate copy. Please hurry and send it!

That BOMC[2] crack about juveniles and the Landmark Books[3] has irritated everyone thoroughly but it is so silly that it shouldn't bother any of us. It certainly shouldn't bother a writer like you, or even an editor like me. I get absolutely wild some days, thinking of you keeping that darn job in that church, so

1. Editor-in-chief of the Junior Literary Guild.
2. Book-of-the-Month Club.
3. In an undated letter to UN that is marked "rec'd 1/23/53," MDeJ told of having received in the mail a promotional brochure from the Book-of-the-Month Club that featured Random House's Landmark Books. Much to the author's consternation, the advertisement boasted that Landmark Books, unlike the "vast majority" of those published for young readers, were written by "serious adult writers."

you can write your wonderful books. But you are praising the Lord in your own fashion, Mick, as even I am doing in my own modest, harassed, untalented fashion. And I can assure you that you are a happier and more successful human being than most of the authors who hack out those machine-made, tailored to order, bloodless Landmark Books. But why am I telling you all this, Gustave, when you know it already? I'm giving myself a pep talk I guess, because even an editor gets discouraged sometimes. You wrote me "I do know that if you depart from the usual run the librarians and teachers who control the juvenile field are scared" and I guess that is true some of the time but not all of the time. I haven't any author like Meindert DeJong on this list but some of the other books we've been publishing are sort of unusual, and off-beat, and I KNOW the children would love and recognize them, but they come up against some influential and unimaginative and thoroughly grown-up and finished and rigid adults. Some mediocre ladies in influential positions are actually embarrassed by an unusual book and so prefer the old familiar stuff which doesn't embarrass them and also doesn't give the child one slight inkling of beauty and reality. This is most discouraging to a creative writer, like you, and also to a hardworking and devoted editor like me. I love most of my editor colleagues but I must confess that I get a little depressed and sad when some of their neat little items about a little girl in old Newburyport during the War of 1812 gets [*sic*] adopted by a Reading Circle.

Well, you couldn't do anything else and neither could I. Did I ever tell you that several years ago, after the Harper management saw that I could publish children's books successfully, I was taken out to luncheon and offered, with great ceremony, the opportunity to be an editor in the adult department? The implication, of course, was that since I had learned to publish books for children with considerable success perhaps I was now ready to move along (or up) to the adult field. I almost pushed the luncheon table into the lap of the pompous gentleman opposite me and then explained kindly that publishing children's books was what I did, that I couldn't possibly be interested in books for dead dull finished adults, and thank you very much but I had to get back to my desk to publish some more good books for bad children.

And maybe when you finally do get some money from your wonderful books for children you'll be able to afford some time and write a book for adults, but I doubt that you'll love doing it as much as you do your books for children. I want money for you, God knows. But I absolutely believe that sooner or later you will make money with your children's books. In the meantime what you are doing out there in Grand Rapids really amounts to giving the children a present. I haven't written any of this because I think you are discouraged. Your letter made it clear that you weren't and that you'll always want to write children's books. I just felt like spending some time writing to my dear Mick. And I've been a little blue and discouraged myself, I'm ashamed to say, and that is silly. "Discouragement is disenchanted egotism," as some man said.... It is disgusting to realize that I am so egotistic about the sort of books I pick out to publish for children. Anyhow, the walls will come tumbling down one of these days. The Ruth Krauss *Bears*[1] absolutely horrified some people but they've finally had to admit that the children simply love it and Ruth Krauss is gradually finding more and more acceptance and her books are selling better. It will happen with you, too. Meanwhile, dear, we still have each other and you are a great comfort to me, rivers of water in a dry place.

1. *Bears*, by Ruth Krauss, illustrated by Phyllis Rowand, 1948. Some critics found this picture book, with its nonnarrative, singsong text—"Bears, bears, bears, bears, bears./On the stairs/Under chairs/Washing hairs..."—bewilderingly offbeat and insubstantial.

If *Shadrach* doesn't win the Newbery surely *Hurry Home Candy* ought to, if Miss Powers is as right as she usually is.

I've written Sendak to say that of course you and I want him to illustrate *Hurry Home*. He is finishing one book, then has to do one for another publisher[1] (everyone wants him now, since the Marcel Aymé book and *A Hole Is to Dig*) and then he's going abroad in June. But I know he will do the drawings if he possibly can. If he says he can't possibly fit it in to this horribly crowded schedule I'll just have to find someone who can draw exactly like him! By the way, you are quite a librarian type yourself, Lynd Ward's Bear book[2] won the Caldecott for the "most distinguished" drawings this year. I still don't love his work.

But I love your work and you too. HURRY WITH THAT CARBON. HOW COULD YOU HAVE FORGOTTEN A SECOND COPY AFTER ALL THESE YEARS!

TO LAURA INGALLS WILDER   March 17, 1953

Dear Mrs. Wilder:

Thank you ever so much for your last letter and for the letter you enclosed about Garth Williams' pictures for your books.[3] We appreciate your writing. I hope that within a day or so we will have printed sheets of at least one of the books, and I will send you a set immediately.

We are all glad to know that you are well and that you had

---

1. *The Tin Fiddle* by Edward Tripp; see letter to Maurice Sendak, March 3, 1953, page 60.
2. *The Biggest Bear*, by Lynd Ward, Houghton Mifflin, 1952.
3. UN commissioned Garth Williams to reillustrate the entire Wilder series in a uniform edition, which Harper published in 1953. She explained her reasons for doing so in a letter to Doris K. Stotz dated January 11, 1967 (see pages 232–34).

such a pleasant visit from the daughter of one of your friends. You both must have enjoyed it a lot.

These are very exciting days here for us after all the last eight years! Garth sent us in sketches for the new jackets, and final plans for everything are finally taking shape. I'll be sending you more material very soon.

Sincerely yours,

TO KATHERINE BINNEY SHIPPEN[1]   June 2, 1953

Dear Katherine:

It was good to have even a glimpse of you at the *New York Times* tea the other day. It was so noisy there that I don't think you heard me repeating the compliment that you had just received from Mrs. Hamilton[2] of Morrow and Mrs. Frye[3] of McGraw-Hill. I was talking to them with my back to the room when Mrs. Hamilton interrupted me and said, "There's a woman standing over there who has the most beautiful face and the loveliest expression I have ever seen in my life." Then Mrs. Frye looked over my shoulder and said, "Yes, isn't she lovely! Who is she? She looks so familiar." It was then that I turned around and saw that they were both looking at you. I agreed with them, of course, and it was with a great deal of pride that I identified you for them as a Harper as well as a Viking author.

As you know, the *Christian Science Monitor* refused to let us include *Big Mose*[4] in our advertisement because of the cigars. Now I must share with you the fact that the Missouri Synod, of the Lutheran Church, likes the book but is concerned about the

1. Teacher and author specializing in works of history and biography.
2. Elisabeth Bevier Hamilton, founding editor of Morrow Junior Books.
3. Helene Frye, children's book editor, McGraw-Hill Company.
4. *Big Mose*, by Katherine B. Shippen, illustrated by Margaret Bloy Graham, 1953.

use of "Gee" on page 27 and "by holy saints" on page 69. They also disapproved of what they identified only as "expressions on pages 4, 11, 38, 59." It's a funny world, isn't it, Katherine? Here I had been worrying about so many other things and all the time I should have been worrying about the naughty language in *Big Mose*!

Affectionately,

TO MARC SIMONT[1]   September 14, 1953

Dear Marc:

The 'phone just rang and I <u>thought</u> the operator said "I have a call for you from <u>Cornwall</u>[2]." Well, I was <u>so</u> excited for of course I thought it was a call from you stating that your new book[3] is finished. As you have already guessed, the call was <u>not</u> from you in Cornwall, and so I was very disappointed and I thought I would write this letter to tell you so. You don't have to telephone me from Cornwall but the next time you are in New York you could call me up from a drugstore. Or write me a letter.

What are you doing these days? Are you thinking about a new children's book? Thank God *Polly's Oats*[4] has earned back its advance and from now on it will be pure gravy—thin gravy, perhaps, but pure. Also *The Lovely Summer*[5] is going right along. So hurry up with your third book.

1. Among the most sought-after illustrators of his generation, Simont had illustrated books by Margaret Wise Brown, Ruth Krauss, Meindert DeJong, and James Thurber, and had written and illustrated several books of his own.
2. Simont was living in West Cornwall, Connecticut.
3. *Mimi*, by Marc Simont, 1954.
4. *Polly's Oats*, by Marc Simont, 1951.
5. *The Lovely Summer*, by Marc Simont, 1952.

I hope you are not discouraged. I know sales have not been terrific for your books, Marc, but you don't want to write about *Bobby and His Steam Shovel*[1] and, so far as we are concerned, you don't need to. Just don't get discouraged. That's all I ask.

I hope you and yours are well and happy. (I know you're rich.) I'm fine—young and beautiful and also enormously wealthy. I'm very depressed about the state of the union—I mean That Mess in Washington. But I'm glad to have Adlai[2] back safe and sound. The poor man, the newspapers make me so sick with their constant "he quipped" .... Eisenhower makes some dopey remark about his golf game and everyone hugs themselves with delight. And Stevenson says something sensible and they add "wisecracking as usual." I can't stand it, but I have to. Stevenson lands in this country and the paper reports: "'I'm glad to be back,' he quipped." Really, that is almost an exact quotation.[3]

Now aren't you sorry that wasn't you on the telephone????

Yours,

TO RUTH KRAUSS   January 20, 1954

Ruthie:

God bless you, girl. The new version of sandwich-kisses[4] is perfect. Many many thanks.

I talked to Mister Sendak this morning and he says he'll be

1. UN clearly meant this as a jibe at Little Golden Books, of which number 69 in the series was a book called *Bobby and His Airplanes*, by Helen Palmer, illustrated by Tibor Gergely, Simon & Schuster, 1949.
2. UN was a lifelong Democrat and an ardent supporter of Adlai E. Stevenson during his two unsuccessful bids for the presidency.
3. In the margin of the circulating copy, UN wrote: "Aside: he [Simont] is a democrat."
4. This phrase, and the mention of "Love and Friendship" that follows, refer to *I'll Be You and You Be Me*, by Ruth Krauss, illustrated by Maurice Sendak, 1954.

all set for Love and Friendship (the text I mean) on February 1st. So that ought to fit right in with your schedule, shouldn't it? And everything will be done with neatness and dispatch.

Our executive vice-president, secretary and treasurer, is a man named Raymond C. Harwood, and he is a lovely man. He is the one person around here who is not positive he knows all about children's books (and certainly much more than that abstracted spinster who wears glasses and occasionally a funny hat[1]). I'll get to the point of this in just a moment. Just want to give you the background. Anyhow, Mr Harwood in his quiet financial way takes note of all publications by all departments and he makes more sense about books than some of the literary boy editors who would know exactly "what kids want" if they just took half an hour off from their rotten old adult novels written on two levels. And this Mr. Harwood said to me the last time I saw him that he certainly liked those Krauss books. I beamed at him and said I loved them too, and then he said, shaking his head, "All the psychiatrists will be out of business by the time the children who now read her books are grown up. That last one[2] surely takes care of many repressions." Now wasn't that darling? Of course Mr. Harwood's opinion isn't as important to you as it is to me, probably, but I had to pass this along to you because I thought you'd like to know about it. I damn near kissed him, but resisted. I may sneak into the Men's Room after hours though and write on the wall: Ursula N. loves Raymond H.

Love to you,

---

1. Here UN caricatured herself.
2. *A Very Special House.*

TO JIM BLAKE[1]   February 9, 1954

Dear Jim:

Adam [W. Burger] just gave me your letter to him about the new Krauss book[2]. I'm so sorry you have to do business with such cross buyers. But you do, so <u>what's</u> to be done about people who don't like children who do any serious crumb-walking....Of course that particular "activity" could just be taken as sort of a little joke, but also it does make clear to everyone that it isn't a good idea just to brush crumbs off onto the floor, or flick them in your mother's face, or wrap them up with an old orange peel and some coffee grounds and send them to some rich bookstore buyer. As for the children practicing acting, our author MAKES CLEAR that you should always explain what you are doing, and certainly any reasonable adult would understand. As for the poor woman with the hunch back, there are now and there always have been and there always will be children who will imitate physical disabilities and they will do it whether or not Ruth Krauss writes a book. But in the how to practice acting activity Ruth does make clear that you mustn't hurt anyone's feelings. She doesn't say that in so many words but read that section carefully, dear Jim, and see if it doesn't give you an out. Children do "mess around with the telephone" as you put it. But Ruth's telephone activity states that the child must ask the caller if the caller would like to hear some entertainment. The caller can always say NO. I've just reread this and see I'm not being any help. But of course I am crushed to the ground and I bleed at every pore when I read your plaintive statement to the Sales Manager: "I wonder if the book couldn't stand <u>a little editing</u> if it isn't too late." It is too

1. Jim Blake, West Coast salesman, Harper & Brothers.
2. *How to Make an Earthquake.* See page 37, footnote 2 to letter to Ruth Krauss, August 22, 1951.

late for any changes and lateness aside, if we want to publish Ruth Krauss <u>AND WE DO</u> we have to publish pure 100% Krauss. She knows something we don't know, and Constance Spencer even doesn't know (though I adore her and in fact dote on all buyers) and most grown-ups don't know. As for "a little editing," well, Ruth has written a lot of books for us and it has been an exciting and rewarding experience for me, as an editor, to watch her grow and grow and develop and go deeper and deeper. I respect her instinct and her final judgments and when she decides that there is nothing more she can honestly do to a book I have to respect her knowledge and trust her. Because she is the one with talent—and I'm only someone who recognizes and loves creative talent. Well, you poor guy, just out there trying to sell a few books, and you write in for help and get a long lot of balderdash from me. But can't you tell some of those rather limited and thoroughly grown up adults that it is about time THEY accepted and trusted Ruth Krauss? A lot of them thought *Bears* was crazy, a great many of them thought *A Hole Is to Dig* was dopey because it wasn't grammatically correct. What does Ruth have to do to convince some of your customers that she knows something about children they don't know? I know every child doesn't love *A Very Special House*[1], but some children love it and some of them love it more than *A Hole Is to Dig*. She doesn't do the same thing over and over again and if she ever starts she won't continue to be Ruth Krauss. She'll always be good but when she stops blazing new trails, you should excuse the originality of my prose style, she won't be the writer she is now. But I should try to get down to your specific problem, and give you some help. I wish I knew what to say. I don't, though. Can't you just kid them a little bit and point out to them that grown-ups and children together with a Ruth Krauss book can be closer than they can be without a

---

1. Sendak received a Caldecott Honor for his illustrations for this book.

Ruth Krauss book? I mean that. I think it is true. I don't <u>know</u> how important adults and children feeling close together is but I <u>guess</u> it wouldn't do adults or children any harm not to feel far apart for a little while, just long enough to enjoy a Krauss book <u>together</u>.

Oh hell, it all boils down to: you just can't explain this sort of basic wonderful stuff to some adults, Jim. It is a shame that you don't have sheets to sell from, and I know it. But, as you know, we couldn't help the lack of selling material. I saw the finished book, type and pictures, yesterday, and it is really swell. The pictures are delightful. There will be a couple of "activities" that some grown-ups will object to but the book as a whole is a book of freshness, imagination, love, originality, humor, pathos, and—well, take your pick of flap-copy nouns. Just look at the last line of the How to Entertain Telephone Callers— which ends "or whatever is your talent." Believe me, that is so close to children, so exactly right, so damn warm and perfect that any little child can't help but feel happier at the moment when it is read to him. "Happier" isn't the right word. I guess I mean that "or whatever is your talent" can't help but make any child feel warmed and attended to and <u>considered</u>. And, believe me, not many children's books make children feel considered. No child would define it that way but you'll know what I mean.

I bet Quail Hawkins[1] at Sather Gate doesn't disapprove of *How to Make an Earthquake*. Does she? You can tell any buyer who seriously objects that Ruth wouldn't put anything in a book which would encourage children to be mean or cruel or unkind. I talked over the bugs in the ice-cubes with her and she pointed out to me that it wasn't mean, it was good fun, etc. etc.[2] She

1. Author; manager of the children's book department of the influential Sather Gate Bookshop, Berkeley, California. During the late 1940s one of Hawkins' friends and part-time employees was an aspiring young writer named Beverly Cleary.
2. On the carbon copy of this letter that circulated among UN's staff, UN had under-lined this sentence and written in the margin: "I begged her to take it out."

knows why children will like the How to Be a Whale thing, reasons I will not go into with you in this much too long letter, but which are good fundamental reasons! There isn't a careless or thoughtless word or phrase or drawing in the whole book, Jim. Don't be sorry that "a little editing" couldn't be done. Anything that's in the finished book is there for a reason, a reason which seems good and important to an author we love and trust. I'm so terribly sorry this isn't a helpful, brisk letter, assuring you that large sections are being ripped out and revised. Just try to get the buyers to trust Ruth and to trust us. After all, they've done all right with Ruth's books and with some other Harper books. I'm glad you wrote, and I'm aware of your problems, and I'm just sorry there aren't any easy answers to send you. But we have to go along and trust Ruth. As for that cross fellow at BOOKS, INC. I'd love to have half an hour with him, and his fury at *A Very Special House*. I bet his children will grow up into wretched, neurotic, frustrated adults. Krauss books can be bridges between the poor dull insensitive adult and the fresh, imaginative, brand-new child. But of course that only will work if the dull adult isn't too dull to admit he doesn't know all the answers to everything. Krauss books will not charm those sinful adults who sift their reactions to children's books through their own messy adult maladjustments. That is a sin and I meet it all the time. But there are some adults who don't sift their reactions to children's books through their own messy maladjustments and I guess those are the ones who will love and buy Krauss.

Well, I certainly did not intend to write you such a vague and wandering letter. As a wise man once said, "I'm sorry this letter is so long. I didn't have time to write a short one."[1] Neither did I. And this one has been interrupted by three

1. Blaise Pascal: "I have made this letter longer than usual because I lack the time to make it short." In *Provincial Letters, 1656–57*.

appointments and one thousand telephone calls. Try to forgive it and me.

I've just reread your letter to Adam and I must ask you to give your maid my love. She makes real sense and I'm crazy about her. Can't you buy BOOKS, INC. and fire that guy and put the maid in as president?

Lots of love,

And this has been sitting in my typewriter, and it is now February 11th and I'm about to go to the Supervisors' Convention in Atlantic City. Life is so full.

Your request for information about *Hurry Home Candy* was just given me by Adam Burger. No, it did not win the Newbery Medal. It was a strong runner-up but it didn't win. DeJong will win it one of these days, maybe in 1955. (And I'm a Dodger fan, too.)

You'll shortly receive a memo saying that the Children's Library Association of the A. L. A. has instituted a new award, The Laura Ingalls Wilder Award, and it will be given to an author for sustained, creative, distinguished contributions, and Mrs. Wilder will be the first to receive it. I'm so happy about this recognition for her wonderful books. And it is wonderful that such an Award will bear her sacred name.

TO GARTH WILLIAMS   February 11, 1954

Dear Garth:

Just back from the mid-winter meetings of librarians in Chicago. The Children's Library Association has instituted a new award (not to be confused with the Newbery and Caldecott) which is to be called the Laura Ingalls Wilder Award, and will be given to an author who has made a distinguished, creative, sustained contribution to children's books. (I'm not using the right words here but I haven't the specific phrase at the moment.) Anyhow, the first person to receive it will be Mrs. Wilder and we are ..

Interruption of several days, during which I have attended a supervisors' meeting in Atlantic City. Letter left unfinished on my desk. To continue: this award will not mean so much to you personally but it certainly wouldn't have been thought up and inaugurated right now if your pictures for the new edition hadn't been so perfect that the beauty of all the Wilder books was brought anew to the attention of influential persons. I'm sorry my prose isn't better, Garth, but it is sincere! Anyhow, again, in Chicago I certainly heard beautiful things about your drawings for the Wilder books and even though the award will go to Mrs. Wilder it won't hurt you a bit!

Rosemary Livsey, Director of Work with Children, Los Angeles Public Library, asked me if I thought you'd design a medal for this award.[1] I said I'd ask you and that even though the Children's Library Association can't pay you for such a design I thought you'd consider it seriously. How about it? I know it is asking a lot of you and you know I'd never urge you to do anything without getting good money for it. But if by any chance you'd like to contribute a design for the Laura Ingalls Wilder Award it will be a simply superb gift to children, children's librarians, everyone concerned with the best in the field of children's books. This Award will not necessarily be given every year. It will, I think, become a more important award than either the Newbery or the Caldecott because it will only be awarded when it can go to some author of real stature. I

---

1. Garth Williams did design the medal. The Wilder Award was given every five years until 1980, and has been awarded once every three years since 1983.

thought that if you could consider making a design for a medal (and if you just made a rough design we could get some plain— as opposed to brilliant genius-type—artist to do the actual drawing, maybe) you could use some motif from one of the 8 Wilder books, either as is or adapt it slightly. I can't write more now. It is now February 19th, and I started this on the 11th! Think it over and let me know whether you could even consider doing a design for the librarians to give over the generations.

Love to all. I'll answer your last letter soon. I understand uranium is all under Colo. and Balmoral will make you rich and if so I hope you know I will have no silly pride about accepting any money you care to give me as your dear friend. I'd feel funny about taking $10.00 (though I'd take it!) but something like $50,000.00 when you become a rich millionaire will be per- fectly all right, and I'd spend it unwisely. Love.

TO JANETTE SEBRING LOWREY[1]   April 14, 1954

Dear Janette:

I've had you on my mind for weeks. How are you, I wonder. I wrote you from Chicago and haven't had one single word since! We've had gaps in our correspondence before but this does seem an excessively long one. Do let me know how every- thing is going.

You know how much I hope the sequel to *Margaret*[2] is going well! But I won't press you for details. I guess you want to finish it almost as much as I want you to. (Joke.) I am hoping you

---

1. Author, best known for her Little Golden Book *The Poky Little Puppy*. JSL first pub- lished with Harper during Ida Louise Raymond's tenure as department head; UN regarded her primarily as a young-adult novelist of exceptional promise.
2. *Margaret*, by Janette Sebring Lowrey, 1950. The sequel, *Love, Bid Me Welcome*, was a long time in coming. Harper published the book in 1964.

haven't been ill, that Fred and Alfred[1] and his family are all right. Do send me a letter soon.

I must keep off politics in this letter. But I did read that someone said President Eisenhower had "delusions of adequacy." Is Texas thrilled with the presence of Senator McCarthy now at the Pegler ranch? I'm wondering if you did go ahead with your tentative plans to get a television receiver. The Edward Murrow programs[2] have been splendid lately. But I thought the other day "Oh, I almost hope Janette doesn't have television," because one of the commercials was more terrible (even) than commercials usually are. The commercial was for a wristwatch, named the (you won't be able to bear this) "Benrus Embraceable." It was advertised on the wrist of a pretty blonde starlet who said, and this is an exact quote: "I believe in the Benrus Embraceable. I admire it and—yes—I wear it." It was the "I believe in the Benrus Embraceable" that was so glorious, you know "and in the country for which it stands."   Have just reread and as usual it doesn't look funny written down.

Janette, please write. Bring me up to date! I've missed your letters.

Affectionately,

TO JANETTE SEBRING LOWREY   June 9, 1954

Dear Janette:

Thanks so much for your wonderful letter. I laughed over the stories—especially the one about the woman with the career

---

1. The author's husband and grown son respectively.
2. Edward R. Murrow, in his CBS television program *See It Now*, gave a sharply critical account of the hearings conducted by the virulently anti-Communist Senator Joseph R. McCarthy into the political beliefs and affiliations of a variety of Americans.

bristling with high points. I wonder if she met the Emperor. Your letters are marvelous.[1]

I'm so sad that your personal life has interfered with your writing. There seems to be no solution to that sort of problem, unless a writer is ruthless which you could never be. But there should be some answer! It is a crime for you not to write, and I don't use that word lightly.

Well, I do hope that you'll have both books[2] done by the end of the summer. You wrote that might be possible. Do let me know. At luncheon the other day Helen Ferris asked me about the sequel to *Margaret* and I was sorry to have no hope to give her.

It is good news you send about Alfred and his family. I'm happy to know that all is well there. It is unbearably sad about your nephew.[3]

You must know, of course, that I agree with all you say about the Republicans. Your paragraph on the bunglers and on the "creature" with "his bag full of windy tricks and poisons" was absolutely brilliant.[4] I won't mention his name either. I've tried to keep up with the hearings as much as any woman with a more-than-full-time job can. In any free time I have I write letters to senators—not just to New York senators but to any and all I can think of. I am in constant touch with the abominable Dirksen, Dworshak, Mundt.[5] And I write accusing notes to Potter[6] who could conceivably straighten up and do right if

1. In a letter dated May 25, 1954, JSL had written UN about a colorful San Antonio dowager who hoped to arrange a meeting between herself and the emperor of Ethiopia, Haile Selassie.
2. The sequel to *Margaret* and a book for children about the poet John Keats.
3. This child, who UN had heard was seriously ill, died soon afterward.
4. This evidently was JSL's caricature of Senator Joseph R. McCarthy, whose nationally televised hearings angered and disgusted JSL and UN alike.
5. Senator Everett McKinley Dirksen, Republican from Illinois, later Senate minority leader, famous for his oratory; Senator Henry Clarence Dworshak, Republican from Idaho; Senator Karl E. Mundt, Republican from South Dakota.
6. Senator Charles Edward Potter, Republican from Michigan.

he'd ONLY read my letters. And I write to the Democrats, of course. I'm sure the post-mistress in the Republican village in which I live is mystified...

It just so happens that all the Harper authors and artists of children's books are ardent Stevenson Democrats. This really is a coincidence for I do not specify that in the contracts, you understand. However, I think this fine record may be broken. I'm terribly pleased (and honored) that the editor of *The Horn Book* is writing a book[1] which we are to publish. (I think you know Jennie Lindquist by name?). We have talked about every subject under the sun EXCEPT politics and I think that this means she is a Republican. For everyone in the children's book world knows that when I went to the Library convention in California last year I had a framed picture of Adlai Stevenson in my bedroom on the train going and coming and it stood on my hotel bureau during the convention. Well, I will love Jennie just the same. But I wish I could be sure. It is the uncertainty that kills me.... Forgive this nonsense and write me again, Janette dear. (And don't mention this Lindquist part to Leah Johnston or the Rosengrens[2]—I doubt you would—I wouldn't mention it to anyone but you!)

Affectionately,

TO MARC SIMONT   August 15, 1954

Dear Marc:

I'm sorry I was on the telephone when you called. I'm glad you will be in with the pictures "early Thursday afternoon." I

---

1. *The Golden Name Day*, by Jennie D. Lindquist, illustrated by Garth Williams, 1955.
2. The Rosengrens owned a San Antonio bookstore; Leah Johnston, another close friend, helped plan San Antonio's Children's Book Week programs.

have to go to one of those damn department head luncheons here, and they never let out until two thirty or quarter to three. I wish, as a matter of fact, you could come quite early that day and let me conceal you in the grandfather's clock in the corner of the Harper Board Room,[1] where these idiotic luncheons are given, or thrown, rather. Sandwiches, coffee, milk, and <u>small</u> containers of ice cream are passed out. After this delicious repast the various department heads announce future publications which could conceivably be of any interest to any other department or to the *Magazine*. This is supposed to avoid conflict, keep all the dept. heads up to date on what is going on in any field which might be of interest to them, etc. etc. Of course it doesn't, and three departments still come out with books with the identical title, you understand. Anyhow, you could do some fine caricatures and maybe *Harper's Magazine* would publish them. At one luncheon I was sitting next to the head of the textbook department (a very rich department) and he and I were talking about something in the morning paper and I mentioned something about democracy. At which a very imposing department head at the other end of the long table leaned forward and said "What was that, Ursula? What did you say? About Democracy? That's my field, you know." Well, it doesn't look funny written down. Sorry.

Just a line to say to come not sooner than 2.30.

Yours,

---

1. This eighteenth-century clock is now in the gallery on the ground floor of Harper's 53rd Street offices.

Dear Maurice:

I've just been thinking about your fall, 1955, schedule. You're planning your own *Kenny's Window*[2], Ruthie's book[3] probably if she doesn't get her *I Want to Paint My Bathroom Blue*[4] ready in time, the de Regniers picture book[5], and probably a Meindert DeJong book[6]. That's four fall books illustrated by the brilliant young Mister Sendak. I've been thinking that if you've already done a lot of thinking about the de Regniers, and if it is to be just black and white (or simple to print anyhow) you could conceivably get it done in time for the spring of 1955. That would give you 1 spring book and 3 fall books and that would be better if it would be possible. I mean it would be much better for you.

I thought about this last night and have just tried to 'phone you but there was no answer. So I'll send this note. I'll be in and out of the office tomorrow and I leave for Boston at noon on Friday. So if I don't get you between now and the time I leave we can talk about this in Swampscott[7]. Will you make a note right now, at this very moment, to put the de Regniers

---

1. UN's wunderkind was, as this letter indicates, hardworking, versatile, and extremely prolific.
2. *Kenny's Window*, by Maurice Sendak, 1956. The first book written as well as illustrated by MS took longer to complete than UN had anticipated.
3. *Charlotte and the White Horse*, by Ruth Krauss, illustrated by Maurice Sendak, 1955.
4. *I Want to Paint My Bathroom Blue*, by Ruth Krauss, illustrated by Maurice Sendak, 1956.
5. *What Can You Do with a Shoe?*, by Beatrice Schenk de Regniers, illustrated by Maurice Sendak, 1955.
6. *The Little Cow and the Turtle*, by Meindert DeJong, illustrated by Maurice Sendak, 1955. Two other children's books illustrated by MS were published that year: *Happy Hanukah, Everybody*, by Hyman and Alice Chanover, United Synagogue Commission on Jewish Education; and *Little Stories on Big Subjects*, by Gladys Baker Bond, The Anti-Defamation League, B'nai B'rith.
7. The annual conference of the New England Library Association was held that year in Massachusetts.

manuscript and that page lay-out you showed me in Swampscott, in your suitcase? I'd like to take a few minutes to reread the text in Swampscott. You might also bring the Kenny stories if you want to as you may have a few hours of leisure when you're not meeting librarians....

Again, the New Ocean House is very informal. But bring a sweater as the hotel is right on the ocean and it may be coldish to walk by the sea. If you have room in your suitcase I wish you'd bring one of your toys[1] just so we can show them to some of the librarians who would love them. If they are all too fragile don't bring one. But I would love to show one of them to some of the people who will meet you.

Mary Russell will have your ticket and will deliver it to you by messenger or in person if you are in this neighborhood before Friday at 5 p.m. She also has the time of the train from the North Station in Boston to Swampscott. As I have explained, the train from New York to Boston gets to the SOUTH STATION in Boston. Then you have to take a taxi across Boston to the North Station to get the train from Boston to Swampscott. I'll meet you in Swampscott, as I have said one hundred times. I think you will get to Swampscott at a quarter to five on Monday. Don't fail me!

And think about de Regniers' book. If you could finish it soon and get it out of the way I'd feel easier about your fall schedule, and I think you would, too. I believe it will be a relatively simple printing job and Jack[2] could pass his usual miracle......

Affectionately,

---

1. MS and his older brother, Jack, had constructed a number of wooden mechanical toys representing characters and scenes from such children's classics as "Hansel and Gretel" and *Pinocchio*.
2. Jack Rynerson worked in Harper's manufacturing department from 1952 to 1957.

TO CROCKETT JOHNSON   November 22, 1954

Dear Dave:

The dummy of *Harold and the Purple Crayon*[1] came this morning, and I've just read it. I don't know what to say about it. It doesn't seem to be a good children's book to me but I'm often wrong—and this post-Children's Book Week Monday finds me dead in the head. I'd probably pass up *Tom Sawyer* today. Let me keep the dummy a few days, will you? I want Ann Powers to read it. She's young and fresh (not sassy, you understand) and less tired than I am. And I'd like to read it again myself when I'm a little more caught up.

I found myself asking such dumb questions—like <u>where</u> did he draw the moon and the path and the tree? And then when I got far enough to realize he was dreaming, OF COURSE, I was puzzled by the moon in the last picture. You can see from this heavy-handed comment that I didn't read the story with much imagination.

I hate to send you this sort of a nothing letter. But I wanted to send you some sort of word and this is the best I can do today. We'll keep the dummy a little longer and I'll write you again soon, or call you up.

Yours,

TO CROCKETT JOHNSON   December 15, 1954

Dear Dave:

The typed up slightly revised copy of *Harold and the Purple Crayon* has just come. Many many thanks. I think it is FINE,

1. *Harold and the Purple Crayon*, by Crockett Johnson, 1955.

and the little changes you made are just perfect. Thanks for the part about the forest, and for all the other little touches.

I'm awfully sorry my first reaction to *Harold* was so luke warm and unenthusiastic. As I wrote you, I was tired in my head. I really think it is going to make a darling book, and I certainly was wrong at first. This is a funny job. The Harper children's books have had such a good fall, so many on so many lists, etc. etc., and I was feeling a little good—not <u>satisfied</u>, you understand, but I thought gosh I'm really catching on to things, I bet, and pretty soon it ought to get easier. And then I stubbed my toe on Harold and his damned purple crayon....

The contract is being drawn up—and I'm sorry the typing is taking so long.

Yours,

TO MAURICE SENDAK   February 21, 1955

Dear Maurice:

I've wanted to write you a note or tell you over the 'phone that your new ideas for the ending of *Kenny's Window* seem wonderful to me, and I'm sure it is going to be a beautiful book. Keep working on it and when you have all the chapters together you and I can go over it word for word, and get down to brass tacks, you should forgive the originality of my prose style. But the main thing is: thanks for everything I am sure you are doing to the book. The pages you showed me the other day in the Vanderbilt made me very very very happy.

As for your color pictures for the Krauss book[1]—words are no good whatsoever. There are a few peaks in an editor's life,

---

1. MS's illustrations for *Charlotte and the White Horse* were his first to be printed in full color.

and seeing those pictures of yours has been a peak in mine. They are indescribably lovely and absolutely perfect and—well, pure in the best sense.

Ruth is coming in this morning to go over the text and make some changes I hope. When we agree on commas, capitals, periods—and dashes—I'll send the final copy to you for the handlettering. For the record, we will, of course, pay you for the lettering and Jack Rynerson is finding out what the usual cost is for handlettering. Be assured that we'll make it as much as possible.

We should get the contract drawn up for *Kenny's Window*. We must talk about what sort of an advance you need. I'll call you later this week, and we'll get all the contract details settled.

Oh my GOODNESS I'm so GLAD I went up to old F. A. O. Schwarz that day.....

Affectionately,

TO JANICE MAY UDRY[1]   May 4, 1955

Dear Miss Udry:

I am extremely sorry that I haven't written you before this about your manuscript, *A Tree Is Nice*[2]. It was read in January— a week after we received it.[3] Since then I must have read it myself and thought about it at least a dozen times. This type of manuscript for the picture book age is the most difficult sort for any editor to judge. I like the manuscript very much myself and

---

1. Author of picture books.
2. *A Tree Is Nice*, by Janice May Udry, illustrated by Marc Simont, 1956. This was JMU's first book. Simont won the Caldecott Medal for 1957 for his illustrations— the first Caldecott Medal awarded to a book published by Harper.
3. Department policy was that every manuscipt received would be read by two different readers.

I'm sure children would enjoy much of it. But I haven't been able to write you about it because I still can't be sure how successfully we could publish it with the sort of illustrations it should have. It certainly needs color and it needs a very good artist. And that means we would have to find a wide enough market for it to print a large first edition.

One thing has puzzled me right along with the manuscript. You start off with "Trees are very nice. Even if you have just one tree, it is nice too,"—and then you follow with five and a half lines which just don't seem to make any sense right at the beginning of the book. Can you think of any better way to say what you want to say? The rest of the manuscript all has to do with the positive fact that a tree is nice, and seems much more truly childlike to us than "Without the trees a river is just a river, a hill is just a hill and a valley is just a valley," etc. Will you look at your carbon copy of the manuscript and let me hear from you again about this? The ending seems a little flat to me, but perhaps that's because I'm not four years old.

Please forgive me for keeping your manuscript for such a long time. We are really interested in it and in anything else you may write. I promise you I will write more promptly the next time.

Yours sincerely,

TO MAURICE SENDAK   June 10, 1955

Dear Maurice, I mean Marlon[1]:

I tried unsuccessfully to get you on the 'phone to say Happy Birthday and to find out what the x-ray thing said, etc. Hope

---

1. The reference is to Marlon Brando. UN did not miss an opportunity to remind the young MS that he too was a star.

you have a good birthday. As I explained, I am <u>making</u> you a lovely present but I thought until very recently that your birthday was at the END of June, and so my present isn't ready. (Not to keep you in suspense, dear boy, I am knitting you some galoshes, and I know you will love them.) So here is my I. O. U. for the birthday gift. As I have said to you other years, I am very glad you got born.

Affectionately,

P.S. Mrs. Tooze was pleased to have met you, I'm sure

TO MAURICE SENDAK   October 1, 1956

Dear Mr. Sendak:

I was reading about you in the *Village Voice*[1], and I certainly enjoyed your comments very much, and I like your drawings, and the way you sound in general, and all in all it was a very fine type article.

I was especially interested to hear that you are working on a new children's book entitled *Very Far Away*[2]. I would love to see it, as it just so happens that I am in the children's book publishing game, and I have a big fat spot on my spring, 1957, list for a book called—you won't believe this—*Very Far Away*. So hoping to hear from you soon in reference to your work, I beg to remain,

1. "The Wonderful World of Maurice Sendak," by John Wilcock, *The Village Voice*, September 26, 1956, pp. 3–4.
2. *Very Far Away*, by Maurice Sendak, 1957. The second book that MS both wrote and illustrated.

TO HENRY MILLER[1]   December 5, 1956

Dear Mr. Miller:

I've just read your letter of November 22nd and I was very glad to know that you are so enthusiastic about *A Hole Is to Dig.* It is one of our favorites, too.

I shall pass your comments on to Miss Krauss and I'm sure she will also be pleased.

Yours sincerely,
Editor

TO ELSE HOLMELUND MINARIK[2]

December 28, 1956

Dear Mrs. Minarik:

It was good to see you and your husband the other day, and to have that time with you both and Maurice Sendak. Maurice is happy that you're both happy about *Little Bear*[3], and so am I.

I look forward to receiving the additional words to cover the giving of presents at the birthday party. I agree with Maurice that most can be handled in the pictures but I think

1. The author of *Tropic of Cancer* and *Tropic of Capricorn* had written a fan letter to Ruth Krauss, in whom he evidently recognized a kindred spirit.
2. Danish-born American author. EHM, who taught first grade for many years, came to see UN with a picture-book manuscript in September of 1956. UN realized that the author's story about Little Bear and his mother was perfect for a new type of first reader that the editor had been hoping to develop. At UN's request, EHM submitted some additional stories about the bear cub and his mother; thereafter, *Little Bear*, the first Harper I Can Read Book, rapidly progressed toward completion.
3. *Little Bear*, by Else Holmelund Minarik, illustrated by Maurice Sendak, 1957.

each animal should say something about "Here is a present." Or the courteous equivalent.....

We are wondering if you have written any stories about children, rather than little bears, or a rhinoceros. I remember thinking months ago that perhaps children who are starting to read might think it slightly baby-ish to read about animals, and I think I raised this point with you. Your feeling was that children read about other children in their school primers, and that stories about animals in their own books would be sort of dessert for them. (I think that was the gist of what you said?) I wish there were some way we could be absolutely sure about this, and of course there isn't! You may be completely right. But we tried *Little Bear* on one six year old, who started first grade last September, and he liked it but not so well as his primer because, as he said, he preferred to read about children. Now I know very very well (as does every tired children's book editor) that the reaction of one child shouldn't be taken too seriously. But it made me remember my own earlier thoughts, so I'm passing this on to you. What do you think? Have you tried stories about animals on lots of children? Now that does sound like a ridiculous question! Forgive me. I'm typing this myself on the last afternoon before the long New Year's weekend, and not making too much sense, I'm afraid. Anyhow, you will understand what I'm trying to say, I'm sure.

Again, we want to follow *Little Bear* with other books by you. So let us see anything else you have done or may do. We hope that on one of these books we can give you Garth Williams for an illustrator. I remember you love his pictures. I think no one could have touched what Maurice has done on *Little Bear*, however. It really is a fresh, original, charming book.

Happy New Year!

Yours,

Dearest Moll:

Thanks so much for your loving little note. I hadn't been silent, though! Your note crossed with my letter, I'm sure. You have heard by now, haven't you? I wrote you a longish letter thanking you for my BEAUTIFUL presents. Again, I love them—and you.

I'm living for the moment in a HIDEOUSLY furnished place at 130 East 40th Street, Apt. 10B. I will be there to avoid the hideous weather in Bedford Hills but will be dividing my time in an irregular way. Better write to the office or to 130 East 40th Street. After all, I'll ALWAYS be at Harpers. 40th Street is not a lovesome spot God wot but it is better than worrying about getting up and down that hill. More about this arrangement later. I'll also be in Bedford Hills a great deal. This sort of living arrangement poses all sorts of critical questions. For instance: where do I keep my *Oxford Book of English Verse*— Bedford Hills or 40th Street? I must ask Cass Canfield[1], who also has two domiciles (get me). Well, he probably has an *Oxford Book of English Verse* in Bedford and in New York, and a third spare for the office just in case of an emergency.[2] I brought in the funniest collection of books and unread magazines—As I gathered the batch together to take out to the car I shook my head over the wide range of my interests. Would Virginia Woolf be sickened to know that she is loved by one who also reads *Confidential*?

My New Years resolution is to be more loving. I don't know how it will work out as I have been quite loving up to now with some disastrous, or at least misunderstood, results. Anyhow, I

1. Cass Canfield Sr., editor in Adult Trade and president of Harper & Brothers.
2. Handwritten in margin: "Don't—repeat don't—send me a second copy PLEASE. This is a joke."

will try even more love and I will let you know what happens. So far not so good. But then it is only the second day .... My other resolution is to hell with auld lang syne, I want some new lang syne and I'm tired of and fed up with the auld. (This is rather hard to fit in with the "be more loving" part of my resolution, but I'll fit it in somehow.)

When you return we will have dinner at some smart spot and go to the theatre. And we'll discuss all the affairs of the world and settle them. When are you returning? What do you hear from the Western Front? This is my adorable, old-fashioned way of referring to Pelham.

Give my best to Eileen and to Bill[1], and love to you, and eat good nourishing food and don't drink so much coffee, and don't smoke so much. Hear?

Love,

TO JANICE MAY UDRY   January 21, 1957

Dear Janice:

I really can't keep on with last names. Is this all right? Please call me Ursula if you can. I am older than the oldest redwood in the world, but lots of young people do call me by my first name so you do too.

We've had an awful lot of sickness in this department since the first of the year and we're terribly far behind in our work. I'm writing this to say that we may not be able to write you as promptly as I'd like to about your new manuscript. We'll read it quickly; that won't take any time. What takes time is thinking about it. But before we even look at it I'm rushing this off to you so I can enclose a page from our catalogue for this spring. It shows

1. The author's sister and son, respectively.

you a bit about a Ruth Krauss book with pictures by Maurice Sendak called *The Birthday Party*[1]. I do hope that it isn't too similar to yours, but I thought I should let you know right away that there is this remote possibility..... I must say I like your title, *The Terrible Birthday*[2], but that adjective would particularly appeal to such an ancient redwood, I suppose....

More later. I'm hoping very very much that both books are quite different.

Yours sincerely,

TO MARY STOLZ February 13, 1957

Dear Molly:

I've tried all day to telephone you. I hope you are having a happy day, wherever you are. And I hope you stay home all day tomorrow and catch up on your Harper manuscript. And have a Happy Valentine's Day, dear.

Now, what I'm writing about is your nephew, Emmet, and his pig. I told you not long ago that after all my efforts to get you, or Margaret [*sic*] Rey, or Charlotte Zolotow,[3] or Esther Averill, to do me an "I Can Read" book, I gave up and then Sue

1. *The Birthday Party*, by Ruth Krauss, illustrated by Maurice Sendak, 1957.
2. This manuscript was never published.
3. Author and editor. Zolotow entered the children's book world in 1938 as UN's secretary. One day when she told UN that she had an idea for a book that Margaret Wise Brown might want to write, the editor asked her assistant to commit her thoughts to writing. With some additional work, Zolotow's memo became the manuscript of her own first picture book, *The Park Book*, illustrated by H. A. Rey, 1944. She and UN became lifelong friends.

   Charlotte Zolotow was expecting her first child when she left Harper in 1944. She continued to write, and returned to Harper as senior editor in 1962. She became vice president and associate publisher of Harper Junior Books in 1976; editorial consultant and publisher of Charlotte Zolotow Books in 1982; and advisor to the department in 1991.

Carr[1] brought a wonderful new manuscript in hot off the elevator and it turned out to be exactly right for children in the first grade (about 6 years of age) and we're going to publish it in the fall of 1957 and we hope it will be only the first of many successful I Can Read books for us.

Now, what I was wondering, why wouldn't Emmet and his pig make a delightful I Can Read book[2]? I guess you know what I think of the thought of your turning aside from Young Adult Books for even a half hour. But this might not take you much time, and it might be fun, and it might sell. Unfortunately the author of a book which has to be so lavishly illustrated and also reasonably priced, can't have ALL the royalty. Half usually has to go to the artist, as you know. But this is something I can discuss with Ollie[3]. Anyhow, you think about it. To review what you told me:::

You said Emmet loved pigs, gave thanks for pigs at Thanksgiving Day dinner, longed to have a pig. The zoning laws made that impossible in St. Louis. So his parents arranged to have him own a pig which lived in Tennessee. He has pictures of his pig. He receives letters from the farmer about his pig. He puts aside part of his allowance to provide mash for the pig. And he is saving money and making plans to go to Tennessee on his vacation and see his pig. This could make, perfectly done, a delightful story and you could end it with the arrival in Tennessee and the lovely meeting of Emmet and his pig. Or with his trip back to St. Louis, dreadfully sorry to leave his pig but deeply happy and relatively secure in the knowledge that at some future time he will be able to come to visit his pig

1. Susan Carr [later Hirschman] joined UN's staff in 1955 as a reader and rose to the position of managing editor. She went on to head Macmillan's children's book department from 1965 to 1974, and in 1974 to found Greenwillow Books, an imprint of William Morrow.
2. *Emmet's Pig*, by Mary Stolz, illustrated by Garth Williams, 1959.
3. Oliver F. Swan, MS's agent at Paul R. Reynolds & Son.

again. Of course it sounds like nothing written down flatly like that. But a good writer could write it up real good, I always think......Have just reread my letter. Who dealt this mess? On second thought, I think the ending should be after the visit to Tennessee, for children would want to know what Emmet and the pig did, how the vacation was, what happened on the farm, etc., and it would give you a chance to do the city-type-life (St. Louis) and country life (Tennessee farm). I think it could be about four or five thousand words. Now you shouldn't spend too much time on it, so if any of this seems like too much trouble just tell me and I'll not mention it any more to you. But it would be darling, if you were interested.

Love,

TO MARY STOLZ   April 29, 1957

Dear Molly:

Just tried to telephone but you are out larking around on this beautiful day and I'm glad about that. I'm sorry I had to ring off last night and trust you really did understand. I'd returned from a quite unpleasant weekend—the only bright spots during it were when I turned aside briefly TO READ A DAMN MANUSCRIPT. Then I returned to my mortgaged little gray home on the hill, feeling quite sorry for myself to be frank, and the telephone was ringing and it was an author telephoning long distance to tell me good news about the third chapter, which was better than bad news about the third chapter but frankly no news about the third chapter was what I was longing to hear at that time on Sunday. So I talked and then hung up and then two neighbors dropped in, and there I was in my damn slip, about to take a bath, but I am so poor I don't have a courteous lady-help to go to the door and say "Sorry Miss Nordstrom is at prayer meeting and won't be home all night." I don't even have an upstairs to which I can retire while the neighbors ring the bell and then peer in through the cursed picture window. So I let them in (I put on me wrapper—of <u>course</u>) and they sat. The wife needled the husband and the husband needled the wife. Suddenly the wife said, with a weak smile to me, a propos of something particularly mean the husband had thrown at her: "I just never seem to do anything right," and on the word "anything" her voice broke and the eyes filled up and I thought oh Lord and at that moment the phone rang and it was you and so that's why I didn't want to go on talking too long for fear the lovely couple in my living room would have been in a real hassle by the time I returned...... They were.

I am about to write the adult's *Hole Is to Dig*. I know I've spoken of this project to you before. The first page is: "Self-pity is to wallow in." I was wallowing in it last night.

Today is different. All is well. After all, what is one bad weekend? Or one spring? Or one life, come to think of it? It is a lovely day and I think that this year the purple lilac will be BEAUTIFUL.

I <u>told</u> you Mr. Herrick[1] would make you cheerful and glad and smiling. I smile when I think of the fury in your voice when you said to me through clenched teeth: "Urs, DON'T STAND UP FOR HIM." I will stand up for him with my last breath. And all poor unfortunate lovers ....

Thanks for the letter about death.[2] I used to get so MAD at

---

1. MS, who had divorced her first husband, enjoyed referring to the man she was then dating as "Mr. Herrick," after the seventeenth-century English poet. She dedicated *Good-By My Shadow*, 1957, to "Mr. Herrick."
2. Dick Pearson, head of Harper's High School department and a much-beloved figure within the firm, had died recently. UN was among the many people at Harper who felt the loss sharply.

Margaret Wise Brown for going and dieing [*sic*]. I'd think help-lessly: "How come she ever went and did anything so grown up?" It seemed so needlessly dramatic of her. This is different, though. But thanks again.

Love,

TO VIRGINIA HAVILAND[1] (MNC)   May 7, 1957

Dear Virginia:

I am enclosing proofs of a book we will publish late in August, *Little Bear* by Else Holmelund Minarik, with pictures by Maurice Sendak. As you will notice on the jacket, we are calling this an "I Can Read" book.[2] We think that this book will fill a real need and we hope that you will like the words and pictures as much as we do. We believe that children who have finished the first grade will be able to read this book by them-selves, and that many who are still in the first grade will be able to read most of it alone with very little help.

Would you be willing to give us a comment on this book which we would be able to use on the jacket? As you know, *The Cat in the Hat*[3] by Dr. Seuss has several very impressive endorsements printed on the back of the jacket and we would,

1. Readers' advisor for children, Boston Public Library.
2. Haviland had alerted UN to the need for good books for newly literate children, for those who came to the library boasting, "I can read, I can read! Where are the books for me?"
3. *The Cat in the Hat*, by Dr. Seuss, Random House, 1957. The Seuss book, which unlike *Little Bear* was written from an age-graded list of words (or "controlled vocabulary"), was published earlier that year. VH responded to UN by writing in part: "The story of Little Bear's imaginative play feels far removed from controlled vocabulary; Maurice Sendak's drawings give it special distinction."

of course, like to have our book have the benefit of a few advance comments. That's why I'm rushing these proofs off to you and to two or three others. I do hope that this letter and this request are not too much of an imposition. We have been working on this book for several years. There is not a comma and not a space between the lines over which we have not worried! The author and the artist have done their best to make it right for the children. That's why I want to do everything I can to help it on its way.

Yours sincerely,

TO EVA LE GALLIENNE[1]   May 13, 1957

Dear Miss Le Gallienne:

Thanks for the last two stories[2] which we like very much. I have sent all seven to Mr. Sendak and I hope that he will come in soon to talk over the size of the book, the number of pictures he would like to do and other details of the format so that we can draw up the contract.

I'm sending you copies of some books that Mr. Sendak has illustrated. I doubt that his pictures for the Andersen stories will resemble any of those in these books because he changes his technique to fit each new text. However, I thought you'd like to see the work of this brilliant young artist. Is there any chance that you'll be in town early next week—Monday or

1. British-born American actress, director, and author who in 1926 founded New York's Civic Repertory Theatre. Le Gallienne's first children's book was *Flossie and Bossie*, illustrated by Garth Williams, 1949.
2. ELeG was translating from the Danish a selection of fairy tales by Hans Christian Andersen for a collection published as *Seven Tales by H. C. Andersen*, illustrated by Maurice Sendak, 1959.

Tuesday or Wednesday? If so, perhaps we can talk over a few small points about your translations. If you're not going to be in town we can certainly write you about the possibility of a few changes.

Yours sincerely,

TO MAURICE SENDAK   July 8, 1957

Dear Maurice:

I was so glad to have your note. We sent you last Wednesday, to your New York address, a copy of the *Times* review of *Very Far Away* which finally appeared. I hope your mail is being forwarded? It is a good review. I'll ask Linda[1] to send you a duplicate to Maine in case your mail isn't being forwarded.

Your pictures for *Somebody Else's Nut Tree*[2] are marvelous and once again I thank you for being so talented and for illustrating this Harper book. Really, they are WONDERFUL drawings. We sent photostats to Ruth and I called her up over this long July 4th weekend and she was so happy with them she said she wished she could write you about it. I guess you have heard from her by now?

I am very very glad *Old Potato*[3] and H. C. Andersen are there with you. That *Old Potato* is a perfectly fascinating manuscript and it will be your best book yet, I bet. I'm eager to know what strange sea-change he will have experienced by the time I see him again. I'm about to talk contract with Miss Le Gallienne's

1. Probably a secretary on UN's staff.
2. *Somebody Else's Nut Tree and Other Tales from Children*, by Ruth Krauss, illustrated by Maurice Sendak, 1958.
3. MS did not complete this novel-length manuscript, which was set in Brooklyn and which described the friendship between a boy nicknamed "Old Potato" and a gentle man who lived in the neighborhood.

agent for the Andersen now. Jack [Rynerson] has got some rough figures and we will be able to have 7 full pages in color. I believe I told you this before. I'm very happy about that book, about all your books in fact. About you too, teacher's pet.

Maine sounds lovely but you should be more loving about the "big seated people in khaki shorts." We can't all have navy blue shorts, you know. Forgive silly letter. I just had a long weekend and got rested and that makes me sort of drunk.

Speaking of shorts, reminds me of Kansas City. Let me explain. It was a lovely convention[1] on the whole. You would have been pleased at how many of your librarian friends spoke about you. For instance, good Hokie[2] who sat up with us that night in Philadelphia. Many of the librarians love your work and I trust that I will have the pleasure of hearing you make the Caldecott speech soon. Marc Simont was good but I see no reason to dwell on that in this letter, do you? The Newbery Medal lady[3] was not good, I thought. She spoke for three hours, or maybe it was four, on how she came to write *War and Peace*, *Moby Dick*, all of Jane Austen, and so forth. With sound effects and emotion.   But to get to me, I had a new dress which I loved madly, lavender lace which sounds either too young or too old for me but which really was, the sales lady assured me, "just right." I love the dress and the night of the Newbery-Caldecott dinner (which this year I called the Caldecott-Newbery dinner, of course) I put on my dress and got so carried away with the excitement of the occasion that I decided to try to look nicer for Harper & Brothers and not wear my glasses. (The oculist has told me not to wear them except when I have to see something so this wasn't complete idiocy.) Well,

---

1. The American Library Association convention, where Marc Simont received the Caldecott Medal for *A Tree Is Nice*.
2. Naomi Hokanson, librarian, Alexander Ramsey High School, St. Paul, Minnesota.
3. Virginia Sorensen won the Newbery Medal that year for *Miracles on Maple Hill*, illustrated by Beth and Joe Krush, Harcourt, Brace, 1956.

everyone was very nice to me and even complimentary. Of course I couldn't <u>see</u> any of the people who came up to me and said I looked nice, and probably it was the same person just doing it over and over to cheer me up, some relative probably. Because I've just seen the photographs of the official group. Oh God. There are Mrs. Rollins[1], chairman of the Newbery-Caldecott committee, Mr. Melcher[2], Mr. Simont, Miss McElderry, smiling and carefree, and then, on the right, who is <u>that</u>? Or rather, <u>what</u> is that? Surely it isn't a woman, or even a human being. No, it is more a sort of <u>expanse</u> of something, and so why would it be in the picture? Is it a prairie? No, it seems to be more of an enormous Russian steppe..... Oh, I know what it is, it is Jones Beach—a picture of Jones Beach. Jones Beach Nordstrom.

Ruth telephoned and I gave her your address. She wants to send you her arrangement of photostats. I said I hadn't sent you a set.

Have lots of fun, and write again when you want to, for I love to hear from you. We'll probably never meet again, Maurice, our paths will simply keep crossing, but it was lovely knowing you. I'm going to arrive in (on) Cape Cod July 28th, and I see by your letter that you'll be leaving there the 27th or 28th. If by chance you linger there longer and are near West Dennis, where I'll be, let me know. We could have a big editorial conference, or a hot dog, or something. Oh no, no hot dog for me after that Newbery picture.

And, again, those *Nut Tree* pictures are superb.

Yours,

1. Charlemae Rollins, children's librarian, Hall Branch, Chicago Public Library, who became a figure of national importance in the field; author of *A Reader's Guide to Negro Life and Literature for Elementary and Secondary School Use*, National Council of Teachers of English, 1941.
2. Frederic G. Melcher, editor of *Publishers Weekly* and president of R. R. Bowker Company; cofounder of Children's Book Week; donor of the Newbery and Caldecott medals; who each year presented the awards at the American Library Association's annual convention.

Dear —————:

We are always glad to hear from readers of our books, and we very much appreciate your writing us about *Harry the Dirty Dog*[1] and *Three Little Animals*[2]. We feel as you do that good usage is extremely important—particularly in books for children.

Actually, however, the use of "everyone" in conjunction with "their" in the two sentences you mention is grammatically acceptable and, we believe, preferable. May we quote a paragraph from page 543 of the *Harper Handbook of College Composition*, a college textbook by George S. Wykoff and Harry Shaw, two recognized authorities in their field. "Since or when the sense of *everybody*, *anyone*, etc., is *many* or *all*, the plural personal pronoun referring to these indefinite pronouns is frequently found in both formal and informal English: 'Everybody is expected to do their share of the work.' Such use is preferable to the somewhat artificial and even awkward 'Everybody is expected to do his or her share of the work.' " Incidentally, the *Harper Handbook* has been adopted by more than 125 colleges and universities as an official text.

In the two sentences you mention we feel the use of the singular personal pronoun "his" would have been too formal and would not have been in keeping with the writing style and flavor of the books.

We are very glad to know that, despite your reservations, you enjoyed *Harry the Dirty Dog* and *Three Little Animals*, and we hope that the foregoing explanation will enable you to recommend the books wholeheartedly.

Again, thank you for taking the time to write to us. We will always be glad to hear from you.

Yours sincerely,
Director

1. *Harry the Dirty Dog*, by Gene Zion, illustrated by Margaret Bloy Graham, 1956.
2. *Three Little Animals*, by Margaret Wise Brown, illustrated by Garth Williams, 1956.

TO MARY CHALMERS[1]   October 24, 1957

Dear Mary:

The last time we met you said oh you must learn more about the grain of the paper, the signatures in a book, high-light halftones, electros, repro proofs, etc. etc. You seemed to think that artists who know all that stuff are better than you, and that you are no good because you don't understand just how a book gets bound, etc. I remarked mildly that you had done all right so far knowing just what you know, and you said what was that? And I said and I hereby state again for the record: You know what many many artists will never know and would give a great deal of blood to know. Your stories and your pictures are so much loved by children and by the adults who stand between the creative artist and the child. You have created a whole delightful, charming, original, touching, funny, wonderful little Mary Chalmers world—the flowers and the ferns and the little animals, and the little conversations, and the trees, and the floor of the little forest, and the friendships. You have done and are doing in your children's books the sort of thing very very very few artists can ever do. And so you mustn't forget that, Mary. You have great gifts, and your books are loved more than, apparently, I've ever been able to make you understand. But you must understand now and believe me. And don't forget it! I'm so very glad you're on the Harper list, and I hope you are glad too. I know you are, so don't think you have to tell me!

Write me again and tell me all about everything.

Affectionately,

---

1. Artist and author, especially of picture books about cats. Illustrator of Nordstrom's book, *The Secret Language*.

TO MARY CHALMERS   October 29, 1957

Dear Mary:

Important message: please buy a new typewriter ribbon. The one you are using is so pale that I will soon have to buy a seeing-eye dog for my seeing-eye dog.

I am delighted that you like the idea of a house-hunting book. I think it could be perfectly wonderful. I loved your description of real-life house-hunting. I also enjoyed Mary Chalmers at the Cat Show[1]. One of these days you are going to disappear into one of your own little books—and then where will we be?

Yours,

—Mercy, what sickening whimsy. Excuse it please[2]

TO SYD HOFF[3]   December 4, 1957

Dear Syd:

I'm returning your dummy of *Danny and the Dinosaur*[4] with my penciled notations in it. I'm afraid it is very messy but I am sure you can make it all out. As I wrote you weeks ago, it is very

---

1. MC had recounted for UN a recent experience at a Philadelphia cat show. While the artist leaned forward to read the card of a cat she particularly admired, the cat in question sank a fluffy paw deep into her hair.
2. By hand on the original.
3. Cartoonist, author, and illustrator. Hoff, whose cartoons appeared regularly for many years in *The New Yorker*, went on to have his own syndicated comic strips, *Tuffy* and *Laugh It Off*.
4. *Danny and the Dinosaur*, by Syd Hoff, 1958. UN was unsure how to proceed with SH's first children's book manuscript until she realized that it suited the I Can Read series recently initiated with the publication of *Little Bear*.

good on the whole but it does need more work. We've taken a lot of time at this end but I think that will save you some time in the long run. Manufacturing estimates have taken longer than they should.

First of all, remember that you have 64 pages of text and pictures including front matter. I can't figure out your numbering in this dummy.

First page of text and pictures (numbered 7 in your dummy, for purposes of identification.) I think you should just say "One day Danny went to the museum." (He didn't actually want to "see how the world looked a long, long time ago," as you put it, do you think? Very unchildlike. He might have wanted to go to see the dead mummies, or other specific things in a museum, but I wouldn't mention that here because you mention it on following pages. So just have a simple statement for this first page. "One day Danny went to the museum.") It is pretty short and if you can think of one more short sentence for this page by all means add it. I can't come up with any suggestion myself. Page 8: you'll have to simplify what he saw on this page. NOT THAT I WANT YOU TO GET SELF-CONSCIOUS ABOUT "I CAN READ." I told you I wanted you to let me worry about that aspect and that's all I'm doing now. You could just say "He saw Indians. He saw bears. He saw…" I haven't been in a museum in 150 years and can't think of anything else, but you can. On Page 9: "He saw horses and wagons. He saw mummies. He saw cavemen. And he saw …." (OK? Roman chariot and Egyptian mummies look too hard for a child who has just learned to read and is excited about reading.) Page 10 and 11: I think he should see dinosaurs in the distance—a double-spread with Danny in the foreground as he is but the dinosaurs much farther away across the museum floor, with other museum items slightly indicated. And on Page 11, where you now say "Of course these dinosaurs were stuffed like dolls and teddy bears, and were not real dinosaurs at all," I'd suggest simply: "Danny loved dinosaurs. He wished he had one." Now if you make double-spread Pages 10 and 11 a long distance picture, you could put the close-up <u>now</u> on 10 and 11 on Pages 12 and 13 with the words on Page 12, "Danny was sad. I wish they were real," he said. "It would be nice to play with a dinosaur." Page 13 could have the words "And I think it would be nice to play with you," said a voice, on the bottom of Page 13. Well, of course you can figure this out better than I can, Syd. I'm just being very specific in case it is helpful to you in working out a new dummy for your guidance. On Page 14 I feel strongly that you should put this thought (that the dinosaur can take an hour or two off in a hundred million years) later in the book. On this Page 14 I think you should just have Danny saying something pleased and happy but essentially matter-of-fact, you know, something as flat as "I'm glad to hear that, said Danny." On Page 15 we suggest slight simplification: "Come on," said the dinosaur. "I'll take you for a ride." The dinosaur put his head down so Danny could get on him. Nothing to say on 16 and 17, which are very good—except make traffic light red light. Pages 18 and 19 seem very resistible to me, Syd. The rest of the story is so reasonable, given the fact that a dinosaur came to life, but this stuff about pushing the cloud away with his nose doesn't quite come off, I'm afraid. The same for the wet cement episode on Page 19. Now if both these pages are dear to you by all means keep them in. They just seem not good enough for you, but I could certainly be wrong. Pages 20 and 21 are fine but we'll (you'll) have to simplify the words a bit. Instead of "tangled up in the telephone wires" you can just say the dinosaur was so tall Danny had to hold the wires away from him (or something— that suggestion is awful). But the main thing to remember is that you'll be showing in the picture that he got tangled up in the telephone wires[1], so you can use simpler words under the picture. Page 21, sort of perfunctory words? Pages 22 and 23 are fine, I think. Pages 24 and 25 are fine too. Page 26: the picture is fine but the words are too involved. If you can't fix we'll try. Page 27: Text has to be simpler. Page 28 fine. Page 29, could you think of a better incident for this page? Pulling the ocean liner isn't good enough for you, I think. Page 30 fine. Page 31, I definitely think you should cut this unless you plan to go on and do something with it—what the world was like so long ago. And I think you haven't room to do that so I'd skip that bit and get to the business of Page 32. Pages 32 and 33 are fine. Page 34 fine with the slight change we indicate. 35 fine. 36 and 37 simply wonderful. Same for 36(a) and 37(a) (this is your number duplication), but on Page 37(a) I'd show the tail end of a crowd of people going to look at the dinosaur. 40 and 41 (in this dummy you skip 38 and 39) are OK, I think, though we'll have to simplify the words somewhat—but the ideas are very very good. 42 and 43—absolutely wonderful, that "It's Danny riding a dinosaur," said one child is marvelous! We'll have to worry a little bit about keeping the words simpler but we can do that the next time around if you can't fix it yourself. 44 and 45 are fine. Pages 46 and 47 fine though words can be simpler. 48 good but you can cut text a bit. 49 fine. Page 50 fine. And 51. 52 and 53 just perfect. 54 and 55 also wonderful. 56 perfect, and also 57. 58 and 59 fine but we'll have to get the words simpler. I wish you could think of a more original song for them to sing—something real dopey that they'd make up, instead of "For he's a jolly good fellow." They wouldn't have sung anything like that, I think. Make up some dopey thing they could chant. I can't think of anything but I'm sure you

---

1. In a later edition, the telephone wires were changed to clotheslines in a nod to the dangers of playing with electricity.

can. Children make up such silly rhymes. By the way, I doubt that the children would have done anything so consciously adorable as "join hands and form a ring." Wouldn't they just jump up and down and shout "Hurray hurray for the dinosaur." Oh it is too bad we have to do all this by letter. It would be so much easier (for you too) if we could just go over this page by page. Well, it can be done this way I know; I just don't want you to be confused by any of this. That's why I've tried to take it page by page, which you probably don't need me to do. To go on Page 60 is OK but would you add "Well, good-bye, Danny," said the dinosaur. Then on Page 61 I think you should change it quite a bit so it reads something like this: "Can't you come stay with me?" said Danny. "We could have fun." "No," said the dinosaur. "I've had a good time, the best I've had in one hundred million years. But now I have to go back to the museum. They need me there." "Oh," said Danny. "Well, good-bye." Pages 62 and 63 are fine. And 64 is OK too but I think you should just have one last little sentence to finish the book off cheerfully, like "But we did have a wonderful time," or something like that (only better!).

When I wrote you about the drawings I said we could have 3 colors on one side of the sheet and two on the other. But you used four in the one with all the children and the dinosaur, and I can see that it wouldn't be nearly so good with only three. So we've been trying to figure out ways to let you have 4 colors on one side of the sheet and two on the other, and still keep the list price of the book to $2.50. I can't remember whether or not you and I talked about you doing color separations. Did we? I'm returning to you today the dinosaur with all the children, and some Dinobase sheets on which the Manufacturing Department has indicated on a small area how color separations might be done. This is going under separate cover. I enclose a copy of the memorandum from the Manufacturing Department about this process. What do you think of it? Do you think you could handle the color process because the strong black line would be weakened. I am getting additional manufacturing estimates on the possibility of your giving us a black key drawing, with everything on it which you want to appear in black. If we can afford it we'd send you non-photographic blues and you could put the colors (minus black) right on the blues, and we'd have the camera do the separation by three color process. I know this would be much much easier for you and I certainly hope the figures I finally get make this possible. I'll write again in a day or two (honestly, we've been slow getting going but now we're almost through with the endless figuring and we won't hold you up again).

I wrote you last month that it was all right to have a few double-spreads in the book, but I should have added that it is important to keep those double-spreads to a minimum because library bindings are side-sewn and therefore the middle of the double-spread is simply nipped into the binding and lost to sight. So have some but not too many and don't put any vital action right in the middle of a double-spread. I also wrote you that it is all right for your drawings to bleed but I've just gone over a lot of details with the head of our Manufacturing Department and he says that really it will be much better if the drawings <u>don't</u> bleed. So can you plan to stay at least 1/8th of an inch from the trimmed edges of the page?

I should have said earlier in this letter (and I should have written you earlier) that we love the dinosaur and the children spread. The feeling is just right. I am not so enthusiastic about the one of Danny and the dinosaur's feet, which I am returning with the other picture. I think you're kidding Danny too much; he looks like an adenoidal dumbbell. I think the book will be much funnier if he looks like a relatively sensible, real boy—I can't think of the right word. I mean I think he wouldn't have a great many changes of expression, you know. If he just accepts all this in a pretty matter-of-fact manner it will seem funnier to adults and perfectly reasonable to children.

We agree that crayons are a nice medium for this book.

I hope you will go over these suggestions for changes in the text and make whatever changes you are willing to make and then send a revised text back to me. We can set it in type immediately and that will be a big help to you when you are finishing the drawings. You'll be able to see just how the words fit on the page. I guess a lot of this sounds awfully fussy, but when the book comes out it will look just right and as though this is exactly the way it was meant to be, and then we'll all be happy.

You will notice that though I wrote you I liked the bit about teaching the dinosaur to sit up and beg, and rubbing his stomach, I didn't see any way to fit it into the dummy. After my initial enthusiasm about these two pictures I sort of cooled off on them; maybe they would seem a little forced? I don't feel strongly, though, and if you want them in just say so.

Be sure that you plan the dummy for 64 pages, including front matter. Check your copy of *Little Bear* to see exactly what I mean. You don't need to allow so many pages for front matter as Sendak did, of course. We can do with as few as four, a title-page, copyright page, half-title page, blank, and start first page of text and pictures on Page 5. That would mean 60 pages for the text and pictures.

Best regards and I hope all this makes sense. It is going to be a wonderful book and we're delighted to have it on our list. Write me soon. What is your 'phone number in case I have to call?

Yours,

TO SYD HOFF   December 13, 1957

Dear Syd:

The new dummy is SO good. Congratulations! "He wanted to see what was inside" was a perfect second sentence for Page 5. Everything is fine but at Page 10 I now wonder if you shouldn't take out "Danny was sad." I know I didn't think so earlier, but now that the text is so much better, and I can read it more smoothly as I turn the pages, "Danny was sad" doesn't look or sound right. His "I wish they were real" sort of implies at least wistfulness, without actually saying it, and I think you could leave out "Danny was sad" with no loss. On Page 10 we suggest you add, after "And I think it would be nice to play with you," said a voice that you add another line: "Can you?" said Danny. Then change Page 12 to read:

> "Yes," said the dinosaur.
> "Oh, good," said Danny. "What can we do?"

That simplifies some of the stuff here and we like it better. Hope you agree. If not just say so. But we really think it is better.

Then everything is fine up to Page 22: The dinosaur had to be very careful going around corners on account of his long tail. That picture is lovely, but I don't know exactly why he would have to be "very careful" on account of "his long tail." I mean, why? Not that I expect you to explain why in the actual words, but if you will tell me more what you meant I'll be more helpful right here I think. If he hadn't been careful going around corners what would have happened, that is to say? (Isn't this an idiotic sort of correspondence. I'm sorry!)

Yes, we like the mention of the hour or two off on Page 26. You can still have it later. This makes it sort of nice and casual.   Page 27: change "peeked in" to "looked" at the ball game. All else is just fine but when I got to Page 40 I thought that the line I once thought flawless: "It's Danny, riding a dinosaur," might possibly be better if you changed it to "Look at Danny riding on a dinosaur," said a boy. "It's Danny etc." doesn't really sound so much like a child as "Look at etc." And the matter-of-factness of "Look at Danny riding on a dinosaur" is good. What do you think? We do not love "Little heads looked over the fence." What could you put in here. Something like a lot of children ran to look over the fence. Or something like that? "Little heads" is too cute. Everything fine to Page 46. The word "tummy" sounds so baby-talkish, and stomach isn't good here either. What with the explicit picture I should think you could just say "He's smart," said Danny, patting the dinosaur.   All fine to Page 55 where I'd suggest instead of having "whispered Danny to the children" you say "Danny said to the children," and on this page you can show Danny in a huddle, heads together, with the other kids and the dinosaur slightly to one side, so we can get away from the hard word "whisper." OK? Page 61. Couldn't you show a little bit of Danny and the dinosaur shaking hands goodbye, or something. Nothing sticky, you know. Just goodbye.   And on Page 64 "But we did have a wonderful time" is a perfectly acceptable last sentence but it isn't perfect so see if you can't think of something exactly right.   I will keep the dummy here because I am sure you remember words and sketches clearly enough to decide on these points without having the dummy. If you will let me know what you agree with soon we'll have the text typed up from this dummy, with these changes, and have the book set in galleys at once. Write soon. Are you in your house yet?

Yours sincerely,

TO —————— January 7, 1958

Dear ——————:

We are sorry indeed to learn that you were shocked by Mrs. [Natalie Savage] Carlson's book *The Happy Orpheline*[1]. We know that Mrs. Carlson will want to read your letter and we are sending her a copy of it. She is in Europe at present, however, and I doubt that she will be able to send us her comments for some time to come.

We would be deeply sorry if any book we published offended a child. In your letter you say you understand that the little orphan "lives in constant apprehension of the possibility of adoption." I do think, ——————, that "constant apprehension" is too strong a description of the extremely vigorous and humorous approach to this story. We trust that the situation in this book will not offend any moderately well-adjusted child with a normal sense of humor.

We appreciate the sincerity of your letter. We too sincerely feel a deep responsibility as publishers of children's books. We fear that anyone who thinks that Brigitte lives "in constant apprehension" of being adopted has misread Mrs. Carlson's story.

Yours sincerely,
Director

TO JANICE MAY UDRY June 18, 1958

Dear Janice:

Thanks for your note giving us your new address. We are notifying the Royalty Department and are changing our own records.

---

1. *The Happy Orpheline*, by Natalie Savage Carlson, illustrated by Garth Williams, 1957.

I started to dictate a reply because I am trying desperately to be more efficient and business-like. But I can't bear not to write a personal sort of answer to your little letter of the 12th. You sounded so sad, somehow. Yes, I do live in a house because I have a beautiful and financial relationship with the Savings and Loan Mortgage Association, based on a very high interest rate. But don't be sad about me in a house and me and moon-flowers. I may have tried to impress you at one time with the beauty and general poetry of my existence, and I may have tried to have you understand that I am surrounded by moon-flowers. That is balderdash, dear. The truth is I can't even grow plain blue morning-glories and I love them with all the passion of my pent-up nature. I am a real mess. I can walk onto a lovely green plot of land, and tall strong trees turn brown, and cracks appear in their trunks, leaves crumble. The grass shrivels; even myrtle turns up its toes, and the crab grass shudders and dies. Death and destruction, pestilence and horror, I'm right out of the Old Testament. Moon-flowers indeed! And apartment life can be very lovely, Janice. I mean when a fuse blows the superintendent will come fix it. Or is your husband handy around the house? Well, I don't know whether this letter is cheering you up one bit; it is depressing me terribly, so enough of this.

What are you writing? I am sitting here looking at the jacket of *The Moon-Jumpers*[1] and it is so purely beautiful I wish I could send it to you. It would make you very happy. But we have to keep it and send it off to the plate-maker very soon. Are you writing some more books for us? I haven't seen your Lothrop book[2] but I will. Write another GOOD book for us. How old is your daughter now? I should send you some of our books and you can keep them until your child is old enough to

1. *The Moon Jumpers*, by Janice May Udry, illustrated by Maurice Sendak, 1959.
2. *Theodore's Parents*, by Janice May Udry, illustrated by Adrienne Adams, Lothrop, Lee & Shepard, 1958.

enjoy them. I'm going to be in San Francisco at the library thing in July but can't get down to Los Angeles. I would certainly like to, just to meet you. But we'll have to be just pen-pals for a while longer. Write me again and send us another manuscript.

Yours,

TO SUSAN CARR

Mykonos, Greece
March 11, 1959

Dear Sue:

We are on the island of Mykonos[1], which is very beautiful in a bare, craggy way. We go back to Athens tonight—over night on a little boat—and I hope it is better than the <u>horrible</u> one which brought us. There was the most interesting woman on the boat coming over—well, what was interesting about her was that she was completely without <u>any</u> sort of definite personality. I cannot describe this vacuity. She was Mrs. ————— from Philadelphia and she was on a trip—from Feb. 1 to June 1. Ireland, England, Amsterdam, Rome, Athens, Istanbul, India, Japan, Spain, etc. I decided she was a recently widowed person on this trip "to forget." But she wore no wedding ring. She had a guide with her—a very sophisticated and humorous looking woman to whom Mrs. ————— deferred as to an "older girl"—or a governess. They came in from a tour of Nykosia [sic] yesterday when F. and I were having luncheon. The guide started for their table and Mrs. ————— said "Could I—oh <u>could</u> I—wash my hands?" I almost sobbed out loud. She is a girl about in her late fifties

---

1. On a trip combining business and vacation time, UN sailed for Europe on February 6, landing in Naples eight days later. UN was accompanied for most of the trip by Frances Chrystie of F.A.O. Schwarz.

and absolutely kills me. She talked to me <u>shyly</u> on the boat. "Oh I don't know <u>where</u> I stayed in Amsterdam. I get so mixed up on names. And I'm very stupid, I'm afraid. I don't remember." What shocked me was a great <u>vein</u> of Mrs. Elliott Robinson Brown[1] I discovered in myself. "Oh Mrs. —————," I cried. "Don't talk about yourself that way! We mustn't <u>limit</u> ourselves!" Of course I died of shame at this Emmet J. Fox[2] aspect of me. Well, I'll have to tell you how Mrs. ————— pronounced her "a's." Very genteel—not <u>really</u> broad—and all misplaced as in Athens. She didn't exactly say Ah-thens, but it came darn close. And all the while long white bony fingers twisting around each other in her lap. I can't <u>stand</u> not knowing why she is on this trip. Frances is sick of hearing about Mrs. —————. Every time I'd see her on the ship or here on Mykonos I'd give her a great big fat smile to encourage her. She kills me.

Now, dear, we <u>did</u> go to Delphi but the Castiglia is <u>closed</u>! We had luncheon at a lovely place but I saw no one who could have been Caresse[3]. And the town is so much bigger than I thought that I didn't just stop some Greek and ask. But she'll be back in Athens (Ah-thens) when I get back and so maybe we'll meet then. I wrote you I left a note for her at the Grand Bretagne. I meant to say Kay Boyle had suggested I say hello but I <u>may</u> have identified myself as a friend of Susan Carr's!

Yes, I would love to see the pretty picture of my dear old father. If anything about me looks like him I'll be happy. I have

---

1. UN's mother.
2. Prolific Harper author whose inspirational titles for adults included *Power Through Constructive Thinking*, 1940; *Make Your Life Worthwhile*, 1946; and *Around the Year with Emmet Fox: A Book of Daily Readings*, 1958.
3. Caresse Crosby, wife of Harry Crosby and the author of *The Passionate Years* (Southern Illinois University Press, 1968), an autobiography that SC greatly admired. Crosby was a friend of the novelist Kay Boyle, with whom SC had recently worked on a new edition of a children's book, *The Youngest Camel: Reconsidered and Rewritten*, illustrated by Ronni Solbert, 1959. UN did meet Crosby before leaving Greece.

many interesting theories which I will bore you with about how fortunate <u>we</u> are to come from less than blissfully happy homes. Frances has this large, happy family (news flash!) and is <u>absorbed</u> by them. I had to sort of cruise around and find an interesting life and outside people to love, and I think that makes for more—oh, can't go on with this. I'm not saying it right. But a person can take <u>refuge</u> in a large family.

I am sort of depressed. I hope Bronowski[1] is all right on Friday. I'm <u>very</u> grateful it worked out this way. But what if he can't stand me? Well, I mustn't "limit" myself! More later.

P.S. I've written "This kills me" 100 times in this epistle. Sorry! I sound like an ancient Holden Caulfield[2].

TO SYD HOFF   July 21, 1959

Dear Syd Honey:

I love the roughts   I mean roughs for *Oliver*[3]. It will be a dandy book and will sell thousands of copies and make you rich. Many thanks!

---

1. Jacob Bronowski, scientist, humanist, educator, and author, then living in England. Bronowski was contemplating a series of science books for young readers to be published for both the British and American markets. UN met with him while in Europe to discuss the project, but not before having to overcome objections from members of the Harper Trade department, who were eager to count the latter-day Renaissance man among *their* authors. Bronowski did in fact make his first appearance on Harper's list as the co-author, with Bruce Mazlish, of an adult title, *The Western Intellectual Tradition: From Leonardo to Hegel*, 1960. One children's book eventually came of his discussions with UN: *Biography of an Atom*, co-authored by Millicent E. Selsam, illustrated by Weimer Pursell, 1965.
2. The self-mocking reference is to the burned-out young protagonist of J. D. Salinger's *The Catcher in the Rye*, Little, Brown, 1951.
3. *Oliver*, by Syd Hoff, 1960.

Hope you were reassured by Sue [Carr]'s letter, stating that I certainly was not mad at you. I love you dearly. I don't know why Mr. Henry Morrison[1] thought I was "mad" at you. This sort of 4th Grade situation always seems a little dreary to me. Believe, me, son: If I am ever mad at you I will write you a letter and so state. Or telephone you long distance COLLECT. I will never go through a third person. I can't remember our phone conversation—Mr. Morrison's and mine. I guess he said for goodness sake where is the contract and I said for goodness sake the lady who types up contracts is busy typing up the revised copy of the manuscript. Anyhow, little one, I am not mad and I will never be. Or if by any chance I am I will tell you first. All right? But really I think you are very nice, Syd.

Your letter—one of them—came from Las Vegas. I long to go there. Please write me about it. I dream of winning vast sums in the pin ball machines, or at 21. Did you win a big wad? Are your daughters well and happy? Your wife? You? Are you having a good time and a good vacation? But why do I care—your whole damn life sounds like a whole damn vacation to me.

We are returning the roughs to you. Delighted with them, really. Maybe I should keep them around for Dorothy Hagen[2] to measure but she is on vacation and I am sure you have been very accurate in doing these sketches.

Much love,

P.S. We are holding roughs to return to Miami Beach address.

1. SH's agent at the Scott Meredith agency.
2. Dorothy Hagen came to Harper in 1957, succeeding Jack Rynerson in the manufacturing department. When Hagen arrived at Harper, UN was being congratulated for having passed the million-dollar mark in annual sales. As the department continued to grow, UN was given her own manufacturing department, with Hagen in charge. Hagen later served as Director of Operations until her retirement in 1982.

Dear Russ,

First, thanks for coming over with the revised dummy of
the Atomic Submarine book[2]. I think it is going to be a good
book and I hope you will let me have the dummy back one of
these days so I can go over it and the text. Let me have it for a
week during early August, will you?

About *Whose* [sic] *Afraid?*[3] I do think it is better but I'm
afraid it is going to need a lot more work, Russ. You simply
didn't take any time to set the stage, get any characters, think
about the situation. All this sounds very ponderous and over-
serious. And I don't mean it that way. But you should make up
a thirty-two page dummy and rough out how the text would
fall (do this without pictures, just imagining them, just figuring out how to divide the text). Then you will see that this
simply starts bang and goes on with no pacing. The turning-
of-the-pages is so important in a picture book with a story,
you know. Well, I don't mean to sound the least bit cross, dear,
or really disappointed. But I felt so hopeful when you left my
place last weekend, and I <u>was</u> a little depressed by the manuscript when I read it (several times) this week. I know you can
do it better but for heaven's sake take a little time and care. It
isn't easy to write a good picture book story. I wish I could be
more constructive but until you do more on this it is pretty
hard for me to be. I will say (this sounds like Eisenhower,
doesn't it? "Well, I will say this," he says, "and let me make

---

1. Author and artist. RH was a successful commercial artist when he came in to Harper
   one day to show UN a portfolio of large drawings of heavy machinery, done on
   brown wrapping paper. These formed the basis for his first book, *What Does It Do
   and How Does It Work?*, 1959.
2. *The Atomic Submarine*, by Russell Hoban, 1960.
3. This was the working title for the manuscript published as *Bedtime for Frances*, by
   Russell Hoban, illustrated by Garth Williams, 1960.

it crystal clear...”). I will say this: that I think your first "chapter" can't be called "The Tiger," and you can't just say in two lines that this Frances was in bed and she couldn't sleep and then bang go right into the act. Why don't you try it slower—easy and slow in the beginning, for a page or two, it was time to go to bed, she didn't want to go to bed, her mother told her again, her father told her, and finally she went. And then she decided she saw a tiger (don't have her go to sleep and DREAM about the tiger). This should all be stuff in her waking mind. I'd think, because she doesn't want to go to sleep and she starts off almost wanting to be scared and then does become scared. I think it is sort of a good idea not to make her a human little girl but why a vole? I sort of wish any other creature but a vole which looks like a mouse. I think it is terribly difficult to draw ATTRACTIVE mice and I am speaking as the editor who tried eight artists for *Stuart Little* before Garth Williams finally came through for good old Harper.

[...]

And thanks again for that beautiful moonlight picture. I am <u>so</u> glad to have it.

Best to you and Lillian[1] and don't be discouraged or mad at any of this.

[...]

TO JANICE MAY UDRY   August 11, 1959

Dear Janice:

I have 1000 things to write to you about and I absolutely promise I will NEVER again get so far behind with you. I hate

1. Lillian Hoban, RH's wife, later an author/illustrator.

editors who don't answer letters or write about manuscripts and I can't STAND to be this way. Forgive me just this one last time.

First of all, *The Moon Jumpers* is doing very well and certainly has had a marvelous critical reception. Sales are good but not up-to-date enough in our records to give you any definite figures. However, it is selling well in both trade and library editions.[1] We are all hoping that it will win the Caldecott. I haven't seen anything to touch it and I am not the least bit biased.

Next: back to a longish letter from you of last May which I certainly thought I had answered but I can't see that I have. About *A Little Liking Book* .... it certainly sounds publishable as a child would like all the things a child would like (this is really creative editorial comment, is it not?) but it just seems too EASY for you, Janice, and also for us. There've been some faintly imitative books (and what do I mean by "faintly") and several derivative ones. And I think that this "liking" book would end up being sort of you imitating you. I hate to see you doing that and I certainly wouldn't want to see us imitating other Harper books. (This is all coming out much more sternly and stuffily than I mean it, you must understand.) It is just that well, there is one other publisher who seems to do books—no, I mustn't say what I started to say. I do think someone will do *A Little Liking Book* but I think it ought not to be Harper.

I definitely do like the idea of a travel book if not too serious. Well, of course, it could be slightly practical. But if not too much of a how-to-do book (which I can't imagine you doing) it might be very very delightful.

The proposed sky book sounds quite good but we need more to say more.

The same goes for *A Little Book of Baby Brother Care*[2]. Tell

---

1. Most children's books are published in a trade edition for sale in bookstores, and also in a reinforced library binding.
2. This and most of the other book ideas referred to in this letter were abandoned.

me more. I am waiting for the time to be ripe to publish a really sound book about "Isn't the new baby nice" and "how much I love my new little baby sister" which has all about "how I would like to put the new baby in the garbage." Anyhow, tell me more.

NOW I ABSOLUTELY LIKE THE IDEA OF THE MEAN STORIES[1]. I think it wouldn't be easy to do (for you to write or us to publish) but I think it has really good possibilities and I would like to have more. The sample story is simply perfect. What other mean things could happen? Would you have some mean children, I hope? I think this is really a good idea and hope you will put more thought on it soon.

Same goes for the playing-house book. But do more on this too. I hope I have finally answered your questions about the proposed books and that some of this will be helpful. Again, I'm terribly sorry I haven't written sooner. It has been a hellish summer somehow. Yes, to answer the question on your last page, someone usually is at my elbow too. I wish it were Leslie[2] once in a while......

Best always,

TO MAURICE SENDAK   September 28, 1959

Dear Maurice:
    I may have to leave, to go to the dentist, God help me, before you come by with the Krauss-Sendak drawings[3].

---

1. *The Mean Mouse, and Other Mean Stories*, by Janice May Udry, illustrated by Ed Young, 1962.
2. The author's daughter.
3. The reference is to *Open House for Butterflies*, by Ruth Krauss, illustrated by Maurice Sendak, 1960. MS and Krauss worked closely on the page layouts for this book, as they had on those for *A Hole Is to Dig*.

So if I don't see you this is a hasty note to say we all (including Elsa [*sic*]) want to make the Minarik title *Little Bear's Friend*[1]. Hope this doesn't throw off any design you have worked out for the jacket. I really think it is more colorful and warmer than *Little Bear and Emily* and will help sell the book and that will be nice for everyone concerned. Yes?

Ruth is coming in with "stuff lightly pasted down" this afternoon. (This could mean me, come to think of it.......)

Ever thine,

TO JANETTE SEBRING LOWREY November 6, 1959

Dear Janette:

Indeed I would be delighted to see three I Can Read books from you. And everything you write me about the sequel to *Margaret* fascinated me. I'm so very glad you're back at the feeling that you can work. That is very very good news.

We've been stymied in finding exactly the right artist for the reissue of *Lavender Cat*[2] but the perfect one will come along soon. We haven't given up on it, though it must have seemed so to you.

I am so interested to read about you and London, then and now. One of these days you could write about a boy in that Shakespeare <u>time</u>—even though he wouldn't <u>be</u> Shakespeare, in view of the other book you found. (I've left this in my typewriter since last Friday and now it is Monday.)

---

1. *Little Bear's Friend*, by Else Holmelund Minarik, illustrated by Maurice Sendak, 1960.
2. *The Lavender Cat*, by Janette Sebring Lowrey, illustrated by Rafaello Busoni, 1944. The book was not reissued.

I'm afraid Stevenson hasn't a chance[1]. And I've been so puzzled by my own feelings about him. I never loved another public figure the way I loved him in 1952 and 1956. I know "love is not love that alters when it alteration finds"[2] but the 1956 campaign did distress me. And then I realized that deep down I was worrying as a woman about Stevenson. Would he finish the speech on time, before the precious valuable t.v. half hour which we had all paid our poor money to buy was used up? He seldom did. The first several minutes of valuable air time was always given to a bombastic and foolish local politician. And then Stevenson wouldn't ever get to his last few beautiful, well-reasoned paragraphs. And then I'd worry at the way he tugged at his tie. Oh it is the sort of thing that in a private love affair would have drawn us, Adlai and me, closer together. But I just can't feel such a sense of worry about the president. I'm joking, of course, but not absolutely 100% joking. I never worried for one split second about FDR. Of course I was younger then..... Anyhow, I couldn't vote for Johnson[3] or any of the other Democrats and I just hate this situation. I wish Chester Bowles[4] would come from behind as a dark horse. He is a good man, and has a fine record. And I think he could beat Nixon who still looks to me like a shady confidence man—which I've never seen....

Aren't you rather relieved, though, that it was dear sweet clean-cut, All American Ike who invited Kruschchev[5] here?

1. The reference is to a possible third Democratic presidential candidacy for Adlai E. Stevenson. In 1960 the Democrats nominated John F. Kennedy.

2. William Shakespeare, Sonnet 116. The original reads: ". . . Love is not love/Which alters when it alterations finds. . . ."

3. Lyndon Baines Johnson, senator from Texas, fought hard for the nomination that went to John F. Kennedy, and settled for the vice-presidential nomination.

4. Former governor of Connecticut and ambassador to India.

5. Soviet premier and party chairman Nikita Khrushchev's visit to the United States, in the fall of 1959, was covered daily in the press and on American television. The Soviet leader frightened many in the United States when he declared, in a remark aimed at the citizens of capitalist nations, "We will bury you," and when during a meeting at the United Nations he pounded his shoe on a desk.

(I need one more "h" in that name.) I must say I was absorbed by the t.v. programs showing K every night. I realized how much I've missed a STRONG personality. That, at least, he has!   It is such fun to be rattling on to you this way. Sorry my letters are always so jerky and interrupted. But I love to write to you.

[. . .]

Yes, I will write now about Rome. Well, we stayed in a hotel at the top of the Spanish Steps, which lead to the Piazza di Spagna. Rome is too vast, of course, for anyone to see much in less than a year! We were there only from Tuesday to Monday morning. But we did many beautiful and exciting things which I will never forget. The weather continued to be beautiful. Cloudless blue sky, and it was again like May in New York. We went several times to the Coliseum, and spent several hours there one day sitting on stones, writing letters, talking, reading. And Frances [Chrystie] mended a rip in her coat. Such outlandish activities for that bloody place! We saw the steps where Caesar was killed. And the Circus Maximus. And Caesar's Forum. And we went up to the Dome of St. Peters— the narrow winding stone staircase climb was the stuff of nightmares. We wandered through the Vatican and saw the Pope [John XXIII] and I was so amused when he was brought in on the chair. All the Romans cried out "Il Papa!" And they clapped, and held the youngest children up to see and wave. Very cosy. And of course we went to art galleries, and saw the Sistine Chapel, and did as much sight-seeing from the guide book as possible. But best of all we saved time and energy to ride a carriage through the Borghese Gardens, so lovely, and one day we drove out of town to the Villa D'Este, with its miraculous fountains, and we drove home on the Appian Way. We took carriage rides by day and also by night, and by now the moon was almost full. We went to the English Cemetery and I found Keats grave, and it docs say "whose name was writ in water"—and I had brought a purple iris, which I put on the grave, and I was unbearably moved. And at the foot of the Spanish Steps every afternoon we bought armfuls of mimosa (in February) and huge bunches of freesia, which I love madly, and our rooms were full of these flowers always. (A huge bunch of freesia cost about 80 cents!) We went to fascinating restaurants at night, and after dinner we would walk beside the Tiber, and look at the sky and at the water and I suddenly wouldn't be able to BELIEVE that I was actually walking by the TIBER! Then late in the evening we would hail a carriage and drive, speechless, back to our hotel through that vast, exciting city, underneath almost-full-moonlight.   Of course part of my pleasure in the whole experience—well a very LARGE part—was because my companion was delightful. I don't remember if I've told you much about her. Frances Chrystie, the book buyer at F.A.O. Schwarz here, but I must say we didn't talk about children's books. Frances is a little older than I am and she had been to Italy before but not for many many years. And she was a perfect travelling companion, curious, interested, moved as much as I was though she seems a good deal less emotional (almost EVERYONE is less emotional than I was from the day we sailed from New York!). Her only failing is that she always looks perfect, nose powdered, lipstick on, never has to look for the Ladies' Room, and yet never puts on a bit of make-up in public so how is it possible for her nose never to need powdering? She is always perfectly dressed, gloves wrinkling just exactly right at the wrists. While I, stumbling, staggering, hair wild, camera around my neck, bulging shopping bag in one hand, huge tourist-y handbag in the other. But oh I did have a heavenly time! We left Rome very early on a Tuesday and went, by bus, to Perugia, one of the "hill towns." On the way we stopped at Assisi; the other people on the bus had lunch together at a huge hotel next to the big church, but Frances and I went off alone and saw quite a bit of the fascinating little town. We bought hand-made iron lamps from a man who was making them, and we found a funny little trattoria where they didn't speak English and had a delicious lunch of cold meat, salad, cheese, red wine. Then back to meet the group at the church (and again the group was small because February isn't a big tourist month.) We went through the Church of St. Francis in the tow of a tired-looking monk who kept looking at his watch. I wasn't too fascinated as I was beginning to have my fill of churches (I am not mad about the Catholic Church and all the nails and blood, etc.) but Frances was absorbed because she loves animals and has always particularly loved St. Francis. Of course the church is fascinating and the famous murals truly beautiful. But suddenly the monk showed us something in a case which indicated something about St. Francis having the stigmata. I glanced at Frances, wondering if she knew about that as she is such a cool, well-bred, quiet person I couldn't imagine her loving a man who had done something so emotional and hysterical as develop the stigmata. "The what?" she whispered to me. "The STIGMATA," I hissed back, also in a whisper. Her face froze. "Oh," she said clearly and aloud, "I didn't know he'd had THAT!"—making it sound like a loathsome [*sic*] disease. No, doesn't seem funny written down.   Then on late that afternoon to Perugia, with which I fell deeply in love. Our rooms, connecting, hung over the most incredible view of valley and towns—and far away mountains, and we sat on Frances' balcony and watched the sky grow dark and the stars come out, and then the moon rose, and that was the night it was absolutely full. I almost died.   In Perugia we took wonderful walks and saw more churches and some very good paintings. And some very BAD paintings. And we had a lovely picnic in a tiny little square—and again we bought armfuls of freesia and mimosa and violets. We stayed there for a couple of days, sort of recovering from all the majestic sights we'd seen. I loved it. And it is so amusing to see on the main street of Perugia a sign in the restaurant window. "Diners' Club."

Then by bus to Florence. There we shared a huge barn of a room in a pensione, thinking we'd see "real Italians." So foolish of us. It was full of elderly Americans, of course. But I loved it. In Florence we again took carriage rides and walked by the Arno, and crossed and recrossed the lovely bridges. The paintings there were incredibly beautiful, and the famous doors, and the statues of David...... I couldn't recount the things we saw but once again the general impression left is one of flowers, beautiful paintings and statues, the Arno, stopping at a little outdoor cafe for espresso or a glass of vermouth, and again the moon which was still almost full the first few nights. The very first night there we walked by the Arno in the moonlight, then we found the House of Dante (it is really just where his house was, but that's enough!) and then we walked back to the pensione—quite late—and just as we were about to ring for the doorman Frances said "We should have champagne!" So we walked until we found a wine place, bought some ice, went back to our huge room and tried to cool the champagne somehow, and then drank it happily. You know, I can't drink anything stronger than wine, and very very little of that! But this was a lovely evening, and the barely-cool champagne tasted delicious. From Florence we went back to Rome, spent the day there, feeling as though it was a very very familiar and friendly city, and then in the evening we flew to Athens. By this time my emotions were super-charged and I could have flown to Athens without the plane. But that will have to wait. More soon.

Affectionately,

P.S. I am delighted to hear about *Guitar*[1], and I'll read the notices tomorrow with special interest. I love some of the off-Broadway things. Perhaps I will be able to see this one. I'm so glad for Mrs. Rosengren, and the young couple.

I mustn't write any more now.   More soon.

TO RUSSELL HOBAN   November 12, 1959

Dear Russ,

I telephoned Garth in Colorado a couple of days ago, and he assured me that we would get a sample drawing for *Frances* in a day or so. He has decided to make these people badgers.

I am awfully worried about his delivery date of December 1st. But we will try to have everything set up here so that as soon as the pictures do come in the book can be put right through RUSH.

I loved your letter of October 30th. It was very sweet. I am very glad you came in with your brown paper that day, too.

Affectionately,

TO RUSSELL HOBAN   December 1, 1959

Dear Russ:

It is better but not exactly right[2] so give it a little more of

1. *Guitar*, a play by Frank Duane, premiered on November 10, 1959, and closed the following day. Frank Duane was the pen name of Frank Rosengren, the son of JSL's friend Florence.
2. Work continued on the manuscript of *Bedtime for Frances*.

a push. The part about the moth's job being bumping and thumping is good. But then she goes on too long about sleeping is a silly job. She could think her job is to sleep and also she doesn't want to get a spanking. But I do think you should leave out all the part about it being mean of parents to make children go to sleep when they're not even tired. It gets baby-talkish which you have brilliantly avoided in the entire manuscript. It is all so straightforward and sensible (!) up to this sort of cute ending. I wish you'd try this last part again, much shorter, and you can still end it with she fell asleep and did not get out of bed again until Mother called her for breakfast. I sort of wish you could think of some good way to say that the moth's job is bumping and thumping, and her job is to sleep (as you have it here) and she also didn't want a spanking (after all she wouldn't suddenly get so reasonable on the very last page) and couldn't you put in something about she'd enjoyed (not that word) the whole evening very much but would never do it again. Now this is the most horrible way for me to put it, so baldly. I just mean to get that idea across in a straightforward un-goody-goody way. She'd really been having a ball, getting up and making up all those things, and scaring herself, and getting to talk to her parents. But she couldn't do it again the next night, and she wouldn't. I mean, this was a night in several hundred. Now I'm not asking you to end up with a big fat moral thing about "and we know you little children reading this book will never get up and bother your Mommy and Daddie [sic]" (ugh) "so many times," etc. etc.   But you could make it sort of funny, and conclusive, and *good*.

Look at your carbon copy and see what you think. It will be better if you just cut this latest last part. But see if you can't make it even better than that.

[. . .]

One more point about Frances. I am positive she wouldn't,

or shouldn't, be thinking about it is nice and cozy to be in your bed at night, it seems so self-conscious. I mean it might be that even though she wasn't sleepy she pulled the blanket up under her chin, and pulled the pillow down under her head, to give the impression that she was nice and cozy, but I hardly think she should be going on about being cozy in her own mind.   Sorry this is such a messy letter. I hope some of it makes sense. Don't get tense about this, Russ. The perfect ending is right there, somewhere, and we still have some days before the final setting has to be done.

Best,

TO RUSSELL HOBAN   December 21, 1959

Dear Russ:

Ye gods! Thank you for the Christmas present but you shouldn't, and I mean that, and please don't give me anything <u>again</u> but I do thank you very very sincerely for this present! You are too generous.

I am glad to tell you that *Bedtime for Frances* went beautifully at the Sales Conference. I read practically the whole story to the salesmen (something one very seldom does) and really they loved it. And then I held up the black key drawings and they loved them too. I wish to God Garth had been able to do the pictures even more quickly, but Dorothy [Hagen] promises extreme and unusual speed on getting plates, and in the meantime we're having four or five of the most engaging pictures printed up for the men to carry with them when they start out early next month. I really can't tell you how much everyone loved the book at the Sales Conference. Our salesmen are really wonderful, and they love children's books. The sales manager listened to the words of your story so intently and changed his expression as I read, from <u>firmness</u> when Mother and Father spoke, to <u>worry</u> when Frances told about the tiger, and the crack in the ceiling, to delighted <u>smiles</u> at the whack and thump of the moth, and then solid <u>relief</u> when Frances finally went to sleep. I think he could rent himself out to attend other juvenile sales conferences as any ardent children's book editor would be willing to pay for that sort of reaction from a sales manager. I was really convulsed and wanted to say "Shall Mummy come over to your house and read you another story tonight, honey???" What is so amusing is that all these salesmen are tough guys who stay up late and don't miss any high spots while they are in New York. So to have them really go for our rabbits, mice, dogs, and now badgers, pleases me mightily. Well, how I do go on. Anyhow, your book went over real big!

Your drawing in *Harpers Magazine* was good. How are your submarine drawings coming?

And thanks again for the Merry Christmas. Best of everything in 1960 to you and yours.

Yours,

TO GARTH WILLIAMS   January 28, 1960

Dear Garth:

I will write you a good letter soon.

But not today.

Today all I can say to you is why did you decide to put three sleeves on Frances' bathrobe on Page 15 and again on Page 18 of *Bedtime for Frances*........ ????? I didn't notice the three sleeves. Neither did Russ. Or the salesmen to whom I showed the pictures at the Sales Conference. Or Susan Carr. Or Dorothy Hagen in the Manufacturing Department. But the young lady, Joan Lexau[1], who goes over proofs and such in our department just noticed the third sleeve. And she wrote me a note which said "Please note third sleeve. OK?" Should I kill myself? Or what?

Garth, badgers only have two arms in their bathrobes.

We realize that you are a very famous artist and if for the same price you will draw three sleeves instead of just two sleeves I guess we should be grateful. But three sleeves is one too many. It looks like something by Charles Addams[2]. I sure as hell wouldn't go to bed and to sleep in a room with a bathrobe with three sleeves..... And I'm a very OLD badger.

Well, I just went up to show the pictures to Dorothy Hagen and she thinks she can fill in a little white spot with benday so the third sleeve (which, seriously, is the bottom of the robe we all think) won't look quite so obvious.

You are a dear fellow, Garth. Black and white integration[3], or badgers with three sleeves. What minority group will you exploit next?????

Too bad about Diana Barrymore[4], wasn't it. Strange to think of all the time and thought Margaret W[ise] B[rown] and Michael[5] gave that complication. And now they are all dead. Well, makes one decide not to worry too much about too many sleeves in too many bathrobes, doesn't it........

---

1. Later an author, under her own name and under the pen name of Joan L. Nodset.
2. *The New Yorker* cartoonist, known for his distinctively droll brand of the macabre.
3. GW's picture book *The Rabbits' Wedding*, 1958, had caused an uproar with its depiction of a marriage between a white rabbit and a black one.
4. The actress, whom Williams knew through his friendship with Margaret Wise Brown, had recently died at the age of thirty-eight.
5. Michael Strange, the pen and stage name of Blanche Oelrichs, was Diana Barrymore's mother. She and Margaret Wise Brown had a stormy, on-again-off-again affair throughout most of the 1940s.

Keep working on *Bad Morning*[1]. Also a *Tall Book*[2] by you will make me very very happy and you very very rich. Also finish your Moon Book. Work hard. Stand up straight. Don't smoke. Take deep breaths.

Love to all,

TO BETTINA EHRLICH   February 11, 1960

Dear Bettina:

This enclosure is more of a personal note. When I read yours about our doing a book together, words by me and pictures by you possibly, I grinned. And I thought I should tell you that I <u>have</u> written a book[3], a children's story, but it isn't anything you'd have been interested in doing pictures for, actually. It isn't a picture book, but a longish (30,000) story for 8 or 9 year old girls about a little girl who has to go to boarding school when she is 8. It is an unpretentious, simple, rather detailed account of her experiences and emotions and I hope little girls will like it at least moderately but it isn't anything that will impress any adult, I am quite sure. I have felt vaguely uncomfortable because Harper is going to publish it, but while I was abroad an author who has also been a friend of mine for many years and who was at one time my editorial assistant here, Charlotte Zolotow, took the manuscript and had it read by an outside person and then submitted it to Susan Carr, the associate editor in my department at Harper, and then they cabled me

1. Neither this manuscript nor that for the Moon Book, referred to below, was published.
2. Williams was already the illustrator of *The Tall Book of Make-Believe*, selected by Jane Werner, 1950. He did not illustrate a second book in this occasional series.
3. *The Secret Language*, by Ursula Nordstrom, illustrated by Mary Chalmers, 1960. This was to be UN's only published book.

in Athens that they BOTH loved it, and Susan wrote me that it should be done by Harper, and the head of the House also thought so. So that is how it happened. I know it looks odd to have this House do it. But I love Harper and the Sales Department and the Manufacturing Department and, well, I just love this House, I grew up here, and the only other publishing house I'd have even the slightest feeling for is Scribner. But I couldn't submit it to their children's book editor, Alice Dalgliesh, because Scribner publishes a book by her every single year. So how could I submit mine and explain that I'd feel odd if <u>Harper</u> published anything <u>by me</u>???? Well, this is a lengthy and tedious explanation but I do feel sort of uncomfortable about it and you're the only author I've told so far, except of course for Charlotte. I know darn well some of the authors will think it very unattractive for their editor to have written anything. But as a matter of fact trying to do it has made me a slightly better and enormously more sympathetic editor! Oh it is so hard to write a simple sentence. Anyhow, it didn't really take any of my time or energy away from my real true love, the books, the authors, the artists. For years I've been a compulsive writer, just scrawling down things I remembered thinking and feeling and doing, all the way back to when I did go to a dreary boarding school when I was seven, all the details of the disgusting food, the homesickness, the slippery way your feet felt in new shoes, the ugliness of some adult faces, etc. and all the way up to things as recent as that fascinating trip abroad last year.   So there was a lot of stuff just scrawled down which doesn't take any real effort. And I did the reorganizing and polishing in odd moments. You can see I feel sort of GUILTY for having tried to write a children's book, and so I am going on much too much about it, and I want to assure you that it is absolutely not anything "distinguished" or especially interesting—but just a little story I think girls will like, at least

I hope so. It isn't autobiographical, either, just in some of the details.   There, now I've written this and I shouldn't reread it or I will decide it is too idiotic to send to anyone whose opinion I respect as much as I do yours!

Love,

TO RUSSELL HOBAN March 11, 1960

Dear Russ:

We have folded sheets for *Bedtime for Frances* but the jacket was so damn pale (the color I mean) that we're having it reprinted and I didn't want the dear author to see it until it is corrected. I am just crazy about this book and, again, you were very sweet to dedicate it to me and I couldn't be more pleased. Yes, the bookstore man is right, we do think very highly of you here at Harper & Brothers, Established in 1817, and the children's book editor has been awake ever since.

We will want to go over *Herman*[1] with you soon, but not until ye olde editor comes back from a brief vacation. I'm leaving on Thursday, the 17th, and will be gone about two weeks, or maybe only ten days if I begin to get too homesick for this pretty East 33rd Street. We'll get together after I get back, anyhow.

Hope to see *Atomic Submarine* soon. No final figures on the heavy machinery book but of course you'll get a statement by April 1. Don't be discouraged if it didn't sell as well as you and I hoped. It is still a noble book and also it did bring you and Harper together.

---

1. *Herman the Loser*, by Russell Hoban, illustrated by Lillian Hoban, 1961.

Do you love the name Herman? It sounds so sort of comic to me. This isn't of huge importance.

Hope your madhouse painting goes well. I have to tell you that on my ceaseless search for new talent I went late one afternoon to a gallery exhibit of drawings. I was terribly tired that day and sort of depressed, but I pushed myself way up on Madison Avenue to try to find someone NEW who can <u>draw</u>, just black and white line, that's all I asked for! Across the room I saw the most magnificent black and white drawings; my fatigue vanished, a large smile covered my large face, I catapulted my large self across the room. Henri Matisse. I was so mad, because everyone knows he is tied up with Simon and Schuster....

Love to all and we'll meet soon.

TO MAURICE SENDAK   April 15, 1960

Dear Maurice:

We're having the corrections you wanted made in the galleys[1] and will get a new set as soon as possible. I had an idea about that one line "Everybody shook their heads yes"—which was the one that we left even though it isn't grammatical. I tried to call you yesterday and again this morning but no answer, to ask would it be OK with you if we changed it to "Everybody nodded." That <u>means</u> everybody shook their heads yes but it will protect you and your book and your ever-loving, cotton-picking publishers from being ostracised by the English teachers of this here great and gorgeous country with its locked-in goodness. Well, since I couldn't get you on the phone I made this slight change but if it sends you screaming out into

1. MS was completing work on the text of *The Sign on Rosie's Door*, 1960.

the street we <u>can</u> go back to the other. But I do hope you will like "Everybody nodded."

I saw your poster[1] at the Children's Book Council luncheon yesterday and it is terrific. Very very good!

Yours,

TO BEN SHECTER[2]   May 16, 1960

Dear Ben:

I'm terribly sorry to have to say the Magazine[3] feels your story is "picturesque and mildly humorous, but empty of action and feeling. Very fragile." On the other hand, Russell Lynes tells me, in a note, "I do think the drawings have a good deal of charm, and I would indeed be glad to see more of his work. Many thanks." I think you should bring in a LOT of your drawings one of these days and let Mr. Lynes see them. And let me see anything you haven't shown me, too.

About the story, I read it and I think it is delightfully written but so unemotional, which is a ridiculous word for me to use about a story which you did not intend to involve the reader emotionally. (But I'm not an editor of adult stories. I'm an adult reader, but editorial comments on adult stories wouldn't make any sense from me.) Anyhow, I'm afraid I agree the story seems fragile. And I too like the drawings. We'll hold the manuscript and the drawings here for you.

1. MS was honored with The Children's Book Council's commission to design the Children's Book Week poster for 1960. MS's design features a clown walking a tightrope and is rendered in a style reminiscent of the work of André François, an artist he greatly admired.
2. Costume and scenic designer; after 1962, author and illustrator of children's books.
3. *Harper's Magazine*, edited by Russell Lynes.

I'm sort of sorry I talked so freely the last time you telephoned. You ought to know what you want to do—and certainly you are probably doing very well in the advertising field. It was just that you really didn't sound very happy, and I suddenly felt terribly sorry that you were becoming a big shot advertising man and not keeping <u>much</u> time and energy for your own very delightful drawings, and all the things you seemed to be so deeply excited about when you first came into the office. Anyhow, I didn't mean to sound so anguished all of a sudden! (I'd just had another conversation with another young man who said he was only going to keep the 12,000 dollar job until he had a lot of money saved up and then he was going to—oh I don't remember how he put it. And it makes me sick because just because the twenties <u>seem</u> to last forever, <u>they don't</u>, of course. And the thirties go by so fast you can't believe it, after the relatively slow decade while you are in your twenties. And the <u>forties</u>—whooooooosh.   And you brought all that on yourself, of course, when you said over the phone that you'd been walking along a street during a noon hour and you saw all the other people belonged some place, or had just left some place but were going back to some place, and you realized that they had definite places, and security. That is exactly what you said; I have a merciless memory. And so you thought you ought to get this good job. Etc.   Anyhow, bring in some more drawings one of these days. Honestly I don't know if your work is going to be right for any children's book we have ready to be illustrated. But we do like your drawings and want to do a book with you sooner or later. And I know Mr. Lynes would like to see more of your work.   Now go back to making all that money and excuse my gratuitous remarks!

Best wishes,

　　　　　　　　October 17, 1960

Dear Maurice:

Elsa [*sic*] loved the dummy[1]. You could have had it back on Friday but I asked Elsa to change the last story and I'd hoped she would get the new parts in quickly so that if they necessitated any change in your pictures you would know it at once. When Elsa told me about how she was going to finish this book she told me a much better finish than this one is, as I realized when I went over the dummy with you. She told me originally that when the parents came for Little Bear they would arrive while he was supposed to be taking a nap on the couch. They would come in and assuming that he was asleep they and Grandmother and Grandfather would discuss Little Bear, had he been a good little bear? Yes. He is really a good little bear. Etc. Etc. But Little Bear was only pretending to be asleep, and he was listening to every word (or something to that effect)— and <u>then</u> when they pick him up he lets <u>them</u> know he heard all the things they said. I won't reread this mess but the difference between the above and what she actually wrote is that she originally intended to have the <u>child</u> who is reading the book <u>know that L. B. is really awake BEFORE the adult bears know it</u>. That makes it very much better, it still seems to me because all children like to know it when they are the center of attention or conversation (what do I mean "all <u>children</u>"—even some adults do!) and since it was her original conception I wanted <u>her</u>, Elsa, to go back to it. The way it is now it isn't as good as it could be. And maybe if she fixes this and makes it as good as it was intended to be you'll want to show L. B. on the couch with his eyes open—turned toward the back of the couch so no one else in the book can see.　? ????　　Well, whatever you say, but this

---

1. MS was at work on the art for *Little Bear's Visit*, by Else Holmelund Minarik, 1961.

change will be made in the text anyhow, somehow. More later. The other changes are all minor.

On Page 18 Elsa wondered if you wouldn't show in a small drawing or two just what Grandfather Bear and Little Bear did to make Grandfather tired? If you do this you could take an extra page—which could come from the goblin story.   On Page 27 she wondered if you wouldn't agree that as she says "a little home for it (the bird)" was made, a real bird cage isn't so good. She had thought more of a little home-made sort of thing, a little box with a bar to sit on, but not a cage, which does look very store-bought.   Page 46: note she says in story the goblin doesn't look back, so he shouldn't in the picture. OK? The only other thing she said she clearly labeled as a point Wally[1] raised, and that's the way I am labeling it, dear Maurice: Wally says would the robin look at Little Bear on Page 37? I think the robin would do just what you have him doing and I'm passing this on just because Elsa told Wally she'd tell me, and I told Elsa I'd tell you.

(I've indicated on 9 and 10, that first two lines from 10 are to go on bottom of Page 9. OK?)

I'll send the new material for last story as soon as I get it.

TO JANETTE SEBRING LOWREY

November 22, 1960

Dear Janette:

A thousand things to write you. I've loved your letters. But I won't write a "real" letter until I've caught up on a few things here. But must tell you my mother and I have signed a peace

---

1. Walter Minarik, the author's husband.

treaty, over the election. She said that "since the election was so close at least Senator Kennedy will not think he has a mandate, as did <u>R. F. D.</u>" This confusing of F. D. R.'s sacred initials is the ultimate in Republican contempt. I screamed.

Affectionately,

TO JENNIE D. LINDQUIST[1]   December 6, 1960

Dearest Jennie:

It was so good to talk to you on the phone that Sunday. I hope your hand is quite all right now. That was a tough break. Don't even think of trying to answer this letter. I know how busy you must be at the store[2], and any extra time or energy you have, work on your book[3].

As I told you over the phone, Chapter 6 is simply fine and I wish you wouldn't worry. Let me worry. It can be cut, as I said. But it is GOOD! I am glad if you find it helps to send it chapter by chapter. So keep them coming. I will want to reread it all at one fell swoop (tell me, did you EVER hear anything more original than <u>that</u>? Honestly, I don't know how I do it—get off these marvelously witty remarks, I mean. "one fell swoop." Lawks.)   Anyhow, I will reread the whole manuscript when I have the last chapter, and then we'll get down to commas, and "verys." Don't see many "justs." It is going to be a darling book and the children will love it and I am so pleased

---

1. Librarian, editor, author. From 1948 to 1958 JDL worked at *The Horn Book*, first as managing editor, then as editor of that magazine. UN published all three of her novels, starting with *The Golden Name Day*.
2. On retiring from *The Horn Book*, JDL moved to Albany, New York, where she worked part-time at the John Mistletoe Bookshop and continued to write.
3. *The Crystal Tree*, by Jennie D. Lindquist, illustrated by Mary Chalmers, 1966.

to send the enclosed from ———————— of Los Angeles. Sorry I didn't send it to you earlier. We wrote and sent biography and picture, but when you can you'll probably want to write her.

Charlotte Ryer's niece sounds wonderful and I would love to have her come in to see me, us, any time she can during her vacation. You didn't give her name. Is it Ryer too? I'd love to meet her. (I don't know that a young woman who looks like Jacqueline Kennedy would be happy with our ratty file cabinets and antique soap machines.) Some of the oddest people come in for jobs. (And some of us odd ones get them too, come to admit it!) But one soignee dame wanted some free lance work (she didn't say what sort, she couldn't type, copy-edit, had never read an American children's book as she had been brought up abroad) and she wanted to do it at home; no, she didn't need the money, actually, but you know one does get bored at home with nothing to do, and she couldn't really take a job outside because she wouldn't want to leave her poodles alone. I was so tired and I was trying hard to be polite, and all I could think of to do was to start crying. I didn't. But it was hard. (Mrs. Kennedy made me get on to all this, not this splendid young cousin of Charlotte Ryer's!)

Glad you love *The Sign on Rosie's Door* but I am amazed that you are not sure children will like it. I'm so positive on that one. After Christmas you must tell me more. I think it is so good and real and I have been terribly disappointed that it hasn't had more spectacular reviews. They've been good reviews; but I do think this book is one-of-a-kind, and such a good book for the author-artist of *Kenny's Window* and *Very Far Away* to have done. I think it is a terrific stride, much as I loved those more poetic, introspective books.

Thanks for saying some children like *The Secret Language*. I'm relieved, of course, that it's had on the whole good reviews, and God knows some much much too generous ones.[1] I'd dreaded someone saying it is odd that a good house could publish etc. etc. you know. Anyhow, thanks again for reading the mss.—and everything. Susan [Carr] was wonderful as editor and her suggestions certainly helped immensely. But it hasn't been an easy or pleasant experience (for anyone) because I work here. Well, enough.

I am hoping to get a new manuscript from Janette Lowrey, whose *Margaret* and *Lavender Cat* I am sure you remember. She is an enormously talented woman who should have a huge body of work done by now, but she is married and the mother of a son (now grown) and the runner of a household, and she hasn't done anything in years. I have been writing her letters as often as I can because of course she is terribly nervous about her manuscript. And I begged her to send me chapter by chapter, just to get it OUT of her desk. Now she writes that she'll send me half of it by the end of next week. I'm wandering, forgive me. I've been in a meeting all afternoon and stayed late-ish to get some things done at my desk, and I hear strange clankings and echoes, and I guess the old dead Harper brothers will be waiting on the stairs when I walk down. I think I'll ask them for a raise.

Now don't answer. <u>Write.</u> Send chapters. And DON'T WORRY.

Much much love

1. By hand on the original: Some bad ones too, of course!

TO KARLA KUSKIN[1]   March 31, 1961

Dear Karla:

Your copies of *The Bear Who Saw the Spring*[2] are on the way to you. I went through mine trying to pretend I'd never seen it before, and this is a fan letter from me to you to say that I love it and I hope everyone else loves it as much. Honestly, Karla, the words are flawless, I think, and beautiful and droll and funny and just so absolutely original I could almost burst into tears if I were an emotional woman but I am very steely-nerved and <u>un</u>-emotional so I just sob a little over how good you write[3]. And the pictures I like better than I thought I would and the colors are lovely, don't you think? (Rereading that I don't want you to think this is luke-warm about the pictures—many of the pages are simply perfect. But we've always loved the words better than the pictures and so this is to say that maybe we were wrong and gosh that isn't something we like to say more than four or five times in one day, you understand.)

Please remember that this is a magnificently original and beautifully written book. And <u>if</u> George Woods[4] on the New York *Times* doesn't realize it then you know something he doesn't, and <u>he's</u> wrong. And if your mother's friends etc. etc. oh just in general don't forget the lousy notices Keats got for *Endymion* as I always say ......

And <u>we're crazy about the book</u>.

---

1. Poet, author, and artist. KK's first picture book, *Roar and More*, 1956, grew out of a graduate-school project completed the previous year at the Yale University School of Art.
2. *The Bear Who Saw the Spring*, by Karla Kuskin, 1961.
3. UN wrote in the margin: "What I mean is you write good like a good writer should." The reference, complete with faulty grammar, was to a well-known advertising slogan of the time for cigarettes: "Winston tastes good like a cigarette should."
4. Children's book editor, *The New York Times Book Review*.

Now that Nicholas[1] is in college I hope he writes home regularly anyhow. When I get over my last antibiotic stuff, and I'd rather have lung congestion believe me, I will be in touch. What a gay thrilling winter I've had in New York. I don't know how you people take it year in and year out—in bed by 9 p.m. every night so I can wake up at 6 a.m. and seize the day by the throat, and grapple with it. At my desk by 8.30 at the latest; thrilling lunches alone at my desk with a tuna-fish sandwich, or a jolly salad at some unlit noisy restaurant with reviewer, bookseller, librarian. Home around 6 for that delicious glass of low-calorie Metracal [sic] on WHICH I AM GETTING FAT. One long lovely ball....... sorry to whine so. One day I really flipped and I stayed up to look at the Jack Paar show. I should take this out of my typewriter and re-do and just send the fan letter. But forgive me for rattling on.

Love to all three Kuskins.

TO MAURICE SENDAK   August 21, 1961

Dear Maurice:

I've been out of the office with a bad throat and assorted aches, which is why I haven't written you before. Also I spent the entire day Saturday writing you a big fat long-hand letter about Tolstoy, Life, Death, and other items which you can get at your friendly Green Stamps store. And then I left it at home. Will now send the gist of what I think I wrote, and it will be more legible than my handwriting anyhow.

1. The author's son was actually less than a year old. UN's joking reference played on the fact that she had yet to meet the boy and on her well-known conviction that authors were better off having no family life to distract them.

OK about the Zolotow book[1], of course. We're sorry but she is so glad you're illustrating it, and so are we, that nothing can cloud our pleasure.

I was glad to have your note about the Doris Orgel story[2]. She is making a few changes which she thinks will improve it, and it will really be a charming book and quite original. She came to see me. Isn't she an interesting person? I was much impressed with her, and I was irritated all over again with myself for not having been enthusiastic about *Dwarf Long Nose*[3].

Your cabin by the lake, and your own boat, sound fine. Please remember that the moon will be full on Friday, the 25th, and take a look at it. It should be beautiful over Lake Champlain. [. . .]

I loved your long letter and hope it clarified some things for you to write it. Sure, Tolstoy and Melville have a lot of furniture in their books and they also know a lot of facts ("where the mouth of a river is") but that isn't the only sort of genius, you know that. You are more of a poet in your writing, at least right now. Yes, Tolstoy is wonderful (his publisher asked me for a quote) but you can express as much emotion and "cohesion and purpose" in some of your drawings as there is in *War and Peace*. I mean that.   You write and draw from the inside out—which is why I said poet.

I was absorbed when I read you had "the sense of having

1. *Mr. Rabbit and the Lovely Present*, by Charlotte Zolotow, illustrated by Maurice Sendak, 1962.
2. *Sarah's Room*, by Doris Orgel, illustrated by Maurice Sendak, 1963. Orgel was one of a group of author and artist friends living in and around Westport, Connecticut, that also included Ruth Krauss, Crockett Johnson, Miriam Schlein, and Harvey Weiss. Sendak was a frequent guest at their homes.
3. *Dwarf Long-Nose*, by Wilhelm Hauff, translated by Doris Orgel, illustrated by Maurice Sendak, Random House, 1960. UN had been offered this book but declined it.

lived one's life so narrowly— with eyes and senses turned inward. An actual sense of the breadth of life does not exist in me. I am narrowly concerned with me .... All I will ever express will be the little I have gleaned of life for my own purposes." But isn't that what every fine artist-writer ever expressed? If your expression is now more an impressionist one that doesn't make it any less important, or profound. That whole passage in your letter was in-tensely interesting to me. Yes, you did live "with eyes and senses turned inward" but you had to. Socrates said "Know thyself." And now you do know yourself better than you did, and your work is getting richer and deeper, and it has such an exciting, emotional quality. I know you don't need and didn't ask for compliments from me. These remarks are not compliments—just facts.

The great Russians and Melville and Balzac etc. wrote in another time, in leisure, to be read in leisure. I know what you mean about those long detailed rich novels—my god the authors knew all about war, and agriculture, and politics. But that is one type of writing, for a more leisurely time than ours. You have your own note to sound, and you are sounding it with greater power and beauty all the time. Yes, *Moby Dick* is great, but honestly don't you see great gobs of it that could come out? Does that offend you, coming from a presumptuous editor? I remember lines of the most piercing beauty (after he made a friend there was something beautiful about "no more would my splintered hand and shattered heart be turned against the wolfish world.") But there are many passages which could have been cut. But I wander....

You wrote "my world is furniture-less. It is all feeling." Well feeling (emotion) combined with an artist's discipline is the rarest thing in the world. You love and admire the work of some other contemporary artists and writers today but really, think how few of them have any vigorous emotional vitality? What you have is RARE. You also wrote "Knowledge is the driving force that puts creative passion to work"—a true statement, and also very well put. But it would include self knowledge for some as well as knowledge of facts for others. (Is this English I'm writing? I need an editor.)

You reminded me that you are 33. I always think 29, but OK. Anyhow, aren't the thirties wonderful?   And 33 is still young for an artist with your potentialities. I mean, you may not do your deepest, fullest, richest work until you are in your forties. You are growing and getting better all the time.   I hope it was good for you to write me the thoughts that came to you. It was very good for me to read what you wrote, and to think about your letter. I'm sorry you have writers cramp as you put it but glad that you're putting down "pure Sendakian vaguery" (I think you invented that good word). The more you put down the better and I'll be glad to see anything you want to show me. You referred to your "atoms worth of talent." You may not be Tolstoy, but Tolstoy wasn't Sendak, either. You have a vast and beautiful genius.   You wrote "It would be wonderful to want to believe in God. The aimlessness of living is too insane." That is the creative artist—a penalty of the creative artist—wanting to make order out of chaos. The rest of us plain people just accept disorder (if we even recognize it) and get a bang out of our five beautiful senses, if we're lucky.   Well, not making any sense but will send this anyhow.

[. . .] Hope the rest of your vacation is wonderful. I'll see you when you get back. And thanks again for writing.

Ursula

You know one of these days you'll go back to *Old Potato*, or a version of that situation, and it will have "cohesion and purpose" and will have <u>so many universal emotions</u> within its relatively simple framework. Love, fear, acceptance, rejection, re-assurance, and growth. No more for now.

TO FRED GIPSON[1]   September 27, 1961

Dear Fred:

What a terrific story[2]! I am sure you can expand it, and I certainly hope you will want to. It is practically perfect as it stands for an adult short story especially in a magazine called *Western Magazine.* (The readers would understand all the western phrases which aren't quite clear to most of us.) But you certainly could place these characters, Curly and his father and brother, more clearly and give more background, and therefore almost automatically involve a youngish reader more closely with the fact that Curly did some growing up in the course of the story. The action is <u>so</u> exciting, and any young person would enjoy it just for the sake of the action. But if you start the story a little earlier—let us see more vividly what you simply imply now—I think it could be wonderful. I mean you imply now that Curly has a bad temper, goes off half-cocked often, but if you start earlier you can show it either in an earlier incident or just in conversation. And you can characterize his father more fully. At the end of the story you say that what Curly said was just the sort of sentimental reasoning (see Page 27) that his father would fall for—a tantalizing hint at an interesting character. If you start earlier you could give more about that side of the father.   What do you think, huh? I really think it is worth thinking about, Fred.

Now about the points you raised on September 20. The

1. Author, best known for his Newbery Honor–winning dog story *Old Yeller*, illustrated by Carl Burger, 1956. FG had originally submitted his manuscript to the Trade department.
2. Gipson's next book was not based on the story referred to here but a sequel to *Old Yeller* titled *Savage Sam*, illustrated by Carl Burger, 1962. FG did, however, write a book about Curly et al. It was published posthumously as *Curly and the Wild Boar*, illustrated by Ronald Himler, 1979.

title—*King of the Wild Country*—doesn't seem just right to us, either. 2. Yes, the style is a bit "free-swinging" but nothing too much to worry about. 3. Yes, about the swearing. 4. Hate to lose Gawdamighty's name but agree with you. 5. Sure, if Huck Finn's father can drink so much why can't Curly's father keep his jug? 6. No, the episodes don't seem too much alike. 7. As you see by above, I think more descriptive matter, and more about the relationships can and should be added. And there could be more about the dogs and Curly, which would make their being hurt even more vivid.   Let me hear from you, will you? I could check in the margins where the meaning is not just clear to a city-slicker-type (how does a wild hog pop his teeth? what does "pawing sand" mean?) Now you mustn't think we would even dream of ASKING you to PAD, even if you'd consider it which you would not. But you could certainly tell more about hogs, and more about how Curly tended that watermelon and how he didn't want any hogs or whatever to get in through the fence, and then the scene which is now the first scene would be even more terrific. In a rush to get this off. I'll send you a nice formal dictated letter sometime, but not today.

Best to you both.

TO CHARLOTTE ZOLOTOW (CZo)

October 30, 1961

Dear Charlotte—

[Maurice] Sendak's pictures are <u>so</u> lovely for your (untitled) book! Utterly different from anything he's ever done—with a timeless, classic quality. You'll be happy, I know. The little girl is lovely, and the rabbit is <u>funny</u>, a good combination, I think.

Mary [Griffith] and I did go to see *Look, We've Come*

Through[1] last night. I haven't seen a play twice in one day since I was fifteen and saw [Alla] Nazimova in *The Cherry Orchard* twice in one day. Mary <u>loved</u> the play and we both wept, and there were many curtain calls, thunderous applause, many "bravos"—and Collin Wilcox was trying hard not to cry, as she took the curtain calls. What a <u>shame</u>! We are both so grateful to you, Charlotte, for telling us not to miss it. <u>So</u> beautifully written, acted, directed. It depresses me <u>horribly</u> that such a touching, tender, moving, <u>and</u> funny play should close after only 4 days. I missed all the Thursday papers (an unheard of thing in the life of this 4-paper-a-day-reader) so I saw no reviews.

You are <u>so</u> sweet about *The Secret Language* and my writing another. I've never had this exact sort of pleasure before and I <u>love</u> it. I've had the most adorable letters from girls 8, or 9, or even 10. Several sent good new secret words. One sent a word for "grown-up, or parents," and I can't imagine why Iris[2] and I didn't have such a word. We usually just said "they," I suppose. Anyhow, I can <u>never</u> tell you how grateful I am to you, dear friend and author. I've never had anyone—well,—be so generous and <u>kind</u>, <u>certainly</u> no AUTHOR—as you've been.

Will try to enclose a page or two of "the next book"[3]—I really appreciate your asking, and will welcome your reaction. Will you send them back. (No copies.) We must meet <u>soon</u>.

I have to go to Chicago and Cleveland, November 10–19. Can't you come at 5.30 some day for a drink and a look at the (as-yet) unfurnished apartment?

Love,

---

1. A play by Hugh Wheeler.
2. Iris Hartman, UN's best friend at Northfield Seminary. Their shared experiences formed part of the background of UN's novel of boarding-school life.
3. UN wrote most of a sequel to *The Secret Language*, which she titled *The Secret Choice*. However, she could not decide on a satisfactory ending, and over the objections of friends destroyed the manuscript.

TO KAY THOMPSON[1]   January 24, 1963

Dear Kay T:

This is incredible! I opened the envelope containing your manuscript[2] myself and read it page by page, and passed it page by page to my assistant who was standing by my desk, and she numbered the pages as I handed them to her. So this work must have been dropped in Italy and mailed to us in mixed-up shape. Maybe this will be a lesson to me...the next time something seems a bit confusing, I will think that it really is confusing, and not worry and think I must be terribly insensitive. I was so polite: "The manuscript seems to end at Page 69, but there are awfully good things from 69 to 117." etc. etc.

I am terribly eager to see the new version in the right order. Do please get it off to me as soon as you possibly can. I wish you could draw yourself. Do you visualize a personified fig of some sort? I mean you say the fig registers changes of mood, and I'm just trying to visualize this. The fox is no problem. But how do you see the fig? We're eager to see the new version, "a practically perfect edition pasted into a book." Really, this mix-up could be funny, but it isn't because too much time is passing. I certainly wish now I'd said frankly that it seemed sort of hard to follow your thought. But even though the pages were mixed up, we did love lots of it and I'm sure we'll love it a good deal more when we see the straightened-out version. But do send it as soon as possible.

All right, I won't refer to our old copy at all. But I'll keep it here just in case we need it. Please be sure to number everything before you send it!

In haste, sincerely

1. Author, actress, singer, and composer-arranger, best known as the author of *Eloise: A Book for Precocious Grown Ups*, illustrated by Hilary Knight, Simon & Schuster, 1955.
2. KT was at work on a book, never published, titled *The Fox and the Fig*.

TO MAURICE SENDAK   January 31, 1963

Dear Maurice:

Your letter about future Nutshells[1] needs a more carefully written reply than I will be able to make today, but as soon as I can I will do my best to send you an answer that will make sense to you. I want to be able to devote some uninterrupted time to this because I can see it is a serious problem. So all I'll do today is send along some immediate thoughts, with a promise of a "real" letter soon. Yes, I did tell you early in December, or late in November, that nothing would be done precipitately about the next Nutshell, and that we'd talk it over. (I was appalled by your reaction because weeks before that I'd asked Beni[2] if he wouldn't like to do a Nutshell sometime. He said no by the way, but I had asked him.) And then we did talk it over, you and I. And then you told me over the 'phone that finally you really did understand our feeling about future Nutshells, and that you saw we were being perfectly reasonable about it all, that you still hated the thought of anyone else doing a Nutshell Library but that you did have to admit that you understood—particularly in view of the fact that you not only did not want to do another Nutshell in the foreseeable future but that also you would never want to do a Christmas Nutshell[3], or a Hanukah Nutshell at any future date. So of course we are very sorry to hear now that you are distressed

---

1. MS, author and illustrator of *Nutshell Library*, 1962, was disturbed that UN was now contemplating sequels to the miniature four-book set, the concept for which they had collaborated closely on, to be written and illustrated by others. *Nutshell Library* consists of four miniature volumes: *Alligators All Around*, *Chicken Soup with Rice*, *One Was Johnny*, and *Pierre*.
2. Beni Montresor, Italian-born author, illustrator, and designer for the opera.
3. UN commissioned Hilary Knight to create a *Christmas Nutshell Library* following the success of the Sendak *Nutshell Library*. See pages 158–59, letter to Hilary Knight, February 19, 1963.

about this all over again, and it is a particularly ironic note to learn that the House's gift of that beautiful little leather set[1] "triggered" your letter. Well, I am very glad that you wrote me frankly, because I always want to know when something is disturbing you. And I want to do my best to make some sense to you.

Your remark about "the publishing bit" makes me realize that apparently I expressed myself unwisely. Perhaps I stressed the business side of publishing more than I should have. I thought it might make more sense to you. That is not the only side of publishing that concerns me, however. You wrote: "Wouldn't people be bored too easily with too many Nutshells—and wouldn't Harpers come in for its share of cynical criticism?" What people, Maurice? Surely <u>children</u> won't be bored with a Christmas Nutshell in the toe of their stockings. Surely children won't be offering any "cynical criticism." So what people? (Remember this isn't my formal business reply to you, this is putting down some words very informally.) We wanted to do the first Nutshell because we thought <u>children</u> would love some perfect little books. We wanted to do them, for years and years, because we thought children could take them to school, or Sunday School, and read them behind their stupid Sunday School books[2]. *The Tall Book of Mother Goose* (the first in that format) was done because we first of all thought <u>children</u> would like a book in that shape, that they could look at it easily, that they could carry it around under their arms, that it would be convenient for them. We did the *Little Fur Family*

---

1. The occasion for this gift was *Nutshell Library*'s having reached the publishing milestone of 100,000 copies in print.
2. MS collected eighteenth- and early-nineteenth-century children's chapbooks, the characteristically small format of which appealed to him as being well suited to young children's hands. The didactic content of the books was another matter. MS saw *Nutshell Library* as a chance to stand the moralistic children's literature of the past on its head.

because we thought <u>children</u> would love a fur-bound book. We did the I CAN READ books because <u>children</u> wanted good stories they could read to themselves. We wanted to do the *Nutshell* because children would love perfect tiny books. All of those above-mentioned projects were enormous commercial successes, as it happened, and that was very gratifying. But not one of them were [*sic*] done because we thought it would be a smart piece of merchandise or that adults would go for it and give copies to each other, etc. etc. They were all done for children. And adults at first HATED the Tall Books, and the *Fur Family*[1]. So how can we start worrying now about "won't people be bored...and wouldn't Harpers come in for...cynical criticism." If by "people" you mean Mrs. Russ[2], and Miss Chrystie, and Miss Cimino[3], and their ilk, some of your adult friends and non-friends (if you'll excuse the expression, after all, such types do exist), what difference can it make what they think? When should we start allowing what those people think to guide our publishing, or the tempo of our publishing? We certainly have to have a decent respect for the opinions of mankind, as the document said[4], but we certainly can't start now to let

1. In an otherwise favorable review of *The Tall Book of Mother Goose*, Ellen Lewis Buell wrote in *The New York Times Book Review* for November 15, 1942, "The 12 by 5 inch dimensions of the volume give it an oddly appealing, intimate charm . . . although where to put it on the library shelf is going to be a problem." *Little Fur Family* received mixed reviews. May Lamberton Becker, writing in the *New York Herald-Tribune Weekly Book Review* for October 28, 1946, noted that the book "sounds the way it feels, like something soft as one goes to sleep." But Becker also commented, "This is, of course, a stunt, causing one who knows the edition to be large to question in advance whether the story will be worth so many rabbits."
2. Lavinia Russ, influential critic and author; children's book editor at *Publishers Weekly* from 1965 to 1972.
3. Maria Cimino, chief librarian of the Central Children's Room, the New York Public Library, from 1960 to 1967.
4. The "document" was the Declaration of Independence, which states that "a decent respect to the opinions of mankind requires that they [the American colonists] should declare the causes which impel them to the separation."

them tell us what to do and what not to do, or give us guidance as to what we publish and when.   (You know this is a subject I always go insane over—always have and always will. We had this sort of exchange all the way back to Robert Benton[1] and how brilliant he was to put the title of his book at the bottom of his jacket, so chic.)

I don't expect creative artists who do books for children to think about children all the time. They never do—the really great ones—because they do what they do for themselves. (I am certainly at my most banal this morning, I'm sorry.) But I have to worry about the children. I mean, we, here in the department. And the fact that we have published children's books for children (not other adults) and that we have NEVER NEVER NEVER been inhibited by "will this bore adults, will this expose us to cynical criticism" makes it impossible for me not to go on like this to you.

Well, enough for now. I'll send you a better letter soon. I want you to understand, and if I can write the right letter you can keep it and reread it the next time something (or someone?) triggers sad thoughts.

You're not in any "difficult genius" category. In the first place that is a redundancy ("har har har de har har"). You're a genius, but we don't think you're unusually difficult. We'd like you to do all the Nutshells we ever do. You can't[2]. We'd like Else Minarik to write all our I Can Read books. She can't. So we do some I Can Reads by other authors and artists. That doesn't make a new *Little Bear* book less eagerly awaited and

---

1. Benton, who was art director at *Esquire*, co-authored and co-illustrated a number of books for adults and children around this time, but it is not clear which book is the one referred to here. Benton later became well known as the director of such films as *Kramer vs. Kramer*, *Places in the Heart*, and *Nobody's Fool*.
2. Three Nutshell sets were published in all: the original Sendak *Nutshell Library*, Hilary Knight's *Christmas Nutshell Library*, 1963, and Robert Kraus' *The Bunny's Nutshell Library*, 1965.

less ecstatically received by anyone. None of the other I Can Reads can compete with yours and Else's, but all are perfectly sound, good books which children love. And none of them have cheapened *Little Bear*.   We have never published junk just to cash in on quick sales, and we certainly don't propose to do so now.   A business-like letter soon. This is just an interim one.

You said you'd have to think over the new Le Gallienne collection of H. C. Andersen stories[1], that it did present a problem to you. I'm not trying to rush you but I'd like to give her some word in a week, if possible.

More soon. In the meantime, best wishes always,

Oh, one more thing. I told Jan's agent that we really couldn't love *Cabbage Moon*[2] but that if you decided you definitely would illustrate it we would be grateful for the chance to re-consider it. (I hope you won't want to do it!)

Yours sincerely,

TO MAURICE SENDAK   February 19, 1963

Dear Maurice:

I was glad to hear the other day, when you were in the office, that you're hoping to write and illustrate your own beautiful picture book next—instead of doing a lot of illustrating for

1. MS, who had illustrated *Seven Tales by H. C. Andersen*, subsequently decided that Andersen's literary fairy tales had no great appeal for him. Accordingly, he chose not to illustrate Le Gallienne's contemplated sequel. UN eventually abandoned plans for a second collection in favor of publishing her translations as picture books of one story each. Two such books followed: *The Nightingale*, illustrated by Nancy Ekholm Burkert, 1965, and *The Little Mermaid*, illustrated by Ed Frascino, 1971.
2. MS chose not to illustrate this book by Jan Wahl, which Holt, Rinehart and Winston published in 1965 with illustrations by Adrienne Adams.

other people. That will be wonderful. You can do something beautiful and I hope you will soon. You were speaking about something, or someone, or some little animal, getting out of some enclosure—and I think that might grow and develop into a basic and beautiful story. From the way you spoke I really think it will. When ever there is anything at all to show me I'll be very happy.

I hope Bob Keeshan's[1] letter arrived. He is so thrilled with the book—as he should be, thanks to your pictures.

As ever,

TO HILARY KNIGHT[2]   February 19, 1963

Dear Hilary:

We have prices on the box for *Christmas Nutshell*[3] now, and the gilt will be possible—rather than just gold ink. I enclose a sample of the gilt (flowered thing) and one of the gold ink. I'm sure you'll agree that the gilt is much much more attractive.

The Production Department hopes to have proofs of the thistles picture early next week. But can you get started now on the box? I return your drawing herewith. We think it is absolutely enchanting and have only one request—that you make the nut on top different from the one Maurice used on his

---

1. Harper had just published *She Loves Me, She Loves Me Not*, by Bob Keeshan, illustrated by Maurice Sendak, 1963. Keeshan was well known to television audiences as Captain Kangaroo.
2. Author, illustrator, and designer best known as the illustrator of Kay Thompson's books about Eloise.
3. Boxed set of four miniature books: *Angels and Berries and Candy Canes*; *A Christmas Stocking Story*; and *A Firefly in a Fir Tree*, all written and illustrated by Hilary Knight; and *The Night Before Christmas*, by Clement Clark Moore, illustrated by Hilary Knight.

Nutshell Library. I think we mentioned this to you and you suggested a walnut.

We'll return the little dummies to you in a day or two. You can't start on those drawings, though, until the Production Department finds out about the size of the finished drawings. But in the meantime I hope you'll be thinking about the plot of *A Tale of Ten Christmas Stockings.*[1] As you know, we think it has great possibilities but that as it now stands it is a bit too involved for the little book. It seems terribly contrived that each of these ten creatures would get out his Christmas stocking, find it rumpled (or whatever) and send it to the same laundry to be washed. ???? I mean could there be a simpler way to mix them up? And do you think cutting the number of animals down would make the whole thing more wieldy? Well, think it over anyhow. On second thought I will now return all 4 dummies to you with this letter. We think *A Firefly in a Fir Tree* is going to be perfect, and you'll surely think of the few things you left blank in the near future. (Excuse this messy letter.) The ABC looks great.

With the drawing of the box, and the 4 dummies, we are also returning the 3 *Eloise* books[2] you let me borrow from you. Sorry I kept them so long. I wish the lady would send me her revision of *Fox and Fig*, so we could get going. It seems to me I first heard about this book a hundred years ago ......

Again, we're delighted with what you're doing with *Christmas Nutshell.* The Sales Department will be very happy too.

Yours,

1. Later simplified and renamed *A Christmas Stocking Story*.
2. Besides this 1955 *Eloise*, HK and Kay Thompson had thus far published three other books about the girl who lived at the Plaza: *Eloise in Paris*, Simon & Schuster, 1957; *Eloise at Christmastime*, Random House, 1958; and *Eloise in Moscow*, Simon & Schuster, 1959.

TO EDNA EICKE[1] March 4, 1963

Dear Edna:

That book with a hole in it[2] was published in 1906 [*sic*] and has been on the Harper list ever since. That's what I mean when I say books last.

About "you and deadlines." Dear Edna, you told me in the summer of 1961 that you worked slowly, that you could not do the Hoff book[3] quickly. I assured you that we did not want to—would not dream of trying to—hurry you. I asked you if you thought you could do it by February or March of 1963, and you seemed so relieved that we could wait as long as that. You said that would be perfectly all right. If you hadn't I'd have (1) discussed it with Syd and (2) probably given you a later date. I'm reminding you of this background because I'm terribly afraid you now have the idea that we've been pushing you. I did not make one 'phone call, I did not write one letter, to get your reassurance that work was coming along well. At Christmas you wrote on your sweet card that you were glad I hadn't been asking you about it, and that you'd have something to show us in plenty of time. So to receive your letter of February 15th was certainly a blow. But I do want to remind you that you told us originally you would feel relaxed and happy about the book if you didn't have to finish it until February 15th, 1963.

I am enclosing typescripts of *Bears*, by Ruth Krauss, *The Happy Day*, by Ruth Krauss, *A Tree Is Nice*, by Janice Udry. I

---

1. *New Yorker* cover artist known for genre scenes.
2. The reference is to *The Hole Book*, by Peter Newell, 1908. In this novelty picture book a small hole punched in each illustrated page figures playfully in the narrative.
3. UN had sent EE a short, lyrical picture-book manuscript by Syd Hoff titled *When Will It Snow?* The text was in a completely different vein from earlier Hoff books such as *Danny and the Dinosaur*, for which Hoff's own cartoon style of illustration had been appropriate. UN teased Hoff, referring to the author of *When Will It Snow?* by addressing him as "Margaret Wise Hoff."

hope you will look at these few words. All three of them came to me in this form. Then I found the right artists. Then we published the books. Then they sold. Look at the text for *A Tree Is Nice*. It isn't as brief as Syd's, but it isn't much longer. And it won the Caldecott Medal and has sold about 90,000 copies and it is still selling and will go on selling for many many years. Look at *Bears*. It doesn't look like much in typescript. But it made one of the most original books we ever published when we had it illustrated. I am writing you this, Edna, because I think someone has convinced you that we are trying to exploit you by giving you such a short little number of words by Syd Hoff. We are not. I want you to see the words in these other picture books so that you can see this is not the first time we have accepted the briefest sort of "manuscript" secure in the knowledge that with the right pictures we could publish a beautiful, or funny, or original book.   I remember you told me when you'd signed the contract that Mr. Geraghty[1] thought you were being asked to "make" a book out of absolutely nothing. Look at these brief manuscripts and tell me you agree with him! The words, no matter how few of them there may be, are important.   When this book is finished Syd's words will owe a great deal to your pictures. But if he hadn't written the words I'd never have hoped anyone would do the pictures. I think Mr. Geraghty has jumped to a lot of conclusions without knowing anything about the publication of picture books. Edna, I bring his name up because you told me over the 'phone he'd been calling you and telling you to "forget Syd's book."

You know I'm not the sort of editor who pesters authors and artists. I love creative people, and I never want to do anything to make life harder than it is for creative people. I don't try to put pressure on. If I had been that sort of editor I'd have been able to break this news to Syd months ago. On the contrary, I

---

1. James Geraghty, art director, *The New Yorker*.

wrote him that you'd told me (on your Christmas card) that work was coming along well and that you'd be finished in plenty of time you thought.   You said for me not to write to Syd until you and I had luncheon together. I did write him saying you wouldn't be on time, and that I was sort of depressed, but that the cover was utterly magnificent, and that I thought you were worth waiting for.   I'm still hoping we can get the book out for this year, and we will wait as long as possible[1]. Otherwise, as *When Will It Snow* is hardly a spring sort of book, we'll have to wait to publish it a year from this September, in September, 1964. But I don't want to have to tell Syd that unless I absolutely have to. Especially in view of what I told him you'd written me in December!

I've <u>had</u> to write you this letter in fairness to Syd and to my responsibilities here. I hope you will understand that.

Yours,

TO MAURICE SENDAK   April 15, 1963

Dear Maurice:

I phoned you several times over the weekend but you had the good sense, I guess, to be out in this beautiful weather. I'm hoping that your 1963 picture book[2] is slowly forming in your

---

1. EE withdrew from the project. UN had extraordinary difficulty finding an artist she considered right for Hoff's manuscript. *When Will It Snow?* was finally published in 1971 with illustrations by Mary Chalmers.
2. *Where the Wild Things Are*, by Maurice Sendak, 1963. As MS's biographer Selma G. Lanes has shown, the artist had sketched out a preliminary version of the fantasy in late 1955, in a dummy titled *Where the Wild Horses Are*. According to Lanes, MS considered the books he had written and illustrated prior to 1963 to be "illustrated books," rather than "picture books," in which text and art are inseparably intertwined. He now felt ready to produce his first true picture book.

mind so that it can get formed soon on paper. Let me hear from you when the spirit moves you, please!

What I wanted to talk over with you this weekend was: I hope one of these days you'll do something which could be as short and poetic as *Moon Jumpers*, but with more substance (which anything by you would automatically have). The dreamy rural aspects of most picture books are lovely but you could do something about a little boy on a Brooklyn street, the stoops, the entry ways, the backyards, street fires, street games, little stores, slightly older children one of whom might call the little boy Old Potato—and visually it could be as beautiful as *Moon Jumpers*—the sun against some of our horrible old buildings is as lovely as lots of things in these wholesome rural backgrounds. And there could be old people, and middle aged people, as well as kids. And I wish you'd think it over.   That *Old Potato* background was always wonderful. But when you wrote about it you wrote it too long and too much and it was too weighted (for you) at that time. But a sort of urban background picture book could use some of that background, without any psychiatric overtones (not that we don't just adore psychiatric overtones, please understand, Mr. Senlak[1]). Anyhow, there were lovely and exciting and interesting things going on, on that Brooklyn street, and they might make an extremely exciting and beautiful and original picture book. Think about it, will you?   (It's really quite a good, casual thing to have an older friend call a younger one Old Potato.)

I'll try to call you later, when you've wakened up, but in case I don't find you in, I'll send this letter.

Best wishes,

---

1. Referring to MS as "Mr. Senlak" became a running joke between the artist and editor after a clerk at a hotel where they were staying during a library convention jumbled both their names. In the confusion "Ursula Nordstrom" had become "Ersella Norcross."

Dear Kay:

Sorry that connection was so awful. What I should have said clearly is that I hope my letter didn't give you the impression that Tomi[1] wanted to do pictures that had nothing whatever to do with the text. He was just terribly excited by the possibility of doing pictures which would connect the fox and fig in some sort of a relationship. I know he would welcome your suggestions if you are not <u>absolutely</u> against his illustrating the book.

I just talked to Andy Warhol[2]—he had promised to bring something in this morning, or to let me come to his place today to see what he has done. However, he now says he won't have anything until tomorrow. I told him that this was URGENT. I had already told him that when I sent him the galleys. He was recently written up in *Time* Mag., and he has an answering service and is out a great deal. But he promised to let me have at least a double-spread tomorrow a.m. I will airmail it to you at once.

I enclose part of a letter I wrote you last week, before Tomi came in. He came in very late Friday and I wish now I'd written you more slowly than I did late Friday afternoon. If you just hate Tomi's sketch A you will also feel awful about us. I think Ferd[3] and I over-reacted because it was so wonderful to see Tomi all lit up and glowing with excitement. Also he would do

1. Tomi Ungerer, French-born illustrator and commercial artist, who came to live in the United States in 1956. The following year, Harper published his first picture book, *The Mellops Go Flying*.
2. Pop artist. Warhol's first *Campbell's Soup Cans* paintings had been shown in Los Angeles the previous year. Warhol submitted sample illustrations that UN found to be overly decorative; she decided against offering Warhol the assignment.
3. Ferdinand N. Monjo, editor of special projects in UN's department.

it in a week i̲f̲ you give the green light.   I don't know why he made the fig green, when you do say it is blue. His fig isn't very fig-like anyhow. But again and again, sketch A was just a quick one. The anachronism of the box of matches on the other sketch was noticed—but then he didn't intend actually to include such a picture and asked me not to send it to you. But I did anyhow, and now I wish I hadn't. Oh gosh.

I'm terribly nervous.

Love,

TO MAURICE SENDAK   July 3, 1963

Dear Maurice:

I've not been able to get you on the 'phone today, so here's a hasty note before I run for my train, and vacation.

Dorothy [Hagen] says that having just some of the pictures for *Where the Wild Things Are* won't be any help, because the printer will want to photograph all at the same time, to be sure of the same degree of—oh etc., etc., you know. Anyhow, it won't hurry up anything for you to give her ten or 15 before they are all finished. So relax a little, keep them all by you, and when you are all through bring them all in. August 15 would be dandy, Sept. 1 would be less dandy, but do what you can and if necessary I will personally stitch the folded sheets into the cloth binding of several thousand copies (I am a very good seamstress), and take them by taxi to the various NYC stores.   If you finish in time, beautiful. If you don't the book will still be magnificent in 1964. But I know you'd like it on this fall's list and so would we, of course. The paper is being ordered and Susan [Carr] will be writing her usual brilliant flap copy as soon as she comes back from her vacation, and everything will be ready. And at the very last minute we can go over the words one last time, but don't worry about them until the pictures are all done.

I had wanted to talk to you to tell you a bit about luncheon with George Woods. When we meet again. (Leave an address with Barbara[1], will you, where we can reach you if necessary?) If you come in to the office talk to Ferd who was at lunch with Mr. Woods, Miss Buell[2], and me too.

In haste, take care, be happy.

TO MAURICE SENDAK   September 23, 1963

Dear Maurice:

We just rushed by messenger a pasted up *Where the Wild* to George Woods, so it can at least be considered for TEN BEST ILLUSTRATED[3]. Of course the Holt Sendak[4] will be included, and it seems dreadful for your *Where the Wild Things Are* not to be too.

Spencer Shaw[5] is on the Newbery-Caldecott Committee. Just found out. Did he dote on you? But natch!

Maurice, before I sent the paste-up I went through it,

1. Barbara Alexandra Dicks, UN's office manager, more often referred to by the acronym of her initials, BAD.
2. Ellen Lewis Buell, children's book editor of *The New York Times Book Review* from 1935, when the *Times* first established a regular weekly page devoted to children's literature. Buell, who had shared her duties with Anne Thaxter Eaton until the latter's departure in 1946, retired from the *Times* in July 1963 and was succeeded by George Woods.
3. The reference is to *The New York Times Book Review*'s annual awards for the year's ten best illustrated children's books.
4. *The Griffin and the Minor Canon*, by Frank Stockton, illustrated by Maurice Sendak, Holt, Rinehart & Winston, 1963. Harper reissued this book in 1986.
5. Spencer G. Shaw, children's services consultant, the Nassau County, New York, library system.

rereading the words, and looking at the pictures again. It is MOST MAGNIFICENT, and we're so proud to have it on our list. When you were much younger, and had done only a couple of books, I remember I used to write you letters when the books were finished, and thank you for "another beautiful" job—or some such dopiness. Now you're rich and famous and need no words of wonder from me. But I must send them, anyhow, when I look through *Where the Wild Things Are*. I think it is utterly magnificent, and the words are beautiful and meaningful, and it does just what you wanted it to do. And you did just what you wanted to do.

I've felt sort of down in the dumps about picture books lately, (and about those who write and illustrate and buy and review them, too, to be frank!). But this bright beautiful Monday your beautiful book is exhilirating [*sic*], and it reminds me that I love creative people and love to publish books for creative children.

As for creative plate makers, more later.

Yours sincerely,

TO MARY V. GAVER[1]   November 21, 1963

Dear Mary,

I can't tell you how much I appreciate your note about Maurice's *Where the Wild Things Are* and the comments from the children. I'm not the last [*sic*] bit surprised that no child was frightened by the wild things (except for that 4 year old girl who is an "extremely nervous child who has a great deal of difficulty getting to sleep at night"). I think this book can frighten only a neurotic child or neurotic adult.

---

1. Professor, Graduate School of Library Services, Rutgers University.

I'm delighted to hear that two of the mothers were so enthusiastic about the book. It is always the adults we have to contend with—most children under the age of ten will react creatively to the best work of a truly creative person. But too often adults (including children's book editors in general and this one in particular) sift their reactions to a creative picture book through their own adult experiences. No, I'm not saying this right. I mean that most children under ten will react creatively to the very best picture books by truly creative artists. And as an editor who stands between the creative artist and the creative child I am constantly terrified that I will react as a dull adult, which is all that I am, of course. But at least I must try to remember it every minute! Excuse me going on like this—but it is all so interesting.

I think Maurice's book is utterly magnificent and that it will live forever. We were so glad it was Number 1 in the *New York Times* list of 10 Best Illustrated Books of 1963. But in addition to the pictures, the story—well, enough. I meant to send you just a brief note to thank you for yours, and for the comments. But I never can seem to be brief when I get on the subject of picture books, especially this one by Sendak.

Thanks a lot for writing.

Yours sincerely,

TO ——————   December 6, 1963

Dear ——————:

Thank you for your wonderful letter of December 2nd.[1] We appreciated your kind words and understand what prompted

1. The writer praised Mary Stolz's 1963 book *Who Wants Music on Monday?*

you to write us. We know Mrs. Stolz will enjoy your letter so we are going to send a copy to her.

We have over the years published books in which Negro characters appear. *Call Me Charley* (1945) and *Charley Starts from Scratch*[1] (1958) are by and about a Negro. The author is Jesse Jackson. He also wrote *Anchor Man*[2], which we published in 1947. *A Summer Adventure*[3] is also by and about a Negro. Richard Lewis both wrote and illustrated it. In two of our I Can Read Books, *Tony's Birds*[4] by Millicent E. Selsam, pictures by Kurt Werth, and *The Case of the Hungry Stranger*[5], story and pictures by Crosby Bonsall[6], the artists have included Negro characters. Oh, yes—our Spring catalogue features several Negro children on the cover. We will send you a copy when our supply comes in, if you would like that.

The preceding paragraph is simply to assure you that we feel all segments of our country's life should be presented naturally, particularly in books for young people.

Thank you again for writing us.

Yours sincerely,
Director

---

1. *Charley Starts from Scratch*, by Jesse Jackson, 1958.
2. *Anchor Man*, by Jesse Jackson, illustrated by Doris Spiegel, 1947.
3. *A Summer Adventure*, by Richard Lewis, 1962.
4. *Tony's Birds*, by Millicent E. Selsam, illustrated by Kurt Werth, 1961.
5. *The Case of the Hungry Stranger*, by Crosby Bonsall, 1963.
6. Author and illustrator, noted especially for her contributions to the I Can Read mystery series and for her witty texts for the American editions of Ylla's later photographically illustrated picture books.

TO KAY THOMPSON   December 26, 1953
                                   —wishful thinking,
                                   I mean 1963

Dear Kay:

Your letter about Kennedy[1] was great. Even the typing. Yes, it is utterly unacceptable and we have to accept it. Unbearable and we have to bear it. Unbelievable and we have to believe it. Etc. It doesn't get any less incredible. I was sitting here talking to an out-of-town artist, and a couple of people came to my door and said the president had been shot, and I explained that the radio always got things all wrong, and exaggerated, and then I went back to the out-of-town artist, and then others came to my door and said it was his head, and I explained carefully that he was a very strong extremely healthy person, and just a little old shot couldn't possibly be serious, and then someone came and said the president is dead, and I felt terribly angry that anyone would say anything so ridiculous. I always thought that scene in Shakespeare's *Antony and Cleopatra* where Cleopatra gets so damn mad at the messenger over the content of the message is silly. But that day I saw, again, Shakespeare is unfallible[sic].... We closed the office and I walked up Park Avenue and saw the flags at half-mast and wept all the way home. I was watching t.v. when Ruby walked up and shot Oswald. The ultimate nightmare. I felt the whole country was unravelling. I still feel it. I've always believed in an idiotic way that the ultimate perfectibility of the human race was perfectly possible, it would only take a lot of patience, but you know, the children will be better than their parents, and their children will be still better, and wiser, and the children of THOSE children will be better still. But I don't believe it any more. Anyone can have a surly crazy son who can hoist a cheap rifle and put a bullet in a

1. President John F. Kennedy was assassinated on November 22, 1963.

beautiful, reasonable, intelligent head. Oswald's mother on t.v. was one of the worst horrors—a coarse neurotic stupid person, primped up for the cameras, touching her ear-rings, being almost arch. Of course one can understand—oh understand nothing.

OK, Poody, chin up as you say.

How about the book about Fenice[1]? That title is fine, *Kay Thompson's Darling Baby Boy*. I am extremely eager to have that or *Kay Thompson's Fox and Fig* on 1964 list.[2] So if Fenice's book rolls more easily off your typewriter, rush it to me. [. . .] I wish you were learning to draw. You could also write a book about ballet ex-star Romana Gaz, and illustrate that. You are very very smart and witty.

Love,

TO HELEN L. JONES[3]   January 23, 1964

Dear Helen:

Your call about asking Arnold Lobel[4] to illustrate a book for you came on a day when we'd all been a little miffed over two other publishers who had been courting artists who had done their FIRST books for us. Otherwise I wouldn't have sounded so crabby to you, dear Helen, for you are surely a fine good citizen and one of my few favorites in the Sisterhood.

1. The author's pug dog.
2. One book came of UN's years of work with KT: *Kay Thompson's Miss Pooky Peckinpaugh and Her Secret Private Boyfriends Complete with Telephone Numbers*, illustrated by Joe Eula, 1970.
3. Children's book editor, Little, Brown and Company.
4. Author and artist. Lobel began his career in children's books in the late 1950s as the illustrator of several books of Jewish interest published by Ktav. In 1961 he illustrated *Red Tag Comes Back*, an I Can Read Book by Frederick B. Phleger. *A Zoo for Mister Muster*, 1962, was the first book written and illustrated by him.

Of course we have no right to say "Thank you for calling, Helen. We appreciate your query and in answer we wish you would not ask Arnold to do a book for you because we love his work and we plan to keep him as busy as possible." We have no right to say such a thing, of course. And I shouldn't have sounded cross with you because at least you told us you wanted to use him! As I have said, several of us in the department had been talking that day about some of the other houses who are always glad to give work to a young artist AFTER they have done some books for us. But who never give any time and energy and concern to the work of someone brand new. I am not thinking of you in this, Helen. But some artists have told me the names of other editors who look quickly through a portfolio and say, "Well, come back after you've illustrated a couple of books." Susan Carr saw Arnold's work when he came in unannounced one day, loved it, gave him the manuscript of an I Can Read book she was working on, and encouraged him to write and illustrate his own picture books. So of course we hope to keep him busy on Harper books. Right now he is working on an I Can Read book by Nathaniel Benchley[1], which is to be published in early fall, and he is then going to do a Science I Can Read book by Millicent Selsam[2]. We hope that then he will give time and thought to another of his own picture books. We want to publish the Selsam early in 1965 and Arnold's next picture book in the fall of 1965[3].

Again, I'm sorry if I sounded cross. I usually try to be nicer than I was when you called.

Affectionately,

1. *Red Fox and His Canoe*, by Nathaniel Benchley, illustrated by Arnold Lobel, 1964.
2. *Let's Get Turtles*, by Millicent E. Selsam, illustrated by Arnold Lobel, 1965.
3. *The Bears of the Air*, by Arnold Lobel, 1965.

TO RUSSELL HOBAN   January 30, 1964

Dear Russ old pal:

I was just going through the correspondence folder and saw your note to BAD about your germs having an infectious humor. This is such a beautiful lousy joke I have to stop working and write to tell you so. Hope throat is better now—better than your jokes, at least. (Joke, I really think you are very clever.)

You were exchanging palindromes with BAD or me or someone not long ago. Do you know the most beautiful one ever invented? About Goethals and the Canal:

"A man—a plan—a canal—Panama!"

Now back to work—you too.

Yours,

TO KLAUS GEMMING[1]   February 25, 1964

Dear Mr. Gemming:

Thank you for writing to us about your daughters' reaction to the inconsistencies in the artwork in *Emile*[2] and *The Case of the Hungry Stranger*[3]. We do not think the *Emile* jacket is really a mistake—Emile's eyes are black and white throughout the book, and the red in the eyes on the jacket probably seemed to Tomi Ungerer a good way of making the jacket a bit brighter. Jacket drawings, as you know, are often not literal recreations of the inside pictures.

As for the errors in *The Case of the Hungry Stranger*, we have

1. Book designer and photographer.
2. *Emile*, by Tomi Ungerer, 1960.
3. KG's daughters had noticed several discrepancies in the illustrations, including a cookie bag that inexplicably changed colors and a cardigan that mysteriously lost its dots.

nothing to say except what excellent eyes your girls have! Mrs. Bonsall hadn't noticed her omissions, no one here had noticed, and we are all horrified. Mrs. Bonsall says your daughters can come and inspect her art before she turns it in to us whenever they want—if there weren't child labor laws she would hire them. As I am sure you know, this is the sort of thing we try our hardest to avoid—for it is the sort of thing that infuriates children. We, and the artists who do books for us, recognize our responsibility to the children who read the books, but occasionally we make mistakes and something slips by our notice. Our apologies to you and your girls, and our thanks to them and to you for calling these errors to our attention.

We have long been admirers of your design and we are delighted that you find so many of our books of interest to your children.

Sincerely yours,
Director

TO CROCKETT JOHNSON   March 6, 1964

Dear Dave:

As you have doubtless assumed, from our silence, we have been thinking and thinking about your *The Emperor's Gifts*[1]. I was slightly baffled as to what age child it would really interest—as the type of format would appeal to a younger child than could possibly enjoy the ideas. Susan [Carr] also was of the opinion that it is more adult than juvenile (she put it more gracefully) and that you'd almost have to keep explaining things to anyone under ten years of age.   Well, here we are, puzzled and wishing we could express love and enthusiasm. But we can't.

---

1. *The Emperor's Gifts*, by Crockett Johnson, Holt, Rinehart and Winston, 1965.

Hurry up and write another book soon, that we can accept, and send you a big blue contract and a big fat check.

What do you think of good old Harper having published books the authors and artists of which won both the Newbery and Caldecott medals[1]? We are so happy—unaccustomed as we are..... We've been living in this sort of cold-water flat for a long time, trying to keep things scrubbed and neat, and the rats under control, and doing the best we can, don't you know, and everyone's braids neat, and fresh pinnys on, and not getting discouraged or bitter—not gambling or swilling cheap wine. And finally we got moved out into a better neighborhood.....   It's been a long wait, but finally we're respectable, and all.   Forgive effusion. We're all slightly light-headed.

Love to you both. And again send us something else soon. Mss. returned herewith.

TO CROSBY BONSALL   April 14, 1964

Dear Crosby:

You just get better and better and better: I've just looked through *I'll Show You Cats*[2] and am blissfully happy with it. I just wish Ylla[3] could see it. She would have appreciated you.

1. Maurice Sendak won the 1964 Caldecott Medal for *Where the Wild Things Are*; Emily Cheney Neville won the Newbery Medal that year for her first novel, *It's Like This, Cat*, illustrated by Emil Weiss, 1963.
2. *I'll Show You Cats*, by Crosby Bonsall, photographs by Ylla, 1964.
3. The pen-name of Camilla Koffler, Hungarian-born animal photographer, who died in 1955. Years earlier Leo Lerman, of Condé Nast, had shown UN several Ylla photographs and suggested that they might somehow make a good book for children. UN then asked Margaret Wise Brown if she would write a text to order for which the photos might serve as "illustrations"; Brown did so and the happy result was *They All Saw It*, 1944. Brown wrote three more books in this way; following her death in 1952, first Arthur Gregor and then CB took over the assignment.

More than that I cannot say.

What you have done with that *Seesaw* book[1] is just great. We love it and we thank you very very much. I know Susan [Carr] has told you all this but I just wanted to add my thanks too.

How about a better ending (more upbeat? Is that what I mean?) for the girl who finally gets measles? Or how about a longer story about this character? A chapter-type book? It is basically a very amusing idea but the way it ends now is sort of unfriendly. It is nice for that girl to get her come-uppance but after she does couldn't some pleasant situation occur?

I've just (oh Lord!) reread this letter and counted all the times I've used the word just. With all these good editors around here wouldn't you think I could do better? Excuse me, please.

Affectionately,
Just Urs.

TO LOUISE FITZHUGH[2]   August 14, 1964

Dear Louise,

We hear through the grapevine—oh I'm so original—that the Virginia Kirkus Bookshop Service[3] is very enthusiastic

---

1. *Seesaw*, by Joan Kahn, illustrated by Crosby Bonsall, 1964. Joan Kahn was an editor in the Adult Trade department, specializing in mysteries.
2. Author and artist. UN and Charlotte Zolotow first met with LF after her agent at McIntosh & Otis, Pat Schartle, sent Harper pages of what was to become the notebook contained within *Harriet the Spy*, by Louise Fitzhugh, 1964. Prior to the publication of *Harriet*, LF had been known as the illustrator of a send-up of *Eloise* called *Suzuki Beane*, by Sandra Scoppettone, Doubleday, 1961.
3. Kirkus, who was the founding editor of Harper's Department of Books for Boys and Girls, launched this review publication in 1933 following her departure from the house the previous year.

about *Harriet*[1]. Also, we have good quotes from Elizabeth[2] and Phyllis McGinley[3]. I do not dote on Miss McGinley but everyone here is pleased that she likes your book. She says: "Thank you for letting me see *Harriet the Spy* which I read in one happy session and which I found wonderfully funny, touching and original. Harriet is quite a girl and I wish both her and her creator, Louise Fitzhugh, very well indeed."

What are you working on now? Or are you just having a good time? I hear you fell in with some poison ivy. I'm so sorry and hope you are fine now.

I look forward to seeing you when you come back to town.

Yours,

We're enclosing the comments from Elizabeth Janeway, and also Virginia Chase of the Carnegie Library of Pittsburgh.

TO MAIA WOJCIECHOWSKA[4]   August 28, 1964

Dear Maia:

Thanks for your letter. We are not afraid of sentiment. I think I didn't use that word. I believe I said that the description of some of your emotion-filled episodes seemed too explicit. Sentiment is fine and we are delighted to cry over books.

1. *Harriet the Spy* was generally well received on publication, and it has come to be recognized as a watershed book that marked the beginning of a new level of emotional frankness and realism in the children's novel. Fitzhugh had drawn an unflinchingly honest portrait of an angry, impertinent eleven-year-old whose parents drank cocktails and took their daughter to a therapist when they reached their wits' end.
2. Elizabeth Janeway, author.
3. Poet and author.
4. Polish-born author, primarily for young adults. MW had won the Newbery Medal for 1965 for *Shadow of a Bull*, illustrated by Alvain Smith, Atheneum, 1964.

Sometimes we even cry when a book isn't sad, but just written perfectly. (Your book only has to be perfect. So weep along with us.)

Interesting about Hemingway and you.[1]

Best regards,

TO HILARY KNIGHT   September 18, 1964

Dear Hilary,

I hesitate to worry you, but I thought I should tell you that some enemy of yours is writing me very angry letters, and signing your name to them.[2]

Have a good week.

Love,

TO ANITA LOBEL[3]   September 25, 1964

Dear Anita,

Here, with great pleasure, is a contract for *Sven's Bridge*[4]. We hope it will be the first of many contracts we'll be sending you.

If you have any questions about the agreement, Barbara

1. In a letter to UN dated August 26, 1964, MW recalled a conversation she had had with Ernest Hemingway. Hemingway commented that writers should vigilantly guard against sentimentality until they reached the point in their careers when the barbs of critics could no longer damage their reputations.
2. After a seemingly endless series of delays relating to the completion of *Eloise in the Bawth* (see footnote 1, page 182, to letter to Kay Thompson, November 4, 1964), nerves were getting frayed all around.
3. Polish-born author, illustrator, and actress; married to Arnold Lobel.
4. *Sven's Bridge*, by Anita Lobel, 1965. AL's first book.

[Dicks] will be glad to help you, although as you have an expert on our contracts much closer to home we doubt that this will be necessary!

Welcome to the Harper list.

Yours sincerely,

TO LOUISE FITZHUGH   November 2, 1964

Dear Louise:

I tried to call you Friday. And this morning. I wanted to be sure you don't miss the ad in today's *New York Times* for *Harriet the Spy*. Everyone thinks the McGinley quote sells, so that's why it was used.

We've gone over the fascinating material you left with us a week ago, and I sort of think you might consider taking the very best things out of the various little books, and perhaps making one book of it. It really should be done as an adult book and so would you consider getting some of the things together so we can present it to an adult editor, I mean an editor of adult books?

We all adore Norman and think you should write a great deal more about him. Charlotte [Zolotow] wishes it could be an older brother but I doubt that any mother and son ever had such a healthy you should forgive the word relationship that this could take place. Anyhow, let's talk some more. Alice in her green dress is fascinating but we can't figure out what to do about her. All the other things you left are fascinating, too.

Are you working on *Mimi*[1] now or on one of the other ideas you took back with you? You never answer the telephone. (I just reread this and it looks as though I had just

---

1. This manuscript was apparently abandoned.

discovered the word fascinating and had to use it all the time. Excuse me.)

We want to publish *Mimi* or something by you in 1965, and we want to publish it earlier than we were able to publish *Harriet*. Then it will get earlier and better review space, than *Harriet* is receiving. So don't forget—two NEAT typescripts, with good margins. The little bit you have told me about *Mimi* is marvelous (fascinating) and I long to hear more. We all do.

Happy Children's Book Week, and many happy to returns to us all.

Yours,

TO MELVIN ARNOLD[1]   November 3, 1964

Dear Mr. Arnold:
    A friend of mine who is out voting for Goldwater[2] this

1. Associate director, Religious Books department, Harper & Row. UN had recently received a letter of complaint from a California school official concerning *The First Christmas*, by Robbie Trent, illustrated by Marc Simont, 1948. UN's correspondent wondered why the jacket copy for the book referred to the "shepherds who followed the star," but no star was shown or mentioned in the illustrations and text. The writer went on to suggest that the inconsistency might be due to ignorance of the Bible on the part of those responsible. This, of course, was more than enough to infuriate UN, who, in preparation for responding to the letter, queried MA as to the facts. He in turn wrote to a professor of New Testament and early church history at the University of Chicago, who reported back that text and illustrations were correct and the flap copy was in error. UN, who was obviously exasperated by the whole affair, wrote a tactful letter to the California school administrator, acknowledging the mistake. For her own amusement, she *also* wrote this parody of the letter of complaint that precipitated the exchange.
2. Barry M. Goldwater, conservative Republican senator from Arizona and 1964 Republican candidate for the presidency, was defeated in a landslide by President Lyndon B. Johnson.

morning has drawn my attention to your sweet little book called *The First Christmas*. He lives in California where there are lots of stars and he is therefore perturbed by the jacket's promise to show us some shepherds following one of them— not fulfilled in text or pix. That doesn't bother me so much since I am a simple student of the scriptures and scholars tell us that things get mixed up. What bothers me more is all that stuff about the moon—endpapers, a special illustration and moonlight obviously shining on the shepherds' road to Bethlehem. Where did you get all that? I have searched the scriptures and I can't find any mention of the moon. If God had wanted us to know about it, He would have told us. I think you are smuggling in naturalistic explanations which do nothing but lead the way toward atheism, Communism, and Lyndon B. Johnson. (I refrain from naming his running mate.)

Someone has sent me a rather solemn letter from some Eastern nut in which the book is defended. Since I don't know Miss Nordstrom, I am forwarding it to you.

Yours in Christ,

TO KAY THOMPSON   November 4, 1964

Dear Kay:

Silence! Silence! That's all I hear from you. I called up Mr. Katz[1]. But he is in Rome. Hilary called and asked if I'd heard from you. I said no. He said he had not heard either. Please please let me know how things are proceeding. I wrote Mr. Katz

---

1. Jack Katz, KT's lawyer.

and asked for a new delivery date for text and pictures.[1] Silence from him, too. I wonder if I'm dead and don't realize it, and that's why you can't get in touch with me.

We had a meeting this morning and people asked about *Eloise*. Do hope I'll have some news about it and you soon.

Are you fine? We are all very happy that Goldwater took such a beating, but I'm shocked that so many people did vote for him. I'm glad it is all over.

Love,

TO ERIK BLEGVAD[2]   November 13, 1964

Dear Erik:

Can we tempt you with the enclosed manuscript by Charlotte Zolotow[3]? Her books for us have been illustrated by such artists as Maurice Sendak, Garth Williams, and H. A. Rey, and she loves your work madly (we all do) and nothing would make us happier, etc. etc. etc...... So please read it and let me know how you feel about it. Also if it would be Number 14 on your agenda, or Number 15.......

1. Although *The Fox and the Fig* remained unfinished, KT and Hilary Knight had begun work on a new book about Eloise, titled *Eloise in the Bawth*, to be published by Harper. It was of course highly unusual for a sequel to a book, especially one as successful as the original *Eloise* had been, to be published by a different house. KT and Knight had, however, already broken with Simon & Schuster once, for the publication by Random House of *Eloise at Christmastime*. The traditional pattern of author/publisher loyalty was rapidly coming to an end, and the intensely competitive UN was fully prepared to take advantage of any opportunity that presented itself to her. In this instance, she was to be disappointed, however. *Eloise in the Bawth*, like *The Fox and the Fig*, was never published.
2. Danish-born illustrator.
3. Although this manuscript, *When I Have a Little Girl*, was ultimately illustrated by Hilary Knight, 1965, EB did illustrate three books by Zolotow, the first of which was *May I Visit?*, 1976.

It was lovely to see you and your wife in Cleveland, and, again, I enjoyed the Chicago evening with you and Emily[1] and ~~Dizzie~~ Dizzy!! Gillespie. I hope you and Lenore[2] will be my guests at some similar evening one of these days. I live around the corner from Basin Street East, and right next door to Jackie Kannon's Rat Fink Room ("no, not here, driver, beyond the Rat Fink Room.") So you can see how convenient everything is ...... Even the garbage-grinding-trucks swing.

Do let me hear from you about Charlotte's manuscript.

And don't forget that if anyone turns down Lenore's manuscripts, and if you and Lenore feel free to let me see them, I—we—would be delighted to have the opportunity to consider them. I didn't mean to sound so pushy that night, just before we went to hear Dizzie. But I am afraid I did, and I'm sorry. I must find some no-calorie beer.....

Love to all,

TO NAT HENTOFF[3]   December 1, 1964

Dear Nat:

Yes, I think *A Hole Is to Dig* was something new. It came from Ruth Krauss' listening to children, getting ideas from them, polishing some of the thoughts, exploring additional "definitions" of her own. It really grew out of children and what is important to them. (A brother is to help you.) Some of the definitions seem quite serious to children but those aren't the

---

1. Emily Cheney Neville, winner of the 1964 Newbery Medal, was touring the annual midwestern children's book fairs with UN.

2. Author; EB's wife.

3. Author and journalist. NH was on assignment for *The New Yorker* to profile Maurice Sendak. The piece ran in the January 22, 1966, issue under the title "Profiles: Among the Wild Things."

ones the adults smile over and consider "cute." For instance, "Buttons are to keep people warm." Adults think oh isn't that darling, but it makes perfectly good sense to children. Conversely, "A tablespoon is to eat a table with" seems a pretty dumb joke to adults, but it knocks most children out, they think it is so witty. *A Hole Is to Dig* was the first of all the *Something Is Something* books, and has been <u>mushily</u> imitated ever since it was published. (*A Friend Is Someone Who Likes You*[1], *Love Is a Special Way of Feeling*[2]) . . . So I think Maurice is right. N.B. Sendak's children in *Hole* have been imitated countless times.

You asked me how "revolutionary" *Where the Wild Things Are* is. There have been a good many fine picture books in the past. (Some by Margaret Wise Brown, and illustrated by one of two or three or four talented artists.) But I think *Wild Things* is the first complete work of art in the picture book field, conceived, written, illustrated, executed in entirety by one person of authentic genius. Most books are written from the outside in. But *Wild Things* comes from the inside out, if you know what I mean. And I think Maurice's book is the first picture book to recognize the fact that children have <u>powerful</u> emotions, anger and love and hate and only after all that passion, the wanting to be "where someone loved him best of all." I'm writing this in a terrible hurry, so forgive me, please. A lot of good picture books have had fine stories and lovely pictures (*Peter Rabbit*[3], the best of Dr. Seuss, Wanda Gág's *Millions of Cats*[4]), and some have touched beautifully on basic things in a child's life, physical growth, going to bed, coming to terms with a new sister or brother (this is making them sound sappy but they are far from that—I'm thinking of Ruth Krauss' *The Growing Story*[5], Margaret

1. *A Friend is Someone Who Likes You*, by Joan Walsh Anglund, Harcourt, 1958.
2. *Love is a Special Way of Feeling*, by Joan Walsh Anglund, Harcourt, 1960.
3. *The Tale of Peter Rabbit*, by Beatrix Potter, Warner, 1902.
4. *Millions of Cats*, by Wanda Gág, Coward, McCann, 1928.
5. *The Growing Story*, by Ruth Krauss, illustrated by Phyllis Rowand, 1947.

Wise Brown's *Goodnight Moon*, Charlotte Zolotow's *Quarreling Book*[1], the Hobans' *Baby Sister for Frances*[2]). But it just seems to me that Sendak's *Where the Wild Things Are* goes deeper than previous picture books. And of course his use of three consecutive double-spreads to show what happened when Max cried, "Let the wild rumpus start!" has never been done in any book.

Yours,

TO CROSBY BONSALL   December 22, 1964

Dear Crosby:

I enclose xeroxed copies of your "We went on a picnic" story and the nonsense dictionary (Arp to Zulpin). I don't dare trust the little books nor the pictures for the picnic andtheriddle [*sic*]—god damn it someone has changed the typewriter or something and I can't type....to the pre-Christmas mail. So I'll keep them here for the present.

As we agreed on the phone, you shouldn't try to rush out some sort of a Nonsense Nutshell for 1965. It is too much work and too little time. Also we are not giving you helpful thoughts about what a Nonsense Nutshell is, or could be.

But you do want to do (and we very much want you to do) a book for the fall of 1965. This could be either a second Greedy Book[3] (*What Did You Bring Me*) or *Susan Says*, with a better ending. I don't remember exactly how the ending was but I do recall that you thought, as we did, that the ending wasn't completely satisfying. Or perhaps you will want to make <u>the nonsense dictionary into a regular book</u> (not part of a Nutshell).

1. *The Quarreling Book*, by Charlotte Zolotow, illustrated by Arnold Lobel, 1963.
2. *A Baby Sister for Frances*, by Russell Hoban, illustrated by Lillian Hoban, 1964.
3. This would have been a sequel to *It's Mine!: A Greedy Book*, by Crosby Bonsall, 1964.

But then you wouldn't be able to use it later if you do go ahead with a Nonsense Nutshell.

Well, this typewriter is the bitter end so I will knock it off (literally, off the table) for now. This is just to say that we hope you will finish a book in time for fall 1965. And let's meet soon in the New Year. I want you to come see me and also meet the Yorkshire[1]. But two months ago she developed a congenital malfunction of the pyloric valve, oh I told you about all that, and she can eat so little she is very skinny. Maybe I'll have a nifty operation to make my pyloric valve malfunction. Then I'd get skinny. Maybe George[2] would like to go in on this project with me? To cut costs?

Dreary note but it is a dreary day and I'm the only one in the city who doesn't simply adore Blessed Noel. I hate it. Tomi Ungerer gave me a present, of a huge gorilla dragging a nekkid Barbie doll along by the hair. She only has one red high-heeled shoe on. Real Christmassy. You can see it the next time you come to the Tot Dept.

Love to you and George,

Ursula Scrooge

TO NAT HENTOFF   January 21, 1965

Dear Nat:

Hope the galleys[3] look all right to you. Sorry to have to have them back so soon, but the schedule is tight.

I just reread the book and think it is darn good. The end

---

1. UN had a series of Yorkshire terriers.
2. The author's husband, executive vice-president of Brodart, a library supply company.
3. The previous year, NH had begun work on a realistic novel for young adults, set in contemporary New York. *Jazz Country* was published by Harper in 1965.

still seemed a bit talky to me (and to Mrs. Shub[1]) but I can't see where it could be changed, except possibly Veronica's long speeches on galleys 38B and 39B could be shortened, or broken up with some remark from Tommy. But it isn't all that important.   On galley 37 "Why are adults always so damn etc." It struck me that "adults" sounds sort of non-conversational—would he say "older guys" or "older people"—If "adults" is OK with you, OK with us. Just thought I'd mention it. As a matter of fact, he could just say why is everybody so damn sure of themselves doesn't have to be perfectly grammatical.   Well, that's all for now from the split-hairs department.

Best regards,

I keep thinking I have forgotten to tell you something especially interesting about Sendak. I discovered a real block because I was afraid he might not like whatever I might say to you. (This is my fault, not his.) One nice thing about him is his generosity to other artists, the good ones, I mean. And to my knowledge he's never said at the end of a job, "Oh, I could do that picture over but it will just have to do, I don't want to bother." (Some artists <u>do</u> say that.

One artist one time showed me a picture book ms. he wanted to illustrate, and I read it carefully and said I was sorry but it honestly didn't seem really original and <u>inevitable</u> and something we couldn't resist—and this artist said "Oh come on, Ursula, we can put it out in a beautiful big format, and have fabulous fantastic pictures, and they will say it is a lovely book, even if the story isn't any good." Sendak would never think or say anything as cynical and disgusting as that.)   You know him well enough yourself by now to know that he is a perfectly brilliant mimic—all the way from (1) a librarian giving a speech

---

1. Elizabeth Shub, an editor in UN's department. See also page 218, footnote 1 to letter to Maurice Sendak, March 18, 1966.

about children's books to a lot of adults (with never one reference to children) to (2) the appearance of the Angel Gabriel—he takes both parts and is brilliant.

TO LOUISE FITZHUGH   February 25, 1965

Dear Louise:

Here is a lovely letter from Polly Goodwin[1] of the unlovely *Chicago Tribune*. I gave her your address and suggested she write you, and give you the number of words she wants and other helpful details. I also sent her copies of some of the most favorable reviews and copies of the silly *Library Journal* letter[2], etc.   Do let me know how you feel about writing a piece for her spring book issue, will you?

I return herewith the original mss. of your second book, (*The Water Mill Mystery*[3], tentative title).   My marginal notes are to be IGNORED until you have finished the whole book. I was going to erase them but then decided I would have to trust you to ignore them. For instance, I scribbled "Mrs. Golly?" on the top of Page 10, and that is just a note to myself to go back and reread the Mrs. Golly chapter in *Harriet*. All this is to say, don't stop to check over the marginal notes. Most of them are utterly complimentary. Just go ahead with the rest of the story, and we can talk over small points later. Small points such as: Harriet is 11 and just wears trunks. ?? Even 7 year olds now

---

1. Children's book editor, *The Chicago Tribune*.
2. A group of librarians from Miami, Florida, had written to say they had found *Harriet* "completely unchildlike" and "more suitable for a *New Yorker* piece than a children's book." *Library Journal*, Vol. 90, No. 4 (February 15, 1965), p. 4 of Children's Section.
3. It was published as *The Long Secret*, by Louise Fitzhugh, 1965.

think they have to have something to cover their non-existent bosoms. But all is minor—so ignore it.

When we meet I'll tell you what Cass Canfield suggests about your commitments to McIntosh & Otis. He thinks you should just talk it over with Miss Otis herself but since you don't know her, I gather, you might just have a friendly talk with Miss Schartle. Probably you are not the first M & O client to have reacted in an un-enthusiastic way to their subsidiary rights department. Let's talk more about this. Apparently it would be very unhelpful for anyone here at Harper to try to work this out.

As I told you over the phone [. . .] I was really touched by Pages 49 and 50[1]. And by the beginning of the next chapter. And when I read that "even Madam Curie did it" I plotzed. I think you have handled this beautifully and we are grateful.

When we meet next tell me more about Jessie Mae's family and the Birchers[2]. This needn't be a real problem at all. Bigots have been in existence for centuries and all of the religious fanatics based their activities on a non-respect for differences. Isn't this the point you want to make? In any event, whatever you do it will come out fine. But let's talk about pinning anything down to a specific group. You know, your books will be selling well in 1985, so generalization will make more sense than 1965 specifics. I think the Birchers will be forgotten by then. But the respectable, cruel bigots will still be with us. I may misunderstand your thought, but I can't believe I do. There were "Birchers" in Salem—???? Well, more later.

---

1. The reference is to the scene, in Chapter 9 of the published book, in which Mary Beth has her first period, and to the following scene, in which she and her friends talk about her new experience. As Janie reasonably points out: "It happens to everybody, every woman in the world, even Madame Curie. It's very normal." UN was well aware of the fact that the subject of menstruation had never before been addressed in a novel for young readers.
2. The John Birch Society, an extreme right-wing organization founded in 1958.

One small thought—you say one of the girls picked at "a hurt place" on her knee. Don't let my question mark bother you. "Hurt place" seemed a euphemism for "sore" or "scab," or something more direct than "hurt place." But that question mark is purely tentative.

I simply loved the thing about the hippo, the mention of pig-noise, the description of the door-knob and its decorations during an emotional moment, the description of the summer house, the description of Beth Ellen following the maid across the lawn when the shadows were dark and cold. I loved Janie working on a cure "for this thing," and Harriet's talk with her father. Also loved Harriet's talk with her mother, and her wanting "everything, everything, everything." Thomas Wolfe took many volumes to express this voracious appetite, and you did it in a couple of lines.

I did think Chapter 1 was too much Harriet and too much Mrs. Golly-ish. The part about the "lining falls out" on Page 52 I thought was a bit tough on expectant 11 and 12 year olds. Later the Biloxi family seemed a bit too grotesque, but you'll know about that better than I will. And on 135 "whore" seemed just a bit too much. But maybe I'm wrong. Nothing important bothers us, really.

This book is going to be sooooooo fine, Louise. We appreciate you!

As ever,

TO JANETTE SEBRING LOWREY   June 4, 1965

Dear Janette:

Your wonderful letter has been read and reread by me. I was absorbed and fascinated and I wish our paths had crossed more often. It does not seem possible that I have not seen you in 20 years. I feel very close to you in many ways. I told you once that you always put me in mind of my mother's people, the Dwyer women. They were strong women and chose with unerring accuracy charming and weak men. (Or did the weak men choose the strong women?) (Or did the women start out weak and have to become strong because their men were weak?) (Or were the men strong to start out with—well, enough of this.....) In any event, your confidences are safe with me but I cannot destroy that remarkable letter at least not for a long while. Your problems are interesting, discouraging, stimulating—but not at all disgraceful and certainly not a patch on some of the problems other authors share with me.

I'm interested in hearing why you don't go to the bookstore more often. There is always a terrible danger in friends "taking sides" in a family matter. But as an editor I simply cannot think about that danger. I love children, young and old. I walk in Central Park and I see children clambering all over the statues of H. C. Andersen and Alice in Wonderland (with her of course are the Rabbit, the Mad Hatter, the Cheshire Cat) and I fill up with tears as I stand and watch those darling youngsters. I read all the letters children send us about our children's books and again I weep over the sweetest sentences. I stop mothers with baby carriages and I talk baby talk to their babies—with many ooooohs and ahhhhhhs, and my aging eyes are again damp as I walk away. But any children or indeed any relatives—husbands, mothers, fathers, brothers, sisters, who are connected in any way with "my" authors are MY ENEMIES.

We have an author, she is around 35 or 36, who is divorced (that's good) but has a daughter (aged 12) and that is bad. The other day we wanted her—I'll call her Mrs. X—to come in and check some changes in the galleys. I'd wanted her to attend to this a week earlier but her daughter (grrrrrrr....) was home for spring vacation and had to be taken to a matinee, or something. Anyhow, Mrs. X came in late one afternoon, gasped out that she couldn't go over the galleys, that she had her daughter waiting downstairs and that she had to take the daughter to a movie (meanwhile our galleys gathered dust, mildew, after neglect). I was furious. "Your daughter!" I shouted. "Why the dickens isn't she married? Hanging around taking up your time!" "Ursula," pleaded Mrs. X, "She is only 12." "Bah," I snarled, "she's just pretending to be twelve, she must be around thirty."........ This is just to explain to you that I love children of any age except those connected with Harper authors. Then I am ruthless and want "my" authors to be the same. Same with husbands. Out! Mothers. Out! Invalid sisters and/or brothers. Out!   I thought I'd be able to add another page of more relevant sentences in answer to your letter, but now I see I cannot. So this is all for now. I'll write again soon. In the meantime I send you much love and I hope all goes well with you and yours, but so far as I am concerned you are the important and talented one and the most valuable.

Ever affectionately,

TO HILARY KNIGHT   September 15, 1965

Dear Hilary:

Thanks for your letter of the 8th. I loved hearing from you and I loved your descriptions of the English—especially about the Grape nuts[1]. Lovely!

---

1. HK enjoyed regaling UN with tales of the eccentric English. One acquaintance of his had fallen in love with Grape Nuts, only to be told by a local shopkeeper that the cereal sold so well (and was therefore so much work to keep in stock) that he had decided *not* to carry it anymore.

I'm sorry you haven't heard from Kay [Thompson], but I haven't either. Cass Canfield was supposed to dine with her last Saturday, September 11th, in Rome. I gave him a bit of the background and I hope that she and he had a good talk. But I haven't heard from him as yet. He was on his way to London and perhaps will write me from there. This was a very very hurried trip on his part but I'm glad he was able to arrange to see Kay. She liked him very much when she met him briefly here.

Yes, I did have a lovely luncheon with Hubbell[1] and I thought that really I should try to see him for at least a half an hour at least every six weeks. He cheered me up so. I've been down in the dumps about children's books for ages, and depressed by some of the minor talents with major egos (you are not among them), and depressed by all the adults who review and pass on the books, etc. etc. And Hubbell was so airy and amusing, and when I started to talk SERIOUSLY to him about doing books with perhaps a bit more "emotional content" and "more levels of feeling" than—say—his *Murdoch*[2], he brushed me off with "Really, Ursula, what is wrong with being superficial? After all some of us preferred Constance Bennett to Maureen Stapleton."   Doesn't look so funny written down but I was delighted. I was at my most ponderous and boring—talking about "his work," but after all he <u>was</u> paying for a darn good luncheon and I thought I should make what contribution I could. But he'd have none of it.

We[3] sold the Bedford Hills house but the lovely (my word for today, apparently) apartment at UN Plaza now won't be ready until January. So we are holed up in a smallish room at a 3rd rate hotel and trying to be darling good sports about this unforeseen delay. I keep reminding Mary that the Gemini V

1. Hubbell Pierce, author, designer of murals, wallpaper, and fabrics.
2. *Murdoch*, by Hubbell Pierce, illustrated by D. II., 1961.
3. UN and Mary Griffith.

astronauts had closer quarters, but as she points out, they are much much younger. Well, this too will pass.

Yes, we think the Zolotow-Knight[1] looks fine. Many thanks. You sound much too busy and happy in London. How about your tenants? Are they nice and responsible? Write me again one of these days.

Love,

TO RUTH KRAUSS   September 16, 1965

Dear Ruth:

You'd be surprised, or would you, to know with what pleasure I see a page with your handwriting on it on my desk....

We are checking once more to see if there are any copies available of *Nut Tree* but I am sure that Miss Gelland[2] and Mr. [Ferd] Monjo did all the combing possible. The Shipping Dept.[3] is now in charge of a big IBM machine named Irving Needleman and I'm not at all satisfied with his work.   More later. But you mention vice-presidential influence and I will tell you something, kid. I have learned 3 things as I have staggered down Life's Roadway. (1) If people ask if you like dark meat or light meat it is OK to tell the truth because they really want to know. (2) If there is only 1 chocolate pastry on the French pastry tray it is OK to say YOU want it because there are other identical ones in the kitchen. (3) Vice-presidential influence isn't on the tray of French pastry.

1. *When I Have a Little Girl*, 1965.
2. Carolyn Gelland, secretary to Ferd Monjo. Later UN's secretary.
3. RK, having had no luck obtaining six additional copies of her book *Somebody Else's Nut Tree* from members of UN's staff, appealed directly to the editor, whom she addressed as "Vice-President in Charge of Warehouses."

You said you wish you would think of a book we would like. You would if you just <u>would</u>, Ruth. Look in the refrigerator[1]. We want another good Ruth Krauss book desperately.

Yes, I am fine. I wish I could lose 100 lbs. But otherwise all is well with your old fan from the 3rd row.

Love,

TO WILLIAM PÈNE DU BOIS[2] November 5, 1965

Dear Billy:

I fear that my immediate reaction to the magic finger[3] in your pictures was a sound one. You talked me out of my feeling that this is an ancient obscene gesture, and I suppose you went grinning up the block.....   The trouble is that this gesture with this finger is constantly employed by boys from the third grade on, and most little girls are quite familiar with it. Well, I don't need to tell you all this, Gustave.....but will you change it, please, to the index finger? I have checked the manuscript and in no place does the author specify the middle finger. How about the index and little finger? Or the index and middle finger in a V?   I loved the pictures so and you are such a smooth talker that I didn't pursue this worry far enough. But as soon as you left Miss Kenner[4] and I began to think more about it. Will you please call me up? I will be out of the office all day Monday but will be in Tuesday.

My first job at Harper was in the College Textbook

---

1. RK stored her manuscripts in her refrigerator.
2. French-born author and illustrator; art editor, *The Paris Review*; winner of the 1948 Newbery Medal for *The Twenty-One Balloons*, Viking, 1947.
3. WPduB was at work on illustrations for Roald Dahl's *The Magic Finger*, 1966.
4. Alice Kenner, copyeditor.

Department, and once in a while I wish I had stayed there. Editorial problems such as this did NOT occur in college texts.....

Your faithful but worried fan.

TO CROSBY BONSALL   December 14, 1965

Dear Crosby,
     Where is the book[1]?

Love,

TO CROSBY BONSALL   December 15, 1965

Dear Crosby,
     Où est le livre?

Love,

TO CROSBY BONSALL   December 16, 1965

Dear Crosby,
     Donde esta el libro?

Love,

1. CB published two books the following year: *The Case of the Dumb Bells*, 1966; and *Here's Jellybean Reilly*, illustrated with photographs by Ylla, 1966.

TO CROSBY BONSALL   December 17, 1965

Dear Crosby,
    Achtung!
    Wo ist der buch?

                                        Love,

Il libro, dov'è?[1]

TO CROSBY BONSALL   December 21, 1965

Dear Crosby,
    Hereway
           isay
              hetay
                  ookbay
                        ?

                                      Ovelay,

1. Handwritten at bottom.

TO RUSSELL HOBAN   January 28, 1966

Dear Russ:

I have you on my mind and know that a good new approach to *Television for Frances*[1] will come to you. I am sure it will. I just hated telling you over the 'phone the other day that the dummy just didn't seem good enough for you and Frances—and Lil[2]. But I had to. And everything you said over the 'phone confirmed my feeling.... I mean if you don't believe what you have Father saying you don't want him to say it. Lawks, isn't it interesting to be so puzzled about these badgers? And doesn't the fact that you are willing to solve this puzzle somehow make your books the good ones they are? I'm coming out very stuffy; forgive me.   I do think that one stumbling block is that you are, so far, really telling about a problem the Father has, not a problem that FRANCES has. Certainly the pattern of your books about F. doesn't have to be the same in every book, but somehow I think that one reason you're having a bit of trouble getting this book PERFECT is that you are presenting Father's problem. I am repeating myself and boring my own teeth out of my own head. I'm really sorry. Anyhow, just a note to say that your loving editor is wid youse and I know you will fix this mss. so that it is exactly right. And don't get tense about deadlines—there's time, (and Lil can always draw 26 hours a day, no????)

Maybe the television problem is just one part of a larger section of Frances' life. Maybe you should think of it without any specific title for the present, and see what happens.

I see you are being published in Japan[3].... Hmmmm

Love to you all,

---

1. The manuscript was published as *A Birthday for Frances*, by Russell Hoban, illustrated by Lillian Hoban, 1968.
2. Lillian Hoban. She illustrated all but the first of the Frances books written by RH.
3. In January 1966, the Japanese publisher Fukuinkan acquired Japanese rights to RH's *Bedtime for Frances*.

TO CLEMENT HURD
January 31, 1966

Dear Clem:

Oh I am sitting here with a big fat lump in my big fat throat and I want to thank you from the bottom of my big fat heart for being able to re-do those spreads for *The Runaway Bunny*[1], and keep <u>all</u> the warmth and love from the originals. FLYING TO THE TREE is perfect now. I always loved it but now it is PERFECT. And THE SITTING ROOM is also perfect, THOUGH I always loved the original. Well, I loved all the originals but how BEAUTIFULLY you have done them again twenty-five years later, and you haven't lost one single bit of the feeling, in fact you have added to it. Well, this is incoherent, I am really practically in tears. The new HAVE A CARROT is absolutely stupendously marvelous, and I never knew until now that the original spread for that great line was so far from perfection.   I think the new black and whites are a big improvement but I haven't had time to do more than just rush through the spreads, and gulp them down and love them. Planning how to do a new edition of this book will take time and undoubtedly European plates, and worries about how big a first printing can we do after all these years, etc. etc.   But "Reflection, you may come tomorrow/ Sit by the fireside with sorrow."[2]   Today all I can do is tell you that I am absolutely thrilled with what you've done, and I know Margaret would have been.   (About whether to bleed or not to bleed the spreads, that too will have to be thought about later, with D. Hagen, too.

1. CH had long been dissatisfied with his illustrations for the original 1942 edition of *The Runaway Bunny*, by Margaret Wise Brown, which he felt had suffered from his relative inexperience in preparing art for reproduction. During the mid-1960s, with the ever-increasing popularity of *Goodnight Moon* as background, UN became interested in the possibility of CH's reillustrating *The Runaway Bunny*. The artist went to work; Harper published the new edition with its now-familiar art in 1972.
2. From Percy Bysshe Shelley, "The Invitation."

She is out with a bad back. She either shoveled snow or hurt herself playing judo.)

Well, editors certainly can be 100% wrong. I knew you could re-do the pictures for *The Runaway Bunny* and that they would be much improved technically. But I didn't really believe that you could get the same feeling into them. I know you're a better artist than you were then, but I couldn't believe that the warm direct emotion could have lasted. I must admit this to you, Clem, because it is such a warm pleasure to admit how wrong I was. I just can't tell you how thrilled I am over all this. I'm happy as an editor, and as just a plain civilian too, because everything good and strong and tender lasted over the last twenty-five years in your work. And I must say that from my end I'm sitting here in this shabby crowded little office reacting just the way I did all those years ago. Rereading this effusion I hope you won't be offended by my utter amazement that you could do this so marvelously. I suppose that isn't madly flattering. But you'll know what I mean, I hope. I always loved that book so much, and it stood for an awful lot for me—when we were all young and sort of nuts. (And now I'm old and sort of nuts!) And it is somehow very very reassuring that you've kept all the best of you 25 years ago and combined it with the best of your abilities now. Really, it can't have happened very often. And I'm grateful.   More later. I know you're anxious to hear about *Dreaming Dog*[1] and *What Whale*[2], and I will write shortly. But I just couldn't postpone writing you this fan letter.

Love,

1. *Little Dog, Dreaming*, by Edith Thacher Hurd and Thacher Hurd, illustrated by Clement Hurd, 1967. Edith Thacher Hurd, a friend and colleague of Margaret Wise Brown's from their student days at Bank Street, collaborated with her husband, Clement Hurd, on dozens of picture books. Their son, Thacher, grew up to be a picture-book author and illustrator.
2. *What Whale? Where?*, by Edith Thacher Hurd, illustrated by Clement Hurd, 1966.

Clement Hurd and Margaret Wise Brown

at Vinalhaven, Maine, 1951

Shel Silverstein,

circa 1964

Maurice Sendak

at Lake Mohonk, New York, 1968

BY NANCY CRAMPTON

Else Holmelund Minarik, 1973

Ruth Krauss

Charlotte Zolotow,

circa 1954

Crockett Johnson

BY JEROME WEIDMAN

E. B. White and Katharine S. White

at the time of the publication of

A Subtreasury of American Humor *(1941)*

Mary Stolz,

circa 1953

Syd Hoff,

circa 1958

Garth Williams,

circa 1955

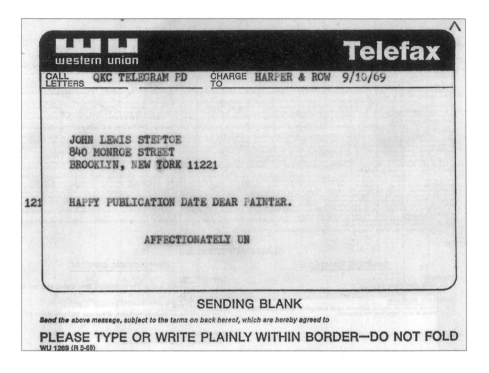

WU

western union | **Telefax**

CALL LETTERS ___ QKC TELEGRAM PD ___ CHARGE TO HARPER & ROW 9/10/69

JOHN LEWIS STEPTOE
840 MONROE STREET
BROOKLYN, NEW YORK 11221

121   HAPPY PUBLICATION DATE DEAR PAINTER.

AFFECTIONATELY UN

SENDING BLANK

Send the above message, subject to the terms on back hereof, which are hereby agreed to

PLEASE TYPE OR WRITE PLAINLY WITHIN BORDER—DO NOT FOLD

WU 1289 (R 5-69)

Telegram to John Steptoe

on the publication of Stevie, *1969*

Telegram sent to Ursula Nordstrom

in congratulations for the awarding of the Hans Christian Andersen Medal

to Meindert DeJong

Sketch by Marc Simont depicting "an episode in the life of U.N.

before she was made a director," and sent to her to commemorate her election

as a director of the company in 1954

9/20/66

Dear Louise:

Nothing special on my mind, just a note to say Hi and hope everything is going along well with you. Also to say again how terribly sorry I am that my long letter and all those marginal notes were the very oppèsite of helpful in your reworking of SPORT. But we are very relieved that Charlotte's two letters did the job for you, and we hope work is going well. As I told you over the phone, of course don't worry about the deadline. You and your books are more important to us than any old deadline or publishing schedule, and we want the book whenever you are ready to let us have it. I thought I'd send you some sizes for drawings, but maybe that would just interrupt you in your work now. If not let me know. Or send me a line anyhow. I hate to feel so out of touch.   As I said, you and Harper will have a long life together, and whenever ahything I do or say burns you up, I hope you will feel free to say so and not steam in silence, as apparently you did after our luncheon. You can always blow your stack and tell us to go to hell and get whatever is on your mind off it and on to ours. Now of course you mayZXXXXXXXXXXXXXXXXXXXXX say Why you big slob if I prefer to steam in silence that is the way I will steam .... OK OK. I just wanted to say that XXXX you don't have to.

     Charlotte hasn't written a picture book for you to illustrate yet, but any minute I bet. She has a lovely book of poetry on the spring list.XXX And she will surely come up with something perfect for your collaborration collabborrationn - ?

     Hope you are all well and happy, Louise, and here's love.

Carbon copy of a letter to Louise Fitzhugh, 1966

Ursula Nordstrom, 1969

Dear Maurice:

I came in from looking at the Winsor McCay exhibit[1] right after you left this morning. Sorry you came to see Dorothy [Hagen] and couldn't—and sorry you are not feeling too well, according to BAD.

Thank you so much for telling me about the Little Nemo things. I had a lovely hour by myself enjoying it all. I liked the one where the bed goes off for that long walk with them, the one you mentioned. But the one where he takes the little girl home from the party, and tries not to admit he is getting afraid of the dark, and all the buildings grew so strange and threatening—oh that one I absolutely loved. I just felt bathed in happiness as I looked at it.

As I said on the 'phone, we all thought your Anderson piece in the last *Book Week*[2] was simply splendid. And I think that one of these days you should let us have copies of all your articles and speeches, and see if you're not pretty near to having a book[3]. I still haven't been able to find a copy of your speech about Beatrix Potter[4], but will make another effort. It was superb, as I remember. Anyhow, some of your articles and speeches certainly should be collected sooner or later and published in book form.

I haven't forgotten about trade bindings on *Kenny's Window*

1. McCay's comic strip art was featured in the Metropolitan Museum of Art exhibition "Two Fantastic Draftsmen."
2. Maurice Sendak, "For Children of All Ages," review of *The Wild Swan: The Life and Times of Hans Christian Andersen*, by Monica Stirling (Harcourt, Brace, 1965), *The Washington Post Book World*, March 13, 1966, 1, 11–13.
3. UN's idea for such a collection was realized years later with the publication of *Caldecott & Co.: Notes on Books & Pictures*, by Maurice Sendak, Michael di Capua Books/Farrar, Straus, 1988. MS dedicated the book "For Ursula Nordstrom."
4. This speech is the first of two pieces on Potter reprinted in *Caldecott & Co.*

and *Very Far Away*. But didn't you want to do new pictures for *Kenny's Window* one of these days? Or did I dream that? It seems to me you said you'd like to re-do the whole book some time. Tell me if I'm wrong.

Yours with high regard,

P. S. We're all so glad about you and Singer[1]. I feel I'm seeing a masterpiece taking place right in front of me. It will be a magnificent book. Oh, I saw some of those Vishniak[2] (sp) photographs. Simply unbelievable. They're like marvelous paintings.

TO EZRA JACK KEATS[3]　　　　　　　　　May 2, 1966

Dear Ezra:

Damn it, here it is bright and early Monday a.m. and I can't get you on the 'phone. I suppose you are out helling around with another children's book editor—and I hate her.

1. MS was at work on the illustrations for *Zlateh the Goat and Other Stories*, by Isaac Bashevis Singer, translated from the Yiddish by the author and Elizabeth Shub, 1966. Singer, the Polish-born Jewish novelist and short-story writer, typically wrote in Yiddish, then collaborated on an English-language translation. Elizabeth Shub, an editor in UN's department and an old friend of Singer's, had persuaded the author to write his first book for young readers, a collection of tales based on the stories his mother had told him as a child.
2. Roman Vishniac, photographic chronicler of Jewish life in Eastern Europe in the years just prior to the Holocaust. Vishniac had photographed the world about which Singer wrote.
3. Author and illustrator, winner of the 1963 Caldecott Medal for *The Snowy Day*, Viking, 1962. EJK, who began his career as an illustrator of books written by others, was accustomed to moving from publisher to publisher. Following the success of *The Snowy Day*, he produced a series of sequels about his young protagonist, Peter, and the boy's friends. Viking published *Whistle for Willie* in 1964, but by the time EJK began the third book about Peter, he had moved on to Harper, which published *Peter's Chair* in 1967 and *A Letter to Amy* in 1968; *Goggles!* was published by Macmillan in 1969.

I wanted to say that Charlotte [Zolotow] and I are both really delighted with the new picture book about Peter[1]. I think Ellen[2] hasn't had a chance to look at it yet but I am sure she will be very happy too about it. Charlotte and I like it even better than the first too [sic] and that is saying a lot.   We both think that you can still think of something a bit better to make Peter change at the end, although —the 'phone just rang and we talked. As you say, with the pictures it will probably be very clear that Peter grew too big for the chair they are painting for the new baby, and then when you show him, Peter, sitting in a regular grown up chair talking with his father, it will be obvious enough.

I hope that you and Dorothy [Hagen] can talk and that you will be able to finish the pictures by July. It would be fine to have some of them on view here at the office during the A.L.A. so that some of your librarian friends can see the originals for the forthcoming spring 1967 publication.

We are simply delighted to have the new book, and we thank you for it. I promise that we will work out production figures as soon as possible, and that if we can go to $12\frac{1}{2}$% before 100,000 copies sold we will. But I cannot make any promises, Ezra. We do want to keep the list price to $3.50 if possible, for a 32 page book of relatively modest dimensions.   That "other department" is not going to be able to make the deals you describe, and at the same time give good production quality, year-round promotion, the relatively lavish sort of advertising we give our children's books. And a lot of other details I won't go into now.

But we will want to do our very best by you, Ezra.

Yours,

1. *Peter's Chair*.
2. Ellen Rudin, an editor in the department, became assistant publisher of Harper Junior Books in 1972 and, the following year, succeeded UN as head of the department.

TO RUSSELL HOBAN   June 20, 1966

Dear Russ:

Glad you're glad about Ohio Head Start, etc.[1] It doesn't sound like such a big deal, but it really is a good sign. Also I was very very happy that Harper had about 23 books out of a hundred. This Title 2 of the ESEA act[2] is going to mean a great deal to all you authors and artists with books on approved lists. For instance, Pennsylvania has just sent us their list of approved Harper books which can be purchased with Federal money, and several of the Hoban books are on it—*Baby Sister*, *Bedtime*, *Bread and Jam*, *Nothing to Do*, *Sorely Trying Day*[3]. And Pennsylvania ALONE has about 4 million bucks to spend on the books on their list.

I'm sorry you had to go to Puerto Rico, but am sure you will get *Mouse and Child*[4] just right in the not too distant future. I hope that with more Hoban books and much more Federal spending you can tell your job good-bye and devote yourself to your own head.

You sounded a little cool in your last. Don't be cool to me; head???? I meant hear!

Yes, it will be fun to see you in July during the A. L. A. The

---

1. The Johnson administration's Great Society program provided massive amounts of federal money for the purchase of trade books (as opposed to textbooks) for children for use in education. This letter gives some idea of the scope of the government's involvement.

2. The Elementary and Secondary Education Act of 1965 funded the purchase by school libraries of children's trade books. For UN's assessment of the impact of federal funding on her own department, see letter to Millicent E. Selsam, June 19, 1969, pages 273–75.

3. *A Baby Sister for Frances*; *Bedtime for Frances*; *Bread and Jam for Frances*, illustrated by Lillian Hoban, 1964; *Nothing to Do*, illustrated by Lillian Hoban, 1964; *The Sorely Trying Day*, illustrated by Lillian Hoban, 1964.

4. *The Mouse and His Child*, by Russell Hoban, illustrated by Lillian Hoban, 1967.

boat ride[1] should be fun—we're going to go down to the Verrazano Bridge. A box lunch, a bottle of wine, and authors beneath the Verrazano Bridge!

Be happy.

Love, your old fan,

TO ARNOLD LOBEL[2]   July 18, 1966

Dear Arnold:

It is so wonderful to think of you all up there having a beautiful summer. We have just come through A.L.A. week and we are all tired and glad the worst heat wave ever is over.   During the A.L.A. I got into one of the elevators at the NY Hilton with one of the Harper men who was on his way to our booth at the convention. The others in the elevator were not library people. The Harper man said to me with the sweetest smile, "Oh Ursula, I just love *Martha the Movie Mouse.*[3]" "Darling!" I cried. "Isn't she <u>darling</u>?" The others looked sort of fearfully at us.... as we rode upward.   Anyhow, everyone loves the book and we think it really looks enchanting and we are hoping you are as happy with it as you deserve to be!

I have *The Great Blueness*[4] right here by my typewriter every day, and I keep thinking that what bothers me about it will float

1. As entertainment for the many children's librarians who would be visiting New York for the American Library Association convention in July, The Children's Book Council chartered a boat for a daylight harbor cruise. A contingent of authors and illustrators, including several published by Harper, was also invited to mingle with the librarians. UN, who did not enjoy events of this kind, managed at the last minute to bump her head, and did not make the trip.
2. See footnote 4 to letter to Helen L. Jones, January 23, 1964, page 171.
3. *Martha the Movie Mouse*, by Arnold Lobel, 1966.
4. *The Great Blueness and Other Predicaments*, by Arnold Lobel, 1968.

up to the top of my mind, and that I will be able to write you a good letter. But I am not smart enough right at the moment. Have you any ideas? This can be the most brilliant book, beautiful and amusing. But why does it bother me that if everything is blue and then everything becomes yellow there ought to be a combination which makes green too????? Barbara Borack[1] and I have been enchanted with so much of it—some of the Wizard's remarks are perfect.   I think that we're (the reader) not quite sure if this is a book about this particular Wizard and what happens to him or what he causes to happen, <u>or</u> a book about color. I think it should be the former and believe you think so too. But as it stands now it is sort of confusing. Charlotte [Zolotow], your big fan, thinks this seems sort of a negative approach to each color. Could everyone love the blue, and then the wizard fools around and gets yellow, and then everyone is even happier at the blue and yellow and green world, and then he gets red, and everyone loves the etc. etc. world. ?????   I hesitate to make suggestions (even if I had any brilliant ones) because I think that if you give this some more thought you will come up with the perfect solution. I do think that you should try to keep it to 32 pages INCLUDING FRONT MATTER.   On the other hand, if you come up with a perfect solution we can certainly go to a longer book. I thought perhaps the limitations of 32 pages might help.   Please don't be discouraged.   In a letter I started to you last week and threw away as hopeless, I wondered if one of the problems isn't that you've made the wizard's activities cover the entire world instead of just a small and mysteriously black and white part of it. And he somehow brings colors back into it. ??????   Would this be any sort of a handle?   It might make the whole thing beautiful and also give it a happy cozy quality children love.   Anyhow, you'll work it out.

1. Editor; author.

We will get the contract drawn up and sent to you in a few days. But what to put down for the delivery date????? Hope you are all well and I know you're happy. Love to you and Anita—and the children too. I will return your dummy but want to keep it for another day or two in case .....

TO ISAAC BASHEVIS SINGER   July 19, 1966

Dear Isaac:

Thank you for your letter of the 14th. I am so glad, we all are, that you will write more children's books for us. To see *Zlateh the Goat* taking shape, becoming a book children (and their parents) will read and love for generations has been a tremendous experience for me. I think your stories have inspired some of Maurice Sendak's very finest work. All of us in the department love your book, and we are so glad that it is on our list. I think that it is going to bring you a special sort of happiness too. You've wondered why Sendak didn't do adult books. And once you asked me if I wouldn't rather be an editor of adult books. But most adults are dead and beyond hope after the age of thirty, and I think with *Zlateh* you will find a new and marvelous audience. God knows too many children's books are routine, cynically produced, coarsely promoted. But *Zlateh* is a complete success artistically. I am sorry to go on in this rather emotional tone but we are all exhausted from the (pointless?) activities of A. L. A. week and I can't help it!

Maurice will be thinking about the Chinese story[1] and I know that will be another magnificent book. Please please

1. Sendak eventually chose not to illustrate the story referred to here, which was published as *The Topsy-Turvy Emperor of China*, by Isaac Bashevis Singer, translated by the author and Elizabeth Shub, illustrated by William Pène du Bois, 1971.

always let us see anything that your commitment to Farrar Straus permits.[1] Of course we understand your loyalty to them. I was awfully fortunate that when I longed to find and publish some good and beautiful stories about Hanukah and/or other mss. with "non-Wasp" backgrounds, Charlotte Zolotow remembered that Libby [Shub] knew you, and asked her if she wouldn't talk to you about the possibility of doing something for children. So it all has worked out beautifully, and if it brings more beautiful children's books by you to the Farrar list, well, I am going to be happy about that too! Especially as you write that you will continue to give some of your stories to Harper.

Affectionate greetings,

TO LOUISE FITZHUGH   August 8, 1966

Dear Louise:

Thanks for your good letter. Love the picture of you hard at work. Good! We are all longing to read the *Sport* mss.[2] We sent the contract to Pat Schartle today, with a Sept. 15 deadline. Glad deadlines make you feel needed because you are. I may knit you a sweater with some embroidery saying LOUISE FITZHUGH'S WORK IS NEEDED—but you'd have to have a chest as vast as god forbid mine to give enough room for such a long statement. Well, I'll think of something.

Interested to hear you may buy that house[3]. It is a great place. Are the taxes terrible? I wouldn't dream of giving you my opinion, because it wouldn't be worth anything, really. (Your

---

1. Farrar, Straus & Giroux published IBS's books for an adult readership.
2. *Sport,* by Louise Fitzhugh, Delacorte, 1979. This novel was published posthumously. LF died of an aneurysm in 1974.
3. LF bought a summer house on a bluff in Cutchogue, Long Island.

letter is at home and I'm in the office so I can't be sure how much of my opinion you were actually asking ......) Anyhow, it is a wonderful place and I'm sure whatever decision you come to will be the right one.

Glad you have the model for Sport and that he, the 11 year old, has fallen in love with you. But how do you feel about him? Maybe you will cut Morticia and her brood[1] off at the pass yet.????

The books are on their way to Mr. Lloyd. I don't mind taking care of any details. But if you want the name of our most efficient office manager, it is Miss Barbara A. Dicks, and she puts things through promptly and with accuracy, while I have a tendency to file things away in my handbag.....

I hope that the news from Memphis doesn't get any worse[2].

You said you were thinking about coming back to town, and mentioned the back to school excitement. How fascinating! I never felt anything but utter horror at the thought of back to school, when all those sinister name tapes came out..... Well, enough. Loved hearing from you. Glad you saw the Sacred Brother's house[3].

Love to you all

P. S. Meant to say, your mother wrote me the most charming note. Said she'd loved meeting some of your friends, etc., and loved being introduced as your mother and Harriet's grandmother. Said she'd never been so proud in her life.

---

1. The reference is to Morticia Addams, mother and wife of the outrageously ghoulish "happy" family created by cartoonist Charles Addams, then being featured on a popular television sitcom.
2. LF's parents divorced when she was a child. The previous year, her father had died. Now, her stepmother was ill; she died in March 1967.
3. LF had no brothers or sisters; it's not clear who was being referred to here.

TO MAURICE SENDAK   August 25, 1966

Dear Maurice:

How is everything with you? Barbara [Dicks] tells me your brother-in-law has to have an operation. I am so sorry and hope it isn't too serious a problem, and that he recovers quickly.

I've thought of you often since you went to Fire Island and hoped that you were getting some good relaxation after all the tensions over *Zlateh*. And of course I hope you've been able to write and get some of the wonderful exciting things in your head down on paper. No need to answer this, Mister Senlak. It is just a line to say I hope you are well, and productive, and enjoying sun, sea, and sand.

We're awfully sorry to lose Phyllis Fogelman[1]. But this is a big opportunity. What with Catherine O'Dea to Dutton, Mary Russell to Bobbs, Janet Loranger and Elizabeth Shub to Scribner, Susan [Carr] Hirschman to Macmillan, I am beginning to feel like the head of a woman's training school. Well, at least none of them ever learned anything bad here.

Take care. Be well. Be happy. We'll rush *Zlateh* to you the moment the first perfect (?) copy comes in.

Believe me ever your fan with regards

Ersella Norstratt

TO LOUISE FITZHUGH   September 2, 1966

Dear Louise

I just read in *Time* or *Newsweek* or *Life* or one of those avant garde journals I devour, about a teacher who writes haiku for

---

1. Fogelman, senior editor in UN's department, left Harper in late 1966 to become editor-in-chief of children's books at The Dial Press.

the children in her class, and she tries to inspire their creativity and get them to write their own, 3 lines, 5 syllables 1st and 3rd lines, 7 syllables 2nd line. And to help the little dollings she sometimes gives them the first and second line out of her own whimsical adorable head and then they fill in the third line. I was practically ill reading about it. Anyhow, one two line thing she presented was the following whimsicalness:

> At the class Picnic
> My friend, Curiosity,

and the little girl who had to fill out the third line put down

> Ate six sandwiches.

Thank god for anyone under 12 years of age. Then everyone goes to pieces. It made me think of Harriet, and that made me think of you, and I thought I would just write you and tell you about it, and say I hope all is well out there.

Love,
Ursula
Old Yorkshire Mother

TO NAT HENTOFF   November 7, 1966

Dear Nat:

Glad to hear from you this morning. Whatever you do, the fantasy or a new teen-age mss.[1], we'll be delighted to see it in the spring. Or sooner. As I told you, we don't want you to worry about any sort of taboos. Just so the book is good, or preferably perfect. It is fine if you want to write about a boy who prefers to go to jail than to join the service... If the story is good, if the

1. NH did not publish another book with Harper.

characterizations are good, then it will always have continuing interest and appeal. What we know you are NOT interested in doing is something that would have topical appeal only if rushed out while the subject is news-y. But a young person having to make some sort of a moral choice is great—

Hope all is well with you. This has been in my typewriter since the day before Election Day, and this morning everything is very depressing. I dreamed about Ronald Reagan[1] last night..... much help that is. But isn't everything awful .... So hurry and write more GOOD books for young people and help the world to get better...

Yours

TO EDGAR AND ANNABEL JOHNSON[2]

December 2, 1966

Dear Johnsons

Have a letter from you on my desk, but this isn't in answer to that. I will write again soon. This is just a note to say we are sending you a copy of *Douglas*[3]. This is a "teen age" novel we published this year and I would love to know what you think of it. I enclose a starred review from *Kirkus*, and have just learned that it is to receive a double-starred review in *Library Journal* in a month or so. We haven't as yet heard from more than a few young readers but those who have read it liked it a lot. Maybe you will find it of some interest. You can see I don't want to stop our exchange of thoughts on books for young adults......

1. Reagan had just been elected governor of California.
2. Married co-authors of novels of history and adventure about the American West, and much later also of science fiction.
3. *Douglas*, by Grace Richardson, 1966.

I still wonder what put you off so about *Harriet the Spy*. Was it the fact that she spied that disturbed you? I think most of us have forgotten the awful things we did or wanted to do when we were 10 or 11 or 12. I was brought up with the most stern drilling of what was right and wrong, kind or mean, thoughtful or inconsiderate, etc. etc., and never tell a lie no matter what. And to this day I would love to read other people's mail and listen to their telephone conversations if it were not for this hideous conscience, well—mustn't get into one of those long wandering letters. But you are all for vigor in children's books and *Harriet* seems to have such vigor and life.   ?????

Hope you are both well and that you have a good productive happy winter

ever affectionately,

TO MAURICE SENDAK   December 6, 1966

Dear Maurice:

You said to send you any questions we had about *Higglety etc.*[1] so here are a preliminary few. First of all, the wonderful thing about this mss. is that the whole thing is quite clear in your head; you have the basic plot all solidly developed. So the only thing left to do is to be sure that what you want to say is said clearly. And you can be sure of that if you answer any questions that occur to you and/or to us. We know you want us to feel free to ask even questions which may seem very dumb. Which I will now proceed to ask a few of:...... On the very first page, is it clear early enough that Jennie intends to go on a trip? You make it beautifully clear that she had all those lovely things,

---

1. *Higglety Pigglety Pop! or There Must Be More to Life*, by Maurice Sendak, 1967. MS modeled Jennie, the canine heroine of the fantasy, on his own dog of the same name.

pillows and windows, and drops, and "he even loved her" but that she "didn't care." However, at luncheon when you first told me about the whole book wasn't the idea that she, nevertheless, in spite of all she had, wanted to go on a trip, very basic? Would you want to add just a short sentence to the first paragraph, just before the sentence beginning "In the middle of the night she packed...."   This may sound like a silly question, "the trip idea is implicit in packing," etc., but I thought I would ask it anyhow.

On Page 13 is it clear enough that they are and <u>have right along</u> been actors in the World Mother Goose Theatre? And that Jennie herself has been in it, so to speak? I am floundering here, but it was all very clear in your mind at luncheon.

One general question: On Page 6 Jennie tells the maid that she has two windows that she left at home. This is a marvelous touch. Would she at other times and places have thought or mentioned other aspects of her previous home, or even thought of the person mentioned in the first chapter? Not often just two or three times?

Why does she say "I am very discontent." ?? If she really feels discontented wouldn't she say "discontented" rather than the faintly literary "discontent"?? But, much more importantly, <u>is</u> what she feels really <u>DISCONTENT</u>? You go on to have her say "I want something I do not have" and that gives the feeling, doesn't it? The feeling of vague longing for she knows not what .... as the poet hath said....? But "I am discontent" seems to have a touch of pettishness, poutiness, does it not?

I know you know we are raising any questions, tiny or large, just because you said we should feel free to do so.

I love this book, Mr. Sendak, I just love it. We know it is going to be funny and beautiful and warm and good with perhaps a touch of classic sadness ..... and that is about all for today, dear sir.

I wondered why the baby turned into that big round-ish Mother Goose and I think Ellen [Rudin] wondered too.   Well these are just a few thoughts and questions to put in the back of your head.   More later. We will keep a copy of the mss. close at hand.

As ever with admiration,

TO MAURICE SENDAK   December 30, 1966

Dear Maurice:

Cass [Canfield] let me see a copy of your letter to him, and his reply to you. It was so darn sweet of you to write him such a good letter, Maurice, and I know such words meant a great deal to him. He is such a fine person. And your letter was so beautifully expressed it brought tears to my eyes. So thanks for being the way you are.

And thanks, dear friend and valued author, for the clipping about Beni[1] in London. I have always thought the Royal Family is Jewish too so I am sure some suitable gala can be arranged while you are in London. But of course even the gentiles do you honor. So how can you miss?

I am going to be out of the office next week but hope to have good news of you, Jennie, drawings, soon after I return. And I also hope that the doctors can do something for your Mother. This has been a terrible time for the Sendaks

1. Montresor, winner of the 1965 Caldecott Medal for *May I Bring a Friend?*, by Beatrice Schenk de Regniers, Atheneum, 1964, was in London for the Royal Opera House production of *Benvenuto Cellini*, for which he had designed the sets and costumes. The gossip columnist Suzy Knickerbocker reported in the *World Journal Tribune* that the artist was being lionized by everyone in the British capital from Mary McCarthy to Princess Margaret.

and we all send you sympathetic thoughts.

I understand the galleys for *Higgledy* [*sic*] will be in a week from Monday, the week I get back. I look forward to rereading them with a fresh eye and a rested head. It is going to be a superb book and every word only has to be perfect.   Are you still wildly enthusiastic about the title??? It may be just exactly right; I just am asking.

I wish you the greatest of everything in 1967. And thank God the Christian holidays are over this year. Everyone on the streets is snarling and scowling and pushing and shoving and hating. So God rest you merry. You will be as always a bright light in the lovely New Year ahead so far as Harper is concerned.

Yours,

TO DORIS K. STOTZ[1]   January 11, 1967

Dear Miss Stotz:

I hope the *Horn Book* reprint[2] arrived safely and that you found some of the material interesting. I am afraid I have been very remiss in answering your letter about wanting to observe Mrs. Wilder's 100th birthday, but your letter came at a particularly confusing time here. Our department is moving (within the same building but to larger quarters) and we have been working in the midst of cartons, shouting, hammering workmen, and incredible noise in general. We are only now getting settled.

I would like to write an article for you, but let me tell you

1. Editor, *Top of the News*, a publication of the American Library Association.
2. The December 1953 issue of *The Horn Book* featured articles by illustrator Garth Williams and others about the Little House books, which Harper had reissued in a uniform edition that year.

in this note the little bit you asked about in yours. And if any of it bears retelling perhaps I can put it into some sort of more formal shape. But I know you don't want anything padded and windy.... and I honestly think that maybe I haven't enough to say to make even a short article.

You asked a lot of questions, and I will try to answer them. After I became head of this department in the early nineteen forties I began to wish we could re-issue the Wilder books in a new and uniform format, and with new illustrations. When the first couple of manuscripts came in to Miss Virginia Kirkus, then the head of the department, she quite understandably selected Helen Sewell as artist. Miss Sewell was, during the thirties, one of the country's most distinguished illustrators. However, her style was extremely decorative and stylized, and as Mrs. Wilder wrote more books the Sewell pictures seemed to me less and less suited to these forthright realistic frontier stories. Also, as time went by Miss Sewell became too busy and then too ill to do all the illustrations herself and so she found a collaborator, a Miss [Mildred] Boyle, who worked on the pictures with her. All in all, by the time the eighth book was published, *These Happy Golden Years*[1], I did feel that eventually we should prepare and publish a new edition. The finding of the right artist was, as it always is, a terrible problem. Garth Williams had illustrated his first children's book, *Stuart Little* for us, and as I came to know him and his wife and daughters, and as I saw more of his work, I became convinced that he could do the perfect pictures for a revised format. He is British and certainly had no roots in any part of the Wilder country. But as we know, thought-kin is closer sometimes than blood-kin, and Garth certainly had all the emotional equipment, as well as the technical, to illustrate these wonderful family books. Well, he

---

1. Originally published by Harper & Brothers in 1943 with illustrations by Helen Sewell and Mildred Boyle.

agreed to do it, and then he and Dorothea, his wife, and their children made the long and careful trip through Kansas, Wisconsin, Minnesota, all the Wilder country, as he tells in his *Horn Book* article.

We had another reason for wanting to re-issue the books. The first four were in a larger format than the last four. I think that Miss Raymond, Virginia Kirkus' successor, thought that the last four appealed to an older age group, than did the first four. At any rate, we wanted to make the size uniform as well as find new illustrations. I may say that the first person I talked to about the new pictures was Virginia Kirkus, and she approved the project and understood our desires. I showed her Garth's pictures and was so happy to find that she was just as enthusiastic about his contributions as we were.

You wrote me about the impact of the books, their lasting quality. The impact has always been and continues to be enormous. Every day we get letters from children (boys as well as girls) many of them addressed to Laura, and all of them referring to the events in the books with great urgency. "Laura, if I'd been you I would have kicked that mean Nellie Oleson." Perfectly wonderful letters.

By the time I came along the Wilder books were well launched and I never met Mrs. Wilder. As a matter of fact I think Miss Kirkus never met her either. The first manuscript I read, when I was Louise Raymond's assistant, was *On the Banks of Plum Creek* and I remember reading it with a big lump in my throat, it was so beautiful. The flap copy for it was the first I ever wrote, and I was terribly nervous and worried about it, I remember that[1]. None of the manuscripts ever needed any editing. Not any. They were read and then copy-edited and sent to the printer.

I remember once when we wanted to have an exhibit of the

1. See UN to Laura Ingalls Wilder, September 9, 1937, page 3.

Wilder books, or take photographs, or something, I wrote Mrs. Wilder and asked her to send us, insured, anything she thought would be of interest. She sent us Pa's fiddle! I stood in the middle of the department holding Pa's fiddle and hardly able to believe it! I looked inside and saw the name AMATI. Goodness, how exciting that was.   And Mrs. Wilder sent us the quilt Mary made after she went blind. We were thrilled but all in a great state of tension until those things were finally returned to Mrs. Wilder.

Is any of this of any interest? If so is there time for me to put it in the form of anything? Even a more formal letter????? Do please forgive me, Miss Stotz. My New Year's resolution was that I was going to be calm, efficient, poised, but I am starting out 1967 the same old inefficient hectic way.   More later about your letter about that panel with Miss Vestal[1] and Miss [Margaret K.] McElderry.

Sincerely,

TO MARY STOLZ

January 12, 1967

Dear Molly:

It is so hard to believe that you want to make this break after all these years[2], after all you and Harper have meant to each other, without even opening my letters, without even talking about it. If it is destructive to your mental peace to read a letter from me, or to talk over the phone even briefly then certainly you must not even try. The most important thing is your work. If you can no longer write for Harper or for what it

1. Jeanne Vestal, vice president and editor-in-chief, J. B. Lippincott. The panel discussion took place later that year at the annual convention of the American Library Association.
2. MS soon changed her mind and was back working with UN.

has come to mean to you (and this is so hard to understand) then of course you must go elsewhere. But isn't there some sort of if not happy at least possible medium? If you were so disturbed about the farm mss. reception here, as you were about our feeling about *Jungle Club*, can't you and Roz[1] and we come to a perfectly amicable agreement that you should send them elsewhere? And let us publish the mss. about the two little girls at camp? Need it be this complete break? Now if a complete break will make you happy and creative and relaxed, I will be the last to give you the slightest bit of argument. But will it make you happy? This department is not just me, if I am the one who is the target right now. This department and this house is full of people who value you, now and in the future as in the past. From Chris through all the sales department right up to the president's office. I know authors can grow resentful if they think a publisher is getting "possessive," and I don't want to say anything that will sound as though that is how we feel about you. But we have valued you and we have valued your work for 17 or 18 years, and I hope you can understand why I feel I must at least hope that you will at least read this letter.

The letter you returned to me unopened was written before I had yours about your resignation as a Harper author. There was nothing in it to upset you, and I hope there is nothing in this one to upset you. Are you really going to be happy to leave us completely? Unless you are going to be completely happy won't you reconsider? I have certainly not shared all this sadness (of mine) with everyone in this department, but the few who do know are just as eager, anxious, as I am to see you or to see your manuscript again. We hope with all our hearts that you will not make this final and complete break. I know Roz and we can work out arrangements which will be right for you. We want to, Molly. We want to try to make you happier than you

1. Rosalyn Targ, MS's agent.

have been recently; can't we both remember that we did make you happy in the past and can't we try to do the same in the future? You can see I, or editorial we, have no false pride and as I told Roz the candle is in the window and will remain there.

As ever,

TO WILLIAM PÈNE DU BOIS   January 23, 1967

Dear Billy:

Alice Kenner assures me that corrected galleys, folios, titles,[1] etc., will be sent to you the first of next week. Do hope all reaches you safely.

The new office is fine but I cannot decide on what color for the draperies so I sit here in a bare white-walled barracks type chamber with piles of unread manuscripts—very odd. Come home soon and help me decide on a color. Of course I don't have much choice—we have to make our selection from one place and why I am telling you all this which is of no conceivable interest I do not know....

Well, they had a memorial service for May Massee[2] and I went but I think May would not have liked it much. They had it at the Community Church on 35th Street and the man who spoke was sort of an actor-ish type who read poetry with embarrassing elocutionary effects. Oh awful I thought. I didn't know the word "beauty" could be pronounced in so many different

1. Most likely for *The Horse in the Camel Suit*, by William Pène du Bois, 1967.
2. The founding editor of The Viking Press' children's book department, and before that the founding editor at Doubleday. Massee, who came of age in publishing during the 1920s, was widely regarded as the dean of her profession. UN and Massee, who regarded each other with mutual respect as friendly rivals, occasionally exchanged copies of their authors' latest books.

rather I mean rawther affected ways. It was all terribly depressing. I hope the gent who officiated isn't one of your dearest friends—but I am sure he couldn't be.   I guess you were away when May died—on Christmas Eve in her sleep. Sic transit. One of the things I liked about her was that she did beautiful books but she also knew right down to the last decimal point exactly how much the binding costs would be per unit.....
It was always very engaging.   Poor lady, 84 and she couldn't see to read any more.

Do write me soon about *Pretty Peggy*[1] and let me know when we can see the manuscript. Have you chosen the third sin as yet? How is everything at the Three Horse Shoes Inn? What do you do every day? I mean, what is a sample day like? You have breakfast in your room, downstairs? What do you eat? I am dieting madly so details of food are always welcome.....

Write me soon again and tell me about the new manuscript and your life over there in Leek, Staffs.

Love,

TO ——————[2]   May 1, 1967

Dear ——————:
Thank you for your recent letter about "controversial literature" for children, with particular emphasis on *Harriet the Spy* and *The Long Secret* by Louise Fitzhugh.

---

1. *Pretty Pretty Peggy Moffitt*, by William Pène du Bois, 1968. This book, the second in a series loosely based on the theme of the seven deadly sins, concerned the young heroine's vanity. The next book in the series, *Porko Von Popbutton*, 1969, gave the artist's interpretation of gluttony.
2. UN's correspondent was doing research for a graduate-seminar paper in elementary education.

You ask about our future plans for publishing controversial books; we have no taboos, within the limits of good taste. We think that any subject of interest to young readers can be treated, by a creative writer, in books for young readers. It is difficult to find the writers; but if we can find writers who will write the manuscripts, we are sure the children will welcome more vigorous books. And we think there are enough perceptive and sensitive librarians, teachers and parents to help us get them to the children.

As for your comments concerning these books, I remember clearly the day I read the manuscript of *The Long Secret* and came upon the part devoted to Beth Ellen's first menstruation. I wrote in the margin, "Thank you, Louise Fitzhugh!", for it seemed to me it was about time that this subject, of such paramount importance to little girls of Beth Ellen's age, was mentioned naturally and accepted in a children's book as a part of life.

I am sorry to say that we cannot give you Miss Fitzhugh's home address, but if you would like to write to her care of this office, we will forward your letter to her. Since we do not handle direct orders for our books, I cannot send you a copy of *The Long Secret* c.o.d. However, if your bookstore is unwilling to order a copy for you, we will be glad to do so upon receipt of your check for $3.95.

Yours sincerely,

TO JOHN STEPTOE[1] June 19, 1967

Dear John Steptoe:

We were all very very happy the day you came in to see us,

---

1. African-American author and illustrator whose career began, to great acclaim, with the publication of *Stevie*, when JS was eighteen years old.

with your excellent pictures[1]. We think you are tremendously talented and we are delighted to think that your first book will be for us[2]. You will be hearing from Mrs. Colchie[3] that we want very much to have the chance to look at your sketchbook. And she or Miss Ellen Rudin will be in touch with you about your doing a jacket sketch for one of our books. We want you to illustrate a book for us (as well as write many of your own) but to start out with perhaps a jacket would be the best thing for you to do first.

I am leaving tonight for a two-week business trip to California. I will be back in New York July 5th and I hope you will come in to see me soon after that. I was deeply interested in what you told me about someone's mother baby-sitting and I think you should try to turn this into a picture book of your own. The first thing to do is prepare a very very rough dummy. I talked to you about this the day you were in but I will repeat it now. I suggest you take 16 sheets of paper 8 by 10 (say) or 10 by 8 if you prefer. And make a 32 page dummy, starting on the first right hand page as Page 1 and ending on the last left hand page as 32. Allow one page for a title page, one for a copyright, one for a half-title, or dedication, and start the story and pictures on the double-spread made by pages 4 and 5. I think the ideas you expressed so well, and the feeling you managed to communicate to me though it was very late on a very tiring day, could well make a fine picture book. And never forget that what you told me is something ONLY YOU know about; no one else knows just what you know about anything. And that is why it will be so important for you to put down your thoughts and

1. JS, who was still a student at New York's High School of Art and Design at the time, had come without an appointment. A member of UN's staff who reviewed his portfolio recognized his great talent. JS returned days later to meet with UN, who was also impressed both by JS personally and by his artwork.
2. *Stevie*, by John Steptoe, 1969.
3. Elizabeth Colchie reviewed portfolios for the department.

emotions in picture book form.   Even if the first dummy you make doesn't seem to have a great big "plot"—don't worry. It is the emotion which is important. And we will gladly go over it with you whenever you want, go over the dummy I mean, and offer any suggestions we can.

Your mother told Mrs. Colchie that you have a job but we hope that after the school year is over you will be able to take some time to work on your own book. We will want to give you a contract and an advance just as soon as you can show us something in rough dummy form.   Again, we are so glad you came to see us, and we look forward to seeing a great deal more of you and your work in the future. Excuse this hasty letter. I am rushing to get it off before I leave for California.

Yours sincerely,

Please thank your teacher[1] for suggesting that you come to see us. If you will give us her name we would like to thank her too!

TO E. B. WHITE   September 6, 1967

Dear Andy:

Thanks for your letter with the revisions for the brochure. As Nancy Young[2] wrote you, I was away or would have acknowledged it myself. The new material is just fine and of course you will see a proof of it as soon as possible. It is so lovely to have the children continue to write about your two wonderful books. I keep hoping that one of these days the third will come to us. Nothing would make me happier.

1. Naburma Buris, a teacher at the High School of Art and Design, had urged JS to show his work to publishers.
2. Secretary to UN.

I went to a convention of librarians and saw a lot of good souls there and I met a lot of teachers, too. I was really amazed and pleased to discover how many of them (teachers) know and use some of the good children's books—especially your two. One teacher told me that she'd had a principal who didn't care what she did with her students as long as she "got them through the Cumberland Gap by Thanksgiving." But, she said, she was trying to stand firm and trying to use books imaginatively with her students. Or scholars as you put it. She said she had one class of "culturally deprived" you should excuse the expression youngsters, and she was supposed to "teach them Emerson's essay on Friendship." She said it was a lost cause so instead she read them *Charlotte's Web* which, she stated, does everything Emerson could have done...... She put it better, but I thought it was a good idea and wanted to tell you about it.

We long for another E. B. White book.

I hope you and Katharine are all right and that the summer has been a pleasant one for you. I went to Maine for the first time the end of August, drove along Route 1 from Yarmouth to Bangor and fell in love with everything.

No need to acknowledge this scrawl—we'll send you the proof soon. I am sorry that summer has sort of slowed us up here.

Best wishes to you both.

TO MARY CALHOUN[1]   October 9, 1967

Dear Mary:

Your letter of Oct. 4th just arrived. You were sweet to write me so quickly, and so openly. I loved everything you wrote. But

1. Author of picture books and novels.

I couldn't have said in that enormous illiterate letter of mine "don't give too much of yourself away." However I put what I tried to say, I didn't mean that. I read something in a book about Shakespeare's sonnets that I've never forgotten—about "the economy of the closed heart,[1]" and I don't believe in the closed heart whatsoever. I think it is death. I keep a little scrap of paper with part from that book in my handbag and quote it to you now "The open heart must give itself away in order to maintain its existence" (what you say in your last, actually) "It is confronted with a perpetual dilemma: it can know of its being only through self-loss. The alternative is to conserve itself until it has withered away." There's more too but the scrap of paper is so old I can't make it out. I guess what I meant was that it is fine to give freely from the open heart, but just try to save yourself a little block of peace and quiet for your own work. But this must sound very contradictory. I hate a closed heart. I know that when I have an unsuccessful day at my desk it is because I simply haven't loved people and books and pictures enough. That sounds fatuous but I don't know any other way to say it. I do rather envy you your religious faith. Especially about life after death.

Your household sounds perfectly fascinating, and I know how rich and rewarding life must be for all of you, with the bad as well as the good.

I hope Ellen [Rudin]'s letter has reached you and that you find her comments[2] helpful. And I am glad to know you have other ideas bubbling too—as you put it. Let us hear from you when you have thought over Ellen's letter, we must be in touch. I think all this bad time is behind us, I certainly hope so, and I believe you must now be convinced of our deep interest in you

---

1. The passage quoted is from *The Sense of Shakespeare's Sonnets*, by Edward Hubler, Hill and Wang, 1962, page 101.
2. MC was at work on a manuscript titled *Magic in the Alley*, illustrated by Wendy Watson, Atheneum, 1970.

and in your work. Thank you again for your wonderful letter. It meant a lot to me.

We've sent Sendak's *Higglety Pigglety Pop* and I hope it arrives safely. You're right, he didn't have any idea of what he was writing (on a symbolic level) until he had it all thought out—or felt out would be more accurate. In San Francisco I told Mary Lee Keath[1] all about Sendak's book. If you see her tell her Jennie (his real dog) died a few weeks after he came home from England. She was much moved by the story. I like Mary Lee so much!

Affectionately,

TO JOHN STEPTOE   October 17, 1967

Dear John:

Thank you for coming in the other day with the revision of the story about Stevie, and the beautiful pictures. We have typed up the handwritten script[2], and I enclose a carbon copy for you to keep. Please reread it and see if there are not places where you would like to tell a little more. I want to keep a copy here for a few more days and I will go over it and suggest some possible additions which you might find interesting. I remember when I asked you if Robert's mother needed the money which boarding Steven would bring in, you said well she would have taken him anyway just because his mother was a friend, but that the money that Steven's mother would pay her would "help out." I think that this is a little touch which would characterize Robert's mother and which would be good to add. Once again, John, I am not interested in any single thing but

1. Head of Denver public school libraries.
2. UN typed JS's manuscript herself.

· 244 ·

what is IN <u>YOUR</u> HEAD. That first day when you talked to me I was so happy because I felt you could and would write and illustrate your own lovely warm original book. And you will, and it will be as close to perfect as you can make it, I know.   So any letters I write you or anything I say is never never even to try to foist any ideas of my own on you. Please believe that. I have the greatest respect for you as an artist, young as you are. I know you know what you want to do and all I want to do is recognize it <u>when</u> you have done it. You haven't quite got the words right yet but I haven't a doubt in the world that you will get them right. And then with your marvelous pictures there will be a beautiful and glowing book.

Please excuse all these words. I do get a little over-emotional but I can't help it.

Now it is October 19th. I have kept this around a couple of days wondering if it is an all-right letter to send, but I will send it anyhow now and trust you to read it the way I mean it.   I will be in touch with you soon about the manuscript but if you have any additional ideas send them along, or bring them in. I am always delighted to hear from you.

Very best wishes,

TO ELSE HOLMELUND MINARIK   October 19, 1967

Dear Else:

Hope everything is all right with you. Did you get my letter about the birds' house idea for a book?

I was simply delighted to hear over the telephone that you had seen a flying saucer. I look forward to a detailed description of exactly what you saw, how it acted, what you said, etc. etc. This is the best news I have had in a long time.

Maurice is working on the black line drawings for *A Kiss for Little Bear*[1] and I know it is going to be one of the loveliest books in the world, or in any world. (It's too bad they discovered there is no possible life on Venus, isn't it.... I just read that in the morning paper. It's been a rotten day all around if you want the truth.)

Nothing in this letter except just to ask how you are and to say I hope you are writing another mss.

Love,

TO MARY CALHOUN   October 30, 1967

Dear Mary:

Thank you so much for your fine letter of October 24th. I found it of absorbing interest, and I am so glad to have it. First of all—I think that most people in the western world do believe in God, do have faith. And you most surely do have things to say to your readers. So don't doubt that for one split second. Perhaps I shouldn't have written you as I did—it must seem awful for someone responsible for publishing books for children to admit to having no faith. But religious or not I operate from a moral (sometimes stuffy about it too!) base and I think all good children's books have to be moral in the truest sense.   I wish I could feel the way you do, and maybe one day I will. The story of my religious beliefs is a long one and not particularly interesting even to me[2]. But I remember well some words in a book I read a long time ago about a little boy who had had complete faith in God, who prayed, and whose prayer

1. *A Kiss for Little Bear*, by Else Holmelund Minarik, illustrated by Maurice Sendak, 1968.
2. UN's mother brought her up as a Christian Scientist.

was not answered, and he had to face the fact that God had "failed" him. (I am simplifying the situation just to get to the words). He then felt anguish—"that anguish that sleeps all day on the heart like a heavy worm, and wakes up at night to feed." Isn't that terrific? I think the book was *Story of an African Farm*[1].

Your description of Leon[2] and the bishop and the lively discussion was marvelous. And I enjoyed reading about it. Yes, that statement to the Hebrews is beautiful. Thank you again for writing me, Mary.

Ellen [Rudin] is still on jury duty but I am hoping you can get some good thinking and good work going on *Alley* even so.

To repeat—most everyone I know does believe in God. I am sure Mary Lee Keath does—for just one example. I used to be very religious too, as a matter of fact. And maybe I will become so again. But I can't see that it takes courage not to believe. I find the "world so various, so beautiful, so new"[3] that I don't have to count on having all this and Heaven too. Though it would be lovely… But I mustn't write any more about this. I am so afraid of writing seriously in this area that I may tend to sound flippant and—I was about to say "God knows" I am not at all flippant about it.   Anyhow, thanks for your letter. I hope all is going well with you and yours.

Affectionately,

1. *The Story of an African Farm*, by Ralph Iron (pseudonym of Olive Schreiner), A. L. Burt, n.d. (first published in 1883), page 11.
2. MC's husband, the Reverend Leon Wilkins, an Episcopal minister. In a letter to UN dated October 24, 1967, MC described a conversation with a visiting Episcopal bishop during which they had discussed the nature of faith. She then quoted the following lines from Hebrews 11:13, citing them as one her favorite passages from the Bible: "These all died in the faith, not having received the promises, but having seen them afar off, and were persuaded of them, and embraced them, and confessed that they were strangers and pilgrims on the earth."
3. UN mixed two quotes together, making her own rhyme. The first passage comes from Matthew Arnold's "Dover Beach"; the second is from Matthew Henry's *Life of Philip Henry*.

TO RUSSELL HOBAN   January 30, 1968

Dear Russ:

Right after I talked to you this morning a copy of the coming Sunday's *N. Y. Times* arrived, with the enclosed review of *Mouse and Child*. It is respectful but not enthusiastic, for which I am very sorry. I had luncheon with George Woods yesterday and talked, among other things, about you and your work. He likes so much of it though he did not like *Mouse and Child*. Well, you and we disagreed about much that you wanted to keep in that book, Russ, but we lost out in some of our requests. And maybe you were right and we were wrong. After all it is YOUR book; and I've always been interested in seeing you explore and experiment....

As I said on the phone, the content of the first chapter of your father-son story is fascinating but the treatment seems to me to be purely adult in its appeal. But send in at least another chapter. Maybe it will turn out to be a classic adult book which will be taken up by some younger readers—as was *Catcher in the Rye*[1].

But your big THING is the powerful emotional content of your very best books—even the seemingly most simple picture book. When you get cerebral don't you lose <u>some</u> of that Hobanity? At least think about this Russ. You must know how much I think of you and of your work, and I hope you know how much time I have spent really wondering what is the "right" thing to say to you..... So don't get irked with my remark about when you "get cerebral"....

I had a good time at luncheon with you. I have loved the inside of your head for a long time now and am always interested in it. But maybe more so in the heart????

1. J. D. Salinger's famous novel is widely credited with having inspired the genre of the realistic young adult novel, which UN did much to champion.

Oh I wish I were more cerebral myself so I could write you a neater, better letter, with tidier thoughts.....

Love,

Eager to see new Frances![1]

TO LAVINIA RUSS   February 7, 1968

Dear Lavinia·

It was such fun seeing you at luncheon; you make such sense and also look so pretty. Grand combination. You did not talk too much about problems. I enjoyed everything. No, I do not circulate all letters, dear. I use some judgment .....

What I want to say to you today is that I love you all the more for your confession about not loving *The Hobbit*[2]. It is one of the several books I have tried my best to read but I simply could never get in to it and I have had to hide my shame, but now I can admit it in view of the fact that I will have your distinguished company. Bless you, Mrs. Russ, and long may you rave.

Ever affectionately,

TO JOHN STEPTOE   February 20, 1968

Dear John:

I have been wanting to telephone you and ask you to come to see me, but have kept putting it off[3] because I have not been

1. By hand on original.
2. *The Hobbit, or There and Back Again*, by J.R.R. Tolkien, Houghton Mifflin, 1938.
3. UN's previous letter to JS was dated November 27, 1967.

sure of what I really wanted to say about the manuscript, and I didn't want to take a chance and say something wrong. I have just shown the rough dummy and your beautiful color pictures[1] to our new Art Director, Ladislav Svatos, and he is as enthusiastic about your work as I am. I hope that one afternoon next week you will come in after school and meet Ladislav and hear some of his ideas.

The main thing I gained in talking with Ladislav, after all these weeks of thinking and worrying, is that I think we should think of your beautiful book not basically as a picture book for very little children, but as a storybook for slightly older ones. Ladislav helped me clarify my thinking a great deal. You worked out the dummy of alternate black and white spreads with alternate color spreads very well. But now I am beginning to think, with Ladislav's help, that maybe the book should have no more than 6 or 8 color pictures, and no black and whites at all. He sketched out for me a more or less solid page of type, with a color picture opposite it. Then to follow that perhaps two facing pages of type. Then a color spread. He is tremendously enthusiastic about your pictures and feels they are so powerful in their effect that 6 or 8 might well be the maximum.   Well, I am very excited this afternoon and think that after this long wait we are ready to be of a bit more help to you than we have been up to now.

I hope that you and your family are well, that school is being as interesting as possible. And I look forward to seeing you again. I think you will like Ladislav Svatos, John. He is a Czech and very sensitive and appreciative, and he is tremendously looking forward to meeting you.

Best wishes as ever, and again apologies for this long silence, but I think it has been worth waiting for time to pass

---

1. Work continued on *Stevie*.

and to get Ladislav's reactions.   Do call me as soon as possible and let's set a day for you to come in after school.

TO PAT SCHARTLE   February 29, 1968

Dear Pat:

I am so glad you and Louise Fitzhugh came in this after-noon to talk with Ladislav Svatos. I think and sincerely hope that he and Louise established a good relationship for the present and for the future. We want her first picture book[1] to be as close to what Louise has in mind as possible. I think Ladislav's suggestions will help her attain what she wants and that his technical advice will be helpful now and in the future.   I hope that both you and Louise saw what a lot of involved thinking and figuring does go into a book of this sort before a publisher can tell just what they can say to an artist.

Next day—March 1. Well, left this helpless effusion in my typewriter overnight as my brained[2] turned out to be dead after our long meeting. (One of my handicaps is that I hate to dictate and type out most of my own letters. Sorry.)

It is awful to think that Louise feels we aren't interested in her picture books, or however she put it to you. Charlotte [Zolotow] and I have been given some very rough ideas but many of them seemed to interest Louise not nearly so much as her next book (full length book) which she and we thought was going to be *Sport*. (I believe we have a contract for this.) And as we too felt that *Sport* and a new one about Harriet (of which she

1. *Bang Bang You're Dead*, by Louise Fitzhugh and Sandra Scoppettone, illustrated by Louise Fitzhugh, 1969.
2. In the margin of the carbon copy to be circulated within the office, UN wrote: "Freudian error! I felt I had been brained."

has about 80 pages written, I believe) would be the best ones for her to spend time on, we did not urge her to try to revise any of her picture book ideas—several of which were amusing but not as yet close to anything publishable. At any rate, we do want to assure you, and if possible through you we want to assure her, that we are as always and forever deeply interested in any and all of her ideas.   It was awful to realize all over again what a bad state Louise is in, and I hope she felt calmer after you and she left. We will always do everything possible, Pat, to give her what she wants. I could see in the meeting yesterday that she would be absolutely unable to contemplate anything less than full color through[out] and so we will go ahead with this—with her pre-separating the black and indicating the colors on blue bristols which Ladislav will supply to her.   I am awfully glad she could understand our feeling about the black plate. Your presence was valuable to us all, of course.

Do urge Louise to come in or send in the pencil sketches and the manuscript so that she and Ladislav can select type and we can have the manuscript set. This is in no way an effort to impose our ideas on hers, or to try to restrict her freedom. (I am sure I need not say this to you, but there it is anyhow.) We simply want to be sure that everything turns out the way she wants it to. Any publisher in the world would want to have the chance to see some preliminary pencil sketches and to have a hand in choice of type, suggestion for perfect placement, etc. etc.   Pat, we do awfully good picture books—most importantly the children do like them, for the most part, and want them reread and reread. And then they do get recognition from experts in the field of design—we usually lead all other publishers at the Institute of Graphic Arts[1]. We do have a good feel for picture books—as those we have done by Maurice

---

1. The reference is to the American Institute of Graphic Arts' annual list of fifty distinguished books.

Sendak (who by the way has come in and shown me his preliminary dummies ever since his first book for us) and Tomi Ungerer and Garth Williams prove.   I am protesting, I know—and I will cease shortly. But I am really so disturbed by Louise's feeling toward us and I know we cannot reason it away, but I wanted to share some of my thoughts with you since she does not want to be in touch with us.

I fear she will feel threatened if Ladislav wants me to look at the pencil sketches and the suggested placement of the words. But of course, Pat, I will have to see them. That is what I do here. I think Louise feels easier with Charlotte but good editor though Charlotte is she simply doesn't have the technical experience, as she would be the first to admit. Once I thought Louise might be more comfortable with Ellen but then Louise told me (or Charlotte, I don't remember) that though she likes Ellen she thinks of her as being so much younger that she would keep having that in mind.   Well, forgive this long rambling letter. I won't even reread it but just send it off and trust you to understand the spirit in which I write it—concerned, eager to do whatever I can to see Louise's work come as close to perfection as possible, nervous, ungrammatical. And as ever worried.!

Let's talk next week about the contract. I am going over figures again with a sharp pencil. I hate to put a list price of $4.95[1] on the trade edition but I am afraid it will be necessary. Well, we'll talk next week.

Best wishes, as ever

1. The book was published with black-and-white illustrations, at a retail price of $3.95, which was average for the time.

TO ———————— *a school child*   March 19, 1968

Dear ——————— :

Thank you so much for your letter asking us to publish some more books like *Where the Wild Things Are*. We think this is a fine idea and have sent your letter to the author, Mr. Sendak, in the hopes that he will like the idea, too.

We enjoyed your letter and appreciate your taking the time to write to us.

Yours sincerely,

(memo)   March 27, 1968

TO THE DEPARTMENT FROM U. N.

Maurice Sendak telephoned me yesterday to read the following by William Blake. (Yes, THE William Blake):

"The bad artist seems to copy a great deal. The good one really does copy a great deal."[1]

Very interesting, we thought.

We must plan for the talk Sendak is going to give us and selected guests on the whole subject of imitation in children's books.

1. Blake wrote this comment in the margin of his copy of Sir Joshua Reynolds' *Discourses*. Blake was reacting to the author's views on originality: "How incapable those are of producing anything of their own, who have spent much of their time in making finished copies, is well known to all who are conversant with our art." *Selected Poetry and Prose of William Blake*, ed. Northrop Frye, Modern Library, 1953, p. 450.

TO SHEL SILVERSTEIN[1]   May 1, 1968

Dear Shel:

It was a real pleasure to have you telephone today. I have missed you a lot. You are one of my very favorite people and you are a rotten no-goodnik to disappear for such long periods of time. Not even a postcard, you rat.

It is great news that the poems[2] are turning out to be so warm and good and generally great. And I am interested to hear that you think you are not necessarily the right artist to draw pictures for them. As you request, I will certainly get in touch at once with Maurice Sendak and tell him you remembered your talk once long ago on Fire Island, and that you would be overjoyed if he would consider illustrating the book. As I warned you over the phone today, Maurice has told me many times in the past year that with few or no exceptions he wants only to write and illustrate his own books. But of course there always may be an exception, and of course you might conceivably be it. I think a book of poems by you with drawings by Sendak would be simply fine, and I will certainly talk or write to him about it. He can't say anything, of course, until he reads the poems. That is unless he flatly says No at once, and doesn't even want to read the poems. I can but ask and that I will do. But please send me as many of the poems as you can and as soon as you can. We are going to have our sales conference later this month and the longer you wait the more hectic things will be here. Anyhow, I am longing to see them, sales conferences quite aside. I need a good shot in the arm, so far as kiddie boox are

1. Poet, author, illustrator, songwriter, and playwright. UN had seen SS's cartoons in *Playboy*. Tomi Ungerer was instrumental in arranging for a first meeting between the artist and editor.
2. SS's next book would be *Where the Sidewalk Ends: Poems and Drawings*, 1974, which he chose to illustrate himself after all.

concerned. I am sort of in the dumps so help get me out of them. (God an editor will stoop to any sort of appeal, yes?)

You sounded good and happy over the phone. I'm glad. Are you in love again, God forbid? Enjoying the Hefner swimming pool[1] and the bunnies? No need to answer this, Shel. Just hurry and send me copies of the poems as soon as you can.

Love,

TO JOHN STEPTOE   May 3, 1968

Dear John[2]:

I telephoned your home today as I have been sort of worried over not hearing from you. I have your pictures and the most recent version of your manuscript on my desk all the time, and I keep looking at the beautiful pictures and hoping we can get going on some final plans for the book itself. So I wondered if you had moved and if your Mother could give me some news of you as I sent a registered letter to Camden several weeks ago. I was so very glad to hear from her that you are back in town. I hope you are feeling very much better than you were the last time

---

1. The teasing reference is to SS's association with *Playboy*, published by Hugh Hefner.
2. At the head of the office carbon of this letter, UN typed the following: "Sent to his Brooklyn address. Note: I telephoned his home today and got his mother. I said I'd been so worried because I hadn't heard from John, and she was very sweet and friendly. She said John had returned to his home and was living at home now. He is still out of school but promises to go to night school in order to finish and get his high school diploma. She said he had upset them all terribly but that she thought he was in a better state of mind than he had been when he left home and went to get a job in Philadelphia. She said she and her husband appreciated Harper's interest and belief in John, and promised to ask him to telephone me early next week. I begged her not to let John think I had telephoned her just to 'check up on him' and said I was simply and sincerely interested in his great talent. She couldn't have been nicer or more understanding, and I am glad she and I are in touch."

we talked, John. You are tremendously talented and the world is never an easy place for a person as talented as you are. But you know your work is IMPORTANT. And ever since I first saw any of your work it has become extremely important to me. To many of us here.   I am still hoping that you will come in maybe next week and talk with me and meet the new designer I wrote you about, Ladislav Svatos. He has some good ideas for the layout which, I believe I wrote you, I think will be helpful to you and also to me as I try to advise you on the manuscript itself. We would like to get the book in shape so it can be published in 1969 without fail, and with all that color work to be meticulously reproduced we need to give the printer lots and lots of time. So do call me up and come to see me, will you? Won't it be great to see your own book, written and illustrated by you, bound and in the bookstores? And children looking at it and loving it, and looking at it again and again? I can hardly wait myself!

It will be very good to be in touch with you again. I have really missed you and the little talks we used to have.

Best wishes as ever,

TO JOHN DONOVAN[1]   June 21, 1968

Dear John:

We'd be delighted to read your manuscript "about a kid with love problems."[2] I'm going to be away on vacation during July, but please send the manuscript in and it will be read in my

---

1. Attorney turned author; executive director, The Children's Book Council.
2. *I'll Get There. It Better Be Worth the Trip.*, by John Donovan, 1969. JD's realistic novel, set principally in New York, concerned a thirteen-year-old boy's longings for love. It shattered a taboo as the first novel for young readers to contain a scene sympathetically describing a homoerotic encounter between boys and the complex feelings surrounding the experience.

absence and then I will read it myself as soon as I return. It sounds extremely interesting. I have been waiting a long time for a manuscript that includes "buddy-love problems" and it will be fine if you are the one to do it successfully.

We look forward to receiving your manuscript early in July. All the best.

Yours,

TO JOHN DONOVAN   August 5, 1968

Dear John:

Thanks for sending me the carbon copy of your manuscript. I am glad to have this as I want to reread the book myself and I also want Charlotte Zolotow to read it.

I hope that when you went over the original copy of the manuscript you found that some of my marginal notations made some sense. As I said at luncheon, I think that not all the places marked need work, but if you do some of them (give the actual conversations in some of them) the other parts marked will seem perfectly all right.

I know you don't want to hit your readers over their heads, but we do think you can make it clearer, more vivid, that David does suffer from considerable worry and guilt feelings. I completely missed the fact that you meant his seeming casualness to be bravado. And then the final talk with the father needed work, needed deepening and broadening. We can talk about this. But I should also tell you how really excellent so much of it is. I put complimentary remarks in the margins too, as I hope you noticed. It is so well written, and all the school stuff is so good, and the friendship with the little boy on the bus. Perhaps we hear just a bit too much about the mother's drinking. But I want to reread it, as I said. I read it in one swift gulp my first evening back after vacation.

I hope you will be able to do the necessary work on it pretty soon, John. I don't want even to try to rush you, but we'd like to have the ms. in final form well before you leave in September. And I want to be sure that when you are ready to let me see it again it comes at a time when I can drop everything else and read it immediately. So keep in touch, will you, as you see how work goes?   As I said at lunchcon, we're going to meet a lot of resistance to this book and we will be eager to fight that resistance as intelligently and gracefully as possible. I was so glad to gather from everything you said that you want to work to make it the very best book it can be. This letter is growing stuffier with every word I type so no more for now. But I am very glad you wanted to write this book, and I am glad that we have the opportunity to publish it. I think it is going to mean a lot to a lot of young readers, if we can just get it past the adults who buy their books!

Best regards,

TO JOHN DONOVAN August 8, 1968

Dear John:

As I told you over the phone yesterday, we appreciate your doing the revisions so quickly. I reread the whole mss. and think your additions improved it tremendously. I hope you feel happy about them too. Also the few deletions you made helped. Look, if you feel strongly about that scene with Fred's body[1] you keep

---

1. The reference is to a dog run over by a car.

it in. I do not believe in the omniscience of editors! Ferd [Monjo] and I may be quite wrong about thinking it weakened the impact of the earlier scene at his grandmother's grave. Well, there will be plenty of time for you to put it back in, or part of it, or decide to leave it out. Whatever you decide.

I still have a few reservations about a few places, and also a few real worries about others, and we can talk more about them. I want to be sure that I understand what is in your mind, what you think you're saying, before I make a few additional points. But let's not get tense about any of this. I never want to ask you, or any author, to pull punches and if I still flinch over his calling his mother a ball-buster it is because for your sake and ours we want to secure the widest possible acceptance for this book. And why handicap it unnecessarily? Well, we'll talk. Meanwhile, I think the conversations you added are all simply fine and I am particularly happy about the ending.

I am trying to write a letter to Dr. Ilg[1] of the Gesell Institute. It would be good if she would read the manuscript (of which I now have two xeroxed copies) and give us an advance quote to put on the jacket. I will remember your suggestion of Mary Calderone[2] too. Ferd thinks, and I think he is right, that we should get someone in the field of psychiatry to give us a quote too. Charlotte Zolotow has just read the manuscript (the carbon copy of the original version) and even without your changes she is tremendously enthusiastic about the book and very glad that we are publishing it. I am sure that this is going to be an interesting experience we are about to have, you and us. But if it helps even a few tormented youngsters feel a little less frightened all the problems will eventually seem

1. Dr. Frances Ilg, director, Gesell Institute of Child Development, Yale University.
2. Dr. Mary Steichen Calderone, authority on sex education; head of SIECUS (Sex Information and Education Council of the United States). Dr. Calderone did not provide a quote herself but referred UN to others who did.

insignificant. (It says here, in small type.....)

More later. Be thinking about another manuscript.

Best regards,

We must have the <u>perfect</u> title.[1]

TO DR. FRANCES ILG[2]   August 8, 1968

Dear Dr. Ilg:

We are going to publish a novel for twelve to fourteen year old readers, and I wonder if you would be willing to read it in manuscript form and give us the benefit of your opinion of it. It is about a 13 year old boy, the son of divorced parents, who goes to a private school in New York City. The story includes a homosexual experience with another 13 year old, and we think the author has been successful, for the most part, in making real the boy's burden of guilt and worry after this experience. The author has done some revision, at our suggestion, and I hope to be able to persuade him to do a little more. But of course I would be grateful for your opinion and if you like the book as a whole, we would be so glad if you could give us a quote we could use. I do not need to tell you that the book will meet with considerable resistance with certain influential persons in the children's book field. Yet surely this is an experience many boys have, and one that worries and frightens them badly. It seems strange that a curtain has been drawn over this entire subject in fiction for young readers. Our book will be the first. And of course I want

1. By hand on original.
2. FI responded enthusiastically, providing a comment for publication that read in part: "In *I'll Get There* a moment of sex discovery is told simply but poignantly. . . . It is how he absorbs this experience (or any experience) that becomes the key to what will happen next. Davy is able to face the experience and to make his choice."

to do everything we can to get it past the adults and to some young readers who may read it with some recognition and some relief. It breaks my heart to think how such an experience can torture a boy. Forgive the emotional tone of this! The book was written by John Donovan, the widely respected executive director of the Children's Book Council here in New York.

Would you be willing to read the manuscript?

I hope all is well with you. I have always enjoyed my few glimpses of you and I wish our paths crossed more often.

Yours sincerely,

TO RUSSELL HOBAN September 24, 1968

Dear Russ:

How are you? Haven't heard from you in ages and I hope you will write me a note and bring me up to date on your news, your family and your work. Come have luncheon one of these days? Most days I have a sandwich at my desk and I am getting darn tired of that routine, so let's go to luncheon together at some fancy restaurant .....

Best Friends for Frances[1] will be on the 1969 list and I am wondering what you and/or Lil are planning for the next one. How are you doing on the proposed novel about the father and his son?

I haven't seen the royalty statements yet—even though they are due by October 1st. We are all going to miss the Federal funds[2] but good children's books will go on selling somehow (it says here in small print) and we will have to grin and bear it

---

1. *Best Friends for Frances*, by Russell Hoban, illustrated by Lillian Hoban, 1969.
2. The financial burden of the escalating war in Vietnam had taken its toll on federal funding for the purchase of children's books by schools and libraries.

without the lavish Federal spending. If this damn war would just come to an end (NOT just for the Federal dough!) Are you depressed about the election? I have just figured out the way I can vote this year and be very happy. I will vote for Muskie against Agnew[1], and that should do it. I am so sad about Humphrey; he was such a great guy. All the lines of disillusion that I remember from my dramatic teens come back: "Roses have thorns, and silver fountains mud."[2] "Men are we, and must mourn when even the shade of that which once was great is passed away."[3] "The region cloud has masked him from me now."[4] Etc.

So drop a note. I hope you all had a good summer. I had 4 weeks of sun and swimming and enjoyed it thoroughly.

Love, and to Lil too of course.

TO ZENA SUTHERLAND[5]   February 24, 1969

Dear Zena:

I've just caught up with your piece in the Feb. 22 issue of *SR.* Good for you! Everything you said needed saying and you

1. The reference is to Senator Edmund Muskie of Maine, who ran as Hubert Humphrey's running mate on the Democratic ticket in the presidential election of 1968, and to Spiro T. Agnew, who ran as Richard M. Nixon's running mate on the Republican ticket. Humphrey's unwillingness to disavow the Johnson administration's Vietnam War policy left UN grasping for reasons to vote for the Democrats.
2. William Shakespeare, Sonnet 35.
3. William Wordsworth, "On the Extinction of the Venetian Republic, 1802." The exact quote reads:
   > Men are we, and must grieve when even the shade
   > Of that which once was great is passed away.
4. William Shakespeare, Sonnet 33.
5. Author; contributing editor, *Saturday Review*; editor, *Bulletin of the Center for Children's Books*; professor in the Graduate Library School at the University of Chicago. In 1972 ZS became children's book editor, *The Chicago Tribune.*

said it just exactly right—strong and graceful and firm.[1] Congratulations. And thanks for the reference to my indignation....I have just remembered that when I was young I loved the inscription on Jonathan Swift's tomb—ubi saevo indignatio cor lacerere nequit. Can I be remembering it correctly after all these decades?[2] Anyhow—where the savagery of my indignation can lacerate my heart no longer. Bettina H. can still lacerate my heart .... So patronizing. Anyhow, just a hasty note to say we all think your piece was terrific.

Love to you and Alec[3]....

Did you receive my earlier personal-type letter???

TO CLIFTON FADIMAN[4]   March 17, 1969

Dear Mr. Fadiman,

Thank you for your note about *Journey from Peppermint Street*[5]. We did indeed publish the book and Meindert DeJong was awarded the National Book Award for it last week. It was

---

1. In a piece titled "The Persuaded Muse" in the February 22, 1970, issue of *Saturday Review*, pages 46–47, ZS criticized Swiss publisher and author Bettina Hürlimann for having stated in *Three Centuries of Children's Books in Europe* that the eminent writers of adult literature who occasionally wrote for children were to be thanked for setting higher standards for the full-time authors of children's books. UN, like ZS, rejected Hürlimann's premise as both naive and patronizing.
2. Almost: *Ubi saeva indignatio ulterius cor lacerere nequit*: Where savage indignation can lacerate his heart no more.
3. ZS's husband.
4. Author, editor, and anthologist; member, editorial committee of the Book-of-the-Month Club.
5. *Journey from Peppermint Street*, by Meindert DeJong, illustrated by Emily Arnold McCully, 1968.

the first National Book Award made for children's literature. Under separate cover we are sending a copy of the book to you, book post special delivery.

With all best wishes,

Yours sincerely,

P. S. I'm sending you Shel Silverstein's book, *The Giving Tree*[1]. This was published several years ago and though it was one of my favorites (and children like it[2]) few reviewers noticed it. Since publication, however, it has become increasingly popular and sales are steadily increasing. Ministers write me that they use it in sermons. I thought you might be interested in seeing it. It is a far cry from Shel's work for *Playboy*. But it shows how hard we look for creative talent to present to children—most of whom are so creative themselves.

TO GERTRUDE B. HERMAN   March 18, 1969

Dear Mrs. Herman:

Thank you for sending us a copy of your letter to the *Ladies' Home Journal* in which you disagreed with several of Dr. Bruno Bettelheim's statements.[3] We were pleased to know you wrote to the magazine about the article and quite frankly we agree with you. The article surprised and dismayed many of us also.

---

1. *The Giving Tree*, by Shel Silverstein, 1964.
2. By hand on the circulating copy: "I hope this but presumptuous of me!"
3. In his regular column in the magazine, Bettelheim, the well-known child psychologist, criticized Maurice Sendak's *Where the Wild Things Are* for its potential for frightening children with the image of a mother prepared to withhold food from her child. GBH, an assistant professor in the Library School of the University of Wisconsin at Madison, faulted Bettelheim for condemning a book that he acknowledged not having either read or observed in use with children.

It is unfortunate the article will reach so many adults with "normal" children who might love the book, when one of Dr. Bettelheim's main concerns has been "disturbed" children.

Again, we appreciate your interest in *Where the Wild Things Are* and thank you again for sending us the carbon of your letter.

Yours sincerely,

TO JOHN STEPTOE   April 2, 1969

Dear John:

Today I signed the print order for the first edition of *Stevie*, and I was so very happy to be signing that particular print order! I do this on every book for the first edition, and usually it is quite a routine part of my job. I mean, the quantities have all been settled, the format has been settled, and the list price has been determined. But today when I signed yours I had an especial feeling of joy. This is the beginning of a very wonderful career, in painting and in books too. Again, I am very proud that your book is on our Harper list.

I keep hoping I will hear something from you about *In Harlem*[1]. I know you have problems in your own mind about how much you want to say in this book, and I hope that when you have worked them out you will let me hear from you. And, of course, if you ever think that talking about some of your thoughts and problems will help, you have only to telephone me. It is always a great happiness to me to see you, John.

The proof of the picture of you in the mirror turned out very well. We'll send you a copy. Loretta[2] will, of course, receive credit.

1. JS's second book was published as *Uptown*, 1970.
2. Loretta J. Farmer, whose photograph of JS appeared on the jacket of *Stevie*.

Best wishes, and do let me hear from you when you can about *In Harlem*. I want very much to give you a contract on it as soon as we have just a little bit more to go on.

As Ever,

TO VIRGINIA HAVILAND[1] (MNC)   April 8, 1969

Dear Virginia:

I've wanted to write you for ages—for several reasons. Mainly to thank you again for the note you wrote me about John Donovan's book. I must say that the reception it has had so far has been heart-warming. Even *Kirkus* gave it a star and a very perceptive review! And so we are happy and I must admit a bit relieved. I suppose we'll get some crabby notes from East Cupcake, Iowa, but so far there has been nothing but appreciation for and approval of the fine writing and the good storytelling.

Virginia, I can't wait to tell you the following: The young man[2] who inherited all the assets of Laura Ingalls Wilder's daughter, Rose Wilder Lane, came in a few days ago and dropped the casual remark that there is a NINTH WILDER MANUSCRIPT[3], written after *These Happy Golden Years*. I asked why in mercy's name we had never been given it and he explained that it covers the first year of married life for Laura and Almanzo and that there is a faint air of slight disillusion in it, which Laura's daughter thought not suited to the feeling of

---

1. VH, who had been a readers' advisor at the Boston Public Library at the time of the launching of Harper's I Can Read series in 1957, was now at the Library of Congress as chief of the Children's Literature Center, which she founded there in 1963.
2. Roger Lea MacBride, Rose Wilder Lane's adopted grandson.
3. *The First Four Years*, by Laura Ingalls Wilder, illustrated by Garth Williams, 1971.

the 8 published books. He has promised to send it to me as soon as he can get it typed. It is in Laura's handwriting. Isn't that exciting? A voice from the grave! How thrilling it would be to have a new Wilder book! Mrs. Lane died a few months ago and her heir apparently is willing to have us publish the ms. if it is really a finished one. I thought you would be happy to hear about this.

My mother is in town this week for a visit and we are having a good time, and keeping away from politics. She did say something about Nixon and I said I noticed he couldn't even throw the ball at the Senators opening game with the Yankees, and she explained to me that with the country in the terrible state it is in after the Democrats have been in office "we do not need a ball-player," and etc. etc. But otherwise everything is lovely.   I was sorry to have to miss the CBC[1] luncheon at which you spoke. Ellen [Rudin] and Barbara Dicks said they enjoyed your remarks greatly.

When will you be in town again? I look forward to our next visit.

Ever affectionately,

TO ZENA SUTHERLAND   April 18, 1969

Dearest Zena:

Such fun to talk to you the other evening. Among the many many oh Lord how many! temptations I face and resist (usually) every single day of my life are: Sara Lee Brownies, imported beer, subscriptions to new magazines, riding instead of walking, martinis, and now direct long-distance dialling. So anyhow I am

---

1. The Children's Book Council.

glad I gave in to the temptation to call you. I am delighted your incision is fine. And of course I am thrilled to hear you are mentioning Donovan AND the ninth Wilder in your May issue. Great great!

I have a copy of a fine review of John's book in the May 4th *Book World*. Very good. I also have a couple of nutty letters accusing me of probably being from Sweden where "everyone lives as cats anyhow" because I am publishing books "on homosexuality for children." One letter makes it sound like a "How to" book for heaven's sake. The letters are not numerous (two or three) but very depressing. John wrote to one insane woman that apparently some deranged person had got hold of some of her letterheads and was sending out letters on it, and returned the letter to her. He's a great guy.

Anyhow, so glad to hear about the May issue and I'm looking forward to it.

Lots of love to you both.

TO JOHN DONOVAN   April 18, 1969

Dear John:

Thanks for sending me copies of the letters about *I'll Get There*. Betty Johnson's[1] was lovely. And I was interested to read the hate one from California. I haven't answered that particular woman as yet and think I won't. Well, aside from these few insane letters and the cheese-y thing in Leonard Lyons column[2], everything looks great for your book, John. I really

---

1. Children's librarian, Lynn, Massachusetts, Public Library.
2. Writing in his nationally syndicated column "The Lyons Den," Lyons noted the "new uncensored sex trend" in popular culture had "invaded even the field of children's books."

couldn't be happier. And I thought I would write to tell you so. I have really appreciated you over these last months—now almost a year since you wrote me that first little note asking if I'd be interested in reading your novel. It has been a wonderful experience, and I can't write THAT to every author a few days before publication of his book!!!! I wanted to write you to thank you for being so great about making the changes you thought made sense, and for being so sound and un-hysterical about those changes we suggested which you thought did NOT make sense. You have been wonderful to work with and I appreciate you, and I hope this doesn't sound silly and that you won't mind my writing you this sort of fan letter.   The whole experience of publishing your book has been a most rewarding one for me. Everyone in the department was so FOR the book. And the salesmen and our Marketing Coordinator—everyone was so glad to hear about it at our Sales Conference. It is such a good book. So thank you very much for being such a good author, and thanks again for the beautiful pin which I wear often and which I love.

I was thinking about you this morning, and thinking I would like to write you a letter about what I was thinking, and then I thought oh no that would sound so dopey..... and then I remembered Wm. James' "Every time a resolve or fine glow of feeling evaporates without bearing fruit, it is worse than a lost chance. It works to hinder future emotions from taking the normal path of discharge."[1]

As ever,

---

1. *Talks to Teachers*, by William James, W. W. Norton, 1958, page 60.

Dear John:

I enclose xeroxed copies of the *New York Times* review and of the *School Library Journal* (if someone can find the latter which is going from desk to desk in the department.) A copy of the *Times* was sent routinely to you at the Council, but I told you I'd send you one to your home-away-from-home in good old Independence, Mo. I think the first part of the *Times* review is fine and that the last part is ridiculous. I don't know where "almost to the point of bestiality" is. I am sorry the whole review isn't as great as the first part, but I am grateful that on the whole it is a respectful comment.   Oh hell, the whole thing is ridiculous and I can't pretend otherwise. But I had been prepared for an all out damning review, by George Woods, so for this relief, much thanks. The *SLJ* is good.

Bestiality? I had luncheon with Shel Silverstein recently. I don't know if you know some of his children's books for us, or some of his stuff in *Playboy*. Anyhow, he is a great man and I love him. I sat next to him at luncheon and was so impressed with the sense of great at-ease-with-himself which he gave off. He just seemed to be hitting on all 24 cylinders. I was feeling particularly out-of-sorts and displeased with myself that day so I asked him for advice on how to get to be the way he is. "Have you had some psycho-therapy, Shel?" I asked admiringly. "How come you are just so great?"   "No therapy!" he said loudly, in the quiet restaurant. "Why should I? If I were hung up on goats why I would just find myself the sweetest prettiest cleanest goat in the world, that's what I'd do."   Heads turned and I changed the subject.....

I have you and Dave Ross to thank for being asked to be "interviewed" by John Wingate last week. Utter horror. I will tell you more when I see you. He hardly mentioned your book but asked me about the story about "the little boy who ate monsters." I finally identified this as *Where the Wild Things Are* and tried to set him straight. (Excuse the expression.)

Think about your next book.   See you on May 14th.

Affectionately,

TO MARY RODGERS[1]   June 5, 1969

Dear Mary:

As I told you over the phone, Phyllis[2] and Charlotte [Zolotow] and I were in hysterics when we finished the part of your ms. you sent us, and read the rough outline of what happens in the rest of the book[3]. I think it is going to be very very very good and funny and also touching. I adore Ape Face being mad for his sister underneath all his horribleness. Well, I adore great gobs of it. I can see I don't have to worry about bed and Father[4] because I gather it all takes place in one day and by bedtime she'll be back to being herself again. So I won't worry. (Personal news note: When I want to say to someone "how is your charming husband" I INVARIABLY say "how is your charming father?" So you can see why I got a little tense when she was in bed next to hers..... Why am I telling you all this, Genevieve????)

1. Author, screenwriter, composer-lyricist; daughter of composer Richard Rodgers and author Dorothy Rodgers.
2. Phyllis Hoffman, associate editor.
3. *Freaky Friday*, by Mary Rodgers, 1972.
4. In MR's off-center fantasy, thirteen-year-old Annabel Andrews wakes up one morning in her mother's body and proceeds to find out, over the course of a single day, what it is actually like to *be* her mother. UN worried briefly about how the author would handle a possible nighttime scene in which Annabel (if still in her mother's body) might find herself in bed with her father.

So just keep going, Mary, and for heavens sake finish it as soon as you can. It is going to be a marvelous book. I think it can be even funnier in the very beginning, but that may be because I read it with 1000 interruptions the other morning.

God bless Stephen Sondheim[1] for suggesting that I get in touch with you! We love *The Rotten Book*[2], of course, but this new one about Annabel is exactly the sort of thing we were hoping you would do, without having any idea of what it would really be. But I hope it is just the first of many longer "chapter" books you will write for us, Mary. The dialogue and setting are just PERFECT. Bless you, dear author, take care of your health, forget children and husband (there, got it right) and also that adult book, and WORK ON THIS MANUSCRIPT. We cannot wait to read the rest of it.

I wrote Candida[3] and sent her a copy of what you'd sent us and said we were ready to talk contract whenever she was. So more soon. Keep in touch. We love you. We need you.

Your fan

TO MILLICENT E. SELSAM[4]   June 19, 1969

Dear Millie:

Barbara Dicks tells me you spoke to her about current sales of children's books, and as this is a subject about which I have

---

1. Maurice Sendak had suggested that UN contact Sondheim, the Broadway composer-lyricist, about the possibility of writing a children's book. Sondheim proved not to be interested in doing so, but recommended that the editor approach Mary Rodgers.
2. *The Rotten Book*, by Mary Rodgers, illustrated by Steven Kellogg, 1969. This was MR's first children's book.
3. Candida Donadio, MR's agent.
4. Noted science writer for children.

been thinking a lot lately (mostly at three o'clock in the morning!) I thought I would send you a note. The Nixon Administration cut the Federal funds for books from 42 million to ZERO.[1] There is a lot of pressure being put on congress and on the administration to restore at least part of these funds, of course. But I doubt that we will get any of them back for a very long time, certainly not until after this disastrous Vietnam venture is concluded. So sales are down and I can't paint you a pretty picture and say they are not! However, we are adding some men to an institutional sales force and they, in addition to the almost 100 textbook representatives who promote our trade junior books in the schools, will be getting every bit of business possible for our department and our authors should benefit by that effort. The whole swing in the country is simply heartbreaking. The primary election in NYC is an example, also in Los Angeles and Minneapolis. School bonds are defeated over and over again in communities across the country. The whole trend is away from everything we've believed in. I hope the pendulum will swing back and <u>soon</u>. But in the meantime the no-nothings seem in control.

On a more cheerful note. In 1967 this department, and most other children's book departments, had the BIG year. Fiscal 68 was down a bit, and fiscal 1969 (our fiscal year closes end of April) is down from fiscal 68. HOWEVER, fiscal 69 is still higher than 1966, the year before the influx of Federal funds. Not much higher, but some higher. So we shouldn't be any worse off—the authors shouldn't—than before the Federal funds.

Have a good summer. You'll be hearing from Lucille[2] and

---

1. On January 26, President Nixon had vetoed as inflationary the pending appropriations bill of the Labor and the Health, Education, and Welfare departments. This action, which the House of Representatives sustained on January 28, dealt a mortal blow to federal support for the purchase of nontextbooks by schools.
2. Lucille Schultz, an editor who specialized in science books.

me one of these days about Bruno and other items. So happy about *Egg to Chick*[1]. We love your books, Millicent.

Affectionately,

Did I tell you George Woods of the *NY Times* is writing a novel[2] for us? And it is darn good. We are delighted. Other authors express mixed feelings!.....

TO GEORGE WOODS   July 18, 1969

Dear George:

We just talked on the phone but I thought I would send another note for you to have on Monday, or Tuesday if you take the Monday off to honor the astronauts[3].

As I wrote you yesterday, this is the time now for you to try to be patient and for Charlotte [Zolotow] and me to try to be very thoughtful and careful and sensitive in all our reactions. You can start your next book now. Why not? It is absolutely imperative that you write another book soon so you may as well start right now.

I was interested in your talk with Maia [Wojciechowska]. As I told you, she is one of my failures as an editor. I couldn't reach her. I couldn't do a thing to help make her get what was in her head onto the paper. Ellen [Rudin] is now her editor and is doing superbly well by Maia; but I couldn't do a thing with her.

---

1. *Egg to Chick*, by Millicent E. Selsam, had originally been published by International Publishers, with illustrations by Frances Wells, in 1946. In 1970, Harper & Row brought out a revised edition, illustrated by Barbara Wolff.
2. *Vibrations*, by George Woods, 1970.
3. The following Sunday, July 20, was the day that Apollo 11 astronaut Neil Armstrong was scheduled to become the first human to walk on the surface of the moon.

Interesting. I think that's one of the strengths of this department—we have editorial talent in depth and if an author doesn't want to work (or won't!) with one editor he or she can work with someone else.   Which brings me to Meindert DeJong again. I do appreciate your friendly and "loyal" reaction to his leaving me after I put in so much time and thought on marking up his mss. after *Peppermint Street*[1]. It was a terrible blow to me for I have loved his work over a period of a great many years, and I think I never gave him any bad editorial advice. But now I'm cooler and calmer about it all, and you be too. He is a complicated man and he just couldn't stand criticism at that point in his life and wanted to hurt me as much as he felt I had hurt him. Anyhow, I am more philosophical about it all than I was when we first talked about this, so you be too. I don't ordinarily put in as much editorial time and thought on manuscripts that are going to be published by someone else. But live and learn. If he wants to play Thomas Wolfe to my Maxwell Perkins, well, I'll live with it.   But back to you; get on with your next book[2]!   And, again, I was tremendously moved by the editorial[3]. Many thanks. I am always glad to see anything you have written, and this editorial is SPLENDID.

All the best, and if you get moody telephone Charlotte. See you soon.

---

1. There had been previous blow-ups between DeJong and UN, but this one proved to be the last. DeJong had resisted UN's editorial suggestions for the novel that was to follow his National Book Award–winning *Journey from Peppermint Street* on the Harper list. The author withdrew the manuscript and submitted it to Macmillan, which published *A Horse Came Running*, illustrated by Paul Sagsoorian, in 1970.
2. *To Catch a Killer*, by George Woods, 1972.
3. In the *Times* "Topics" column, GW had recently written a mood piece describing the onset of a storm.

TO STUART HARRIS[1] (*internal memo*)   September 3, 1969

Many many thanks for listening to all my ravings about John Steptoe's *Stevie*, and for sending it to your friends at *Life* Magazine. We are having a tremendous reaction to the *Life* piece, and it is making all the difference in the world to the success of the book. Really, we appreciate your efforts in its behalf.

TO GEORGE WOODS   September 19, 1969

Dear George:

Just hung up from our phone conversation. Oh I am so glad you got to talking about being on that bus, and wanting to sit with a girl, almost any girl, and being with the boys[2]. And wondering why—were you too skinny, was it your complexion, were you too much of a wise guy.   Go on thinking about that and write it down. It could be a great beginning—and serve to catapult the narrator into the sort of depressed, obsessed mood in which he begins to think about his entire life, and Bubsy. You amazed me when you said, "Maybe this isn't Bubsy's story, maybe it's mine." Honestly, George! Of course it isn't Bubsy's story! OF COURSE it is your story.   This explains a lot of things about you and the ms. to me.   But to get back to the 16 year old being lonely on the bus. As we said, you get sad if you are not loved, and you also get sad if you cannot GIVE love that you have to give. You know that. So don't forget it. It is important.

1. Advertising manager, Harper & Row trade books. *Life* magazine reprinted *Stevie* in its entirety in its August 29, 1969, issue. Steptoe's first book was also featured on several national television programs.
2. Work continued on *Vibrations*.

OK, you are not thinking about reviews, or sales, or anything but the best book you can possibly write. I am sorry people come up and ask you who is going to review it for the *Times*. And about what it is about. Too bad.

I am so happy about you and your books—there, Freudian slip. I meant to write book, but of course I know this is just one of the books you will write. Anyhow, think more about the beginning, and get down some of this great bus stuff you told me about over the phone.

I've had quite a morning. I just wrote a new author[1] (new to this list) that this week I've been absolutely bogged down in inventory revaluation, printing estimates, budgets for fiscal 1971, etc. And one particular mss. of only 17 pages I have been putting to one side all week because I was so preoccupied with the above business details. And this morning I came in early, in this beautiful weather, and read the 17 pages and it is utterly beautiful and I sit here in shimmering happiness over such a lovely manuscript, and I should have been remembering all this week that this is what it is all about. This sort of mss., and this sort of good talk we had over the phone this morning. I can cope with the inventory and printing prices, after all.....

All best, and all hopes.

---

1. Ned O'Gorman, poet and founder of The Storefront, a Harlem community center, had submitted a manuscript titled *The Blue Butterfly*, which Harper & Row published, with illustrations by Thomas di Grazia, in 1971.

TO JOHN STEPTOE   September 23, 1969

Dear John:

I enclose a review of *Stevie* which will appear in a forth-coming issue of *Library Journal*[1], a very influential magazine in the library field. The review absolutely puzzles me. But it ends up enthusiastically, so we can't complain, I suppose. But some of the review is really baffling. I don't know what she is talking about.

Sorry I missed you yesterday when you came in. I had such a rotten 2 weeks vacation of solid rain that I have been leaving early Friday and coming in late Monday for several weeks. I got here yesterday just after you'd left.

When we were talking not long ago about how you hadn't been doing any painting or any of the pictures for *Uptown* I said something to express my sadness, and you said that, all right, I could go ahead and "curse you out." John, I said then that I wasn't in any sense doing any such thing, nor would I even dream of trying to "curse you out." Maybe that was just a manner of speaking, and you didn't really mean it. I hope you didn't. Maybe one of these days you will be able to trust me a little bit. Maybe not. But I hope you will sooner or later.

Give me a ring, will you, and tell me when you'll come in and talk about some of the problems we might help you with? On *Uptown* I mean.

As ever your friend,

1. In a starred review the New York Public Library's Susan O'Neal found the book to have "universal" emotional appeal but questioned its authenticity as a story typical of the experiences of urban black children. *Library Journal*, Vol. 94, No. 18 (October 15, 1969), p. 3814.

TO MARGARET BLOY GRAHAM[1] September 23, 1969

Dear Margaret:

Glad you had an interesting summer—Vienna and Prague must have been fascinating. I am lunching with Maurice [Sendak] today and look forward to hearing his impressions of his trip.

I'm awfully sorry you think your mss.[2] is not in a shape right now to show me. I'd be delighted to see it, Margaret, and maybe you are wrong, you know. The parrot plus a dog would be a very tempting combination. Why don't you let us see it? Authors don't always know what is what with their work, you know. I remember one day Ruth Krauss brought in 5 manuscripts and had me read them while she sat by my desk and stared at me. I didn't like 4 of them but the 5th was the text of *Bears* (on half a piece of typewriter paper) and I went into hysterics and took it on the spot. "I think you are insane," Ruth said coldly.   And a good thing too.   So anyhow, send it along and let us look at it and maybe have a suggestion or two. We must come out with a second book by you and illustrated by you. Of course we certainly will remember that you are available for illustrating someone else's book. But it would be great for you to do your own.

Yes I'd love to see the drawings you mention, and the "bad Victorian poetry and fake Victorian children's tales." I don't know what department they'd be for—probably not this one???? But I am always glad to see anything and everything from you.

---

1. Author and artist. MBG was married for many years to author Gene Zion, with whom she collaborated on *Harry the Dirty Dog*, 1956, and several other picture books.
2. *Benjy and the Barking Bird*, by Margaret Bloy Graham, 1971. This was the second book that MBG wrote as well as illustrated.

Isn't the country in a terrible mess? My mother came for a weekend and all passed off happily until we both blew up—me against and Mother for President Nixon. I just can't bear it. How can my mother be for Pres. Nixon??? I'd think I was changed in the cradle, but I was born at home. No possibility of error!

Affectionate greetings from all of your friends here and write again soon.

TO JOHN DONOVAN   September 29, 1969

Dear John:

Right after I sent you my illiterate wail about Mrs. Sayers' idiotic letter about your book[1], I have received a copy of your reasoned, well-mannered, well-written reply to her. Well, you are just too great for me. I wish I could be like you but I can't be. You are so right in everything you wrote to her.   I once read something Goethe wrote to a critic of a stand he Goethe had taken (political). He said "But enough of this sorry theme, lest I lose my reason in attempting to reason about anything that is so thoroughly unreasonable."[2] Or to that effect. It must have been better in German.......

---

1. Frances Clarke Sayers, former superintendent of work with children at the New York Public Library (Anne Carroll Moore's successor in that job), had written JD privately to state her objections to the "new realism," of which she considered his first novel a prime example. Sayers believed that such books robbed children of the period of innocence to which they were entitled. JD wrote back that innocence was a luxury that most people in contemporary society could ill afford.

2. The quote is from *Conversations with Eckermann (1823–1832)*, by J. W. Goethe. In John Oxenford's more recent translation (North Point, 1984, p. 344), the passage reads: "However, not a word more upon this wretched subject, lest I become unwise in railing against this folly."

I am longing to hear Lavinia Russ tomorrow. Not to come to luncheon. But come to hear the talk. Is this a possibility? I will pay for the cost of the luncheon.......but not expect to partake or sit at a table. I understand the tickets are all gone and have been for several days. I should have realized that I'd want to hear Lavinia. Is there anything you can do? I will probably call you later today to find out. I will send this to you by messenger.

In the envelope with the letter to Mrs. Sayers was a perfectly beautiful BOGMAERKE[1]. I gather it is from you????? Thank you so very much, John. I really love it and I will use it (in all the dirty books I publish........)   I am just reading a new mss. by a well-known author on our list and she uses the word SHITTY in this manuscript. Are we ready for this? I don't even like it as a plain person, much less a publisher of children's books ......   Wait until Mrs. Sayers sees Sendak's new book[2]. His young hero appears <u>STAKE NARKID</u> from the front. Like, wow!

Love,

TO ———————   October 15, 1969

Dear ———————,

We are distressed to see how deeply you feel that *Bang Bang You're Dead* by Louise Fitzhugh is an inappropriate book for children. We are very conscious here of our responsibility to our readers, and it is our hope that each book we publish reflects that concern.

1. Danish for bookmark; UN was making a light reference to the fact that as executive director of The Children's Book Council, JD was in frequent contact with European publishers.
2. *In the Night Kitchen*, by Maurice Sendak, 1970.

The adult responses to *Bang Bang You're Dead* have been varied[1], but we have had only favorable reports thus far from children.

We appreciate your taking the time and trouble to write us, and we hope that you will accept, with our compliments, a copy of another Harper book which may be more to your liking. Under separate cover we are sending you a copy of *Someone Small*[2] by Barbara Borack. We very much hope you will like it.

Yours sincerely,

P.S. You will find enclosed the biographical information you requested.

TO LOUISE FITZHUGH   October 15, 1969

Dear Louise:

Glad to know you are working on a Harriet manuscript. It is longed for by all your fans. Really, we have never never had so many letters and requests for "another book about" anyone else. You say you "do not like to talk about it or even think about it" so we will say no more about it. But Ellen [Rudin] and Charlotte [Zolotow] and I just hope you know how much YOU ARE NEEDED!!!!

I am glad to hear that you are more settled and that you like Bridgewater[3]. No, I didn't know about Hubbell Pierce (whom I love) and I don't understand it about him or you because I read the "land transfers" in the paper with eagle eyes. As you say, it

---

1. The book, which was published at the height of the Vietnam War, had an antiwar theme.
2. *Someone Small*, by Barbara Borack, illustrated by Anita Lobel, 1969.
3. LF had bought a house in Bridgewater, Connecticut, where UN and Mary Griffith owned a weekend home that later became their permanent residence.

is all a most incredible coincidence. Where is Hubbell building? And where are you on Keeler Road? We are on—or rather off—Curtis Road which is on the other side of the town from Keeler. Yes, of course I will come to see you one of these days. You ask where we are so you can drive past, and I don't mean to sound evasive but it is rather hard to describe. Curtis is at the end of Hat Shop Hill, and our house is one of several on a little dead-end dirt (nameless) road off Curtis. It isn't something you drive past, you see. We have hardly any furniture, rugs, curtains. Two beds. Two chairs. A desk. We just rough it when we are there but sooner or later we will get more furniture and then I'll ask you over. Where are you on Keeler— oh I asked that. I am glad you still have the Cutchogue place for summers.

Yes, Maurice [Sendak] did hit George Woods with a rubber frankfurter sort of toy of Emily's[1]. George is now writing a book for us and I love him dearly as I dearly love all Harper authors. (But I am awfully glad GEORGE didn't hit MAURICE!!!!) The blows were struck at a hastily assembled party at my house for a visiting librarian who had the good judgment to leave early ..... I am told that another librarian turned to Kay Thompson (we are doing the next *Eloise* if it ever gets finished) and burbled: "Oh I love your Harriet books." Silence and the *Titanic* could crash and sink in seconds. The librarian went on: "Your wonderful books about Harriet and the Plaza."

Ellen and Charlotte send much love, and from me too. Write again.

---

1. Emily and Pocket were UN's two Yorkshire terriers.

Dear George:

As I just said over the phone, I wish you could—as you suggest—take a week off from your job and finish the work on your book. I know you can do it working nights and weekends, but it would go more easily if you could work without interruption for several days. I am sure it wouldn't take more than a week.   As I also said, I now am sorry I didn't go through and cut out the notes Charlotte [Zolotow] and I made that no longer have any relevance (!) now that the story is more the narrator's...... But I just didn't do what I should have done, and I am sorry. I am sure you will discover that many of the points are either very very small, or no longer valid in view of the revision you are doing. There are some good points which you will want to consider. Yes, CZ suggested "show" in a few places where I didn't see how it could be done any way but the way you wrote it. We do not consider ourselves infallible, need I say, and just wanted you to have our thoughts. Ignore what doesn't strike a sympathetic note.

I know how you feel about children's books and their "status." But I wouldn't change anything. Do you know that along with their big review space, and their big cocktail parties, and their big fat luncheons with literary agents, editors of adult books refer to something called MANUSCRIPTS FROM THE SLUSH PILE???? Isn't that utterly disgusting? Oh of course I wish authors and reviewers and bookstore personnel realized how important children's books (the good ones) can be. But if I had to choose, I'd never want that rotten adult book publishing world. I am simply chilled by many aspects of it.

I wish you would stop thinking about whether something in your book will make you look "too sensitive." And of course when you finish what you are working on these days, it will be some sort of catharsis. There isn't a thing in the world wrong with that.

Back to children's books, yes I am very fortunate at Harpers. But it wasn't always that way. We were once known as the Kiddie Book Dept. We got the short end of the production schedule. We were given the merest slice of time at the Sales Conference, when all the salesmen were hung over and the then-Sales Manager kept saying, "Ois, why don't you do some flats?" We were down-graded, to use your word. I fought and scratched and screamed and prodded the management. Maybe the same thing will happen for you at the *Times* eventually! I must have told you the old story of how I was patronizingly offered a job as an editor of adult books, "now that you have proved you can successfully do children's books."????? I almost killed the man. Well, maybe I protest too much. But I think not. I think there are tremendous compensations in our field. And I hate it when backbiting to compare with what goes on in the adult field begins to take over in our field. The children deserve better of us.

I reread that *Sounder*[1] review. You have remarked that I have never complained to you about any review, or the lack of any review. And I don't intend to start now. But oh is there any prettier sight in the world than the sight of someone sticking their neck OUT???

Yes, write me any time. You can write me to my apt. if you want. Or telephone. It is awfully hard to do what you are doing now. It was exhilirating [*sic*] and tremendously exciting for you

---

1. *Sounder*, by William H. Armstrong, illustrated by James Barkley, 1969, won the Newbery Medal for 1970. In her October 26, 1969, review in *The New York Times Book Review*, June Meyer Jordan questioned the appropriateness of the book for children and raised a number of questions about the novel's treatment of violence and attitudes to moral outrage.

to create and to recreate, and now the slow polishing must seem like sort of slogging. So be in touch.

All best,

P. S. Send in a chapter at a time, or 2 at a time—or however you want to do it.

TO MARY RODGERS   November 12, 1969

Dear Mary:

I enjoyed our phone conversation yesterday, when I called to read you the review[1] in next Sunday's *Times*.

By all means let us see as much of the mss.[2] as you have written. Then let's get together for luncheon and a talk. I am delighted by everything you say about it. Even the fact that you are thinking about the problem of ADULT PANIC indicates to me that the book is going to be even better than we thought it would be. (That is a problem, and I will be happy to talk it over with you when we meet.) How to treat it, I mean. Awful letter at the end of a wild day.....

I hope the no smoking, less coffee, etc., are continuing to make you feel fine and that work begins to come more easily. We're all funny bundles, aren't we. I am putting through a requisition slip for His and Her strait-jackets to hang up in my office....

Affectionately,

1. *The Rotten Book* was favorably reviewed in the *Times* as "fresh and fun."
2. Work continued on *Freaky Friday*.

Dear Nat:

One of the young people on our editorial staff, Phyllis Hoffman, just asked me if I thought you'd be interested in doing a biography of John Coltrane for us. Does that idea interest you? I don't know anything about his life but Phyllis does and thinks it might make a very good book. When you have a minute drop me a line or call, will you? Phyllis also told me she thought there might be a book in about five not-too-long pieces about some of the street-singers.   Of course I know our black brothers get very angry now if a white writer does a book about a black man! But this too may pass. One young militant fellow came in to see me with some pictures and he bawled me out because Wm. Styron[1] had written about Nat Turner and I got mad and told him I hadn't just been dancing on the levee all my life but that Richard Wright, Ralph Ellison, James Baldwin, and other less famous black writers had been invited by me to write for young people and all had turned me down. I finally got (years ago) Louis Lomax[2] (!!) to sign a contract and accept an advance to do a book about Crispus Attucks for heaven's sake, but that was years ago and he never put word one to paper.   Did you see our *Stevie* by John Steptoe? I think I sent you a copy. He's black but where his second book is I do not know and he doesn't come around here any more, and doesn't answer letters.   Well, forgive me for rattling on; it

---

1. William Styron's historical novel *The Confessions of Nat Turner* became the focal point of a fierce debate as to whether it was appropriate for a white writer to attempt to represent the experiences of blacks. The debate carried over into the children's book world and had in fact been joined a few years earlier with the publication of Nancy Larrick's essay "The All-White World of Children's Books," *Saturday Review*, September 11, 1965.

2. Newspaperman; television commentator, writer, and director; author of *The Reluctant African*, 1960, and other works for adults.

is late on Friday of a hectic week. Let me know if the Coltrane idea interests you.   I haven't read your Lindsay book[1] but plan to.   Nixon and Agnew are so awful; the country seems to be unravelling. A lot of Harper people are going to Washington[2] tomorrow. I hope there is no violence.

All best and excuse this letter.

TO ZENA SUTHERLAND (ZSu)   November 18, 1969

Dearest Zena:

Thanks for your letter and comments on the 9th Wilder manuscript. You ask how much leeway do we have. Well, I think Rose Wilder Lane's grandson, who inherited all her assets including the Wilder books, would let us do some judicious editing, but I think we just better not. I think maybe we can get the grandson to write an introductory note, or something. And just put it out as is. I would hate like hell to tamper with this. Charlotte [Zolotow] says we should do it as is, too.   You say you think clearly that the book should be published and suggest some good ideas for changes. I will think about it some more and consult the grandson, Roger McBride [*sic*]. But as of now my impulse is not to make any changes here. The Wilder books and the two E. B. White books were the ONLY manuscripts I ever published here with no repeat absolutely no editorial suggestions from me or anyone else. Anyhow, I appreciate your reading it for us, I appreciate your suggestions, and if now I am cooling off on the idea of publishing it with changes made by us, that doesn't mean I'm still not very grateful for your advice.   I have been shilly-shallying about this matter for a long time.

1. *A Political Life: The Education of John V. Lindsay*, by Nat Hentoff, Knopf, 1969.
2. A massive protest rally was held in opposition to the Vietnam War.

I am going to a CBC thing this afternoon, to celebrate the 50th anniversary[1] and I understand all of the past presidents will be there. Those of us who are still alive, I should say. And maybe some of those who have gone before us to That Great Publisher in the Sky ..... will also be present though not visible ...... I went to a gathering last week and there saw Ruth Krauss, and I looked at her and remembered when she and I were young and crazy, and I thought dolefully that now we are old and crazy. "We're like in a play, Ruth," I said. "There was the first act when we were young, then the second when we got older. And now here we are in the last act....." She snapped, "Don't say that! Say the NEXT to the last act.".......

Bright spot. M. Sendak is finishing all his preliminary lay-out on his next great opus, *In the Night Kitchen*, and with it he takes another giant leap ..... Thrilling, absolutely thrilling, and makes up for some of the second rate Shakespeares I'm trying hard to love today .....

Love to you and Alec.

TO E. B. WHITE   November 19, 1969

Dear Andy:

It is wonderful to have your letter, and to know that we will receive the manuscript of *The Trumpet of the Swan*[2] shortly. We

---

1. The event marked the fiftieth anniversary of Children's Book Week. Capturing the spirit of that turbulent time, the commemorative poster by Emily Arnold McCully featured the image of an androgynous gamin leading a demonstration for "Book Power."
2. *The Trumpet of the Swan*, by E. B. White, illustrated by Ed Frascino, 1970.

will read it eagerly and I will write or wire you immediately. I know it will be wonderful.

I wrote Garth [Williams] several weeks ago that your manuscript was almost finished. I said we might have to ask for sketches even from an artist of his eminence. I asked him how he felt about doing sketches, and about his work schedule. So far silence. But we will find the perfect artist, I know, whether it is Garth or someone else.[1]

We gave Les Davis[2] a copy of part of an earlier letter from you about *Charlotte's Web* and the movies. If he turns up with anything I'll let you know.

When last you wrote you had been suffering from migraine headaches but were feeling all right again. I hope you are still fine.

Cass [Canfield] is eager to read your manuscript.* We will have several copies made the MOMENT it arrives.

Yours,

*He and Jane are on a cruise, as you may know.

---

1. In part because EBW was in bad health, UN was eager and determined to publish the book as quickly as possible. Williams, who was much in demand as an illustrator, proved to be unavailable in time to meet UN's projected schedule. In *Letters of E. B. White*, Dorothy Lobrano Guth writes that the illustrator was deeply disappointed not to have gotten the assignment; see pages 591–92 for EBW's letter to him. See footnote 1 to letter to E. B. and Katherine White, January 16, 1975, page 363.

    After a frantic search, UN with EBW's approval chose Ed Frascino to illustrate the book.

2. A young filmmaker who had contacted Harper about the possibility of making a movie based on *Charlotte's Web*. EBW had resisted various filmmakers' proposals since 1956. Davis was to be no more lucky than his predecessors. Mounting medical bills later prompted White to relent, however; Hanna-Barbera produced the film version of *Charlotte's Web* in Hollywood in 1973.

Dear Andy:

Ed Frascino[1] came in this morning with seven or eight drawings and I hope to be able to send you good clear stats of them later today. I would send the originals but the possibility that they might be lost in the uncertain mails worries us. I am sure the stats will be good ones and you won't have the bother of returning them. All right? Also the stats will be the size the drawings will be in the book. The originals are much larger.

Phyllis Hoffman and others in the department, and Gloria Bressler, our Art Consultant, and I are very happy with these first few pictures and we hope you will be too. If ANYTHING bothers you about ANY of them just tell us and Ed will re-do what is necessary. I think he has a good light and funny touch in many of them. He absolutely adores the book and is extremely proud to be doing the drawings for it. I do hope you will like the pictures. I am not sure about the one of the boys holding their noses, with the man sprawled on the ground but others here like it and I may very well be wrong.

The galleys haven't arrived as yet but registered mail usually takes longer than unregistered. So I won't worry yet.

More later today, I hope, with the stats. Or Miss Hoffman will write. She was heartbroken that she wasn't at her desk when you telephoned her, and that I had the pleasure of talking with you. You really are everybody's favorite author.

Best to you both.

---

1. Edward Frascino, illustrator associated with *The New Yorker.*

TO MAURICE SENDAK

January 16, 1970

Dear Seymour Forsythe alias Maurice Sendak[1]:

Sorry about your boiler and all other troubles. Do you think the boiler is Jewish too?

Be happy with your beautiful *In the Night Kitchen*. I can assure you that you have these doubts and confusions and miseries whenever you start the finishes of ANY book. I can assure you that this will be a work of genius. I can assure you that it will turn out well.

I understand you and Dorothy [Hagen] and some Neff[2] man will talk next week. Be not disturbed. We would do nothing to harm your book. We will put on it the most reasonable list price we possibly can. We love your work. We love you. We hate your boiler.

Yours ever,

TO GEORGE WOODS

January 19, 1970

Dear George:

I was thinking about you and your manuscript[3] over the weekend. And I wonder if you'd try something for me that has worked well in other publishing experiences of mine. The ending of the mss. still seems unfocussed to me, though I know that books no more than life have to have a neatly stated denouement, good heavens, can I really be writing anything so banal this beautiful Monday morning?????? What I am

---

1. MS had been watching the television adaptation of John Galsworthy's *The Forsyte Saga*. UN, like the majority of the viewing public, insisted on pronouncing (and spelling) it "Forsythe."
2. The reference is to the Neff Lithographing Company, New York, printers.
3. Work continued on *Vibrations*.

trying to say is that it is all right for an ending to be relatively inconclusive. So that is not what bothers me about yours at present. But something which eludes me isn't exactly right. And I think it would help you and me a great deal if you thought about your book and pretended you were writing some catalogue copy for it. How would you describe what it does and says in a seven or eight line paragraph? Why don't you try to put down some "catalogue copy" and see what you get out of that effort? (At the least the perfect title might leap out at you and us!)..... Anyhow, try it. I asked one of our other authors, a distinguished Mr. X., to do just this about one of his books and he realized when he came to write the "catalogue copy" exactly what was missing in his general conclusions, what was missing in what he had THOUGHT he had said, but hadn't. Anyhow, try it and let me see it.

I am sorry Charlotte [Zolotow] and I are having to take a long time at this point but the book will be the better for it, or rather our comments will make more sense. She still feels that only cutting is necessary and I am sure she is right.

Now do your catalogue copy and send it along soon. You won't find it easy to write, but do it anyhow. We can supply the adjectives ("moving" "intense" "full of humor") but you give the gist of what you think the book is about.

And oblige your faithful friend and editor,

Affectionately,

TO ——————   January 23, 1970

Dear ——————:

Thank you for your letter of January 13.

I, too, am shocked now as I look at the picture on page 4 of

SHHhhhh, Bang[1], and I realize that it presents a very unfortunate stereotype.[2] If we reprint this book I can assure you that it will be changed.

It's good to realize, at least, that what was apparently acceptable in 1943 (the year of publication for the book) is completely unacceptable and very offensive now.

Please know that we deeply appreciate your bringing this to our attention, and that we share your concern.

Yours sincerely,

TO CROSBY BONSALL   February 3, 1970

Dear Crosby:

Well, I was all alone in the office eating my low-fat meatloaf sandwich, and so I decided the hell with it I would just telephone you. It was great to talk to you and to hear that you are working on the new mystery book[3]. We will look for it eagerly.

You are kind to say I am a saint, and I readily agree with you. You may, in fact, call me St. Ursula. When I was little I told all the other children, trying to achieve some sort of spectacled status, that I was descended from the great St. Ursula. Only later did I find out that she was a notorious virgin.   Anyhow, no matter what I say I admit I am not a saint but I will always love you and your work no matter how awful you are, and in spite of the fact that you never write or phone me.

---

1. *SHHhhhh . . . . . . BANG: a whispering book*, by Margaret Wise Brown, illustrated by Robert De Veyrac, 1943.
2. In the illustration in question, three African-American railway porters are rendered as though in comic blackface.
3. *The Case of the Scaredy Cats*, by Crosby Bonsall, 1971.

I don't know how you can stand the winter in the country, even with beautiful George. I have been up to Conn. for several snowy weekends and have enjoyed it a little but have been deeply grateful to get back to the civilization of 870 U.N. Plaza. Don't you ever come to town for a couple of days? We could give a party for you—a party for Crosby because she has NOT just written a book. ????? Think it over.

I suppose your new mystery won't be ready for fall. But our fall 1970 list is getting greater and greater. And we would love to have yours on it. But spring 1971 is a good season too. Anyhow, dear silent rotten-to-the-core friend, keep working. And let me know if there is any chance of your being in town later this month or during March. We would all love to see you.

I am still terribly depressed about the veto.[1]

I won't ask you to write, but think of us once in a while. We really miss you. Can't Brodart move back to New York? The air is lovely here, very low taxes, good subway service, lots and lots of empty taxi-cabs with very courteous drivers. Come on home. This is ridiculous!

Love,

TO MARY STOLZ   April 29, 1970

Dearest Moll:

Wrote you yesterday. This is just a postscript to wonder if, as you work on the girl and the stairs story (we must get a better way of identifying this!) you couldn't figure out a very good way to get the gist of *The Jungle Club* into it as a story within a story. I know you told me the last time we talked that you were willing

1. See letter to Millicent Selsam, June 19, 1969, p. 273–75.

to put the thought of the *Jungle Club* as a book by itself aside. But I know the work is dear to you, and the style in which it is written is dear to me. So I was thinking last night maybe it would fit in somehow with something a character in the girl-on-the-stairs story would tell someone else, or write (possibly in a shortened version). Then the comment could be implicit (or explicit) that not banding together into clubs is a very mature idea and that it is—well, I came in early this a.m. to get this and a couple of other letters written and the phones are beginning and a cross author whose second book isn't as good as his first book is coming in shortly. So no more for now. Just a line or two to put this wispy thought into your head in case you see a way to do it. I know you don't want to do anything inartistic just to use the content of the *Jungle Club* but it might fit in somehow in a longer book.

I want you to win the Newbery so much. Willa Cather never won the Nobel Prize, but that is cold comfort. Please please keep going on the girl-on-the-stairs story and think up a name so I can identify it less awkwardly.

Harpers has a new phone operator who asks anyone who telephones me to spell the name, sounds very dubious about anyone named NOSTRAND working here, and gives the general impression that no one ever heard of such a person. Makes me feel odd.

Love from Ersella Nostrand.

TO GEORGE WOODS   May 21, 1970

Dear George:

Patience and fortitude!! As I wrote you, I wanted to put *Vibrations* away for a little while so I could be sure I was thoroughly objective about the latest version. Don't be self-conscious. There are two other manuscripts I've been working on so intently that I am pulling a blank on them too, and have put them aside for a few days. Yours is due back from the copy-editor shortly and I will then be fresh and bright enough to go through all three manuscripts quickly and efficiently. Until then, as I said, patience and fortitude!!!

You know, when Syd Hoff's *Danny and the Dinosaur* came in, years ago, it was roughed out in a 48 page dummy.[1] There was something about it that bothered me and I begged the agent to let me keep it until I could figure out what was wrong. I spent weeks trying to see how it could be cut down to a 32 page picture book; I knew it sagged as a 48 page picture book. No inspiration. Then one day just like in the funny papers it was as though an electric light bulb lit up over my head. "Of course! It doesn't need shortening; it needs to be expanded to 64 and it will then make a perfect I CAN READ Book." And it worked out and we have sold hundreds of thousands of copies of *Danny*. All this just to say an editor can go stale and then get bright again. And I trust this will happen with the three mss. I am now blank on, including yours.

Now don't reread this and think, oh she's going to ask me to make *Vibrations* into an I CAN READ Book. I just got going on that little anecdote and couldn't stop. Forgive me. Relax. Enjoy your jury duty.

As ever,

1. See letter to Syd Hoff, December 4, 1957, pages 103–9, and especially footnote 4 page 103.

Dear Else:

Oh Else, why do you stop writing to me? Why don't you keep in touch??? I have you much on my mind. I hope the beautiful month of May is making you happy, and CREATIVE.

When are you going to let me see the dramatization of *Little Bear* for our I CAN ACT books[1] based on the I CAN READ books? Could I have it the end of the next week? Do you see *The New York Times*? In case you don't I enclose a copy of Lavinia Russ' article on some of our new I CAN READ BOOKS—it leads off with admiration for what you have done, and on the whole it pleased us very much.[2]

Kindly send me a written description of what you do most days.[3] When do you get up? Do you keep the shades down so the light doesn't waken you, or do you sleep with them up so you can tell the minute it is getting light? What do you have for breakfast? Where do you eat it? In the kitchen? Bedroom? Living room? Or is your house so vast it runs to a dining room? Then what do you do most mornings? Read? If so what—not STRINDBERG still for heaven's sake. Did you ever read Shelley as I requested? What about luncheon? And during the afternoon you do what???? What friends do you have? Which ones do you see most often? Are they interesting? Friendly? Loving? Appreciative? What are your relations like now, daughter and son-in-law? How often do you see each other? Do you dine out or fix dinner for yourself, or go to your daughter's or what? How late do you stay up? What direction

1. This project was apparently abandoned.
2. In a review titled "In the Beginning There Was *Little Bear*" in *The New York Times Book Review* (Part 2), May 24, 1970, p. 43, Russ called *Little Bear* "delectable" and discussed the wide variety of subjects found in the nearly 100 I Can Read books then in print.
3. The following series of questions exemplifies a favorite technique of UN's for helping an author focus on a subject about which he or she might decide to write.

does your bedroom face? Are you well and happy? Please be happy, somehow.   What would get you started writing again? We sit here longing for *Hetty*, for the beaver book, for the *Little Bear* play or plays. Do respond to this epistle!!! It is possible that our fine Ellen Rudin, Administrative Editor and great admirer of Else Minarik, may be in or around Boston one of these days. If she came to see you could she bring away a manuscript? I remember going out to see you on Long Island and literally typing the manuscript for our first EARLY I CAN READ, and that's the only way I was able to get it out of you. What can we do? We love and need you.   Kindly respond.

As ever affectionately,

TO JOHN STEPTOE   August 25, 1970

Dear John:

I'm sitting here with a typed version of your adult drug story. Some of it is terrific. Really powerful. It isn't finished, you will remember, though you told me how you were going to end it, and I made some notes at the end of the manuscript of what you said. In case I die.

I am worried because Stephanie[1] said you were sick over the weekend and couldn't come in yesterday, as you'd planned. She said you would phone today. But I haven't heard from you, dear John, and as you can understand I am getting a little concerned. I hope with all my heart that you are all right and that you will be able to get out to phone me and to come to see me soon. We must get going on *Train Ride*. The manuscript itself needs some work, but mainly now it is important for you to do the pictures AS SOON AS POSSIBLE.

---

1. Stephanie Douglass, the woman with whom JS was living.

Uptown is going to be great. I found the little piece of paper on which I scribbled down something you once said to me about *Uptown*. You said: "This is not the type of book that some people would want their children to read. But it is the way that some people's children have to live." You can certainly say something so that it stays said!

I know you are a strong and responsible young man so I shouldn't worry. But I do. Please call me. Or ask your mother to call me. I miss talking with her though I'm glad the reason for our conversations no longer exists. Or does it?

As ever affectionately,

TO JOHN STEPTOE   August 28, 1970

Dear John:

Please call me, or ask your mother to call me. You must still be sick or I would have heard from you.

I've just seen a set of printed pages of *Uptown* and it is terrifically good. Bound books should be in soon. It is really handsome.

You must finish that much more adult manuscript about John and Vinnie and the drugs. It has powerful stuff in it, and when I have more I want to show it to others here and perhaps to a magazine. But I need more material, John.

If you are having problems, or are sick, don't be discouraged! You are young and strong and a lot of people love you and love your talent. And have great faith in you.

I was crabby one day to you over the phone but I never will be again. I will <u>always</u> be your friend and I never will be angry with you. I absolutely can promise that. Do please call me, or ask your mother to give me a call when she can. I think of you and your family more than you can imagine.

As ever affectionately,

TO E. B. WHITE   September 4, 1970

Dear Andy:

Yes, of course we will have that ko-hoh changed to beep on
Page 201.[1] I am so sorry that we didn't catch that here. Forgive
us. However, I'm sure it made your two rich young readers
happy to be able to point it out to you. In a book about an
octopus Tomi Ungerer purposely—in one picture—gave the
octopus only seven tentacles. He said so many children would
have the pleasure of calling it to his and our attention.

Glad you're out of the hospital and that nobody could find
anything wrong. I guess it takes some time to get over the
shakes after an experience such as the one you had.[2] Terrible!

                                    Best regards to you both,

TO VIRGINIA HAVILAND (MNC)   September 30, 1970

Dear Virginia:

I loved your card from Russia! Thank you for it and thank
you for thinking of me. How you do get around! And in those
dangerous flying machines ......

When are you coming to New York again? I would love to
have a visit with you and hear all your news. Everything is fine
here—in the department I mean. Not New York, which is
filthier than ever. Mary [Griffith] and I try to get away to
Bridgewater, Conn., most weekends, and that helps a lot.

1. EBW had received a letter from the father of two boys who spotted a minor incon-
    sistency in the text of *The Trumpet of the Swan*. He asked that a correction be made
    in the next printing. To the author's amusement, the letter had come with a posh
    Fifth Avenue return address.
2. Both EBW and his wife had been in poor health. He had just come home from the
    hospital.

This is a very tense week here. Sendak and Dorothy Hagen and I are all wrapped up in the printing of *In the Night Kitchen*. Maurice and Dorothy go to the printer every day to see press sheets (we're printing on very small sheets so that the register will be perfect). And last Friday the blue plate just disintegrated, at the end of the day. I know, such things cannot happen, but this did happen. Then a big light crashed down from the ceiling and spoiled other plates. I sit by my telephone in my office waiting word from the printer and just hoping that all will go smoothly from now on. The printing should be finished in a few more days, then nothing can go wrong with the binding, I am sure, and we'll have books by the middle of October. But it is a very very tense time. It is a major major work and the world has never seen anything like it. What genius he has! The proofs of the book, early ones, are on the couch in my office and they seem to have a life of their own—just glowing and almost seeming to pulsate. How I do go on! ! ! ! But it is a very exciting experience. But exhausting!

I wonder how you are liking some of the fall books. Our dear *Trumpet of the Swan* is going beautifully, and again we are grateful to you for your advance comment, Virginia. Have you seen Steptoe's *Uptown*? Better than *Stevie*, I think. Steptoe has been besieged by other publishers, of course, to illustrate books for them and so far he has turned them all down. He told me about one mss. he'd read and returned and I said "what was there about it that you didn't like?" And he shook his head and said "Well, it was just untouched by human love." I thought it was a good description of a lot of manuscripts, and of a lot of published books too, alas! Well, enough.

As ever affectionately,

TO CHARLOTTE ZOLOTOW (CZo) November 11, 1970

Dearest Charlotte:

As I sat in my hairdressers under the dryer and thought of you having a good comforting talk with Dr. Eisner[1] right upstairs, I wished we could change places. These are nutty days in my head .....

But what inspires this note is: YOU MUST WRITE IMMEDIATELY, or FIND AMONG YOUR UNFINISHED MANUSCRIPTS, THE PERFECT MANUSCRIPT FOR LOUISE FITZHUGH TO ILLUSTRATE IN FULL COLOR!!!!![2] She can be very funny, as you and Ellen [Rudin] pointed out in our meeting this a.m.   But she also has done haunting paintings—one showing a little girl alone in a field, and I would have given my eyeteeth—ooooooh how original I am—to own it.

Anyhow, if you hadn't called my attention to that Fitzhugh unpublishable picture book we would never have drawn *Harriet the Spy* out of Louise. And so you should have the pleasure and honor of having her illustrate your mss. with her first color pictures. Please please please take up this challenge. I know you cannot write to order. But you can be galvanized by this opportunity to come up with something terrific. Louise will be very difficult for any editor (even her new pal Ellen!) to deal with on a picture book, but if the text is by you she will be more reasonable than she would be otherwise. She has great regard for you as a writer, as a person, and she raved about you as an editor to M. Sendak as recently as a year ago.

Now I want this for you very very much, Charlotte. Your two new Harper books, pix by [Leonard] Weisgard and [Ben]

---

1. Eugene Eisner, CZ's analyst, had his office in the same building where UN had her hair done.
2. CZ made an effort to do so, but the collaboration with LF never materialized.

Shecter[1], are fine fine books. By the beginning of Thanksgiving week I hope you will show me the scripts of a new idea which Louise can see and illustrate.

The fact that your personal life is in a bit of a hectic state right now should only be an advantage. Withdraw from the sturm und drang for one whole evening and concentrate on your OWN WORK.

Love as ever,

TO CROCKETT JOHNSON   November 23, 1970

Dear Dave:

Yours of the 18th just received. I find it incredible that "the managers of this year's fair have been able to get no books by Ruth Krauss or Crockett Johnson."[2] There are channels for fair managers and there are literally thousands of successful book fairs handled every year. We do not consider the sale of any books "an unwieldy nuisance" and of course I resent the way inefficient buck-passers blame the publishers for their own inadequacies. I am passing your letter on to our school library department and know they will do whatever can be done. I wish you'd given me the name of at least one of the "managers of this year's fair" so we'd have someone to write to.   As you can discern I am rather burned up by your local managers telling you a lot of stuff that has evidently made you feel the big unfeeling publishers just don't want to be bothered with selling books. And then too, this is the season of the year when bookstores tell anxious authors "we

---

1. CZ's *A Father Like That*, illustrated by Ben Shecter, and *Wake Up and Goodnight*, illustrated by Leonard Weisgard, were both published in 1971.
2. The reference is to an event in Connecticut, where Krauss and Johnson lived.

ordered your book from the publishers but were told it is out of print."　　This breaks the hearts of the authors, leads to acrimonious telephone calls, and of course it ALWAYS turns out that the book in question is in print, in LARGE supply, and that the bookstore personnel has simply not ordered it or even re-ordered it when called upon by one of our fine and numerous sales representatives.　　So I am ready to be burning with rage at this. You say "I probably am romantic about books and anybody that shows an interest in them, and industry and commerce cannot afford to be." I resent that implication very much. There are a lot of us in publishing who are just as romantic, or perhaps more romantic, about books than many of the authors and artists.　　This stereotype of the grasping and greedy people in book publishing is a horrid one and as one who has fought, bled, and practically died to do good books whether or not they were going to be immediately profitable—oh well, no sense in going on any more about this. But it is so ludicrous for some local lights up there to be able to convince you that their inability to get children's books for their book fair is anyone's fault but their own.

In spite of the above I still love you very much and am so glad you are out of the cast. I think you are great to have sent the crutches to a deserving shrine. I still have mine in a closet in my office. Never can tell when an irate author will come in and kick me in the ankle and break it again.

Love, sincere love, Dave.

Dear Zena:

Loved your letter. Loved you on the Saarinen show.[1] Couldn't stand her. She looked vaguely at *Sounder*, spoke about the medal, and said vapidly, "It's—er—about a—a—dog." We were watching in my office and I shouted, "But he's a NEGRO DOG." But you and John were charming, Zena. You looked lovely and made great sense. I think you are terrific. I also liked N[atalie] Babbitt[2]. John says the older woman is good too, but she struck me as imitating Jonathan Winters imitating his old Maude Fickett.   End of review.

I asked someone to collect xerox copies of everything in Bill Morris's[3] file on *Harriet* and I enclose a large batch. I am not taking the time to go through and winnow it for you, as I want to get it right off. I long to see what you write about "the amoeba in progress." Hope these reviews will be helpful.

Thank you, dear, for your sweet words about a sequel to *The Secret Language*[4]. I would love to finish what I have, and give it to Charlotte [Zolotow] for her advice and help. Maybe I will one of these days. Nothing has given me the sort of happiness that doing that little book did—I mean the letters that come in are so darling. Anyhow, thanks for the nudge. And as for your Newbery-Caldecott possibilities of White and Sendak, any inside dope you have will be gratefully received. I think

1. For the week of November 23rd, Aline B. Saarinen's morning talk show on NBC, *For Women Only*, focused on children's literature. ZS and Dr. Richard Darling, the dean of Columbia University's School of Library Science, appeared throughout the week, and were joined by various authors.
2. Author of children's books.
3. William C. Morris, director of library promotion and advertising, Harper Junior Books; later also a vice president of the house.
4. See footnote 3, page 151, to letter to Charlotte Zolotow, October 30, 1961, for information about UN's contemplated sequel to *The Secret Language*.

they are both great books. But a teacher went into F. A. O. Schwarz yesterday (the buyer phoned me at home last night) and said Sendak must be some sort of GNOME, that the book was shocking, that she wouldn't let her 5 year old son see it until he was at least eight years old. Too bad having children isn't an intellectual exercise, isn't it.

Lovely to see you when you were in town and you were dear to come to the Jane Canfield party. I wished you lived nearer, Zena.

Love,

TO ELESTINE STEPTOE[1]   December 10, 1970

Dear Elesteen [sic]:

I do not know if that is the correct spelling of your name, and if it is incorrect I hope you will forgive me.

I am so worried about John, and I feel I must write you. He promised about two weeks ago to bring in the finished pictures for *Train Ride*[2] and he did not keep the appointment (which didn't surprise me as he has so often simply not come when he said he would) and he has not telephoned me to make another appointment. Our Art Consultant, Mrs. Gloria Bressler, wrote John last week to ask him to telephone but she has not heard from him either.

I know he considers himself a grown man and will probably be angry at me for appealing to his mother for help. But I just don't know what else to do. He can have a tremendous success, artistically and financially, if he keeps on with his books. I also have an author (black) who has written a book about African

1. Elestine Steptoe, John Steptoe's mother.
2. *Train Ride*, by John Steptoe, 1971.

instruments and John said he would be interested in illustrating it. This is a project that would be fine for young black children to have in book form, and it would also make some money for John. Forgive me for writing you. But you just can't imagine the way I feel waiting for John.

Dr. Kenneth Clark[1] telephoned me to ask for John's address. He would like to buy a painting from him. He asked how John was doing and I said I honestly didn't know, that he just dropped out of sight every once in a while and I didn't know what he was doing. Elesteen, is there some phone number where I could call you? I think John said you had another job. It was so good when I could call you at your other job and get some sort of news of John. He is a perfectly wonderful person. I think he is very cynical about me, I can't help being white, and I suppose he can't help not liking me. But I truly love him. I love his talent, but I love him as a person, too. And I love the way he feels about you. It was one of the big disappointments in my life that I couldn't come to the opening of the library[2]. And when I heard you were there I almost wept! Do call me up when you can, and if there is a telephone at your job let me know when it is convenient for me to call you. And do beg John to get that book in to us! It just breaks my heart to have this inexplicable silence, when we've been PROMISED finished work.

Affectionately,

1. Author, psychologist, educator; founder of HARYOU (Harlem Youth Opportunities Unlimited), a program with which John Steptoe was associated. Clark, a member of the Harper Board of Directors, gave influential testimony in *Brown vs. Board of Education of Topeka*, the case that ended segregation in public schools.
2. Following the publication of *Stevie*, the John Steptoe Library was established in the author's honor by District 16 of the New York City public school system. The library serviced the elementary-school children of the Bedford-Stuyvesant section of Brooklyn, where Steptoe lived. The library no longer exists.

TO KATHARINE S. WHITE
January 20, 1971

Dear Katharine:

Well, I just heard that Andy did NOT win the Newbery. It is utterly incredible. What won was a Viking book entitled *The Summer of the Swan*[1]. Did you ever hear of anything so odd? I consider this a terrible thing for the librarians, as nothing can hurt Andy's books in the eyes of children and of intelligent adults. It is selling beautifully and will have a very long long life. I am simply DISGUSTED.

We will now concentrate on the National Book Award[2]. Forgive scrappy letter. I am in a rage.

As ever,

TO JOHN STEPTOE
January 21, 1971

Dear John:

Sorry I missed you the other day. I had a very long manuscript I was reading at home. But it was good to talk to you over the phone.

I looked at the 3 new pictures, and like the double-spread advertising SIX HOT CATS a lot. But I'm afraid the last picture, of the boys on the steps, isn't good enough for your book, John. It kills me to say this, but I think that you would not be happy, in the long run, if we included this picture just for the sake of having a final picture in the book showing the boys talking. Excuse my honky self, I mean RAPPING, of course. Anyhow, that picture just isn't good enough for John Steptoe

---

1. *The Summer of the Swans*, by Betsy Byars, illustrated by Ted CoConis, Viking, 1970.
2. The award went not to White but to Lloyd Alexander for *The Marvelous Misadventures of Sebastian*, Dutton, 1970.

and I hate to have to admit it. Then we are concerned about the drawing of the boys in the train itself. The right hand of one of the boys with his back to us seems oddly drawn. I have tried to hold a pole with my thumb in that relationship to the rest of my hand and I can't seem to do it. However, I will show it to Dorothy Hagen and others around here and get their reactions. If they agree with me is there any chance you can come in and fix that hand? Your books have been so fine, John, and *Uptown* is so very much better than *Stevie*, that we certainly don't want most of *Train Ride* to be less than your best.   You said very bitterly to me once that you could bring in a lot of garbage to me and I wouldn't know the difference and would accept it. So now maybe you are testing me, dear? At any rate, I can't accept that picture of the boys on the stairs and I will hate to include the subway interior unless you can come in and correct the hand here. We cannot say anything else.

When are you going to finish that long manuscript about the drug addict? It is a crime for you not to give me enough more to show one of the adult book department people. I do need more for them to go on. Try to get more written down. I will re-type it myself!

Love, as ever,

TO E. B. WHITE   January 22, 1971

Dear Andy:

I see that I did not answer your question about how one recognizes the first edition of a book. An authority (Barbara Dicks) explained it to me as follows: "If you look at the last page of *The Trumpet of the Swan*, you will find a row of numbers. The left-hand number gives the year of the printing; the right-hand number gives the particular printing. If your copy has 70 on the left and 1 on the right, yours is a first edition." Also, we thought you might be amused by the reference to *Stuart Little* on page 3 of the enclosed *Red Devil* publication[1].

As ever,

<u>Many</u> thanks for the true-to-life bird and shoe-lace. Nature copies art.

TO EDWARD GOREY[2]   April 13, 1971

Dear Edward:

I phoned yesterday but didn't leave my name with your answering service. Also tried to phone this morning a little after nine but no answer. I just wanted to say that I really enjoyed seeing you last week, and I am still very enthusiastic about *Hubert's List*[3] and hope you still are too. It can be a delightful, funny, beautiful and altogether marvelous book!

I wrote Candida[4] and told her that we'd been talking recently about your doing books for us, and that you had a wonderful idea for one, gave her the title, and said we wanted to give a contract now for it, or rather as soon as we had a few details from you as to what size you would like it to be, and how many pages you think would be in full color, etc.

I mentioned all this to Maurice Sendak for it was at his suggestion that I presumed to telephone you. He was delighted to

1. A quote from *Stuart Little* was published by the William Underwood Company, makers of Red Devil sauce and other food products.
2. Author, illustrator, and designer, known for his outré sensibility, droll wit, and fascination with things Edwardian.
3. Working title for a book never published.
4. Candida Donadio was also EG's agent.

hear about our recent meetings and about the new book. I am very happy about it too, and hope you are, Edward. Do decide on what size you'd like as soon as possible. You said you'd like it to be oblong, and so it must be that if you really want it. It did occur to me over the weekend that an upright book might look more like a <u>list</u>—but I certainly don't feel strongly about it.....
As you could see in our window on 33rd Street, we have done lots of oblong books.

I read the Grimm story and think it isn't honestly worthy of publication in book form with your pictures. Wouldn't you love to do your own *Hubert's List* and then do others? I will still reread the Lear poems you suggested, of course. I don't want to sound unenthusiastic about any of your ideas but I must admit I am terribly eager for you to do your OWN books and illustrate them.   Call me up and tell me how everything is with you. I am so happy to have met you, Edward.

All best,

TO MAURICE SENDAK   May 17, 1971

Dear Maurice:

Thank you for letting me be present at the unveiling[1] yesterday. I was much moved. I was tempted to go to Natalie's[2] with all of you, because I feel very close to the Sendak family. But it did seem to be such a family group I didn't want to intrude.

I must tell you before you sail about my chat with Natalie Orkin (spelling?) and her sister Anita.[3] Also about my chagrin

---

1. The traditional Jewish ceremony to dedicate a gravestone, which takes places one year after burial. The unveiling referred to here was for MS's father, Philip.
2. The artist's sister.
3. Cousins of MS.

that my driver turned out to be the wrong kind of Jewish man to be the tenth man.[1] I don't understand his inability to put on a yarmulka for God's sake and stand in as tenth man. He (Max, the driver) and I had entered into a very close relationship on the drive from NYC to Woodbridge. As a driver he is not much, being unable to tell north from south or right from left. But he told me he was in a labor camp all during the 2nd World War. He is a Jew of Rumanian descent and the Rumanian Jews were not put into concentration camps but just into work camps. Nonetheless, he had been persecuted. His sister committed suicide two years ago, leaving a fine husband and two children, both daughters. His mother died at age 81 in Israel of a quick heart attack, not having suffered a day's illness in her life. His father was lost in World War I, and he, Max, had "a complex" when he was a child because he had no father. He, Max, has no religious convictions, does not fast on Yom Kippur, and goes to synagogue only once or twice a year. For Christ's sake why couldn't he have forgotten he was a cohane or whatever and stood in as the tenth man? I felt so inadequate. I felt sure that if Judy Taylor[2] had been there she would have revealed herself as a fully circumsized [sic] Jewish male of the proper group and been able to fill in. (No, forgive me for any of this if it comes out like a bad joke. I felt terribly emotional about the whole thing and I am not trying to make any of this funny.)

I got there, in spite of Max's inability to find the way, at 11.15 and had rushed up to at least two other groups, extending

1. According to Jewish law, a Kohen, or man descended from the Jewish priestly class, is barred from participating in funerals other than those of members of his immediate family, on the ground that to do so would render him ritually unclean. This prohibition does not, however, apply in the case of an unveiling: Max appears to have been in error.

2. Children's book editor, The Bodley Head, MS's British publisher. MS had suffered a heart attack while visiting England in 1967. Taylor was with the artist at the time and helped save his life.

my hand eagerly and introducing myself as Maurice Sendak's publisher. One group was the Itkins and wanted no part of me, and the other was the Landes and they too did not care to have me in their group. So by the time the Sendaks did arrive I was all over-extended and soaking wet too.   I remember Philip in the hospital, and his notebook with the Yiddish manuscript on which you worked. He was so gentle and such an attractive human being, and as the man who sired you, true genius, he was and always will be important to me. And in his own right he seemed so fine. I remember him with great tenderness the day you brought him up for a sandwich at my desk, and he brought me some flowers. He looked so lovely, and he sat there eating that awful sandwich with so much dignity and charm. We were all so happy to see him.

And then I saw a part of you I'd never seen before, the manly tenderness and love with which you treated him in the hospital.   That will always give you happiness, dear, that you did so much for him in the final years, gave him so much love and understanding and support.

I don't know if it is all right to write this sort of letter to a Jewish person, but I wanted to say some of it. And I think I am just about as Jewish as you are anyhow.

When Philip's book[1] is finished it will be a beautiful one. And that will be a great happiness to everyone.

For heaven's sake take care of yourself on this trip.[2]

Love,

1. *In Grandpa's House*, by Philip Sendak, translated and adapted by Seymour Barofsky, illustrated by Maurice Sendak, 1985.
2. MS sailed for Europe later that month in preparation for illustrating a book of tales retold by the Brothers Grimm. The book was published as *The Juniper Tree and Other Tales from Grimm*, translated by Lore Segal and Randall Jarrell, illustrated by Maurice Sendak, Farrar, Straus, 1973.

TO ———————   May 24, 1971

Dear ——————:

Mr. Grillo, Manager of our Mail Order Department, very kindly shared with me your letter about *Harold and the Purple Crayon*. It gave us such pleasure to read how much your son Philip and your whole family enjoyed the book years ago, and that you are giving Philip a new copy of it now on the occasion of his graduation from high school. We are sending your letter to Crockett Johnson, to whom it will mean a great deal, I'm sure.

All good wishes.

Yours sincerely,

I well remember the day the manuscript and rough layout for *Harold* came to my desk. We still love that book![1]

TO CROSBY BONSALL

August 9, 198oh my god I mean <u>71</u>

Dearest Crosby:

Back from the best 4 weeks I ever had. Weather perfect. Lightning didn't hit the pump during the vacation (it did just before but was fixed before I left NY.) Pool perfect. Oh I had such a lovely time!!!!!   I kept hoping I would get bored, but I didn't. Had a lovely lazy routine of sleep, swimming, reading the paper, watching t.v. in a daze of relaxation. About the 3rd week I started coming to and sat by the pool and thought about

---

1. UN added this postcript by hand on both the original and the copy she forwarded to Crockett Johnson.

the past year and about the year ahead. And one of the bright spots is the new Crosby Bonsall.[1] I absolutely mean it. It was such a great happiness to have you come in that red-carpet day and give us that darling new book, and it is going to be SUCH FUN to publish it in the fall!!! I thank you, we all thank you, and do please write another one soon. We can't wait that long again. We simply cannot.

One bad moment in the vacation was the day I went to the public library. The librarian introduced me to a woman and identified her as the children's librarian. "OH, I am particularly happy to meet you," I said pleasantly, "because I publish children's books." "Oh, I know all about YOU," this person said loudly. Several heads turned and I thought OH Kee-rist what part of my checkered past does she know about God forbid? "I've sent you many manuscripts," she continued in a loud and cross manner, "and you have sent them all back." It was a crushing experience in the middle of a supposedly carefree vacation. I said weakly that I make bad mistakes every day in the week and that perhaps her manuscripts should not have been returned, I could be very wrong, oh forgive me for living and for existing this particular moment in the library in my rather shabby slacks and tacky sneakers, I beg your pardon, moddom, I crawl, I apologize for not loving your work.   Etc. I wish there were some sort of damn PILL I could take so as not to be the way I am. No shrink could help, I am too far gone.....

But anyhow, I love you and your work and also your husband. And I wish you would hurry up with the new ms. about walking each other home.   You said you didn't know [if] it would make a book. OF COURSE IT WILL MAKE A BOOK!!! YOU DUMMY!!!!   You said it would just be talk back and forth. How great!!! They could be straightening out a mis-understanding—discussing a boy, or another horrid girl, or all

1. *The Day I Had to Play with My Sister*, by Crosby Bonsall, 1972.

sorts of IMPORTANT matters. Catapult yourself back to 8 or
9 or even seven.   Call me up some time. I miss you.

Lots of LOVE,

TO NATALIE SAVAGE CARLSON   September 9, 1971

Dear Natalie:

How great to hear that you are working on a new book!
Barbara Francis[1], Charlotte Zolotow, and all your other fans
here will be as delighted to hear this as I am. Just splendid.

So glad you and John [sic][2] had a good trip to Canada. I'd
have loved to see the dramatization of *The Talking Cat*. I am in
a reminiscent mood this morning as several of my colleagues in
the department surprised me with flowers and cards (and a red
crepe-paper "carpet" from door to my desk) to mark the 40th
anniversary of my coming to Harper & Brothers in 1931. (Of
course you understand I was only about three or four years old
at the time......)   And here is your note and I am remembering the great excitement I felt when I read the manuscript of
The Talking Cat in—what was it—1950[3] I think??? I know I was
living in Hastings and reading at home that day, and we'd had
your manuscript a disgracefully long time and I telephoned you
in Rhode Island and told you we loved it and would take it. A
very wonderful and happy relationship all these years with you,
Natalie, and I am so glad that you are ours and we are yours.

I should have written you more often but I know you are in
good and sensitive hands, and I eventually see all letters, etc., so
still feel in very close touch.

1. Editor in the department.
2. UN apparently meant "Julie," the author's daughter.
3. UN began work on the manuscript in 1951.

How is your daughter enjoying life at Storrs[1]? We have been hearing about interesting work done for children's books by a woman there named Butler. I believe Julie knows her. Someone said to me, "Yes, she (Butler) has good ideas, but she is so positive we are afraid she will make some enemies." An odd observation. As one stumbles down life's roadway it seems to me one should be as proud of one's enemies as of one's friends ....

Well, you can see I am in an odd mood this morning.

As ever affectionately, dear "durable author."

TO E. B. WHITE   October 18, 1971

Dear Andy:

You have written one of the "Recommended Non-Sexist Books about Girls for Young Readers." How about that? It is *Charlotte's Web*, and the copy in the pamphlet compiled by Feminists on Children's Media reads as follows: "Charlotte is a spider who, through her intelligence, calm, and wit, saves the life of Wilbur the Pig." The name of the pamphlet is "Little Miss Muffett Fights Back" and I thought I should let you know right away about this.

With this, and favorable notice from that zoo keeper at the Philadelphia Zoo,[2] you are having a fine year. We are proud, too.

Everyone is going crazy down here and you and Katharine are fortunate to be up in Maine. We are getting a lot of

1. Julie Carlson was an instructor in education at the University of Connecticut at Storrs, where Francelia Butler, a professor of English, was becoming well known for her pioneering scholarly work in children's literature studies.
2. EBW had written UN about a fan letter he had received from a keeper in the Bird Department of the Philadelphia Zoo.

complaints about a little naked 6 year old in Sendak's *In the Night Kitchen*, and I have had several requests for a revised edition in which the little boy is clothed or covered in some graceful way.

End of message.

All best to you both and thank you for a non-sexist book.

TO E. B. WHITE   November 12, 1971

Dear Andy:

Well! No work done this morning with all the news of your new honor[1]. Mr. Jack Frantz of the National Book Committee is the one who telephoned me the good news that you had won the National Medal of Honor for the body of your work. This is a very prestigious, can't spell it, award. During Democratic Administrations the award was made at the White House. Of course Dick What's-his-name couldn't care less. So it is now held in the library of Lincoln Center. It will be a small group of not more than 100, on Thursday at 5.30, Dec. 2nd. You need not make a speech. The entire little reception will be over by 7.30, Mr. Frantz told me, "except for the boozers."

I telephoned him right after I spoke with you the second time this morning and told him that asking Bill Shawn[2] to introduce you mightn't be such a good idea as he is quite shy— or something. I made it sound all right, really. They were glad to have this information.

They are writing directly to you. Of course I never should have told you that Vladimir N[abokov] was part of your competition. So forget this literary tidbit. The person at the National Book Committee was horrified that I might tell you

1. EBW had been named the 1971 recipient of the National Medal for Literature.
2. William Shawn, editor of *The New Yorker* from 1952 to 1987.

what your competition consisted of.

Again, if you do decide that in a bit more than 3 weeks you will be quite over your battle fatigue and can come to receive the medal and five thou in person, we can arrange a car and driver to New York and back to North Brooklin, and make the trip as pleasant and untiring as possible.

I called Cass [Canfield] who is in the country today and he was delighted. Well, it is always lovely when excellence is recognized. And also you are as pretty as Gloria Steinem on her best day.

Good wishes to you and Katharine. More soon. We don't have all this excitement in Kiddie-Book-Land and I find myself quite dizzy. The whole building is buzzing with the news. You wouldn't believe it . . . . .

TO WILLIAM PÈNE DU BOIS   November 12, 1971

Dear Billy:

I just have to put in writing our appreciation of the marvelous pictures you gave us yesterday for *William's Doll*[1]. They are absolutely perfect and with Charlotte [Zolotow]'s words they will make the book a tremendous success, and make a lot of children very very very happy.

I was telling a friend last night about the book, and your coming in with the pictures, and saying what a happy day it was on the whole. She then told me that her brother asked for a doll when he was very little, and his mother gave him one, which he named Rosie. He loved Rosie very much and took her around with him, and slept with her every night. One day when he was about 8 he went to his mother, with Rosie, and told her that he

---

1. *William's Doll*, by Charlotte Zolotow, illustrated by William Pène du Bois, 1972.

thought he was getting too old to sleep with Rosie any more (I don't know what someone said to him, or what caused this) and then he asked his mother if she would mind letting Rosie sleep with her, since she couldn't sleep with him any longer. The mother said of course, she would be glad to let Rosie sleep with her, and she did. My friend's brother grew up to marry four times, twice to the same woman, and is generally an all-around All American Male. Well, it doesn't look so sweet written down, but I thought I would share this with you.

You always laugh and think I am kidding when I give you compliments..... but you really are one of the nicest persons I have ever known (faint praise, looking back at the many real stinkers with whom I have to cope).... And I love the inside of your head and I honestly think you are a lovely man.

Love from your fan,

TO MARY STOLZ   November 17, 1971

Dearest Molly:

Hope things are getting quieter on your home front now. So very relieved that Tom's[1] son isn't seriously ill. I know what a fright you must all have had.

As I told you, Joanne[2] says your jacket sketch[3] will be in tomorrow, Thursday, and we will rush it to you to look at and return with your comments. Unless we hate it and know you will too—which I doubt.

I tore out a little thing from A. P. Herbert's[4] obit in the

---

1. Dr. Thomas Jaleski, MS's husband.
2. Joanne Ryder, editor in the department, later an author of picture books.
3. For *Leap Before You Look*, by Mary Stolz, 1972.
4. English poet, playwright, and novelist known as "the wittiest man of his time."

Times the other day. I loved it and wanted to share it in case you missed it. We've talked about "prior to" instead of "before" and "I emerged from the vehicle to find the perpetrators," etc. Well, Herbert said that if Lord Nelson had lived during World War 2 he would not have uttered his famous "England expects every man to do his duty." It would have been "England anticipates that as regards the current emergency personnel will face up to the issues and exercise appropriately the functions allocated to their respective occupation groups."

Now back to work. More soon about the jacket.

Love to all. Isn't it lovely to be happy with each other?

TO MAURICE SENDAK   December 15, 1971

Dear Maurice:

I'm glad the Yale thing[1] is over but I know it must have been a tremendous experience for the students. Don't forget one of these days we should publish *Sendak on Picture Books* or *Sendak on Children's Books*. You make so much sense.

I liked our unexpected little visit the other day and loved hearing about the English woman's comments on *Wild Things* and Charlotte [Zolotow]'s *Mr. Rabbit* (Charlotte's and yours!) When you think of it, put a copy in the mail, will you?

I enclose another letter about *Night Kitchen*—and a copy of my reply. I do this not to upset you but to share some of this with you. I have engaged in "a dialogue" with a woman who hated *Charlotte's Web* because the spider loved drinking the fly's blood. So this woman wouldn't give the book to her 8 year old

---

1. In the fall of 1971 MS taught a semester-long seminar at Yale College on picture-book making. Among the students enrolled in the class were Paul O. Zelinsky, Eve Rice, and Sandra Boynton.

neice ? niece? Anyhow, I wrote her an impassioned letter saying that it was in the nature of spiders to drink the blood of flies, and that indeed in the book Wilbur shared her (the woman's) distaste at Charlotte's eating habits. But I begged her to give the little girl the book, to give the book a chance. Etc. etc. Blood all over the typewriter. Well, she wrote back and said if I were a gambling woman she would bet me the price of the book that the niece would hate the book. I told her that gambling was the one bad habit I did not indulge in, but please to try it anyway. Happy ending: she had the decency to write me that the niece loved the book and she took back what she'd written. Which is why I always like to answer insane letters. We are in the field of wanting to communicate so I must be consistent and try to communicate. But you mustn't let this turn you against your old pals, dear! Many many librarians love and treasure you, and even if they don't always understand exactly what you are doing they know they can trust you as an artist.

I dreamed last night that you were talking some more about a little book of three or four Sendak things like the *Family Circle* little story[1]. You were doing one called *The Search*. What does this mean, doctor?

Crosby Bonsall's new book is called *The Day I Played with My Sister.* Our president Win Knowlton[2] jovially observed in a large meeting where new contracts are announced, "Well, I see Ursula is now going into the field of juvenile incest." I had noticed the title could be taken that way but had thought I had just developed an unusually dirty mind, which any children's book editor has to have.

I am a great social success with your Mme. DeGaulle story.

1. MS created a puzzle, called *The Christmas Mystery*, for the December 1971 issue of *Family Circle*.
2. Winthrop Knowlton became president of Harper & Row in April 1970. It was a sign of the times that Knowlton's background was Wall Street and government, not publishing.

You give me so much! I'll let you know what I hear from the attached school librarian. She may try the book with children, and then she will have learned something from you. As I have so often, Maurice, and as I continue to .....

Seasons greetings and love.

TO EDWARD GOREY   December 23, 1971

Dear Mr. Gorey:

I wonder if you will remember me? Perhaps my name is vaguely familiar to you? I am the editor at Harper & Row who wanted you to finish your book, *List*, so that we could publish it in the fall of 1972. We wanted to get the book out early so our excellent sales force could spread out across the country and show it to booksellers VERY EARLY, and thus build up a good sale and make you very rich.

Really, Mr. Gorey, I think it would be easier for you to finish the above mentioned book than to have to receive mournful phone calls from me. And now this letter. Hope is still flickering within my heart—but it is a guttering flame and at any moment may go out.

Won't you start the New Year RIGHT and finish your book in January? We want to give it the best production we possibly can; we don't want to rush the plate-making or the printing. Do, dear Mr. Gorey, try to cooperate a little.

I think you go to movies all the time. Please pull yourself together, and kindly oblige your ever devoted,

Dear ——————— :

Your letter about Sendak's *In the Night Kitchen* was delayed in reaching my desk as you sent it to our Scranton, Pennsylvania, division. I am sorry not to have written you more promptly.

I am indeed distressed to hear that in the year 1972 you burned a copy of a book. We are truly distressed that you think it is not a book for elementary school children. I assume it is the little boy's nudity which bothers you. But truly, it does not disturb children! Mr. Sendak is a creative artist, a true genius, and he is able to speak to children directly. For children—at least up to the age of 12 or 13—are usually tremendously creative themselves. Should not those of us who stand between the creative artist and the child be <u>very careful</u> not to sift our reactions to such books through our own adult prejudices and neuroses? To me as editor and publisher of books for children, that is one of my greatest and most difficult duties. Believe me, we do not take our responsibilities lightly! I think young children will always react with delight to such a book as *In the Night Kitchen*, and that <u>they</u> will react <u>creatively</u> and <u>wholesomely</u>. It is only adults who ever feel threatened by Sendak's work.

I will send you a few positive comments on this book within the next few days, and I hope you will read them and that you will give the children in your school a chance to enjoy Mr. Sendak's book.

Yours sincerely,

Dear Edward:

Thanks for your card telling me you are having a nervous breakdown. Welcome to the club. I think you know that I have His and Her Straitjackets hanging in my office. Come down and slip into one and we can have a good talk.

Honey, I hate to pester you, but we do so want to do beautifully by your book *The Interesting List*. And we were supposed to get it in November so we'd have plenty of time to have printed and folded sheets for the Sales Conference early in May. Now it is almost February and I've seen nothing.

If you are stuck, or discouraged, or something like that I might be able to help get you unstuck, or encouraged. I thought I had experienced all the editorial experiences an editor could experience. But you are a brand new experience for me, and it makes me feel all young again..... I mean lots of brilliant artists are happy to let me see their work in progress, and they know I am not going to say anything to throw them off the right track. Won't you trust me? Must I send you certificates of editorial integrity from Ungerer, Sendak, and others?

We want *The Interesting List* to be one of the BIG BIG BIG Harper books for the fall of 1972.

Love, genius dear.

You gave me that frog and you said you MADE it. But when visitors come to see me and admire it I say the great Gorey gave it to me, and then they say they have one just like it. Are you leading me up the garden path, Edward? Kindly call. As Miss Warner[1] told you, I am about to be discharged for inefficiency because I can't get your book out of you. I am a nice person and I have worked too hard to have to be fired now.

1. Margaret Warner, UN's assistant from 1971 to 1973. See also page 348, footnote 3 to letter to her, August 31, 1973.

TO MARY RODGERS   March 22, 1972

Dear Mary:

Tried to phone. Here's a favorable review of *Freaky Friday* from *School Library Journal*. They should have raved more, but this is a good review and librarians will buy.... The review is on a piece of paper with another review of Nat Benchley's new book[1]. You and he must meet sometime. You'd love each other ..

The great Shel Silverstein told Marlo Thomas[2] the great Marlo Thomas to look me up while she is in NY making a t.v. special. She came in and Charlotte and I both saw her. She is an absolutely delightful young woman and Charlotte [and] I both liked her a lot. She is very caught up with Women's Lib (which I know you are not particularly) and she has been upset by some of the "sexist literature" being fed to children. She had seen a couple of particularly obnoxious books [*sic*] called *I'm Glad I'm a Girl* and *I'm Glad I'm a Boy*.[3] What she wants to do is make a record for Caedmon Records (very good people) that people can play to their children, and she hoped I could find her some writers who would contribute brief stories and/or poems which will in some way counteract the sexist stuff.[4] I showed her *William's Doll*—which is at least against sexual stereotypes, and another book in which a little boy was told he would only be a sissy if he felt it was sissy of him to cry (the author said it better!!!!) and I told Marlo that we just didn't have a lot of

1. *Small Wolf*, by Nathaniel Benchley, 1971. This was one of the author's many I Can Read books.
2. Actress.
3. It was actually all one book, *I'm Glad I'm a Boy! I'm Glad I'm a Girl!* by Whitney Darrow, Jr., Windmill, 1970.
4. This project developed into a record, a 1974 McGraw-Hill book, and a television special all titled *Free to Be...You and Me*, conceived by Marlo Thomas and developed and edited by Carole Hart et al.

authors who write therapeutic material for the sake of the therapy, but that I would try to think of a few who might be interested at least in talking to her. Would you be? There's one book called *Mommies at Work* and it is utterly ghastly. That's the trouble when you get writers who write didactic books. But Shel seems to have given Marlo the impression that Ursula can solve the problem.... And so I am writing a few people (Charlotte too) to ask if they have any ideas. Of course if the ideas are good they would also make good books. Anyhow, if the idea appeals to you I will tell Marlo to get in touch with you. Maybe you already know her. She referred to "my boy friend Herb Gardner[1]" and of course I've been trying to get a book out of him for ages. I asked her to write a book herself but she flatly refused to consider it. She had a very interesting child-hood and adolescence—as who hasn't when you come down to it????—and I think she could write. Anyhow you and Hank[2] and she and Herb would make a cute double-date.

Love,

TO FRAN MANUSHKIN[3]   March 29, 1972

Dear Fran —

I am sorry that work on your next Harper book is not going easily. But that happens, you know! Second books are never easy, and *Baby*[4] is such a knock-out that you will tend to keep thinking you have got to top it. You can't top it, of course. There is no other book like it, and you will not write another book like it. But you will write one just as good <u>in its own way</u>.

---

1. Playwright, best known for *A Thousand Clowns* (1962) and *I'm Not Rappaport* (1985).
2. Henry Guettel, MR's husband.
3. Editor in the department; author.
4. *Baby*, by Fran Manushkin, illustrated by Ronald Himler, 1972.

You simply <u>must not let</u> the thought of *Baby* come into your mind when you are working, or when you are trying "to keep the channel open."

You are one of the most gifted persons I have ever known, and I have known a lot of them. You have marvelous emotional equipment and that is what the finest creative artists have. You are going to have to write out of your emotions and you are going to have to trust your emotions. You are a terrific person, with vitality and creative energy and there isn't the slightest chance in the world that you are not going to write many many many wonderful books. So try to get through this frustrating time without becoming discouraged. I can absolutely promise you that you will do your next book sooner rather than later, and that it will be good.

As ever affectionately,

TO RUTH KRAUSS AND CROCKETT JOHNSON
May 25, 1972

Dear Ruth Krauss and Crockett Johnson:

I do not know if my name will be familiar to you but I knew you both once, and I published many of your great books. I find you both in my thoughts these days. We are busy cleaning out desk drawers, etc., preparatory to the great move from this rickety old building to lovely quarters at 10 East 53rd Street. Harper Junior Books will occupy two floors, connected by an open central stairway, and we will have a terrace just for our department. (There will be another terrace for the horrid non-Junior Book Department personnel, but we will have our own.)

I thought I would write you a note to mention that I just saw a printing order go through for 10,000 more *Carrot Seed*.

Isn't it great that such a good book should also sell so well and for such a long time? So, with all the bad news in the papers and chaos all around us, I thought a note with this pleasant news would make you a little happy.

You both must come to New York once in a while. Let us know a little [in] advance of the trip in so we can invite you to our new quarters, and open a small bottle of something.

As ever with love,

TO MAURICE SENDAK   June 2, 1972

Dear Maurice:

I think of you often and hope the new apartment and new house in the country and the new car (and the new driving license) are all making you happy.

This is our last day at 49 East 33rd Street. It has been somewhat demoralizing to have been trying to work for weeks in a department without any books, any pictures on the walls, any posters, and with very little furniture. So we leave with no regrets and look forward to the future at 10 East 53rd Street where we hope you will be one of our first callers.

But of course I have a lot of memories—I remember the day the receptionist came in to my office and said "E. B. White is outside and wants to see you." And I was surprised as I'd had no idea he was coming in, and I rushed out and he said "Here's my new manuscript. It's called *Charlotte's Web*." And the day Else Minarik came in with a terribly ugly all blue crayoned dummy containing what is now Chapter One in *Little Bear*. And Ruth Krauss getting off the elevator to discuss the race problem with me and proving to be so funny and original I begged her to leave the race problem to others and do some other books. And

Tomi Ungerer—so tense, and Russ Hoban with his heavy machinery drawings. So many others, coming into this building. So this is just another of my many fan letters to you over the years to say the time <u>I love the best</u> is when you came down to talk over doing some sketches for Aymé's *Wonderful Farm*. And then eventually you wrote your own *Kenny's Window*, and then there was a period of time when you came in to the office and read manuscripts for us a few hours a day. I remember the girl, Doris Something, who practically threw her pelvis out of joint when she saw you sitting there, and she was on her way to the water cooler. Well, dear Mr. Senlak, just to say we're glad you came to this old building and we want you to come soon to the new one. I've learned much from you, and hope to continue to do so.

Your fan,
Ersella Norcross.

TO M. E. KERR[1]   June 7, 1972

Dear Marijane:

I laughed and bled all through *Shockproof*[2]. You are terrific! Others in the department now want to read it so Barbara A. Dicks will not get her copy back for quite a while. I didn't read all of *Sudden Endings*[3]. I have a big thing about death—I don't even like to go to sleep at night. But I will get it back when Charlotte finishes it and read the rest of it. You certainly write well, Ms. Kerr!

I am so disgusted with myself for writing on that manila

---

1. A pen name of Marijane Meaker, author of young adult fiction and fiction for adults.
2. *Shockproof Sydney Skate*, by M. J. Meaker, Little, Brown, 1972.
3. *Sudden Endings*, by M. J. Meaker, Doubleday, 1964.

envelope your name as M. J. Meagher. I have gone through a long life being called Ersella Nostrand, Uneeda Borstum, and other variations. I think your M. E. Kerr pseudonym completely disorganized me. So please forgive me.

Note I wrote the above on June 7 and it is now June 20 and this note has been in my typewriter ever since while I took some time out to have pneumonia. I was very smart, I guess—after a spring of virus-y ailments and flu which they can't treat except by telling you to stay in bed, it turned into pneumonia and they can give you penicillin for that. But the penicillin leaves you feeling very rotten. Through this entire experience I have gained 2 lbs. so the hell with it.

Since I started this note I received a very sweet note from you about the Skinner Award[1]. I went to the dinner the second day I was up and around after the pneumonia so I am not too clear about the event. I have the awful impression that I seized the citation and little gold engraved thing and said "I won! And I'm glad glad glad!!!!!!" Anyhow, it is over now and I am back to being kicked and buffeted by life. But it was a lovely evening.

Glad the rewrite is going well.

As ever,

PRESS RELEASE   June 9, 1972
from Harper & Row, Publishers, Inc.

IMMEDIATE RELEASE
On behalf of Maurice Sendak, Ursula Nordstrom, Publisher of Harper Junior Books, recently sent the statement quoted below

---

1. UN was the 1972 winner of the Constance Lindsay Skinner Award of the Women's National Book Association. The award honors the recipient's contribution to society through books.

to some 380 librarians, professors, publishers, authors and artists throughout the country. The response was extraordinary: 425 signatures. Many were accompanied by personal notes underlining the signer's indignation at this reported exercise of censorship by a librarian through alteration of the illustrations of *In the Night Kitchen*. It is hoped that this protest will alert all those concerned with children's books to the invidiousness of such censorship.

> "The following news item, sent to *School Library Journal* by a Louisiana librarian and published in a recent issue of that magazine without any editorial comment, is representative of several such reports about Maurice Sendak's *In the Night Kitchen*, a book for children, that have come out of public and school libraries throughout the country:

>> Maurice Sendak might faint but a staff member of Caldwell Parish Library, knowing that the patrons of the community *might* [italics added] object to the illustrations in *In the Night Kitchen*, solved the problem by diapering the little boys with white tempera paint. *Other librarians might wish to do the same.* [italics added].[1]

> At first the thought of librarians painting diapers or pants on the naked hero of Sendak's book might seem amusing, merely a harmless eccentricity on the part of some prim few. On reconsideration, however, this behavior should be recognized for what it is: an act of censorship by mutilation rather than by obvious suppression.

> A private individual who owns a book is free, of course, to do with it as he pleases; he may destroy his property, or cherish it, even paint clothes on any naked figures that appear in it. But it is an altogether different matter when a librarian disfigures a book purchased with public funds—thereby editing the work of the author—and then presents this distortion to the library's patrons.

1. Italics were added in the original letter UN sent out, not in the present volume.

The mutilation of Sendak's *In the Night Kitchen* by certain librarians must not be allowed to have an intimidating effect on creators and publishers of books for children. We, as writers, illustrators, publishers, critics, and librarians, deeply concerned with preserving the First Amendment freedoms for everyone involved in the processes of communicating ideas, vigorously protest this exercise of censorship."

TO MAURICE SENDAK   October 31, 1972

Dear Maurice:

Happy Hallowe-en. I suppose you don't get troops of trick or treaters in that classy neighborhood of Ridgefield.

I have just read the children's book issue of *The N. Y. Times* and am irritated by the way I was misquoted in an article on why children's books cost so much.[1] I told the man (and I didn't "growl" as he states) that parents paid for expensive records and toys that didn't last, and that books such as yours were powerful emotional experiences and that they would be part of a person's entire life. Oh, you know the way I go on. I said publishers of mass market $1.95 books couldn't—in the nature of things— take first books by creative but unknown artists, and supply the climate in which they could grow. Etc. This comes out that Miss Nordstrom growled and referred to "publishing a Sendak and letting him grow." I never said that, and I hope you know

1. UN had seen the forthcoming November 5 issue of *The New York Times Book Review*, with its special Part II supplement devoted to children's books. In an article by Thomas Weyr, "Why Are They So Expensive?" UN was asked to comment on the rising cost of picture books. UN remarked that children break their toys and record albums, "while a child's book is read and reread and becomes part of the child's emotional experience for his whole life." UN, according to the reporter, then "growled" that a book such as Maurice Sendak's *Where the Wild Things Are*—which cost $4.95 in 1972 as compared to $3.50 in 1963—was far more likely to have this impact on a child than was a one-dollar mass-market children's book.

that the phrase "a Sendak" is not one I have ever heard. There is only THE Sendak. Well, you've been misquoted enough to know how these things happen.

I hope you are OK. What about your friend Sheila? Call me up one of these days and give me your news. Judy Taylor writes Barbara Dicks that she knows how happy you are in Ridgefield because all your letters since you moved to the country have been such happy ones, etc. "All your letters." I admire Judy's needlework very much.

Hope Grimm is almost finished and that you and Ma Goose[1] will be getting together soon. Or you will be getting together with your own next Sendak. What a wonderful thing it has always been for me to hear about the first stirrings of a new Sendak book. After, of course, you'd told me you were never going to be able to write another one. I remember sitting in Ten Park in September after you'd planned out everything in *Higglety*..... and your face which had been the last time I'd seen it tense and worried, was smooth and serene, and you knew you had the book under control.

Lots of love, she growled.

TO SUSAN HARRIS[2]   December 1, 1972

Dear Susan Harris:

Your name has been given to me as the scriptwriter for the *Maude* episode in which *Goodnight Moon*, by Margaret Wise Brown, and published by Harper, was mentioned.

To many of us who watch *Maude* it meant a very great deal

1. UN had discussed with MS the possibility of his illustrating a collection of Mother Goose rhymes.
2. Writer for television.

to hear one of our favorite books mentioned, and if you were the one responsible here are thanks from us. So many wonderful children's books are ignored by TV that we were really tremendously pleased! Was it your idea to include *Goodnight Moon*? And did you know it as a child? I hope so because children do love it. And of course I've been in love with that book ever since Margaret and Clem Hurd came in with the first rough dummy—so many years ago.

Best wishes to you in what must be very interesting work. If you ever want to think of doing a children's book we'd like to hear about it.

All best,

TO EDWARD GOREY   December 14, 1972

Dear Mr. E. Gorey:

I withdraw my proposal of marriage. I couldn't be married to a man who refuses to answer his telephone. What if I wanted to phone home to say I was going to dine and spend the night with Spiro Agnew?

However, I do adore the drawings—few though they are— for *An Interesting List*. I think this will be a simple and elegant and classic book, and I beg you to finish it before you start on anything else. Please, Edward. You have a brilliant book started here. Don't put it aside and go to the movies and the ballet, and illustrate books for other publishers.

PLEASE FINISH THIS BOOK. You could finish it during January and February, and we could do a terrific job of selling it as a fall 1973 book.

I am sending a copy of this S. O. S. to your agent. Perhaps

he can persuade you to finish this Harper book before turning to other things.

I wrote Sendak what a joy it was to see you operating at that Showcase jury day.[1] I said you were very strong. He replied saying yes you were indeed a mensche which if you don't know is Yiddish for good person.

But on deadlines you are rotten to the core.

Much love from your ex-fiancee

P. S. Will you let me know when you'll be home so that we can return these pictures by messenger?

TO PAT MYRER[2]   January 10, 1973

Dear Pat:

I just heard from George Woods that he has a favorable review of *Dinky Hocker*[3] which will appear in the *Times Book Review*. I'm glad, because George himself was very luke-warm about the book. However, the reviewer to whom he sent it reacted with enthusiasm (so George says) and so it will be good to have a good review in the *Times*. George likes *If I Love You* etc.[4] much better than *Dinky*. Very interesting. Our salesmen all loved *If I Love You* (they also liked *Dinky Hocker*) but they seemed to like the second book even more because they sympathized so much with the young gentleman who "got shot down." I think I told you, but in case I didn't, I was bowled over

1. An annual event sponsored by The Children's Book Council from 1972 to 1977 during which a selection of the year's books were reviewed on the basis of their design and production.
2. Formerly Pat Schartle; agent at McIntosh & Otis.
3. *Dinky Hocker Shoots Smack!*, by M. E. Kerr, 1972.
4. *If I Love You, Am I Trapped Forever?*, by M. E. Kerr, 1973.

with the way Marijane went over with the salesmen—at the conference and at the luncheon afterwards. One bald man came up to her and said "I liked it because the bald guy got the girl." "Don't they always?" asked Marijane demurely. He melted with pleasure.....

I have written Marijane about the George Woods thing. Just wanted to let you know too.

All best,

TO MAURICE SENDAK   February 16, 1973

Dearest Maurice:

I phoned Morley Safer's office and asked when the segment with you would be telecast on *60 Minutes*.[1] I am tired of having to watch the whole program every minute every week! The young woman who answered said the interview was still being edited and thus had not been scheduled, but she took my name and phone number and said she would let me know when it was definitely scheduled. "Now whose secretary are you?" she asked pleasantly—female chauvinistic sow. "I am Mr. Sendak's editor," I said with simple dignity. I don't plan to be buried but it would be nice on my tombstone.... "She was Mr. Sendak's editor."

Now, honey, the formal announcement about my new role and Ellen [Rudin]'s new role[2] is being circulated to the Harper people today. And Joan Robins[3] will be sending a story to *P.W.* shortly. It has been great to have been able to share this good

1. The CBS News magazine *60 Minutes* aired Morley Safer's profile of MS on April 1, 1973.
2. UN had decided to take early retirement as director of the department and to become a senior editor with her own imprint, Ursula Nordstrom Books. She had chosen Ellen Rudin as her successor as director.
3. Director of Junior Books publicity.

news with you in such confidence for such a long time, and to know that the thought that I'd have more time for the things I really love to do made you happy too.

I enjoyed your last phone call very very much. It was—as always—tremendously exciting to hear that you are getting flashes and signals in your head about your next book, and the little you told me was—again—TREMENDOUSLY EXCITING. I know how privileged I am to hear about what is going on in your head. It has been and is the greatest happiness of my professional life. Now I'm getting stuffy sounding, so enough of this.....

And don't forget one detail of the luncheon with Julia McRae[1] and Steig[2], and you. Did you cook??? Well, save the story until we meet again.

Love,

TO ———— *a school child*   February 16, 1973

Dear ————:

Your letter about Charlotte's death has come to me because I published the book, *Charlotte's Web*. When I read the manuscript I felt exactly the way you now feel. I didn't want Charlotte to die, and I too cried over her death.

What I think you and I both should keep in mind is that Charlotte had a good and worthwhile life. And she was a true friend to Wilbur. And something to be glad about is that she had all those children. I think the author knows that in due

1. Julia MacRae, editor, Hamish Hamilton Children's Books, Ltd.
2. William Steig, author and artist; winner of the 1970 Caldecott Medal for *Sylvester and the Magic Pebble*, Windmill, 1969.

course a spider such as Charlotte does die, but her children live, and so will her children's children.

This may not be of much comfort to you now, but perhaps as time goes by you will understand why E. B. White had to tell Charlotte's story the way he told it.

Thank you very much for writing, and for sharing your feelings with us.

Yours sincerely,

TO ROBERT LIPSYTE[1] March 6, 1973

Dear Bob:

I was delighted to hear from you again. Many thanks. But I don't think of you as a "Nordstrom Wandering Fellow."[2] I know you'll do another fine book for us one of these days. Yes, *The Contender*[3] was an extremely happy experience for us as well as for you, and of course books in this field do have great impact for "people still open to new thoughts and experiences." End of quote!

The new idea for a novel for this department sounds most interesting. I hope that when you finish the novel you are working on now you will get down to work on the one about the adolescent fat boy and the crippling experience he has living in a walking ghetto[4]. (And again I quote.) We can substitute this for the *Fifer* one? Were you by any chance an adolescent fat boy? Hardly seems likely but there is an intensity of feeling in

1. Author, television journalist, reporter, and columnist for *The New York Times*.
2. RL had used this phrase to describe himself in light of his failure, till then, to write a second book for UN, for which he was under contract and for which he had received an advance.
3. *The Contender*, by Robert Lipsyte, 1967.
4. *One Fat Summer*, by Robert Lipsyte, 1977.

your paragraph about this proposed novel that makes me feel it has special meaning for you.

As you will see by the enclosed I am going to stop going to a lot of budget meetings, sessions about inventory revaluation—and this summer will become an editor again. Ellen Rudin who will become head of this department is a fine young woman—a good administrator as well as a splendid editor. But I will still be active as senior editor of the House, and so I will hope to hear from you when you get closer to work on your next Harper Junior Book novel. I'm also enclosing a letter I wrote to some librarians about a new young author on our list, Alexis Deveaux[1]. I'm sending you a copy of the book under separate cover. It isn't a novel, but I think you'll find it interesting and completely original.

Again, it was great to have your warm and friendly letter.

All the best as ever,

TO M. E. KERR   Bridgewater
                                                May 14, 1973

Dear Marijane:

I stayed out of the office Friday to read some long manuscripts in peace and quiet, and I read and reread the ms. with revisions of *Son of Someone Famous*[2]. I do think you are terrific, and a real pro, and everything you added is just right. Many many thanks. I will send a copy of this to Pat Myrer so she will know all is great. The new material is really fine, and this is going to be a terrific book.

---

1. Alexis Deveaux, a young African-American poet, playwright, and illustrator, published *Na-ni*, her first picture book, with Harper in 1973.
2. *The Son of Someone Famous*, by M. E. Kerr, 1974.

I enclose a good review of *If I Love You…* from a recent issue of the *Christian Science Monitor.* I wonder how the Christian Scientists are making out with Haldeman, Erlichman,[1] and what's-his-name, the third C. S. on the White House staff. Did I ever tell you that I was brought up a Christian Scientist? I think I did …. Anyhow, when I was about 12 or 13 I asked my mother, "Why if we deny the existence of bodily pain don't we also deny the existence of bodily pleasure?" She replied, "Don't be impertinent." (I was thinking of trying to demonstrate over my fondness for banana splits, as a matter of fact, but how could she know?)

I tried to telephone you this afternoon but you and Zoe[2] are out having a fine time in the country, I guess. I wanted to hear a friendly voice and to see if we could arrange to have an open telephone line between you and us when the Watergate hearings start on Thursday. I will go nuts trying to concentrate on work here and not knowing what is going on with my new hero Sam Ervin.[3]

Do you hear from mutual acquaintances in Bridgewater[4]?

Love, and thanks for being such a good writer and such a professional reviser. We really appreciate you.

1. H. R. Haldeman and John D. Ehrlichman, aides to President Nixon and later convicted in the Watergate scandal.
2. Zoë Kamitses, a friend of the author.
3. Senator Sam J. Ervin, Jr., Democrat of South Carolina, chair of the Senate Judiciary Committee, who presided over the Watergate hearings.
4. The reference is primarily to Louise Fitzhugh, who had introduced MEK to UN when the novelist was looking for a publisher, and with whom UN was no longer in touch.

TO MARY RODGERS   June 22, 1973

Dearest Mary:

    Good to talk to you the other day and to sense that you were working happily and well on the new ms. about Boris, and Annabel.[1] I know you'll get back to the Exeter book one of these days but if you feel you've gone stale on it, Charlotte and I both agree a new *Freaky Friday* type book is the thing for you to work on.

    The part you read me sounded awfully good, Mary—funny and breezy and really dandy. I should have told you, though, that though I was <u>glad</u> to listen I actually never take things in well except visually. You may be flattered to know that ordinarily I pay people a small fee NOT to read aloud to me. (This is one of the many reasons I never married—young men wanted to read poetry aloud to me and I would start to scream.) But the reading by you over the phone did sound <u>good</u> and I hope you got a lot more done during the rest of the week.

    Now it is Monday, the 25th. I left this in my typewriter over the weekend. Will send it along anyhow, not that it says much. But as usual it brings you lots of love. I really appreciate you, Mary.

As ever,

TO MAURICE SENDAK   Bridgewater
                                                    August 7, 1973

Dearest Maurice:

    As I told you over the phone, the office sent me the copy of your father's manuscript. It is your first rough un-cut translation

---

1. *A Billion for Boris*, by Mary Rodgers, 1974.

from the Yiddish. I have gone over it carefully but of course the next best thing is for you to send me your revised version so that I don't make comments on parts you may have already changed or cut entirely. In this letter I am referring to the only version I have seen, untitled, and running to 43 pages including some pages marked "additional chapters."

I said over the phone that parts were not clear to me, and you agreed, and we both felt there was too much repetitive material. Then I said I thought the ms. needed much much more dialogue and I believe you agreed. Then you said something to the effect that you were finding it a little difficult to decide how much of your father's story you could really change, really re-write; you wondered almost if you had the "right" to do much re-writing. Dear Maurice, this is a most delicate point for me to discuss [with] you in a letter but I must. And you must and will, I am sure, take it in the loving way it is meant. I would never even try to intrude into the relationship you and your father had. But I can't help but feel especially close to his story, and to your working on it. One of the clearest memories I have of you, and of Philip, is going to St. Vincent's Hospital with you and seeing Philip looking so fine in his handsome pajamas, and on one visit he let me see the notebook in which he was writing his story in Yiddish. I seem to remember that it was one of those black and white boardbound notebooks, with lined paper, and on the cover he had written next to the printed word "Student" his own name, and next to the word "School" he had written St. Vincent's. (I may have dreamed this, though)[1] There was just always something about your father that touched me deeply, and that is why I feel I won't offend you if I write you this so frankly. I remember when you and he came to my office and ate sandwiches at my desk. He was so neat about his sandwich (you and I weren't particularly!) and he looked so handsome in his

1. By hand on original.

dark suit, and I remember he bought a bunch of especially lovely flowers, no two the same. Well, anyhow, all this to say that I know you approach your work on your father's manuscript with all sorts of special feelings, and that I understand them and—as much as a non-Sendak person can—I share many of them. I am absolutely sure that if Philip were with us today you and/or I could ask him what he meant by certain passages, and he would either explain and make them clear to us, or he would, as most fine story-tellers can do, say "well that part isn't really important so let's leave it out." So now that he isn't here for you to talk to about certain parts of the manuscript I think and hope you must feel that anything you do to make this story marvelous and worthy of Philip and more accessible than some of it is now to young people (and old reviewers) is what you want to do and what your father would want you to do. My God I hope I do not offend you by writing this way.   A few specific comments. On Page 3 I wrote next to the first paragraph (the big hand pulling David and the bird down) "Marvelous." It is a fantastic picture. Page 4, middle of page, not too clear perhaps because this photo-copy is not too clear. "We were a very wild tribe and we killed each other off. And whoever went (what?) we killed." Bottom of Page 4, I think you can say this better. Page 5 where the lady giants served the food you will not be surprised to hear I wrote M.C.P[1]!!! (Joke, but I will let it stand as I know you are not a m.c.p.) Page 6, I wrote "lovely" where David looks out through those eyes (of the fish) and he never saw such a lovely world. Beautiful. The ms. is full of beautiful passages, Maurice, and at present (in this version) they are not easy to find with so much repetition and so little dialogue. The story needs shortening and at the same time opening up. Don't you agree? Isn't it in fact the story of a boy's

---

1. Male Chauvinist Pig.

search for his parents? There are at present too many digressions and we lose sight of the basic story, which is so important. I'll skip a few more marginal notes and go to Page 17. Could the parents be mentioned in the first paragraph? There should be some sense of urgency to his journey. Bottom of Page 17, could you expand (about rabbi and Torah etc.) or tell more about it earlier? Here it seems to slow up movement. Page 18, middle of page you say "they aimed their bows and arrows and shot at the animals …… The children cried 'David saved the sheep!' Because his aim was fine and he had frightened away the animals." Can you make clearer above that it was mainly David's ability with the bow and arrow that killed almost all the wild animals? A small point but again the clearer you can make it, the better. Page 19. "Then he (David) told them wonderful things." Now if you and/or I could ask your father, "Tell us more, what sort of wonderful things? Give us a for instance or two" I am sure he would tell us some SPECIFIC "wonderful things." So I think it isn't your taking any liberties with your father's work to tell us more here, as he would have been able to. Page 20, I wrote "is this episode important? It's sort of a little bit too much?" Of course you may have already cut out and changed a lot of places so perhaps I won't go on giving specific notes. For instance top of Page 28 is really very unclear and dense. And very very important, and more about this later, bottom of Page 26, were the parents dead or not? The ghastly dream convinced me! Oh it wasn't a dream—I just went back to the first two pages. Dr. Freud help! Page 32 (in an additional chapter) so good about people who take things for granted "as though everything was due them." So good, I hope you can keep this somehow.

I hope this week with your family in Conn. is as happy a one as it can be under the circumstances. You can see I have left this in my typewriter for several days, going over and over the manuscript and getting jittery about what I have already written in this letter. It is now Aug. 11.   I hope the music for *Nutshell*[1] is moving ahead. I hope you won't mind anything I have written in this letter. Phone or write me when you want to talk. I will be here through August.   Lots of love, and regards to your family. I will write Jack[2] later today or tomorrow. I am not quite accustomed to this typewriter so forgive all typos!

As ever,

TO MARGARET WARNER[3]   Bridgewater
                                                  August 31??, 1973

Dear Margaret:

Just talked with you on the phone and am so glad you can rush that note off to Billy [Pène du Bois] about *Grandson Lew*[4] this afternoon. I think your ideas all excellent and—as I said on the phone—shifting pics on Pages 25 and 31 and getting him to add a loving little spot for Page 32 will be fine. The size of the type on title page and 1/2 title doesn't bother me. But will go with what D. Hagen thinks.

I never told D. Hagen that there would be color just on

---

1. *Really Rosie, starring the Nutshell Kids*, a half-hour-long animated film, with music by Carole King, first aired on CBS in February 1975. Harper published a companion volume containing the TV script, the four *Nutshell* texts, and the music for Carole King's songs under the title *Maurice Sendak's Really Rosie: Starring the Nutshell Kids*, 1975.
2. Jack Sendak, author; MS's older brother.
3. UN's editorial assistant since 1971 left Harper in late 1973 to become a journalist. MW began her new career as a reporter for a New Hampshire newspaper. She later became well known for her work on the PBS *NewsHour with Jim Lehrer*.
4. *My Grandson Lew*, by Charlotte Zolotow, illustrated by William Pène du Bois, 1974.

one side of the sheet. I think I told her it would be just like *William's Doll*, and I believe that has color on both sides of the sheet. Haven't got a copy here. She shouldn't try to make a liar out of me when I am 80 miles away and can't give her a karate chop.

Glad you agreed about the Crawford novel.[1] I will return it tomorrow. Mary is rushing to get *Grandson Lew* stapled and she will drive me to the post office. Don't dare rely on a neighbor to drive it in to you on Tuesday, and I am sure it will arrive safely on your desk Tuesday a.m. via this great book bag arrangement you cooked up.

Working out of the office on a picture book isn't like the work on the [Pat] Myrer submission, or on Crawford, on Sendak or Lil Hoban's partial ms. of jr. novel.[2] Especially when there is all this rush as it should get on the spring list (*Lew*, I mean). I was so dumb about this ms. for years. At least it seemed like years—and to CZ[3] too. I kept picking it up and reading it and rereading it and I kept referring to it to CZ as "I don't know what to think about your Death Manuscript." It drove her wild. Of course I later saw it is the opposite of a Death Manuscript, and I am now very sentimental in a good way about it. And I really do think Billy's pictures are good. And I think your suggestions are all simply fine, Margaret. I wrote a few notes on the margins of the artwork so look through it again, will you? You are a dandy girl, and I do not have a gravelly voice or a growly one.   Love to all, and thanks for all the super ideas and efficient help on this book!

1. The reference is to Charles P. Crawford, who published three novels with Harper Junior Books, including one, titled *Three-Legged Race*, that was published the following year.
2. *I Met a Traveller*, by Lillian Hoban, 1977.
3. Charlotte Zolotow.

Dear —————— :

Ellen Rudin has given me your recent letter about Tomi Ungerer's *No Kiss for Mother*[1], in answer to hers of September 20th. I am the person who accepted Tomi's first book for publication by Harper many years ago and I also accepted *No Kiss for Mother*. I wish I could give you a good concise paragraph about "the sorting out process which certainly must take place," but I would find it difficult to do so. Of course we have standards and I think the Harper Junior backlist proves that we do. But every book is subjected to individual judgment. We all share your concern for good books for children.

Tomi is a brilliant, creative person and this book was very important to him. I think it is a book to which boys (and men) may respond more positively than will women. But a lot of little girls think it is just as funny as boys do. I didn't like the character of the mother and her relationship with his son. But that was the whole point of Tomi's book, and I had to face the fact that Tomi was writing a story he HAD to write, to get certain emotions and feelings off his chest. I did ask Tomi not to make the mother-son relationship quite so unpleasant. Tomi felt he couldn't change it. He felt very strongly about it.

Yes, there was one unfavorable review in *School Library Journal*. I enclose a copy. But the other reviews, including the ones Ellen Rudin sent you, were favorable. Perhaps we (and I include myself—an ardent feminist) are being too serious about what is basically a rambunctious, funny book about a bad relationship that is somehow somewhat improved by the end of the book.

I know that this is not a satisfactory answer to your letter, and I am sorry. I have thought about this more than you can

---

1. *No Kiss for Mother*, by Tomi Ungerer, 1973.

possibly imagine. As I said above, we truly share your concern for good children's books.

Yours sincerely,

TO RUSSELL HOBAN January 16, 1974

Dear Russ:

First of all I would be DELIGHTED to see the pages of *Najork*[1], even though it has gone to Atheneum. I guess you may be right that we might have been more enthusiastic if we'd seen it with pictures though I've always thought we, in this dept., could visualize a book with often nothing more than a one-page typescript, take it, and then find the right artist. But apparently we missed the boat on this one. It did have several readings and much thought and we hated not to accept it. Of not much interest to you at this point!

Yes, I do feel sad about not taking *Numbering Around*[2]. Can't help it. You spoke of the changes in the character of your work and in our mode of "doing business." I very much miss seeing you as an author and knowing a little bit about what was going [on] in your mind about your work. I do know editors go to London to see authors and publishers and I'm glad to tell you that Ellen Rudin will be going to Bologna in April and then to England and I know she wants very much to see you and have a talk.   I never did make a lot of trips abroad. Once I went to the Frankfurt Book Fair and was so horrified at the amt.

---

1. *How Tom Beat Captain Najork and His Hired Sportsmen*, by Russell Hoban, illustrated by Quentin Blake, Atheneum, 1974.
2. This manuscript may have been the one published as *Ten What?: A Mystery Counting Book*, by Russell Hoban, illustrated by Sylvie Selig. The book was first published in England by Jonathan Cape in 1974, and was brought out the following year in the United States by Scribner's.

of the firm's money I was spending (and of the complete confusion at the booths which were always manned or womanned by no one with any real authority to buy or sell) that I got tense and bought a magnificent color picture book entitled *Gaetano the Pheasant* by Guido Rocca[1]. It was a beautiful book but by the time we got through producing it in this country I wonder whether it was wise to take it on or not.   Anyhow, our talks about your work, as you describe them in this last letter, meant much to me and perhaps were mutually valuable. I know I always got more from you than you ever got from me, but I think it did help you once in a while to think out loud to me, however. And I'm sorry that letters will have to do for the present. But there needn't be the long gaps you mentioned in our correspondence. That was a real foul-up last summer. It was an adjustment for me working out of the office when I'd always been here in the eye of the hurricane so to speak for so many years. But it is an adjustment I have made and it is a good one for the authors with whom I still work. Of course you can have my Bridgewater address. BAD gets my mail here just because some days I am at home working in the NY apt. and some times I am working in Bridgewater. But BAD always knows where I am. Anyhow, I will be in New York except for a few snowy days here and there in Bridgewater so you can always write to my apt. 870 United Nations Plaza, Apt. 9A. If you don't get an IMMEDIATE answer just assume I have gone to Conn. for a few days.

Dimmed-out London must be bad. The 3 day week must be awful. We are getting messages from D. Hagen about paper shortages, and I just heard from an author of ours who makes a tremendous amount of dough on paperback sales that the shortage will make it necessary for the paperback houses to cut

1. *Gaetano the Pheasant*, by Guido Rocca, illustrated by Giulio Cingoli and Giancarlo Carloni, 1966.

down on printings and therefore on advances.   But for some reason I keep feeling optimistic, that it is not as bad as we are being told. If we could just get rid of Nixon! Bad as Gerald Ford might be it would be better than having this dreadful man as president.

About Bridgewater, 53rd St., and UN Plaza. It will soon be all much simpler. In May we are hoping to sell the apartment and then I will be in Connecticut most of the time, coming to NY only when absolutely necessary. But this winter I am in NY most of the time (and in the office part of almost every day). I will hate to give up the apt. which I love, but it will be a pleasure not to see New York City except very infrequently.

I try to keep off personal questions but do you plan to stay in England for the foreseeable future?   Aside from Ellen's trip this April it <u>might</u> be possible for me to come over some time on my own, combining a vacation trip with some good time with you. I don't know. The thing is, Russ, that what was so great with our working relationship over the years was the cumulative effect of frequent, informal meetings. So many great things came out of your head during luncheons at repulsive 10 Park! And that long day at Bedford Hills when we went swimming and you put *Bedtime for Frances* together in such a perfect way. So a few days visit in London by me wouldn't at all be the same thing.   Well, write me again. Sounds as though work is going well on *Turtle Diary*[1].   Yes, you did write me in your last summer's letter about your workshop. I wish I could attend it..... So let's keep in touch by letters, and send the *Najork* when you can. Looking back I probably have missed good things by not going to London but I was able to take a lot of awfully good things just being available at that succession of crumb-y offices on dirty old East 33rd Street.

---

1. *Turtle Diary*, a work of adult fiction, was published in England by Jonathan Cape in 1975 and in the United States by Random House in 1976.

Anyhow, Ellen will be there and will see you and that will be great for you and for her.

Love,

TO EDWARD GOREY   January 25, 1974

Dear Edward:

I hope you have opened the envelope and that is why I am writing on the envelope THIS IS NOT ABOUT *THE INTERESTING LIST* BUT ANOTHER BOOK.

We loved your jacket for *Freaky Friday* and wonder if you would like to do the jacket for Mary Rodger's [*sic*] next book? It is about the same characters in *Freaky Friday* and so of course we would like the jacket to be done by you too. If your schedule is too full I better hear that now so I can (1) kill myself and (2) find another jacket artist.

Now here I am with a lot of space left on this paper and so in spite of my promise on the envelope I will ask you what about your *An Interesting List*. It is one of my strongest hopes that you will finish it and let us publish it as soon as possible and consistent with beautiful reproduction of your marvelous pictures. Any chance of it within the next month or so? What is blocking you? Edward, I see your name as illustrator of books for all other publishers and this doesn't help my inferiority complex one bit. After all, we were at one time engaged and though the engagement was broken by mutual agreement, I am still an admirer of yours and would very much like to get *An Interesting List* on the interesting Harper list before a truck knocks me down and kills me. I am going to be out of the office for a few days next week but you can always leave a message for me with Miss Dicks, 595-7015, or drop me a line. On a chance I just phoned, but as usual got your answering service.

Do let me know about the Rodgers jacket. We'd need it by the middle of March. There's no immediate rush because we still haven't got a title. But I want to know if you think you can do it or do I have to start to find someone else. And compared with you there is no one else …….

As ever,

TO MAURICE SENDAK   May 20, 1974

Dearest Mr. Senlak:

I should have written before this to send a bread and butter and roll and tuna-fish letter. I enjoyed my visit with you tremendously and I loved hearing the cassette of the t.v. project.[1] It is going to be marvelous. I have told lots of Harper people about it, and told about hearing the words and music when we had our sales conference. Everyone is really excited and I hope all goes smoothly with absolutely no complications.

Fran M[anushkin] wants me to ask you about the last page of *Where the Wild Things Are*. As you know, new plates are being made and before the new edition comes out we wonder if you want to change the last word from "hot" to "warm." I can't for the life of me remember the history of all this but I believe we heard from a couple of children (or their rotten parents) that "and it was still warm" would be better than "and it was still hot" because children don't like hot foot [*sic*]. Listen, have you ever had such great editorial comment in your life? Anyhow,

1. Work continued on *Really Rosie*.

just a note to ask you if you ever cared one way or another. If you want to keep it hot that is OK by me and by us, of course. I just couldn't remember if you even wanted to give the "still warm" idea a second thought.

Maurice, it did me so much good to see you looking so well and strong and healthy. When I give you a little hug now it is all just solid rock. Well, you were always perfect but in earlier years there wasn't quite SUCH solid rock. What am I saying? I mean it as a compliment, dear sir.

I'm going to be in Bridgewater from this Wednesday on until about Tuesday the 28th. Give me a ring there if you feel like it and tell me about the last word in *Wild Things*.

Lots of love.

TO KATHARINE S. WHITE   Bridgewater
                                          June 26, 1974

Dear Katharine:

Yours of June 24th arrived with a copy of the paragraph from Louise Bechtel[1]. I was so glad to have this reaction from Louise. We never spoke of A[nne] C[arroll] M[oore] and *Stuart [Little]* in earlier years. It was always somehow so embarrassing that ACM had been so awful about *Stuart*. One averted one's eyes if possible. I remember when I was a child and something awful happened on the street, you know, one didn't look. Absolutely didn't look—ACM and *Stuart*, well, it was like a

1. Louise Seaman Bechtel, founding editor, from 1919, of Macmillan's pioneering children's book department, and later a reviewer for the *New York Herald-Tribune* and other publications. In both her professional capacities, Bechtel had had occasion to take strong exception with the views about children's books expressed by the New York Public Library's Anne Carroll Moore. See footnote 1, page 20, to letter to Clare Turlay Newberry, November 28, 1947.

dreadful accident, a horse fallen down. No, that doesn't say what I mean.

You say the strike[1] should be arbitrated, and I'm glad to be able to tell you that both sides met with the State Arbitrator yesterday. I haven't the latest details. But at any rate, there was an arbitration meeting. The newspaper accounts are garbled, as you will not be surprised to hear. Yes, there are a lot of women who are vocal and militant. But actually the strike hasn't to do with the woman's movement. I am in complete sympathy with the woman's movement even though some of our sisters make not as much sense as some of us wish they would. I've been working for over 40 years and the worst curse I could put on any man is: "In your next life may you be born a talented and creative woman." I gather from the way you write that you are not in much sympathy—but I guess your career at *The New Yorker* was never hindered by the fact that you were a woman. Enough of this, however.

Publishing is, as you say, a sacred trust. And particularly so I feel when one is involved with publishing for children. Teaching is also the same sort of field. So strikes are terribly disturbing for us here. But I must say no more. I hope it will all be over by the time you receive this. And thanks again so much for sharing Louise Bechtel's note with me. I may write her myself one of these days, to be in touch. I never knew her well but admired her greatly.

Love to you both as ever.

2. On June 17, 1974, members of the Association of Harper & Row Employees, then an independent union, went on strike in a dispute with management over the terms of a new three-year contract. This strike, the first to affect the United States publishing industry since the 1930s, ended seventeen days later, on July 3, when a new contract was agreed to. The episode, which included crossed picket lines and implied threats of imminent firings, was a bitter one for all concerned. UN's fierce, and by then rather old-fashioned, loyalty to Harper prevented her from expressing, and perhaps from feeling, much sympathy for the strikers.

TO BARBARA ALEXANDRA DICKS

Southbury
December 26, 1974

Dearest BAD. I enclose a note to E. Gorey which I hope you will mail to him. As you see I wrote it earlier in Dec. but didn't want it floating around in the Xmas mish-mash. I will send you other epistles I have written and not sent you. As you know, I am carrying on a correspondence with George Woods none of which needs to be seen or circulated. He writes about various subjects and encloses clippings of things he has written, but nothing to do with a future George Woods book. If something comes up in the correspondence that I think would be of editorial interest to Ellen [Rudin] and/or others in the dept. I will let you know. I think *Catch a Killer* hasn't sold so badly.....

As I told you, I am going to see Sandy Rabinowitz[1] in her Conn. place this coming weekend. She says the whole house is decorated for Chanukah and Christmas and I am looking forward to seeing it. I believe she has abandoned the idea of Paul Revere and his horse for the bicentennial, and that she has some other ideas. I will try to "draw her out.".......

I also have letters to Marijane [Meaker] that I will send in (mailed from Conn.) As I said over the phone, I think to you but it may have been Edite[2], I want to type up brief summaries of the notes from Marijane when I send in my carbons. Marijane also includes fascinating little personal items not for carbon circulation, but the gist of the rest should be on record in the office.

I am so happy to have the colored picture postcard of Billy Pène du Bois in his antique Rolls Royce at the rally in Monte Carlo. God, how I miss seeing his beaming face and hearing his

---

1. Author and illustrator, whose first book, *The Red Horse and the Bluebird*, was published in 1975.
2. Edite Kroll, editor in the department; later a literary agent.

silly half-sentences, concluded only by waving his arms or giving me a blow on the shoulder. Anyhow, this card will enable me to shout at his demon agent, Mike Watkins, when he tries to hold us up at gun-point. I don't know any children's book publishing people who have a Rolls Royce ......

I enclose a reprint of an article by H. A. Rey, author of the great *Curious George* books. As you circulate this Ellen will of course see it and decide if she does or does not want to sound out someone who reads *Scientific American* (L[ucille] S[chultz]?? not UN, anyhow). Please everyone remember that in addition to the *Curious George* books H. A. Rey also did an adult book for Houghton Mifflin, about *The Stars*[1], and then they did a jr. edition of it which continues to sell. I mean he is a scholar and student and a subscriber to the *Bulletin of Atomic Scientists* and all like that. ..... He is not just a dear man who does wonderful picture books. (This is coming out very snobby about picture books and Heaven knows I don't mean that. I just want Ellen to know that he is an extremely erudite person, though he may have a little age on him.) Anyhow, I was fascinated by his article on Wind-power and I looked up fly-wheels in the *American College Dictionary* but part of the definition used the word "piston" in it and as I don't know from pistons, I don't know really what a fly-wheel is. But maybe there is a science I Can Read book in "windmills" or perhaps a book for older readers about wind-power in general. Rey's little article was extremely interesting and stimulating to me, and perhaps it will seem so on East 53rd Street. Anyhow, here it is. I will write Rey that I am sending it in. He may not want to do anything about it himself, but if not and if the idea is appealing to Ellen, he would be happy to have anyone else do it, I am sure. I met him and Margret (correct spelling that, MARGRET) when they were

1. *The Stars: A New Way to See Them*, by H. A. Rey, Houghton Mifflin, 1952. Rey's children's book on the subject was *Find the Constellations*, Houghton Mifflin, 1954.

refugees early in the forties, and he did a couple of books for us—not too successful. *Curious George* went to HMCo. before I met them because their London editor, Grace Hogarth, was there for the duration of W.W.2. He promised to do for Harper a pictorial history of the world, and in my feckless fashion I gave him a $500.00 advance and a set of the *Encyclopedia Britannica* (my personal gift—I must have been nuts then as now). But he never did it. It was going to be marvelous—in full color, and showing pictorially by interesting little figures in charts what was going on at the same time over various parts of the world— for instance, A. Lincoln was born the year Napoleon went over the Alps (or somewhere, it was so long ago I cannot remember it exactly). But it came to naught. However, it did cement relations and Mrs. Rey wrote *Spotty* which had a very very good sale, as did *Pretzel*. His *Elizabite*[1], about a carnivorous plant, frightened some of the adults and never sold well. Anyhow, here is the reprint and I send it just in case it may interest others there as it does me. I will write Rey that I'm sharing this with Ellen and the rest of the dept. but put it so that if he doesn't hear anything more from anyone there he won't be surprised.....

I am carrying on a rather interesting correspondence with Helen Sims. She is the young woman Jane Langton[2] told to write to me, and she did and sent me the first chapter of a proposed jr. novel. I told her she'd have to let me see more before I could give her any constructive reactions, and I also asked her to write me at length and in whatever personal detail she cared to. I received a five page single-spaced perfectly typed letter from her and I am answering it in some detail and with care. No way of telling if she has any real writing ability or not but she certainly has some interesting material. (Pocket just walked in

1. *Elizabite: Adventures of a Carnivorous Plant*, by H. A. Rey, 1942.
2. Novelist for children and adults.

and kissed me on the ankle and I'm sure she sends love to everyone there. Pass it on.) Helen Sims' letter is full of fascinating sidelights and I have read it several times. It is a little self-conscious, as why wouldn't it be. I do hope something comes of all this as it would be great for Helen Sims and also a shot in the arm for me. I have adjusted to not being in the eye of the hurricane (of course I have created my own UN hurricane at this desk and in this bedroom-office) but I do miss the opportunity of LISTENING to young hopeful writers and artists..... Also to the young people in the Jr. Book Department, of course. Well, I listen by phone and by letters, but the head-to-head meant much to me. Everyone always gave me so MUCH stimulation and excitement that I almost had to give some of it back or I would have overflowed, and so much stuff going back and forth all the time ...... Phone just rang, where was I. Again, sorry to miss Shel [Silverstein] on Xmas Eve (such a great time for his oft-postponed visit) but he sounds happy over his book, at least when he last called me he sounded blissful. We should get it in writing ..... Anyhow, back to Helen Sims and this burgeoning correspondence. I am not sending it in to the office because I think she feels she is writing from her heart to my heart and includes things not for carbon folders. But I wanted to mention this new activity in this letter so you'll all know what's going on here at the moment.

I told Marijane that I was so thrilled to see that Martha Graham quote ("Keep the channel open") on the program of Louise Fitzhugh's memorial service.[1] She said Louise had always carried it in her wallet and I believe I gave her a copy some years

1. Fitzhugh had died suddenly, at the age of forty-six, of an aneurysm. At the memorial service held at St. James' Episcopal Church in Manhattan, tributes by Maurice Sendak, the novelist Peter Taylor (who was her uncle), Marijane Meaker, and the poet James Merrill were read. For the text of the Martha Graham quotation referred to here, see Introduction, page xxxiv.

ago when she was blocked. Made me feel warm, somehow.

It's beautiful here and the *NY Times* is delivered to the door in Heritage Village[1], and there are many Chanukah-Christmas parties going on all the time.

Oh, another news note which I've told to B[arbara] B[orack] and CZ. On Christmas Eve at 10.30 a.m. Crosby Bonsall called in a great fury and said she was in Bridgewater and they were driving up and down Curtis Road and they couldn't find us and couldn't get us by phone, so they went into the General Store and Mrs. Gowan there (the village crier) .. (I mean she knows all about where a fire is, where the ambulance is going, etc.) told her we were in Heritage Village. So over they came, Crosby and George, and we had an absolutely marvelous re-union. We sat around here and talked and had coffee and then they took us out for Christmas Eve luncheon, and it was lots of fun. She wasn't writing anything these days, just couldn't somehow, but I didn't pursue it. She stopped smoking in November and that can throw you off your stride a bit, I think. Anyhow, she's been not able to write before and has always snapped back and I trust she will this time. She said not to tell B. B. any of this but of course I did and of course Crosby already had. I said vaguely, "I hear you're thinking of writing a chapter book" and she said quickly, "And I'm not working on THAT either." Anyhow, it was a lovely interlude and so different from those noisy Christmas Eve luncheons at New York restaurants where the waiters are always half-drunk, to say nothing of the customers, and the service is rotten, and it isn't at all what Jesus had in mind, I always felt ...... Well, there's my news for now. More later. Am dying for a detailed account of your N. H. trip. Lots of love to all and esp. to you, my dear liaison wonder-person. [. . .]

---

1. The condominium community in Southbury, Connecticut, where UN was spending winters.

TO E. B.   Southbury
AND KATHARINE WHITE   January 16, 1975

Dear Andy and Katharine too:

I hear great things about the *Letters*[1]. I can't wait to read
them. I know you will be sorry to have Beulah[2] leave, but as you
know Frances Lindley[3] is a terrific person, warm and wise and
of course an all-time E.B.W. fan. So you'll be OK. I hate
changes myself. And I don't think it is necessarily a sign of age.
In 1952 a "weather girl" on t.v. was replaced by someone else
and I found I would have preferred re-runs of old and out-of-
date weather forecasts by the original. Oh why do I get started
on an idiotic sentence like that. Sorry.

As you know but may have not remembered, I now work
and live in Bridgewater, Conn. I go into NY once in a while to
go to a sales conference and present the books for which I am
responsible, but otherwise it is the country, and I like it very
much. The little house in Bridgewater is not really good for
a New England winter so I am spending the snow-and-ice
months in Heritage Village, a condominium community near
Bridgewater. Now I am giving you all these unnecessary autobiographical details because Heritage Village has a very sweet
little library, and there I found your sub-treasury of American
humor[4]. My own copy was borrowed AND NEVER
RETURNED several decades ago, and I fell upon the library

1. *Letters of E. B. White*, collected and edited by Dorothy Lobrano Guth, 1976. After
   Mary Griffith commented on how delighted UN always seemed to be to receive a
   letter from White, UN wrote to the author proposing that Harper publish a book
   of his correspondence.
2. Beulah Hagen, longtime assistant to Cass Canfield and editor, retired in January
   1975.
3. Lindley worked first in advertising for the Adult Trade department and then as an
   editor.
4. *A Subtreasury of American Humor*, edited by E. B. White and Katharine S. White,
   Coward, McCann, 1941.

book with delight. The introduction made me feel I was right in a room with you, and I loved it. It is such a good book! One thing I found depressing—the acknowledgments mentioned publishing houses long gone, or merged, or sold.

Andy, if you suddenly write another children's book, which we all long for, let me know. A note to me c/o Barbara Dicks will always be forwarded promptly. Or 1031B, Heritage Village, Southbury, Conn. 06488. At least until April. Thank you for your Christmas card. I didn't send any this year.   Oh, one good thing about Heritage Village is that the *N. Y. Times* is delivered to one's door at 7 a.m. In Bridgewater it is a 4 mile drive into New Milford. Though the *Times* doesn't seem the same now that Dick[1] has gone back to San Clemente....

Hope you are both well, and again I am looking forward to reading the letters at least in galleys.

TO ETHEL HEINS[2]   Bridgewater
                                                         June 16, 1975

Dear Ethel:

I have meant to write you before this about the piece about M[argaret] W[ise] B[rown][3]. I have made several very false starts—every one interrupted by emergency trips to New Hampshire where my parents, both well into their eighties are quite ill, and will not be moved out of their old New England farmhouse. Bad bad time of life for them and a darn difficult one for their only daughter who is now well into her hundreds ......   Anyhow, I haven't forgotten the article

1. President Richard M. Nixon had resigned in disgrace on August 9, 1974.
2. Editor of *The Horn Book* from 1974 to 1984; librarian, educator, critic.
3. UN never completed the article.

and I will keep trying. I have written Clem [Hurd] and Garth [Williams] and am going to write Leonard [Weisgard] to help refresh my memory about some of the books they illustrated with her. I asked Barbara Dicks at the office, my liaison with the department but more importantly about the most efficient and capable person imaginable with an incredible memory, to send me the MWB file. Unfortunately BAD didn't know MWB so her memory is no help, and the file itself is pitifully bare. Most of MWB's business with us was done verbally, at breakfast or luncheon. I remember meeting her at a restaurant at 12th and 5th one morning at 8 a.m. for breakfast and she ordered some sort of fish—which came with its head on and its eyes in. I almost fainted but the children's book editor went cheerfully ahead and devoured the whole thing.   Actually, as I looked through this skimpy folder and thought back to those days with MWB I realized one of the reasons I still am so emotional about her is that she was such a big part of a still young editor's beginning to learn to try to be a children's book editor. I followed Louise Raymond at Harper, who followed Virginia Kirkus, and my taking over the department came at a time when an influential California librarian told me "they" couldn't even consider any of the Laura Ingalls Wilder books for the Newbery "because we don't like series books." I babbled "but these are hardly Bobbsey Twin books," (traitor, for I loved the Bobbsey twins when I was little). Anyhow, there were all sorts of rules and regulations and inhibitions and MWB helped to blow them away—which of course you know and which is why you want an article about her. But I was still following what I'd had drilled into me about what the librarians would not like, by Louise Raymond, and I kept worrying about MWB's refusal to let me put in commas.   Well, none of this makes sense but I am just trying to explain why it is really terribly hard to write anything very objectively about MWB's Harper work. I hope Garth will tell me a bit about *The Friendly*

Book[1], which he and MWB did for Golden (Harper couldn't keep up with her output and Golden offered her thousands and thousands of dollars which she could always use, of course, as she lived extravagantly.) Anyhow, Ethel, something will be coming along one of these days. I haven't wanted to do anything right this much in a long long time, so be patient???

All best wishes.

BAD does her best to send me *Horn Book*, *SLJ*, etc. after they have circulated in the department, so I do see them eventually but late. I've just caught up with the issue which has the article about excellence in books by Mary Steele,[2] and want to compliment you and your staff on that whole issue. Truly interesting and lively. Your job must be absorbing, but not easy.

TO BARBARA ALEXANDRA DICKS   Bridgewater
September 25, 1975

Dearest BAD:

Glad you had a good vacation and very glad you're back. SAF[3] was most helpful while you were away and fortunately there wasn't too much going back and forth between the office and me during your absence. As you will see when you catch up on the carbons, I wrote Molly [Stolz] two long letters about her most recent ms.,[4] and this is for the record: she called me

---

1. *The Friendly Book*, by Margaret Wise Brown, illustrated by Garth Williams, Simon & Schuster, 1954. This book was Little Golden Book 199.
2. Mary Q. Steele, Newbery Honor–winning author of fiction and fantasy for children, and an occasional contributor to *The Horn Book*.
3. Sara Ann Freed, permissions editor, Harper Junior Books.
4. *Ferris Wheel*, by Mary Stolz, 1977.

yesterday—or asked JRR[1] and/or Liz Gordon[2] to have me call her—and she said she was completely rewriting the book, completely overhauling it. She sounded very good and very "up" and appreciative of all the time and effort that went into the marginal notes I typed up and sent her. At least she was at the exact time we talked yesterday! I hope it will last.

I enclose a carbon copy of a letter to Andy [White]. I know you will be stuck with a lot of royalty problems for days but will send this along anyhow. Yesterday SAF was going to send me copies of the 1952 letters as of course I don't remember much about the contents of the exchange. I will send on to Andy from here. As requested on the carbon, maybe you or someone could share my letter to Andy with Corona[3] so she can see that more is coming. I am very happy to know she is being eager with Andy over *The Letters* as he and Katharine some months ago gave me the impression that they had the impression that Harper wasn't really interested in the forthcoming book of *EBW Letters*. I tried to tell them they were wrong, but having Corona's eagerness obviously pleases Andy and therefore Katharine. I do think it will be a fascinating book.

Well, you will see my note to Shel [Silverstein]. Yesterday he phoned me (he's talked to Barbara Borack) and told me he was sending *The Missing Link*[4] to you so you could send it to me with the proper return envelope etc. Of course Barbara B. should look at it before it comes to me. Shel promised me that it was in really good and almost final shape—none of the thousands of pieces of paper and none of the millions of changes, etc. etc. that *Sidewalk*[5] involved. I hope with all my heart that

---

1. Joanne Ryder.
2. Elizabeth Gordon, editor; in 1983 she was to become the head of the department.
3. Corona Machemer, Harper & Row Adult Trade editor who oversaw the publication of *Letters of E. B. White*.
4. *The Missing Piece*, by Shel Silverstein, 1976.
5. *Where the Sidewalk Ends*.

this is really the case. When he came out to see me in H. V. he recited the whole thing to me and at that time I thought it was very very good (in fact terrific). I hope he hasn't messed it up—and I am pretty sure he hasn't. At any rate, I am hoping it can be a fall 1976 book and if it is as close to final form as he said over the phone, it can be.   I was sorry yesterday not to be at either phone number for several hours. I was going to be in H. V. all day and at my phone post, and working, but went in the a.m. with Mary [Griffith] to the car repair place and it took hours instead of minutes, and then it broke down on the way back. Another country living complication—in Bridgewater all the mailboxes near us on Curtis Road were knocked off their stands by some bums from New Milford, so the mail can't be delivered, and we have to go to the post office to pick it up. Nothing yesterday (Wednesday) and SAF told me she'd sent me several things on Monday. Of course the situation is most irritating. Molly Stolz rec'd her copy of *Cat*[1] and I haven't mine as yet. I am also very anxious to get whatever SAF sent, and also the EBW copies of 1952 letters.   No more for now. Mary is going out and will mail this. Lots of love and please stop taking these frequent and lengthy vacations—it is very unsettling to this country. So just stop it.

P.S. Could you send me more envelopes and some more stamps, please? To H. V. as we will be spending more time there from now on, though for the moment still in Bridgewater. We go to H. V. a couple of times a week to transfer stuff.   The rain continues!!!!!

---

1. *Cat in the Mirror*, by Mary Stolz, 1975.

TO MARY STOLZ   Bridgewater
                                          September 12, 1976

Dearest Molly:

I have misplaced your last letter. My filing system is unbe-
lievably chaotic—it is non-existent. Anyhow, this is to say that I
am glad you are enjoying the Florida life so much but I personally simply detest your being there. What is that phrase? I find
it "personally obnoxious." Something like that. I hate it, I hate
it, I hate it, hear?????

I hope you are all set with your typewriter and that the next
ms. is in the works. I know you think I am not interested in the
Haunted Cuckoo Clock[1] but that is not true. I just want you to
write what you want to write, of course, but I am simply worried when you decide you want to do a very young PICTURE
book because you haven't been satisfied yourself with how your
younger books have done. And now picture books with even
two colors have to be listed at $6.95 unless the publisher can
print a huge edition, and all in all I don't know how this picture
book thing is going to end up. I was able to do one of Ruth
Krauss' first crazy books at $1.00, in an edition of 5000. I
remember thinking, well, we can sell at least a couple of thousand copies, and if we get stuck I can gradually buy the rest of
that first printing myself because at that time the employees
could get a 50% discount........   Why am I going on
like this. Just thinking on paper to you that I'm glad I had the
chance to take chances when to do a picture book in color didn't
cost a fortune......

An author spent most of the day here the other day going
over a long long ms. line for line with me, and whenever she
disagreed with one of my (really quite good and thoughtful)

---

1. This manuscript was later published as *The Cuckoo Clock*, illustrated by Pamela
   Johnson, Godine, 1986.

points, she'd say that her house-guest had particularly liked that special part I was criticizing. I resisted the desire to ask her what publishing house her house guest had been an editor at. Anyhow, I wish it had been you here with me, talking about a ms. Didn't we have a GREAT DAY in Washington that time? It all went so well and smoothly with the Egyptian ms.[1], and then the pandas and the sunshine, and the LOVELY dinner you treated me to! We've had a lot of fun, haven't we, Molly. Well, this has a dismal autumnal tone to it. Doubtless we'll meet again and have good times talking about your work, among many other things. But right now I wish you were here with handsome Tom, and we could sit on the little patio and look at the hills and then go swimming. The pool is still open. I've had a nasty little interior upset of a horrid sort, unsuitable for a dame with a poetic soul, need I say more. But today I feel OK physically and had a marvelous swim. The air is about 75 degrees and the heated pool is 80. DELICIOUS!!!!!!   Write me, and tell me exactly how you are and how Tom is, and do you miss me too??????   Did your tenant survive the move into 52 Pride's Crossing? I must say I'm glad we don't have that special street address any more, though I found it better than the earlier Birdsong Lane. But for heaven's sake, stop moving until you come back to Conn. and STAY PUT.   How was Eileen?

Lots of love to you both, always.

1. *Cat in the Mirror.*

TO MARY RODGERS (MRo)   Southbury
                                      January 28, 1980

Dearest Mary:

I loved your letter in answer to my formal note of sympathy.[1] Bloomingdale's note on the envelope touched me
deeply. No, I didn't have any psychic kicks and am glad you
haven't too. Glad everyone is being fine and sensible, and of
course that dear Hank [Guettel] is such a lovely human being.
I did love your letter, Mary, not the least because your salutation was "oh Urs, I adore you." Naturally I love it that you
adore me—it certainly is mutual—but especially because of the
way you spell Urs. A lot of people spell it Urse and this makes
my fingernails turn back. Or the unspeakable URSIE, or URSI
(European affection.) Well, enough of me and my pleasure in
your dear letter.

Please don't avoid me or anyone at Harper because of the
"dumb-assed movies."[2] My big question mark was sent just
because those men on the bottom line asked. But Barbara
[Dicks] had a good talk with Shirley[3], apparently a pearl among
agents, and Harper will want the ms. when you get to it. Notice
I say when—not if. Your important part of your creative life will
be attended to, and I do care about it because, you said it yourself, I care about you.

Charlotte [Zolotow] is doing a terrific job, naturally, and
the department is zooming. I am planning to slope off in my
activities in about another month or so. But of course Charlotte
is there and has a very fine staff. Also Joan Robins and Bill
Morris, and many of your other admirers. So you will be in the

1. The author's father, composer Richard Rodgers, had died recently after a long illness.
2. MR was involved in a variety of projects, including screenwriting. The author's
   third novel for children, *Summer Switch*, was published by Harper & Row in 1982.
3. MR's agent, Shirley Bernstein, of Paramuse Artists, Inc.

best of hands. Aside from Charlotte's brilliant editorial ability (which you already know about) the sales and promotion people love you and your books and will always be supportive—there's that word again. Charlotte understands my desire to slack off and has asked me, however, to be available to her on occasion which I will certainly agree to. But I won't be signing contracts or go on with this idiot "Ursula Nordstrom Book" gavotte, or dealing with agents, and I can forget about those tiny tiny little persons who live on the well-known bottom line.   Do you know that most publishers think one should pass up taking "marginal books"???? Fantastic. One could think *The Rotten Book* would have seemed a marginal book, and look what it led to! *Freaky Friday* and *Billion for Boris* will sell forever, and so will *Ape-Face*[1]. Also I think I printed about 7000 first edition of Silverstein's *Giving Tree*, and it sells more every year and is now approaching one million. Really. So I may, in my leisure time, start a small press called MARGINAL BOOKS, INC. Sendak said he would design a logo for it. What nonsense, excuse me. I expect to have little leisure time, I walk enormous distances each day, and of course in the summer I have to swim for a long time, and now of course the *N. Y. Times* has taken to publishing the equivalent of the Sunday *Times* every weekday. Then I may look at daytime television, some soap opera, and keep enough time for any odd jobs Charlotte wants me to do. So MAR-GINAL BOOKS, INC. may have to be postponed for a while. But I do think it is a nifty idea.

I am writing several of these "I'm sloping off" letters to authors with whom I have worked particularly closely. But none goes with as much love as this one to you. I will NEVER forget the friendship you showed me when I hit a low point in my professional life.

---

1. This is a reference to the book published as *Summer Switch*.

No need to answer this—you must have a thousand letters to write. I will send it to Charlotte to forward to you as she may want to enclose a note of her own.

L'amour toujours, you dolling goil,

[. . .]

TO SUSAN CARR HIRSCHMAN   January 29, 1980

Dear Susan:

Just a hasty note to congratulate you from the bottom of my heart on having the Honor Newbery book[1], and on the Honor Caldecott book[2], and—what did Charlotte tell me—EIGHT books on the Notable list[3]? Ye gods, that is simply terrific, and only 5 years after you started Greenwillow! You must celebrate with another box of Mallomars. Maybe they no longer make them, though. A ghastly thought.

Now I have the rest of this page, empty, and really nothing to say of any interest except the congratulations given in paragraph one. But I will rattle on anyhow. I understand you approve of Mr. Pomerance[4] and I certainly hope he is a great guy and that everything goes smoothly for our dear Charlotte [Zolotow]. I

1. *The Road from Home: The Story of an Armenian Girl*, David Kherdian, Greenwillow, 1979.
2. *Ben's Trumpet*, written and illustrated by Rachel Isadora, Greenwillow, 1979.
3. American Library Assocation Notable titles published by Greenwillow in 1979, of which there were nine, included: *Ben's Trumpet*; *Blue Sea*, by Robert Kalan, illustrated by Donald Crews; *Fast Friends: Two Stories*, by James Stevenson; *Living With a Parent Who Drinks Too Much*, by Judith S. Seixas; Kherdian's *The Road from Home*; *Seeing Is Believing*, by Elizabeth Shub, illustrated by Rachel Isadora; *The Talking Stone: An Anthology of Native American Tales and Legends*, edited by Dorothy de Wit, illustrated by Donald Crews; *A Treeful of Pigs*, by Arnold Lobel, illustrated by Anita Lobel; and *We Hide, You Seek*, by Jose Aruego and Ariane Dewey.
4. Norman Pomerance, group vice-president, Harper & Row trade imprints.

am enjoying this sort of country life immensely but around Christmas I got my usual psychosomatic flu—how I hate Charistmas [*sic*], and I remember you loved it so much, and you made copies of the words of a million Christmas carols, and made us all stand around in the department and sing the damn things. I tried to catch The Spirit from you, but never succeeded. Anyhow, the post flu depression hit me and I realized that I had entirely wasted my life. I should have been living this sort of peaceful-in-the-head existence all these years instead of trying to cope with—well, I needn't list for you, especially— all the various temperaments. I have now recovered from that extremely transient state of mind, thank you, and then Mary and I went to see *Kramer vs. Kramer*[1] and it hit me like a ton of bricks, especially when the little boy said "Where will my bed be. Where will my toys be?" I cried and couldn't stop. Then we picked up a copy of the book so I could cry (and wallow) even more. And there it was—the little boy wanted a story read to him called *The Runaway Bunny*..... I always loved that MWB book, even better than *Goodnight Moon*. It was so sweet that the mother always would go after the little bunny. So that sent me off again. I thought I had remembered EVERYTHING about divorce, but I hadn't remembered the frightening sense of self-preservation until the boy said "Where will my bed be?" Oh this is coming out like balderdash. But I'll send it along anyhow. Sometime tell me how old you were when your parents parted[2], and if it gave you pain then. This is ridiculous at my age but I was so flabbergasted by my reaction. I didn't mean to put down all this dopey autobiographical stuff but there isn't much (anything) you don't know about me so I'll let it stand.

1. The 1979 Academy Awarding-winning best feature film, starring Dustin Hoffman and Meryl Streep; based on *Kramer Versus Kramer: A Novel*, by Avery Corman, Random House, 1977.
2. SCH was five at the time of her parents' divorce.

Kramer etc. is an amazing movie and I'd love to hear your re-action to it. When, big Honor and Notable winner, your time permits.

Love,

TO MARY STOLZ Southbury
February 25, 1980

Dearest Molly:

Thanks for your beautiful card and friendly message. Glad you liked my exchange with Mary about my hair. In my next life I will be one of those wonderful women who are clever about their own hair. I blame this particular shortcoming on the fact that I had a devoted nurse until I was about eight. So now everything to do with my person seems impossible. Looking back I can blame all my shortcomings on my mother, of course. On vacations from school I was taken to Central Park to have rides on some poor little pony who simply buckled under my hugeness. I felt foolish and that has lasted into my great old age.   You are right, please let's not observe or mention birthdays. I will remember yours because of your Peggy and my Dick, but I won't mention it.

Molly, I told Charlotte Zolotow many months ago that I wanted to slope off my job with Harper, and not be an editor any more. There are good things about it, always have been, but no more working with authors, dealing with contracts, worrying about the lack of reviews, or when there are bad ones, for "my" authors. Charlotte, as head of the department, is a brilliant and sensitive and creative person. She will see that you and your work get the good attention I think you have always had from the dept. You know and like Robert Warren[1], especially Liz Gordon who saved my life on *Cider Days*![2] and wonderful Frank S.[3], dear BAD, and Bill Morris, Joan Robins, and other key people. Charlotte wanted me to keep some authors but that wouldn't be fair to her or to the dept. for me to pick and choose. She, Charlotte, did ask me to keep some sort of connection with the dept., and we have agreed that I will be a consultant on any odd jobs she wants me to handle. But I will be working directly with her. As my friend you will be glad that I will have much more time for the inside of my own head. Please remember that you and I will continue to be friends and I will always be interested in your welfare and interests, and current reading, and always everything about beautiful Tom. But I don't want to have anything to do with anyone on the subject of manuscripts or turn into one of those horrors who sit up in the country and second guess things in New York, or look as though that's what I am doing. The department is in great shape and all is and will be well for you. I am sending this letter to Charlotte so that she can add a message, and I am writing Roz [Targ] whom I have grown really to love.   New subject: was it *Bleak House* that you recommended so highly? We have a huge, paperback copy, bought on your recommendation, but I can't get into it. I've been reading and rereading a lot of poetry lately. End of page. Please write me and be in touch.

As ever with love, Moll, and to Tom.

1. Editor in the department. He became MS's editor.
2. *Cider Days*, by Mary Stolz, 1978.
3. Frank Scioscia, sales manager, Harper Junior Books.

Dearest Molly:

My typewriter has been out of order and I have been going insane. I can't write handwritten letters and I've been wanting to write you for weeks. Finally I found a place in Waterbury who sent a man to fix the machine. I always typed my own editorial letters and answered my own phone, but I never changed a typewriter ribbon. Crazy! This is a borrowed machine and unfamiliar and so this will be a mess but I hate being out of touch with you.   I loved your message saying that you felt like an Urs-while author—no I didn't LOVE it but I felt touched and rueful. You are a real writer, Molly, and I was interested to hear that you may write an adult novel next. Tell me more.

How did you like the flap copy for *Time of Night* that Robert Warren sent you? I thought it was good. And are you going to send him a new picture? Write and tell me all your news. I love your letters but you never really write as though you'd heard from me. I wrote you that terrible thing about the shrimp, etc., and you never said "Oh, how awful but interesting about the shrimp somersaulting back to the ocean when they get washed up on the beach." Like that, Molly. Then I know you have read my epistle. I am NOT criticizing you— just observing. And you never wrote "Glad you remember my insane swimming caps." Etc. Do try to do better. I am joking, of course. The weather is superb after a ghastly rainy and cold April. Now we have forsythia, daffodils, lilacs about to bloom, lovely dandelions, dogwood beginning to blossom, and I am ecstatic. I love the slow, incredible, New England spring.   We are about to move back to Bridgewater but write to Heritage Village until about May 23. I have to go to Colorado Springs next Friday because the Association of

American Publishers which gives an award for Innovative Publishing[1], or something like that, is giving it to me and I have to take a parachute and fly out to Colo. Springs. Dread it. But it is nice actually because it is the first time the award has gone to someone who is (a) in the junior readers publishing field and (b) a woman. So we've come a long way, baby, as the headline says..... No more for now as I must rush to get this in the postbox before the man comes. Isn't the state of our country maddening? I can't vote for Reagan or Kennedy. I'm not mad at K about Chappaquiddick, I believe in redemption. But he said in Maine to a group, "When I'm president I will not send your daughters to fight in the Persian Gulf." Pure Nixon. Love to you both, and write soon and at length and tell me all about everything. <u>Lots</u> of love. How did you like the Hazard[2] [*sic*]?

TO MARY STOLZ[3] (USM)

Southbury
May 22, 1980

Dearest Molly:

So many things to write you, and ask you, and I have misplaced your last so welcome letter. We are about ready to move back to Bridgewater. [. . .] Anyhow, I can't find anything but I believe I remember most of what you wrote.

1. UN won the Curtis Benjamin Award for 1980, given by the Association of American Publishers in recognition of exceptional contributions to innovation and creativity in publishing.
2. UN had sent MS a copy of *People in Glass Houses: Portraits from Organization Life*, by Shirley Hazzard, Knopf, 1967.
3. The following letter was written on Harper stationery, on which UN placed a slash mark through the printed words "Senior Editor," and wrote in "Consultant." Next to the date typed in at the top of the third and final page, UN added: "can't stop writing you!"

Yes, I would vote for Bill Moyers for anything. Yes, I did see the Iran programs and was interested in Farhang. The Iranian culture is so different from ours that I wonder if we will ever understand each other. Anyhow, I do watch Moyers regularly, also MacNeil-Lehrer. Also Dick Cavett. I have an unreachable ambition, however, which is that I wish I could look EXACTLY like Dick Cavett. I heard a rumor that he has six toes which is a bit bizarre. But I dote on his neat, tidy spare face. And speaking of faces, I don't feel old at all, even physically, but especially in the head. However, I am reminded by others of the great passage of time. (My face looks 1000 of course due to the recent loss of weight.) But what was I saying; oh about Fred Astaire. He is now 81, and I remember him so clearly because he married Phyllis Baker Potter who went to boarding school with me, and so I have always felt very close to Fred. But with the passage of years he now looks nothing like himself but increasingly like Boris Karloff in the movie *Frankenstein*. The same small sunken eyes, and the bony protruding forehead. This metamorphosis really hurts me, more than my own facial deterioration. I don't know what I look like now—I guess like an OLD Dame May Whitty, on a good day.

I am so exhilirated (sp?) to have my typewriter back that I can't write sensibly. I just wrote an idiotic letter to the glorious BAD, and I am sure she will think I am stoned out of my dome on marijuana. I'm not. I just feel very euphoric.

Robert [Warren] sent me a copy of your last letter to him. *Atlantic Monthly* quote just right. Isn't it awful the *A. Monthly* was sold to a Boston real estate man? He probably is a lovely gent, but still....

I am interested to hear you are working on a short story. A wonderful form, but I wonder why you abandoned your novel. Please don't dwell mentally on how you can't write if you don't smoke. That really isn't possible, Molly. Do you have a title for the short story? You've started some of your best books with just an idea for a good title—*No Music on Monday*[1] comes to mind. I'm touched that you keep remembering that thing about "the darkening light." The copyeditor at that time gave me the argument that light cannot darken but Charlotte Zolotow, my brilliant and sensitive editor, fought for it. (Come to think of it, "Light Cannot Darken" wouldn't be a bad title for something. You are welcome to it, dear!)

I thank you for the dear dedication[2] to your novel. It touched me deeply. It doesn't seem such a long time since I sat in that crowded dark little office on East 33rd Street and laughed myself silly over the Mexican jumping beans on the streetcar (I think?) and I was so grateful to you that girl didn't get boy at the end. I do believe that *To Tell Your Love* was the first "girl's story" in which girl didn't get boy. Of course these days I read that the happy ending is when at the end girl gets girl. Oh well, the planet is overpopulated anyhow.

Of course you MUST have received my letter about the shrimp somersaulting back over the sand to the water. In it I also referred to my desire to see you and Tom again on our patio, and with you both in the pool, and with you wearing one of your silly, impractical, but fetching bathing caps. I wrote it in answer to Tom's darling (though sort of illegible, doctor!) letter to me about my becoming just a consultant. Speaking of shrimp, have I shared with you the meaning of "happy as a clam"????? It means nothing without the rest of the sentence, "happy as a clam at high tide." I love it. Mary Rodgers told me that. I owe so much to "my" authors.

---

1. *Who Wants Music on Monday?*, by Mary Stolz, 1963.
2. MS dedicated *What Time of Night Is It?*, published by Harper & Row in 1981 and the last book that she and UN worked on together, "To Ursula—For a Wonderful, Terrible Time." The internal reference is to MS's 1967 novel *A Wonderful, Terrible Time.*

Of course I am stricken that you won't vote[1]. You knew I would be so why did you have to write it down and thus turn the knife more cruelly in my heart? I won't argue, no use to argue with you except on editorial matters. However, I do beg you to study and see if you can't see one-tenth of one per cent difference between Reagan and Carter. Surely one is at least that much more preferable to the other. I ask not in my name, but in the name of those courageous sisters who preceded us— those fine, sensitive, brave suffragettes who chained themselves to buildings, who suffered ridicule from the male chauvinists, who spoke and fought and stood up so that we could vote. In the name of Carrie Chapman Catt[2] I beg you to reconsider. John Anderson urged as recently as 1963 that the Congress pass a resolution, or an amendment, or something, to the effect that the U. S. of A. was a Christian nation and acknowledged Jesus Christ as its savior. Or something like that. I do believe in re- demption and John A. has since recanted but that is a bit much. I am as sick as you are about the election this fall, but I am going to vote and I think Carter the lesser of two evils.   Tough about Hazzard. What is so too bad is that no reviews notice things like that. I read a lot of novels (for adults) these days and aside from basic editing even the copyediting is awful. ("Get out," she hissed.[3])

Yes, I went to Colorado Springs and flew out alone and wasn't at all nervous. Also didn't mind the flight back. Two rich friends of mine (Mary and a Bridgewater neighbor) gave me a

---

1. The reference is to the upcoming presidential election, in which President Jimmy Carter was being challenged by Republican Ronald Reagan and by third-party can- didate John Anderson.

2. American suffragist who in 1919 organized the League of Women Voters.

3. While she gave her authors every latitude, UN demanded that language be used with uncompromising precision; a pet peeve was characters hissing bits of dialogue that contained no *s* to his*s*, or otherwise using as verbs of utterance actions that had nothing to do with speech: "Yes," she pointed.

present of the difference between economy and first class, and I must say I can't imagine what economy is like because 1st class was ghastly. Oh for the dear old 20th Century with its glorious dining car, sparkling glasses, rose on the table, tiny orchid for the women, boutonniére (sp?) for the men. And the darling drawing room with its interesting though puzzling sanitary arrangements! I saw a revival of *The Sting* on t.v. recently and when Paul Newman was ushered by the porter into his drawing room I almost sobbed. I can sob over Paul Newman anyhow, but Paul Newman in a DRAWING ROOM—oh gawd. How old does one have to be before the sap stops rising, and I do mean sap????

The visit to Colo. Springs was great and the overly generous and marvelous introduction by Erwin Glikes, the distinguished publisher of Simon and Schuster,[1] really moved me. He mentioned so many books, and authors—including you, OF COURSE. And I really got quite emotional and when I got up to accept the plaque I was so moved my voice shook when I uttered my few words, and I was ashamed of myself. But anyhow, it was all lovely, and the hotel was magnificent, and Pike's Peak really is terrific. Charlotte Z did all sorts of lovely things to make the award possible and for me to be there (no Harper doesn't "spring" for much these days—publishing is going through a tough time). Erwin Glikes read a letter from Sendak, and all in all it was a happy evening for me. Oh God, my typewriter is now squeaking—that can't be a good sign????   I have heard about those cartridge typewriters and I've asked BAD if I could get a discount on one through Harper. I doubt it, but no harm in asking.   We have had terrible expenses, but I won't go on about that.   Charlotte sent me a bunch of articles by and about me, copies of the stuff

1. Glikes had been the publisher of Basic Books, a Harper subsidiary, before moving to Simon & Schuster.

she sent for use in Colorado, and Mary Griffith threw things together and rushed off to a Heritage Village friend and he organized an official looking release and sent it off to weekly papers around here. You wouldn't believe the results. Headline: "Local lady wins Award." Result: the phone is ringing and as I type I am awaiting the visit of a man who wants to write a book on successful retirement. I told him I knew very little about publishing and that little was entirely about books for young people, but he is approaching anyhow, and so I must bring this mess to an end. I love hearing from you, and want news of you and Tom, and so you should write me often just rattling on off the top of your interesting and extremely creative head. I love you both, and if Mary weren't off doing Bridgewater stuff she would send love too. Wish you both were back in New Canaan. Again, much love as ever.

TO JOAN ROBINS   July 28, 1981

Dearest Joanie:

I am sorry I haven't sent you some stuff about Louise Fitzhugh for that woman in Winnipeg[1]. If she'd sent us a sort of little questionnaire it would have been relatively easy to answer, or fill out. But here goes about what I know, and I will have to trust you—and I do—to get one of your eleven assistants and/or secretaries to edit it and omit portions you think should not be shared with Miss Winnipeg. I also have been trying to answer a two page letter of questions from a graduate student someplace in Ohio, about Louise. Among the questions: "Why did Louise

---

1. UN mistakenly assumed that the correspondent here referred to, Perry Nodelman, was a woman. Nodelman, a children's literature scholar at the University of Winnipeg, later published an essay on Fitzhugh in *American Writers for Children Since 1960: Fiction*, Vol. 52 of the *Dictionary of Literary Biography*, edited by Glenn E. Estes, Gale, 1986.

never marry?" Can you imagine? I remember someone once asked that question of Margaret Wise Brown, in my presence. Margaret who was then having a flaming affair with one of John Barrymore's ex-wives[1] said haughtily, "Because I am emotionally immature." Well, enough of my wandering on.

Louise was born in Memphis. Her father was a rich man and one of great importance in Tenn. I think he was Attorney General of the state[2]. Her mother came from—shall we say—a rather different walk of life, and I believe the marriage was an unhappy one. One evening when Louise was at my U. N. Plaza apt., after one of our Harper parties, we were playing records and Louise—who then looked like a twelve year old little boy with short curly hair and she always wore pants long before everyone else did—got up and started to dance by herself. She was marvelous—such rhythm, and on her face a rapt inner contemplation of the music and the beat, and the general pleasure she was experiencing. I was in those days a pretty damn good dancer myself and I really was able to appreciate her performance. When I expressed admiration she explained simply, "Well, my mother was a hoofer." Anyhow, she got out of the south as soon as she could, came north, went to Bard College (I think she didn't stay there long enough to be graduated) and concentrated on losing every single trace of her Southern accent. When I first met her—when she was working on *Harriet*—she sounded not just like a well-bred New Yorker but she had also tacked on an almost Brooklyn accent, "Yeah," etc. When she died so suddenly and tragically it was found that in her papers, or indeed I think perhaps it was in her will—the definite request that she be buried ABOVE the Mason-Dixon line.

---

1. See footnote 5 to letter to Garth Williams, January 28, 1960, page 132.
2. Fitzhugh's father, Millsaps Fitzhugh, served as U.S. Attorney in Memphis.

There were many things in her well-born southern upbringing and experiences that she didn't like. I remember she told me one day, in horrified remembrance, that well-brought up boys and girls in their teens who had dates would, after dinner, decide it would be fun to go down to "coon-town" and throw rocks at the heads of young Negro boys and girls. Anyhow, by the time I knew her, she hated all that, was completely "liberal" and had many black and white friends. As for her not marrying, I can only say that I think she was so committed to her writing and to her drawing and painting that she couldn't possibly have had the inclination to commit herself permanently to any one person. She was a brilliant painter. And toward the end she was drawing the most magnificent black and white pictures you can imagine. As you know, we didn't publish her last book, or two, but it was just one of those inevitable misunderstandings that do occur once in a while between one who is a genius, and the most devoted editorial staff. Anyhow, it ended up that we both, unbeknownst to each other, bought houses in Bridgewater, Ct., a tiny village, and we met one day by accident in the same restaurant and there was a rapprochement and happiness and emotion on both sides. After she died I was so grateful that we'd had that last meeting, at which we were both moved, and at which all past silly hurts and misunderstandings disappeared.

Her father died before she did and I believe she came in to a great deal of money—several million. But when she first came to NY her family did not approve and apparently gave her little or no financial backing, and she lived very simply and the small advance we were able to give her on the first few pages of *Harriet* meant a great deal to her.

It was Charlotte Zolotow, then senior editor, in the dept., who wrote me a report on the first sample pages of *Harriet* and said "You have to get this writer to come in and talk. This isn't a book, but it could be." As I remember it the agent sent us, at first, material that really eventually became the contents of Harriet's notebook about her classmates. I asked Charlotte to sit in with us and Louise sat sullenly, hands jammed into her pockets, while we expressed enthusiasm over what we'd seen, over her drawings, and we began to ask questions. "Why these drawings? Why these comments?" We talked for about an hour trying to draw her out. Trying to share with her our eagerness to help her expand whatever it was she had in her head and make a real book out of it. After at least an hour she looked up and said "So you're not really interested, are you?" We almost died. Anyhow, she did begin to write more and more. She mentioned Old [sic] Golly but with no background for her, or explanation, and we asked for more about Old Golly. At any rate, she finally did enough that we gave her a contract, a decent advance, and published *Harriet* with great happiness. It was a controversial book, at first. As I remember George Woods of the *Times* hated it and wouldn't let his children read it. But he gave it to an outside reviewer who raved about it and, to George's credit, he published this favorable review.   Louise inscribed a copy of *Harriet* to me with the poetic remark about to Ursula, and the only publishing house without finks.   Then came *The Long Secret*, and by that time Louise was recalcitrant about certain revisions we felt it needed. For instance I thought the character of the preacher was a little too farcical, but Louise disagreed and for all I know she was right and I was wrong. I do remember that when I read the ms. and came to the page where the onset of Beth Ellen's first menstrual period occurred, and it was written so beautifully, to such perfection, I scrawled in the margin, "THANK YOU, LOUISE FITZHUGH!" It is incredible that Louise's *Long Secret* contained the first mention in junior books of this tremendous event in a girl's life. Of course the following scene with Harriet screeching "Oh, I'm not going to do THAT!" was delicious. But that scene with Beth Ellen thoughtfully going out and spending that first morning in the garden, or arbor, or whatever (I haven't a copy of the book in Bridgewater, it is in Heritage Village). Anyhow, after *Long Secret* came out Louise and I and Mary Griffith and a friend of Louise's drove out to Water Mill on Long Island, which is mentioned so often in *Long Secret*, and we went to have a drink, or luncheon, or something at the place identified in the book as "the Evil Hotel" and there was indeed something sort of Charles Addams-ish about the place. We could hardly wait to get our bill paid and get out. It had changed hands but the owner had taken in payment a magnificent painting Louise had done, of a little girl standing alone in a meadow. It expressed all the essential loneliness I think Louise always felt, and it tore me apart. Sorry to sound so emotional, but I have never pretended to be Madam Ice-Cube!

I went to Louise's funeral in the little Episcopal church here in Bridgewater, and she is buried in Bridgewater in a little cemetery Mary and I pass once in a while. I always get out of the car and go to her grave—there are always flowers growing around it spring, summer, fall. And think of her. She would have been 53 this coming October 5th and she wouldn't have liked that at all! But what a terrible loss children's books suffered. Though, I don't know. After the big success of *Harriet* and *Long Secret* her "friends" tried to get in to the act and gave her advice, which didn't always seem good to us, and the "friends" kind of tried to take her career over. She was a brilliant, erratic, moody, often extremely thoughtful and endearing person and I loved her—through the bad times as well as the good. She included me among her favorite "fanatics" in the dedication to *Long Secret*. The Dr. Slaff she mentioned was her psychiatrist and she adored him. Well some of this may be helpful. Give the gist of what you think right to Winnipeg.

Love,

TO CHARLOTTE ZOLOTOW (CZo)   Southbury
March 18, 1982

Dea

Dea

Damn it what is wrong with this damn typewi w= type-writer? Dear CZ: well, it seems to have healed itself. It is the very devil to get repairs in this place.

We have talked on the phone and this is sort of a business letter so I will send a carbon to BAD for the record. I do not mean to shy away from your dear questions about *The Secret Choice*. I do think I can pull it together and get something to you before I die of this dislocated shoulder complication. I am sorry Norman sent me back the advance I returned to Harper via him, but his letter was so sweet, and my bank balance was so low, I didn't give him any argument! Have you thought (god knows there's no rush) of someone who could give you a (favorable) advance quote for the jacket? George Woods will be waiting to jump all over it with swords, I know, and so will a few influential others. I am very nervous about it although you did like the parts you have seen (or heard) and I trust you more than I can say.

I wish you would work on your own manuscripts but I know your time has been broken up with the job and with personal appointments. But it is AWFUL that you don't get the *Early Sorrows*[1] out of your way and let me see what you have, and then get on to your own young adult novel[2]. The days go back [*sic*] so quickly "and at my back I always hear time's winged chariot hurrying near, The grave's a fine and quiet place but none I think" do finish their books from there.[3] I

---

1. *Early Sorrow: Ten Stories of Youth*, edited by Charlotte Zolotow, 1986.
2. This book was never completed.
3. The quote is based on two passages from Andrew Marvell's "To His Coy Mistress":
    But at my back I always hear
    Time's wingèd chariot hurrying near. ...
    The grave's a fine and private place,
    But none, I think, do there embrace.

have mis-quoted this but no matter. You get the idea.

I have found a poem by an English poet I haven't known before. Stevie Smith—she died in 1971. It is called "Not Waving But Drowning" and I think it is so splendid I will copy it here for you. Maybe others in the dept. will read the carbon copy and be moved by it, as I was. But they are all so young probably not. I remember reading Thomas Hardy's poems *Winter Words in Various Moods and Meters* when I was 18. Then years passed and when I was in my early fifties I found it in the library at the Cosmopolitan Club one late evening, and sat down and re-read it through, and it was so interesting to re-read the poems which meant so much to me in my late teens, and still meant a great deal in my fifties, but reading them with a lifetime of experience and feelings behind me it was a different and more rewarding experience. Well, back to Stevie Smith

> *Nobody heard him, the dead man,*
> *But still he lay moaning:*
> *I was much further out than you thought*
> *And not waving but drowning.*
>
> *Poor chap, he always loved larking*
> *And now he's dead*
> *It must have been too cold for him his heart gave way,*
> *They said.*
>
> *Oh, no no no, it was too cold always*
> *(Still the dead one lay moaning)*
> *I was much too far out all my life*
> *And not waving but drowning.*[1]

Well, nothing to cheer one up but I thought it beautifully done, and it made me feel good. Frank S[cioscia][2] found a copy

---

1. From *Collected Poems of Stevie Smith*, by Stevie Smith. Copyright © 1998 by Stevie Smith. Used by permission of Oxford University Press, Inc.
2. Scioscia, in addition to working at Harper part-time, was now the proprietor of riverrun, a used bookstore in Hastings-on-Hudson, New York.

of Edna St. Millay's [*sic*] (out-of-print) letters[1] and I am so grateful. After her husband died the woman who worked in the post office in the little village (Austerlitz, I believe) helped her a lot with correspondence and with answering condolence letters. Millay wrote her a note to thank her and said something in answer to the post office woman's statement that she missed seeing Boissevain coming down the hill. Millay answered her, "I know you must miss him coming down the hill. He doesn't come up the hill any more either." I may have misquoted this. I shouldn't try to quote from memory. But even so it has a lovely cadence.

1. *Letters of Edna St. Vincent Millay*, edited by Allan Ross Macdougall, 1952.

BIBLIOGRAPHY

& INDEX

By Ursula Nordstrom

BOOKS

The Secret Language, illustrated by Mary Chalmers, Harper & Brothers, 1960.

ARTICLES

"Assorted Thoughts on Creative Authors and Artists." *Library Journal*, Vol. 99 (September 15, 1974), 2211–14.

"Editing Books for Young People." In *Celebrating Children's Books: Essays on Children's Literature in Honor of Zena Sutherland*. Ed. Betsy Hearne and Marilyn Kaye. New York: Lothrop, Lee & Shepard, 1981, 143–53.

"Honesty in Teenage Novels." *Top of the News*, Vol. 21 (November 1964), 35–38.

"The Joyful Challenge." *Saturday Review*, Vol. L (November 11, 1967), 39–40.

"'Perhaps Even Cheerful.'" *The Retail Bookseller*, Vol. 51 (August 1948), 69–70.

"Re-issuing the Wilder Books." *Top of the News*, Vol. 23 (April 1967), 267–68.

"Stuart, Wilbur, Charlotte: A Tale of Tales." *The New York Times Book Review*, May 12, 1974, pp. 8–9.

"Ursula Nordstrom's Comments About the Fifties." *The Horn Book*, Vol. XLV (December 1969), 708–9.

Articles about and Interviews with Ursula Nordstrom

Freilicher, Lila. "PW Interviews: Ursula Nordstrom." *Publishers Weekly*, Vol. 201 (June 19, 1972), 32–33.

Fuller, Muriel. "Ursula Nordstrom of Harper." *The Publishers' Weekly*, Vol. 152 (October 25, 1947), 2090–91.

Natov, Roni, and Geraldine DeLuca. "Discovering Contemporary Classics: An Interview with Ursula Nordstrom." *The Lion and the Unicorn*, Vol. 3 (Spring 1979), 119–35.

"Ursula Nordstrom—and How Harper's Children's Books Come to Be." *The House of Harper* (company newsletter), August 1963, 3–4.

Zolotow, Charlotte. "Ursula Nordstrom." *The Calendar* [of The Children's Book Council], November 1981.

Other Sources Consulted

Alderson, Brian. *Ezra Jack Keats: Artist and Picture-Book Maker*. Gretna, La.: Pelican, 1994.

Anderson, William. *Laura Ingalls Wilder: A Biography*. New York: HarperCollins, 1992.

Bader, Barbara. *American Picturebooks from Noah's Ark to the Beast Within*. New York: Macmillan, 1976.

Bliven, Bruce, Jr. "Child's Best-Seller." *Life*, Vol. 21, No. 23 (December 2, 1946), 59 ff.

Canfield, Cass. *Up & Down & Around: A Publisher Recollects the Time of His Life*. New York: Harper's Magazine Press, 1971.

Cech, John. *Angels and Wild Things: The Archetypal Poetics of Maurice Sendak*. University Park, Pa.: Pennsylvania State University Press, 1995.

———, ed. *Dictionary of Literary Biography: American Writers for Children, 1900–1960* (Vol. 22). Detroit, Mich.: Gale Research, 1983.

Cerf, Bennett. *At Random: The Reminiscences of Bennett Cerf*. New York: Random House, 1977.

Coser, Lewis A., Charles Kadushin, and Walter W. Powell. *Books: The Culture and Commerce of Publishing*. New York: Basic Books, 1982.

Cummins, Julie. "'Let Her Sound Her Trumpet': NYPL Children's Librarians and Their Impact on the World of Publishing." *Biblion*, Vol. 4 (Fall 1995), 83–114.

Elledge, Scott. *E. B. White: A Biography*. New York: W. W. Norton, 1984.

Exman, Eugene. *The House of Harper: 150 Years of Publishing*. New York: Harper & Row, 1967.

George, Jean Craighead. *Journey Inward*. New York: Dutton, 1982.

Gottlieb, Robin. *Publishing Children's Books in America, 1919–1976: An Annotated Bibliography*. New York: Children's Book Council, 1978.

Hentoff, Nat. "Profiles: Among the Wild Things." *The New Yorker*, Vol. XLI, No. 49 (January 22, 1966), 39 ff.

Jagusch, Sybille A., ed. *Stepping Away from Tradition: Children's Books of the Twenties and Thirties*. Washington: Library of Congress, 1988.

Jones, Dolores B., comp. *Bibliography of the Little Golden Books*. New York: Greenwood Press, 1987.

Kerr, M. E. *Me Me Me Me Me: Not a Novel*. New York: Harper & Row, 1983.

Kresh, Paul. *Isaac Bashevis Singer: The Magician of West 86th Street: A Biography*. New York: Dial, 1979.

Lanes, Selma G. *The Art of Maurice Sendak*. New York: Abrams, 1980.

———. *Down the Rabbit Hole: Adventures & Misadventures in the Realm of Children's Literature*. New York: Atheneum, 1976.

Larrick, Nancy. "The All-White World of Children's Books." *Saturday Review*, Vol. XLVIII (September 11, 1965), 63–65, 84–85.

Lorenz, Lee. *The Art of The New Yorker, 1925–1995*. New York: Knopf, 1995.

Marcus, Leonard S. "An Interview with William C. Morris." *The Horn Book*, Vol. LXXI, No. 1 (January–February 1995), 37–46.

———. *Margaret Wise Brown: Awakened by the Moon*. Boston: Beacon, 1992.

———. *75 Years of Children's Book Week Posters: Celebrating Great Illustrators of American Children's Books*. New York: Knopf, 1994.

Neumeyer, Peter F., ed. *The Annotated Charlotte's Web*. New York: HarperCollins, 1994.

Rennert, Jack, ed. *The Poster Art of Tomi Ungerer*. New York: Darien House, 1971.

Ross, Clifford, and Karen Wilkin. *The World of Edward Gorey*. New York: Abrams, 1996.

Sendak, Maurice. *Caldecott & Co.: Notes on Books & Pictures*. New York: Michael di Capua Books/Farrar, Straus, 1988.

———. "For Children of All Ages," review of *The Wild Swan: The Life and Times of Hans Christian Andersen*, by Monica Stirling (Harcourt, Brace, 1965), in *The Washington Post Book World*, March 13, 1966, 1, 11–13.

Silvey, Anita, ed. *Children's Books and Their Creators*. Boston: Houghton Mifflin, 1995.

Sutherland, Zena. "A Change for the Better." *Saturday Review*, Vol. LI (March 16, 1968), 38.

———. "The Persuaded Muse." *Saturday Review*, Vol. LII (February 22, 1969), 46–47.

Tebbel, John. *Between Covers: The Rise and Transformation of Book Publishing in America*. New York: Oxford University Press, 1987.

Weyr, Thomas. "Why Are They So Expensive?" *The New York Times Book Review*, Part II, November 5, 1972, 40–42.

White, E. B. *Letters of E. B. White*, coll. and ed. by Dorothy Lobrano Guth. New York: Harper & Row, 1976.

Wilcock, John. "The Wonderful World of Maurice Sendak." *The Village Voice*, September 26, 1956, 3–4.

Wolf, Virginia. *Louise Fitzhugh*. New York: Twayne, 1991.

N = Newbery Medal;   C = Caldecott Medal
Numbers in *italics* refer to illustrations.